3 July Seventh Month hath 31 Days

	D	H	M	
New ☽	8	0	3	Morn
First ☽	16	2	0	Morn
Full ○	23	2	47	Morn
Last ☽	29	6	51	Aft

☊ { 1, 11, 21 } ℞ { 9, 8, 8 } Deg.

Planets

D	☉	♄	♃				
	♋	♉	♏				
1	10	13	23				
7	16	14	23	♋ 1	6	29	4
13	22	14	23	5	9	♌ 9	1 N
19	27	14	23	9	14	19	5 N
25	♌ 3	14	23	13	19	28	0 N

M D	W D	Remarkable Days Aspects weather &c.	☉ rise	☉ Set	☽ Long	☽ rise	☽ South	☽ Age
1	2	Days Decrease 2 m.	4..39	7..21	0-23-0	12..59	19-28	23
2	3	Visitation of V. Mary	4-40	7..20	1-6-50	13..32	20-19	24
3	4		4-40	7-20	1-20-19	14..10	21-12	25
4	5	St. Martin	4..40	7-20	2-3-29	14-51	22-1	26
5	6	* ☉ ♄	4-41	7-19	2-16-21	15-39	22-56	27
6	7		4-41	7-19	2-28-53	16-24	23-41	28
7	F	6th Sund. past Trin.	4..42	7-18	3-11-13			29
8	2		4-42	7-18	3-23-18	Sets	0 27	☽
9	3	Lyra South 11-15	4..43	7-17	4-5-17	8-27	1-17	1
10	4		4..43	7-17	4-17-10	9-2	2..1	2
11	5	Days 14..32	4-44	7-16	4-29-0	9-36	2-45	3
12	6	♃ Stationary	4..44	7..16	5-10-50	10..6	3-30	4
13	7	* ♀ ☿	4..45	7-15	5-22-46	10..37	4..12	5
14	F	7th Sund. past Trin	4..45	7-15	6-4-50	11..8	4..48	6
15	2		4-46	7..14	6-17-5	11..39	5..34	7
16	3	Spica ♍ set 10..58	4..47	7-13	6-29-29	12..12	6..25	8
17	4		4..47	7-13	7-12-20	12-46	7..12	9
18	5	Arcturus Sets 1-25	4-48	7-12	7-25-24	13..26	8..4	10
19	6		4-49	7-11	8-8-48	14..10	8..57	11
20	7	Margaret	4-49	7-11	8-22-31	14-56	9..52	12
21	F	8th Sund. past Trin	4..50	7..10	9-6-35	15-44	10-31	13
22	2	Magdalene	4-51	7-9	9-20-55		11..49	14
23	3	☉ enters ♌	4-52	7..8	10-5-26	rise	12..45	15
24	4	~~Dog Days begin~~	4-53	7..7	10-20-7	8..20	13..45	16
25	5	St. James	4-54	7..6	11-4-48	9..4	14..40	17
26	6	St. Anne	4-54	7..6	11-19-32	9..39	15..33	18
27	7		4-55	7..5	0-4-0	10..14	16..26	19
28	F	9th Sund past Trin	4..56	7..4	0-18-18	10..49	17..14	20
29	2	Days 14..6	4..57	7..3	1-2-17	11..27	18..9	21
30	3	~~Days 14..4~~ Dog Days begins	4..58	7..2	1-15-58	12..5	18..58	22
31	4	Days Decrease 42 m.	4..59	7..1	1-29-18	12..44	19..50	23

July 30 is the true time the Dog Days begins
for that morning that Star rises with the Sun
Sept. 5th Dog Days end.

THE LIFE OF
BENJAMIN BANNEKER

Published with the Support

of the

Joseph Meyerhoff Family Charitable Funds

Benjamin Bannaker's
PENNSYLVANIA, DELAWARE, MARY-LAND, AND VIRGINIA
ALMANAC,
FOR THE
YEAR of our LORD 1795;
Being the Third after Leap-Year.

BANNAKER.

—PRINTED FOR—

And Sold by JOHN FISHER, *Stationer.*

BALTIMORE.

THE LIFE OF
BENJAMIN BANNEKER

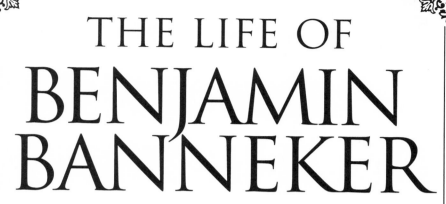

The First African-American Man of Science

· SECOND EDITION ·

REVISED AND EXPANDED

SILVIO A. BEDINI

MARYLAND HISTORICAL SOCIETY

BALTIMORE

First edition 1972
Second edition revised and expanded 1999

Copyright under the Berne Convention

Printed in the United States of America

05 04 03 02 01 00 99   5 4 3 2 1

LIBRARY OF CONGRESS CATALOGING-IN-PUBLICATION DATA

Bedini, Silvio, A.
    The life of Benjamin Banneker : the first african american man of
science / Silvio A. Bedini. — Rev. ed.
        p. cm.
    Includes bibliographical references and index.
    ISBN 0-938420-59-3 (hardcover : alk. paper). —ISBN 0-938420-63-1
(pbk. : alk. paper)
        1. Banneker, Benjamin. 1731. 1731–1806. I. Title.
QB36.B22B4   1998
520' .92—cd21
[b]   98-22848
                                                                CIP

End Papers. Pages from Banneker's manuscript journal, the left containing a projection for an eclipse, and the right the calculations for a month's ephemeris. *Maryland Historical Society.*

Frontispiece. This purported portrait of Benjamin Banneker, not from life but the only known image of the amateur astronomer, appeared on the title page of *Banneker's Almanac* for 1795, printed for John Fisher. The appearance of an African American on the cover of an almanac in that period was a novelty intended to help promote sales. *Maryland Historical Society.*

For
LEANDRA and PETER

I have been the more careful to investigate those particulars, and to ascertain their reality, as they form an interesting fact in the history of Man.

—Senator James McHenry
(letter quoted in *Banneker's Almanac for 1792*)

CONTENTS

PREFACE

M Y ATTENTION WAS FIRST DIRECTED TO BENJAMIN BANNEKER MORE than forty years ago in Connecticut while engaged in research on early American clockmakers and makers of mathematical instruments. The story of an unschooled tobacco planter who had constructed a successfully operating striking clock, supposedly without ever having seen one, invited further investigation. It was soon apparent that the homemade clock was only one, and perhaps among the least, of Banneker's achievements. Fairly late in life, this son and grandson of African slaves had undertaken to teach himself mathematics and astronomy sufficiently to be able to calculate ephemerides for almanacs, and furthermore, he had participated in the historic survey of the Federal Territory (now the District of Columbia). Obviously, Banneker was not just another of the early American mathematical practitioners—surveyors, navigators, science teachers, philomaths, or makers of instruments whose science helped shape the new republic—but one whose accomplishments merited closer study. And thus began the search for the full story of Banneker the man of science, requiring pursuit and investigation of countless research resources not only on the state of the sciences but also on the question of slavery and abolitionist movements.

An excessive amount of sleuthing proved to be required in the exhaustive and exhausting search for the rare surviving documents recording his life and work, of the tangible memorabilia and ephemera of this memorable eighteenth-century African American. A first step was the search for copies of all published references known to mention Banneker. Eventually this compilation grew to more than a hundred items, ranging from brief notices to substantial biographical sketches in periodicals or as chapters in works on African-American history, as well as one book-length fictionalized biography for children. Most proved to have been based on one or more of the same four sources, without further study or evaluation, and often with added exaggeration or misinformation.

The four primary published accounts were based on sources contemporary to Banneker. The earliest was a sketch by Senator James McHenry, then a memoir by John H. B. Latrobe published forty years after Banneker's death, and finally, two useful sketches by Martha E. Tyson derived from her own recollections, those of family members, and information obtained from others who had known the self-taught astronomer during his lifetime.

The numerous other biographical pieces contributed relatively little new information and reported the magnitude of Banneker's achievements according to the climate in which they were written. No new research was conducted, and earlier errors were not only perpetuated but frequently exaggerated. This practice has continued to the present time, so that the modern reader has had no accurate resource readily available. It matters little that the writers may have erred in the number of pounds of tobacco paid by Banneker's father for his farm, for instance, or that the year of his death is incorrectly given. Far more important is that Banneker's attainments, which were impressive and substantial, should be truthfully reported and evaluated, and that his philosophy should be properly understood in order that it may serve as an example to others. Better than any other lesson to be derived from Banneker's life and work is the one he so admirably exemplified: that the thirst for knowledge is not limited to youth, and that the process of learning recognizes no barriers of race or creed.

Banneker has been brought into prominence from time to time as a reflection of the popular interest in the cause of antislavery and the role of the African American in American society, rather than for the substance of his scientific achievements. In due course he has been credited with things that he did not in fact achieve. Today erroneous exaggerations continue. Consequently, because of outright misstatements, Banneker's name has occasionally become clouded with doubt, instead of being the source of inspiration that it could be.

Actually, Banneker was a man of modest ability and performance, who, by means of his efforts, contributed a tangible bit to the fabric of American science in the late eighteenth century. The never-ending problem has been that writers hasten to copy already existing information without making the effort to verify it. The problem persists to the present day. Compilations of erroneous statements continue to appear in printed form, and public addresses relate that Banneker, described as "a mathematician and inventor," was hired by none other than President George Washington to assist Pierre Charles L'Enfant in laying out the nation's capital. The fact of the matter is that Major Andew Ellicott, with Jefferson's approval, hired Banneker to work as his assistant on the preliminary survey.

In the best of times, Banneker's life might have been similar to that of many other men of his generation who found inspiration in the sciences and seized the opportunities at hand to pursue them. But he lived in difficult times, for he was a free black man in an era when people of African descent were held in subjugation, and the world was just beginning again to realize, as it had in classical ages, that black skin was an accident of nature and not an indication\ of inferiority. At any other period in history, his work would have merited a far more accurate appraisal.

Originally I had not contemplated a full-length biography of Banneker. The work began as an attempt only to present his attainments in proper focus and to evaluate their importance in comparison with those of other early American men of science. The publication in 1964 of an account of early American scientific instruments and their makers in which Banneker was included brought requests for more information about him from scholars and students. Inevitably the awakened interest led me to review the materials collected for a more substantial presentation.

The research that followed, and upon which this biography is based, was divided into several major segments. There was, first of all, the story of Banneker's family and his early life. The investigation of civil records and the search for personal papers began in the Maryland Historical Society, then moved to the Maryland Hall of Records, and eventually into many other county and community archives in the region. The enthusiastic participation and dedicated cooperation of librarians, archivists, and officials were essential in bringing about the completion of this work.

The dramatic story, often retold, of how Banneker's precious astronomical notes and borrowed texts escaped destruction at the time of his death raised the question of whether they still existed and where they were to be found. Such materials might help to adjust and bring into focus the image of the man and the value of his work. Presumably these materials had been left to a descendant of the neighbor who had encouraged Banneker and to whom they had been returned. But where to look? The search for descendants assumed forbidding proportions, but the recurring expressions of interest from others encouraged renewed attempts to locate Banneker's missing journal of notes, his commonplace book, and other memorabilia. The logical repositories failed to yield up these treasures, leading to the inevitable conclusion that they no longer existed. It was not until the manuscript was well in progress that a stroke of unbelievable luck led to the discovery of all the known memorabilia and more.

Another segment of the research was the careful investigation and analysis of Banneker's calculations for ephemerides. There is relatively little information in published form explaining how eighteenth-century almanac-makers arrived at their calculations, made forecasts of the weather, or gathered together the other components of the published almanacs. Beginning from the beginning, using copies of the same texts that Banneker had borrowed, it was necessary to teach oneself the equivalent in mathematics and astronomy in order to duplicate Banneker's calculations, from time to time calling upon the expertise of other specialists.

A third aspect of the research dealt with the process by which Banneker's almanacs reached publication—a significant achievement in itself for an African American in his time and region. The trail led from Baltimore to Philadelphia and to the records of the Pennsylvania Society for the Abolition of Slavery preserved in the Historical Society of Pennsylvania. This repository proved to contain a treasure trove of manuscripts and published material concerned with Negro history, some of which has not been fully studied. The lack of a systematic index or catalogue of these papers made it particularly difficult, inasmuch as they had to be searched by means of time periods and names of individuals known to have been associated with Banneker.

Several appendices containing supplementary materials have been added for readers with special interests. Many of the manuscripts described or quoted are privately owned or form part of large public collections which are not fully indexed or catalogued. Accordingly, certain texts of particular interest or importance have been fully quoted in the appendix of *Documents*.

The listing of published references to Banneker with annotations compiled in the appendix on *Bibliography* presents a timesaving resource for the reader. Because the sequence of the dates of their publication reveals how the world remembered Banneker, and when and why, this compilation is presented chronologically instead of alphabetically.

The Life of Benjamin Banneker, first published in February 1972, has remained in print to the present, having been reprinted in 1984 by Landmark Enterprises, Inc. The exhaustion of the second printing provided an opportunity to produce a revised and much enlarged edition incorporating all new materials that have come to light since the book first appeared.

Occasionally the story dwells upon the apparently unimportant minutiae and details of Banneker's daily existence. This may seem unnecessary, but there is a reason for it. In reviewing his life, the evidence of the tedium of "the even tenor of his way" has emerged as an important element in understanding the simple pleasures he found in the world of nature around him and in his studies. These minor details were essential to his existence, the savor of which can be preserved in a general narrative only with the greatest difficulty. In the course of fitting together the fragments of fact as they were recovered, Banneker emerged in the mind's eye as an impressive being of flesh and blood. Here I have told, as carefully as it was possible to re-create, what is known of what Banneker thought and believed, what he attempted and what he achieved.

In the years since this biography first appeared and generated interest in the life of the tobacco planter turned amateur astronomer, recognition of the first African-American man of science developed at several levels in his native state and nationally. This led eventually to the establishment of the organization of the Friends of Benjamin Banneker Park, dedicated to the mission of preserving his former farm, situated less than a mile from Ellicott City, Maryland, a historic community representing the advent of technology that changed the economic future of the state. This endeavor has had the support of the State of Maryland, which has provided funds for the purchase in 1985 of the tract of 42.5 acres of the farm that includes the home site. Preliminary archeological research, also funded by the state, successfully identified the site of his home and outbuildings and the confines of his land. From excavations made by archeologists of the Maryland Historical Trust a number of artifacts have been recovered that reflect Banneker's life style and various preoccupations. A Benjamin Banneker Museum has recently opened on the premises.

As always, the assistance of the many librarians, archivists, and museum curators who have contributed substantially to this endeavor is gratefully acknowledged.

SILVIO A. BEDINI

September 1998

ACKNOWLEDGMENTS

The re-creation of the life and times of such an elusive figure as Benjamin Banneker has involved extensive research and considerable historical detection pursued over a number of years. The book therefore owes its existence to the many individuals whose contributions small and large have been assembled into the whole, as well as to the countless others who offered encouragement. It is not possible to identify all with whom the writer has corresponded on this project, but he takes this opportunity to extend his appreciation, while making grateful acknowledgment of those contributions which have been particularly substantial and rewarding:

First of all, to the American Philosophical Society, for the grant which it provided from the Penrose Fund.

To the late Dr. Robert T. Fitzhugh, a descendant of the George Ellicott family, for his generosity in making available for study, reproduction, and citation in the present work original Banneker, Ellicott, and Tyson family materials and memorabilia in his possession.

Equally to the late Elizabeth M. Fitzhugh for her splendid cooperation that contributed so substantially to the completion of this work. To various other descendants and members of the Ellicott family, for generously granting me permission to study, quote, and otherwise reproduce manuscripts, correspondence, and other original and published materials and memorabilia relating to Banneker and to the Ellicott, Tyson, and Mason families.

To the Maryland Historical Society, which has been deeply involved with this project since it was first initiated in 1955. Among past members of the staff who have contributed materially to this effort were Dr. Harold R. Manakee, Director; P. William Filby, Assistant Director and Librarian; Lois McCauley, Curator of Graphics; Francis C. Haber, former Librarian; and Ellen Lee Barker, former Curator of Manuscripts, and Robert I. Cottom, Editor, who has substantially improved the manuscript..

To Warren J. Danzenbaker, for invaluable assistance in many aspects of this project in ways too numerous to mention, who deserves particular recognition and my sincere gratitude.

Finally, to the numerous scholars, librarians, archivists, curators, and private citizens who have assisted so willingly in this research and have made available materials which have been embodied in the present volume: the mention of their names here is a very inadequate recognition of their generous cooperation:

Dr. Thomas R. Adams, Librarian of the John Carter Brown Library, Brown University; Louisa R. Alger, Cambridge, Massachusetts; Dr. Betty Bandel, Professor Emeritus, University of Vermont; Dr. Whitfield J. Bell, Jr., former Librarian of the American Philosophical Society; the late Charles H. Berger, Smithsonian Institution Libraries; M. Berton, Académie des Sciences, Institut de France; Lela Bodenlos, Smithsonian Institution Libraries; the late Dr. Julian P. Boyd, Editor of *The Papers of Thomas Jefferson*, Princeton University; the late Dr. Clarence S. Brigham, former Director of the American Antiquarian Society; Louis de Broglie, Secretaire perpetuel of the Académie des Sciences, Institut de France; Dr. Lyman H. Butterfield, Editor of *The Adams Papers*, Massachusetts Historical Society; Dr. Henry J. Cadbury, Haverford, Pennsylvania; Dr. David Clark, geophysicist, Maryland Historical Trust; Dr. Josephus R. Coan, Gammon Interdenominational Seminary, Atlanta, Georgia; Winifred Collins, Massachusetts Historical Society; R. Courrier, Secretaire perpetuel of the Académie des Sciences, Institut de France; Caleb Dorsey, Baltimore, Maryland; Dr. Ron Eglash, Ohio State University; the late Dr. Charles Ellis Ellicott, Jr., Baltimore, Maryland; Dr. V. L. Ellicott, Baltimore, Maryland; the late Peter Farb, New York, New York; Dr. Florence Fasanelli, Washington, D. C.; Robert Fellows, Jackson Heights, New York; Dr. Bliss Forbush, President of the Trustees of the Sheppard and Enoch Pratt Hospital; Mrs. LaVerne Hill Forbush, Towson, Maryland; Dr. Owen Gingerich, Smithsonian Astrophysical Observatory; Jack Goodwin, formerly of the Smithsonian Institution Libraries; Dr. Arnold E. Grummer, Curator of Museums, The Institute of Paper Chemistry, Appleton, Wisconsin; Mme. L. Hautecoeur-Milliez, Conservateur en chef of the Bibliothèque de l'Institut de France; John B. Hench, American Antiquarian Society; Dr. Brooke Hindle; Dr. Oliver Wendell Holmes, Chairman of the National Historical Publications Commission at the U.S. National Archives; Samuel Hopkins,

Baltimore, Maryland; the late Mrs. Robert J. Fitzhugh, Craryville, New York; Cherry Miller Fox, Banneker-Douglass Museum; Dr. Richard B. Hughes, Chief, Office of Archeology, and Dr. Robert J. Hurry, Maryland Historical Trust; Mrs. Bryce Jacobsen, Archivist Emeritus, State of Maryland Hall of Records, Annapolis, Maryland; Mary M. Johnson, Research Division, U.S. National Archives; Frederick W. Jones, Washington, D.C.; John D. Kilbourne, Curator, Historical Society of Pennsylvania; Charles W. Koontz, Ellicott City, Maryland; Jim Leggett, Hudson, New York; Mrs. Howard Lewis, Washington, D.C.; Mrs. Lilian Lewis, Trevor Arnett Library, The Atlanta University; Nancy R. Long, College Park, Maryland; Dr. Beatrice Lumpkin, Professor Emeritus, Malcolm X College, Chicago, Illinois; Dr. Marcus A. McCorison, Director, American Antiquarian Society; Dr. Keith E. Melder, Washington, D.C.; Dr. Uta C. Merzbach, The National Museum of History and Technology, Smithsonian Institution; Jean-Claude Nardin, Paris, France; Susan Nettles, former Archivist, State of Maryland Hall of Records, Annapolis, Maryland; Elmer J. O'Brien, Librarian of Garrett Biblical Institute, Evanston, Illinois; Roger Pierrot, Bibliothèque Nationale, Paris; C. Frank Poole, Department of Legislative Reference, City Hall, Baltimore, Maryland; Dorothy B. Porter, Librarian, Howard University; Dr. Emmanuel Poulle, École Nationale des Chartes, Paris; the late Derek J. de Solla Price, Avalon Professor of the History of Science, Yale University; R. Joyce Ramey, Falls Church, Virginia; Clayton E. Rhodes, George Peabody Branch, Enoch Pratt Free Library, Baltimore, Maryland; Albert L. Rogers, Library of Congress; Charles H. Rowell, Vienna, Virginia; Edwin Schell, Baltimore Conference, Methodist Historical Society, Baltimore, Maryland; Lee E. Sellers, Librarian, Wilberforce University; the late William A. Smith, Pineville, Pennsylvania; Janet M. Stanley, Librarian, National Museum of African Art, Smithsonian Institution; Catherine Dietz Tucker, Oella, Ellicott City, Maryland; Dr. Charles Wagandt, Oella, Maryland; Jean Walsh, Friends of Benjamin Banneker Historical Park; The Reverend B. J. S. Watkins, formerly Rector of Lydford Parish, Okehampton, Devon, England; Charles J. Weiker, Findlay, Ohio; Charles H. Wesley, Director of the Association for the Study of Negro Life and History, Inc., Washington, D.C.; Mrs. Charles E. Wilde III; Conrad Wilson, Historical Society of Pennsylvania; the late Edwin Wolf 2nd, Librarian, Library Company of Philadelphia; the late Laurence C. Wroth, John Carter Brown Library, Brown University.

To my wife, Gale, I owe the greatest debt of all, for sharing with me the pleasures and obstacles of the research as it progressed, and for devoting countless hours to the usual chores of revising the manuscript and preparing an index.

ILLUSTRATIONS

THE LIFE OF
BENJAMIN BANNEKER

I

THE HERITAGE
AND THE LAND

There is nothing that is less in our power, and less our own,
than our birth. Therefore of all pretences a man takes hold
of, to value and prefer himself to others, that of his birth
appears the most groundless; and the truth is, a man does
seldom insist upon it, but for want of another merit.

Banneker's Almanac for 1794

BENJAMIN BANNEKER LIVED his entire life, which spanned three quarters of the eighteenth century, almost to the day, in Baltimore
County in tidewater Maryland. During his lifetime he witnessed
major changes in the development of Maryland, from an English province
to a state in the new republic. He and the members of his family were at the
same time victims and beneficiaries of many of the colony's problems and
their resolutions during this period, so that the story of Banneker's life
becomes, in many ways, the story of eighteenth-century Maryland.

Much of that part of central and southeastern Maryland known as the
tidewater was still a wilderness at the end of the seventeenth century. It was
a rich, wild region divided by a waterway which created the eastern and
western shores. In contrast to the lower horizon of the opposite side of the
bay, the western shore was more elevated and undulating, presenting vistas
of open fields in green valleys against a dark background of dense forest
that studded the sturdy, low hills.

Separating the shores was the great Chesapeake Bay, from three to
eight miles wide and extending from the capes at its ocean entrance 170
miles north to its head at the mouth of the Susquehanna River. Feeding into

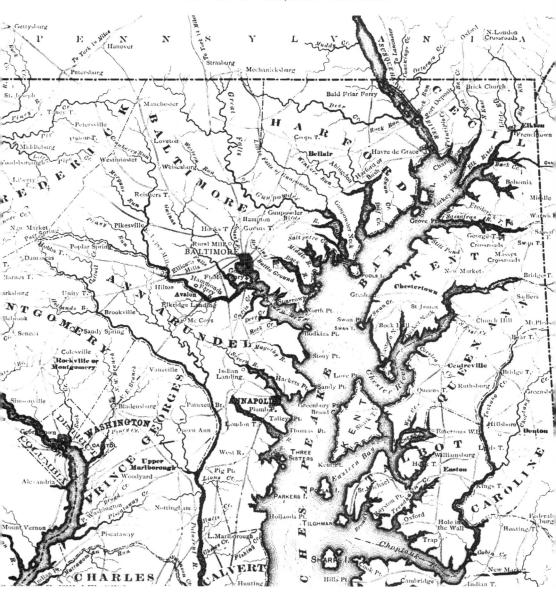

Map showing Baltimore County, Maryland, in which Banneker lived. Ellicott's Upper
Mills is situated in the upper central portion of the map, just below Baltimore. From
Charles W. Evans, *Biographical and Historical Accounts of the Fox, Ellicott and Evans
Families . . .* (Buffalo, N.Y., 1882).

this great body of water were forty-eight tributaries, from two to one hundred miles in length. Many of these rivers were navigable and sufficiently wide and deep to permit seagoing vessels to penetrate them for considerable distances.

The bay's tides moved up the western shore for a distance of approximately thirty miles, seeking the openings of major waterways such as the Severn, South, Rhodes, and West Rivers, and finally the broad mouth of the Patapsco River. The tides crept fully twenty miles up the Patapsco from its entrance between Rock Point and North Point, until the river narrowed considerably as it turned westward. It began to lose its tides at the mouth of a great gorge at the river town of Elkridge Landing. The larger vessels that came to trade with the surrounding countryside could not proceed up the Patapsco but lay at anchor off North Point, where they received their cargoes by river transport.

"Patapsco" was an Indian name that appears in at least nineteen variations in the colonial records. It derived from the word *pota* in the Algonquin language, meaning "to jut out," *psk* meaning "a ledge of rock," and the locative *ut* meaning "at," so that the original form was *Pota-psk-ut* or "at the jutting ledge of rock" or "at the rocky corner." Originally this was applied not to the river itself but to a place on the river that has been identified as "White Rocks." This was a formation of limestone ledge which projected over the river opposite the point where Rock Creek joins the Patapsco River. Still prominent today and well known to fishermen, it rose much higher out of the water and displayed a more extensive surface when white men first came into the region. Captain John Smith did not use the name Patapsco, and when he explored the Chesapeake region in 1608, he named the river Bolus. Patapsco first appeared on a map in 1660, and in the land records only several years before that date with the first grants made in the region.[1]

Scattered along the river were occasional towns or seaports, now extinct, which were established in thinly settled sections of the tidewater region after the mid-seventeenth century. Created by an act of the Assembly, the towns were directed to be self-supporting, and the inhabitants of neighboring regions were required to bring their products to the towns to be sold in the warehouses established for that purpose. By the same token, ships entering the rivers from the bay were required to anchor at these ports and unload their cargoes in exchange for local products. The towns thus supported themselves on warehouse fees. In addition to the warehouses, agents of merchants in Glasgow, Bristol, and London maintained stores that sold clothing, hardware, stationery, agricultural tools, and other imported goods that provided comfort and luxury to the primitive community.

Each town had its own "husting," or court, with jurisdiction over ordinary offenses and civil suits. The first buildings to be erected in each new river town were a church, a guildhall or courthouse, and warehouses. A town council governed the community. Market days were established several days a week, during which an active business was carried on. Autumn fairs of four and five days' duration attracted inhabitants throughout the region. Buyers and sellers came together to negotiate the sale of farm and plantation produce. Minstrels and mountebanks furnished entertainment, and common games of chance competed with a variety of outdoor sports and horse races. Slaves and tracts of land were frequently raffled during these gatherings. Many towns contained a slave market, where slaves were unloaded from the ships and sold for labor on the plantations. Londontown, for instance, was designated in 1706 as a port for the unloading of Negroes in addition to wares and commodities, and cabins of unusual construction existed east of the town and survived until recent times.[2]

Such river towns sprang up along the Patapsco's shores at the end of the seventeenth century, but none existed very close to the area in which this story takes place until the first quarter of the eighteenth century. Probably the most important community in the area was the first county seat of Baltimore County. It was a small community, also called Baltimore, established on the Bush River in what is presently Harford County. The old Baltimore was originally intended to become the capital city of the province of Maryland. In 1674 an act of the Assembly authorized the erection of a courthouse, and two years later an ordinance was passed designating sites where inns could be kept. Old Baltimore was the county seat for twenty-five or thirty years, after which it was removed to Gunpowder, where it remained until 1712. Few records were maintained during this early period because of the sparseness of the settlements, thus creating particular difficulties for the historian.

The tobacco plantations on both sides of the Patapsco were farmed by slave labor. Because communication was limited, each one formed a separate community independent of the outside world. Large numbers of artisans—blacksmiths, coopers, housewrights, cobblers, and millers—supplied the plantations' needs. Although the major crop was tobacco, many of the plantations harvested a substantial amount of grain for their own use, and some operated their own gristmills. Millers were brought from England, either as free men or as indentured servants. Those larger plantations situated at a distance from the river towns found it necessary to make their own importations. The planters sold their tobacco through English or Scottish agents, and as part of their return they imported goods that were delivered to their plantation wharves by the English vessels calling for tobacco. If prices on the London market were favorable, the planters frequently ordered more goods than they required for the plantation's needs. The surplus was kept in a storehouse from which it was later distributed to non-importing planters and farmers in the region. Sale of such items was announced by the plantation cannon.

Large plantations summoned all workers to begin each work day by firing a cannon at sunrise. When a planter had selected those items which he needed from the shipment and was ready to dispose of the balance, he fired his cannon at sunset. This was a signal recognized by other planters and farmers throughout the area, and during the next several days they would find time to call at that plantation to purchase or trade for their needs. Included in such sales was a wide range of agricultural implements, a variety of cloth, from the most common sort to fine brocades and silks; china and glassware; books, wines, shoes, and many other goods which were not produced in the province. Planters and farmers arrived on horseback, sometimes with one or more pack horses in tow if they anticipated making substantial purchases.

The plantations were connected with each other and with the river towns by horse trails and by the "rolling roads" in a network that branched out in all directions, like the strands of a cobweb. The "rolling roads" were an unusual form of thoroughfare created for the transportation of hogsheads of tobacco by hand from the plantations to the docks. The method employed was quite ingenious. Each hogshead served as its own means of transportation by having a pin or gudgeon fastened into each end; hoop shafts were attached to these, and fastened to the collars of horses, which thus rolled the load to the docks. Often a similar device was used for hauling the hogsheads by laborers. Another simple means was to have the hogsheads rolled merely by manpower.

These "rolling roads" survived to become the basis of the highway system throughout the region. At the beginning of the eighteenth century, the law required that all public and main roads be cleared and grubbed fit for travel twenty feet wide. The roads that led to the county courthouse were to be marked with two notches on the trees on both sides of the road, and another notch at a distance above the other two. Any road leading to a place of public worship was marked with a slip cut down the face of a tree near the ground. Another important means of travel was provided by the river and its tributaries. The province maintained ferries over the rivers and other large streams, which provided a means of transporting the hogsheads of tobacco by water when it was more convenient.

Tobacco dominated the lives of most people in the province of Maryland from the earliest period of its colonial existence. The crop was grown upon at least one-half of Maryland's arable land and provided the chief product and support of its people as well as the foundation of its trade and commerce. Tobacco culture severely limited the cultivation of grain and prevented the introduction of manufactures. The currency of the colony was in tobacco, and even the county payment was made in this tender.

The emphasis of an entire province on a single commodity had additional unfortunate results. Tobacco production soon increased beyond its true value, and its price consequently fell until a new code regulated its production and retarded its depreciation. It was not until 1763 that the colony passed a "tobacco code" "to amend the staple of tobacco, for preventing frauds in His Majesty's customs and for limiting the fees of officers." This act provided for the most minute details of inspection, warehousing, and shipment of tobacco, as well as punishment for opening hogsheads, burning, and stealing. Every provincial officer as well as every laborer in the province was to be paid in tobacco, all debts could be discharged in tobacco, and all duties were to be paid with it. Because of the importance of the product, stringent laws for its purity and for its inspection were strictly observed.[3]

The production of tobacco did not, however, totally obscure other needs. From time to time the Assembly passed laws to encourage industry and manufactures. Efforts were made to promote the raising of provisions and the erection of water mills for producing flour for export. However, it was not until the eve of the War for Independence that these efforts achieved some success.

Few communities existed on the Patapsco River in the late seventeenth century. Occasional large plantations flourished on both sides of the river in the mountainous regions. The upper reaches of the Patapsco with its great falls provided a wealth of water power which was harnessed to operate small mills, but large sections remained virtually unexplored and uninhabited. Farther up the gorge from the site of Elkridge Landing, steep hills rose on both sides of the river, with rocky ledges overhanging the impressive mountain torrent.

A low valley that extended just below the great falls was locally known as "The Hollow." It was enclosed on all sides by sloping hills densely covered with trees and undergrowth. Wild turkeys were plentiful, and herds of deer found shelter there. Among the major threats to travelers were wildcats living there in rocky ledges and caverns near small streams, unhindered from the time of the Indian settlements. Before the land became thickly settled, wolves roamed the region, sometimes in packs of forty or fifty. The unfortunate sometimes encountered bears and snakes, including the black snake, red-bellied water snake, corn snake, and rattlesnake.

It was in this region that our story begins, with the arrival of an Englishwoman named Molly Welsh, at about the turn of the century. There is no certainty about the correct spelling of Molly's last name inasmuch as no documents relating to her have survived. Both "Welsh" and "Walsh" have been used, but it is likely that the former is the correct version. Young Molly, a servant or milkmaid on a cattle farm, said to be in Wessex County, England, was doing her chores at milking time, when a cow knocked over a pail of milk. Her employer accused her of stealing the milk, and for this offense Molly was arrested.

According to the criminal code in England at that time, stealing was one of more than three hundred felonies for which the penalty was death on the gallows. Cruel as the system was, it was mitigated by two means, the pleading of clergy and royal pardon. A person convicted of a felony had the privilege of "calling for the book." If the prisoner could read the book, sentence of death was reduced to branding of the thumb. The other method was the judges' submission, after each session, of a list of persons considered worthy of mercy. A pardon under the Great Seal could then be issued for those listed. It was the ability to read that saved Molly from death on the gallows.

Conviction as a felon during this period was not necessarily evidence of crime; the least excuses were used to gather involuntary convicts for shipment to the American colonies to supply labor for the plantations. Although it was not legal to penalize a felon with transportation or exile, a pardon was possible on the condition that he or she leave the country. Soon after the beginning of the seventeenth century, Parliament modified the common law to enable certain classes of offenders in clergy to be sentenced to transportation. By the middle of the seventeenth century a system of conditional pardons was refined and continued in use for a century to come. The new system required that after each major assize the justices submit to the secretary of state a pardon signed by two justices for those convicts believed worthy of reprieve from the gallows. When the document was signed by the king, countersigned by the secretary of state, and passed to the chancery, it was issued. The prisoners then appeared in open court to plead their pardons; if successful, they then became available for shipment overseas, for a period of exile fixed at seven years. The sheriffs made arrangements for transportation with merchants trading in the plantations, and the latter realized their profit from selling the convicts as indentured servants overseas.[4]

No organized system for transportation of convicts existed, and they frequently underwent great hardships before they arrived in the colonies. They were often made to await the next jail delivery while held in the care of sheriffs who made no provision for their support. The sheriffs were not permitted to deliver felons to the transporters without a license. Despite repeated petitions that Parliament enact legislation to improve the situation, many years passed before any action was taken. Selection of the ship on which the felons were to be transported was left to the discretion of the sheriffs, who consigned the prisoners to one of the captains who had petitioned to transport convicts. Payment of a bond was required from the merchants to give security to the sheriffs for the safe conveyance of their charges.[5]

The voyage from England to the New World was a terrible experience for anyone, but for the transported convicts it was almost unbearable. Judged by modern standards, the vessels were extremely small, few being over two hundred tons. The number of passengers they carried varied from 150 to two hundred, including as many as twenty-five under twelve years of age. The ordinary price for passage from England to Virginia and Maryland was six pounds, although it was sometimes reduced for large parties. The length of the voyage varied from 47 to 138 days. Often after the ship's departure from London, it could be delayed by storms which detained it in another English port for several weeks before getting under way.

The great uncertainty about the length of the voyage invariably caused problems in providing sufficient food and water for passengers and crew. Since the food consisted chiefly of bread or ship biscuit, salt meat, peas, and cheese, the difficulty arose primarily from lack of space for storage. The passengers generally received the same rations as the sailors, consisting of a weekly allowance of seven pounds of bread, cheese and butter, and a weekly allotment of one half pound of pork, with peas on five days. After arrival in Chesapeake Bay, a vessel might spend three or four months calling at various ports to deliver English goods and collect tobacco for the return voyage to England.[6]

Shipmasters disposed of the felons and indentured servants as their vessels moved up the Chesapeake Bay to the river landings, their planned arrival duly announced in the local newspapers. For example, a notice in the *Maryland Gazette* told of the arrival on June 29, 1767, of the ship *Blessing's Success* from London with "a parcel of healthy country servants, for seven years; amongst which are many valuable Tradesmen . . . to be disposed of on board the said Vessel laying in the North West Branch of Patapsco River on Friday the Third Instant."[7]

A similar announcement which appeared several years later read:

> Just imported from Bristol, in the Ship Randolph, Capt. John Weber Price, One Hundred and Fifteen Convicts, men, women, and lads: Among whom are several Tradesmen, who are to be sold on board the said Ship, now in Annapolis Dock, this Day, Tomorrow, and Saturday next, by Smyth & Sudler.[8]

The transported convicts were popularly called "Seven Year's Passengers" or "King's Passengers," and frequent advertisements in the local newspapers announced their arrival. The announcements varied, and occasionally a writer with a wry sense of humor reported the arrival of "Eighty passengers, sent in for the term of Seven Years on account of their Ingenuity," or the arrival of "Sixty-eight of His Majesty's Seven Years Passengers, who had too much Ingenuity to be suffer'd to live in England."

Often their countracts were sold, and they became indentured servants. Molly Welsh arrived in the province of Maryland around 1683 on an English vessel that docked at one of the major ports of entry, which may have been Providence (later re-named Annapolis) or Londontown. There she was sold, in accordance with the custom, to defray the cost of her passage. Purchased by a tobacco planter with a plantation on the Patapsco River, Molly was required to work seven years as an indentured servant to pay for the voyage.[9]

The role of the "servant" in the colonies requires definition. A servant was in fact any person brought into the colonies for hire, and great numbers in this category arrived who indentured themselves for varying periods of time in order to to work off the costs of transportation and board of the overseas voyage. There was great need for workers on the plantations and in the cities of the New World, and English shipmasters searched out and assembled persons in all conditions of poverty from the English cities and the countryside of England. They transported them at their own expense, well aware that they would recover their investments and with profit on the colonial shores. Those transported included not only farm laborers and house servants but also tradesmen and craftsmen, such as carpenters, masons, mechanics, shipwrights, and members of the educated but frequently impoverished class, teachers and clerks, who were eagerly sought as tutors or as clerks on the plantations.

The period of indenture ranged from five to seven years and was a form of voluntary slavery. During the period of service the employer was required to provide clothing, food, shelter, and washing, and in return the servant was required to be obedient at all times, to serve his master well, and particularly not to steal. A master could not punish a servant with more than ten lashes for a single offense. No servant was permitted to travel a distance of more than ten miles beyond his master's premises without a written pass.

Upon completion of the period of servitude, a reasonable provision was made to enable the servant to establish himself or herself in gainful employment. In the province of Maryland, the freed servant was entitled to receive fifty acres of land, an ox, two hoes, a gun, and clothing. Clothes, in the case of a man, included a new suit of kersey, stockings, a hat, and shoes. Each woman was provided with a skirt and waistcoat of penistone (a coarse woolen cloth), a linen smock and a blue apron, two linen caps, stockings, shoes, and three barrels of Indian corn. Although the new landholder received the land without cost, he was thereafter required to pay an annual quitrent in order to keep the land for himself and his heirs. Shortly after the first landings in the province, however, the land allotments were reduced to one half of the original acreage, and the system was abandoned altogether in 1683. Thereafter land was available only by purchase.[10]

Molly worked out the period of her indenture faithfully and without incident. She was reasonably well treated by her master, and she made use of her time by learning as much as she could about this new country, so different from her own. Whether she was a house servant or a plantation hand is not known, but the latter seems more likely. Finally, around 1690, Molly won her freedom. There was little that a single woman could do in the wilderness by herself with the few items she acquired with her freedom rights; it must have been a bewildering prospect. Molly was a courageous and strong-willed woman, however, and after considering all possibilities, she decided to establish a farm of her own. She had neither money nor other forms of legal tender with which to purchase land, and had received none as part of her freedom fees. Her only prospect was to rent a small farm for a modest fee, to be paid annually in tobacco, located on a suitable and inexpensive tract of land in the undeveloped region not far from the edge of the Patapsco and adjoining a tributary called Cooper's Branch. It was situated conveniently near the rolling road, approximately twelve miles north of the mouth of the Patapsco.

Her new home was in the midst of wilderness, but it held few terrors for a woman who had already survived such experiences as Molly had undergone. At first she worked alone, clearing a small section of the land that was relatively free of large trees, and planting her bushels of Indian corn as well as some tobacco. She concentrated on the care of her crops, and she had rewarding harvests. She had no friends, and there were in fact very few people living in that region. There may have been one or two Indian families living in cabins some distance away, but there was no Indian settlement of any size at that time. Occasional references occur in the Baltimore County court proceedings to Indian residents of the county, and reports of the Baltimore County Garrison noted the existence of Indian cabins from time to time. Indians were attached to the fort built in the county in 1692 and paid in a type of garment called "green matchcoats" instead of money.[11]

Although Molly worked alone, she probably received some assistance in the beginning from friendly neighboring planters or their employees. She was evidently very industrious, and became a successful farmer. From time to time she put aside a little tobacco or money until at last she was able to purchase land of her own, perhaps the very piece of ground she had been farming. This was an impressive achievement, and her new status as a landowner gave Molly impetus to carry on. After several years had passed she had put aside enough tobacco, besides that which she sold to fill her needs, to purchase some assistance for managing the farm.

Molly had deliberated over this action for many months. She could not afford the highest quality of slaves, because they brought good prices and were quickly sold after arrival at the major ports of entry. She had taken the time to visit the nearby river towns when English or New England ships moved northward up the bay to sell their slaves. She had also given thought to buying one or two male slaves from one of the "soul drivers" or "soul agents" who came along the rolling roads several times each year, driving gangs of slaves that had remained unsold on shipboard. Too frequently these were ill or otherwise in poor physical condition. The system prevailed into the nineteenth century, and Robert Sutcliffe, for one, reported having encountered such gangs several times during his travels between Baltimore and Georgetown between 1804 and 1806.[12]

Molly was opposed to slavery on general principle, particularly after her own experience, but when she evaluated the alternatives she found herself without choice in the matter if she meant to survive and prosper in this strange new world. Once her decision had been made, she planned to carry it out when she next delivered her tobacco crop to the landing. Tradition handed down in the family reported that in 1692 Molly purchased her two slaves "from a ship anchored in the Bay." This would have been one of the larger English or New England slave ships that could not navigate the Patapsco and anchored outside North Point. It would have been necessary for Molly to make her way down the river, which she may have done with her tobacco crop at the end of the summer.[13]

In the late seventeenth century, traders purchased slaves at a prime cost of £4 to £6 per head and sold them in Virginia and Maryland at prices ranging between £16 and £20. The prices rose to £40 per head by the mid-eighteenth century. Prices fluctuated according to age, sex, physical condition, and particular accomplishments of the slaves, and also with the season. Higher prices for slaves were realized in the Chesapeake during the spring and early summer, due to the need for extra labor on the plantation during the working months. Prices dropped sharply after the crops were harvested near the end of the year.

Molly was able to pay only modest prices, and then in tobacco credit. She finally selected two young male Negroes from those offered. One of them looked particularly healthy and strong, and she quickly visualized his usefulness on the farm. The other lacked these characteristics, but there were qualities about him that she could not identify but which appealed to her. Furthermore, his price was particularly reasonable and she was certain he would be a good investment.

Molly's hopes were quickly realized in her first choice, and her fears were confirmed with the second. The strong slave, whose name has not survived, proved to be extremely energetic and willing to work, and he soon adapted himself to the climate and the farm labor. He seemed to enjoy felling the great trees to clear another section of the farm, and he assisted her in erecting the new tobacco building she needed, as well as with other chores.

The other slave was otherwise inclined. He was neither as strong nor as adaptable as the first, and although Molly assigned him the lighter tasks of the farm, he was not disposed to work willingly. Molly gradually managed to communicate with him and learned a little of his background. His name was Bannka or Bannaka, he told her, and he claimed to be the son of an African chieftain. Molly spoke of him later as an African prince, the son of the king of his country. He had been captured by slave traders, sold to a slave ship, and brought to the American colonies. Because of his royal blood, Bannka was unfamiliar with manual labor, and Molly had great difficulty in utilizing him on the farm. All that is known about Molly and Bannka relies on descriptions and anecdotes handed down in the Banneker family from one generation to another, and subsequently collected in interviews with survivors and contemporaries conducted by Martha Tyson decades later. According to one description, he was "a man of bright intelligence, fine temper, with a very agreeable presence, dignified manners, and contemplative habits."[14]

The origins of Bannka have been the subject of much speculation, concerning his nationality as well as the actual spelling of his name. According to contemporary records, his name was Bannka, Bannaka or Banneka, and his claim to have been a prince was resolved as being the son of a tribal chieftain in Senegal, on the western coast of Africa. Subsequent research conducted in Senegal by Dr. Ron Eglash confirmed that Bannaka was a native of Senegal, of Wolof ethnic origin and probably a member of the Poular or Fulani tribe. A Wolof given name or first name of *Banne* is to be found in Senegal, and appears to have a semantic relationship to the term "nectar," inferring a person of sweet or serene disposition. The name *Banne* in Wolof dialect is a feminine given name or first name sometimes given by Wolof mothers to their sons; it cannot, however, be passed on from that son to one of his sons.

Although *Ka* is not a surname in the Wolof language, it exists in the Peul dialect, and there had been intermarriage between the two ethnic groups. It is not likely that one would have the name of his ethnic group, but it is possible that when Molly Welsh first asked her slave his name that he answered with the name of his people. This seems to be unlikely for the son of a tribal chief, however. Wolof men are sometimes given their mother's first name, so that it is possible that Bannaka's name derived from that of a Wolof mother and of a Peul father. That the Bannaka name was derived from a Wolof-Peul combination seems likely in view of the prevalent caste system maintained during this period, which permitted members of different ethnic groups to marry if they were of the same social caste. Furthermore, Banneker's extremely dark skin color is associated only with that of the Wolof ethnic group in the Senegambian region.[15]

Eglash has pointed out that stronger identification comes from the linguistic historian Pathé Diagne, who cited the Wolof name *Banakas* as being derived from the royalty of the Wolof kingdom of Walo, presently in the St. Louis region of northern Senegal. Daigne states that the name *Banakas* can be traced to the Arabic word *Tanakas* meaning "belongs to the place" which was later west-Africanized with the consonant B replacing the T. There were many chiefs under each ruler and there was in fact a ruler of the Walo region in northern Senegal named Yerim Mbanyik Aram Bakar, who reigned in the years 1640–74. The names "Mbanikas" and "Banakas" also were names associated with royalty of the Walo region. "Banakas" is an Africanization of the word "Tanakas."[16]

During the period that the Senegambian slave trade prevailed and for years thereafter, slaves from that region—described as tall and slender black-skinned people standing straight and proud—were favored among American plantation owners and generally given preferential treatment and assigned light work around the house instead of labor in the fields. The Walo region became a considerably more vulnerable source of slaves since its economic situation was much more fragile than that of other Wolof kingdoms, and because its location exposed it directly to the European slave traders.

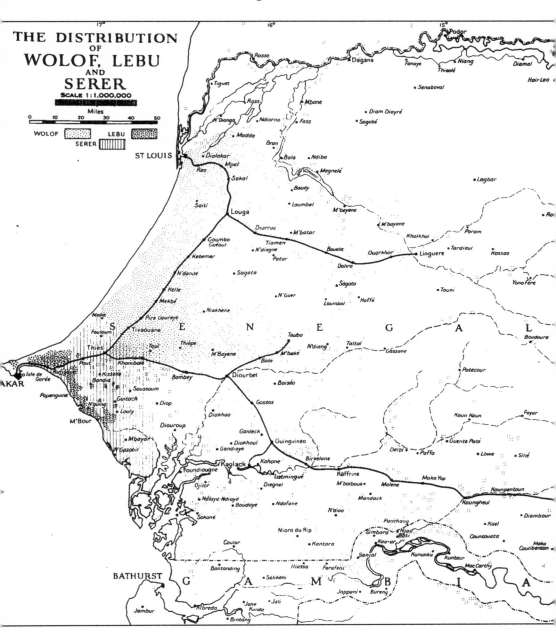

Map of Senegambia. The Wolofs inhabited the coastal region shown. From Peter D. Gamble, *The Wolof of Senegambia* (1957).

That a member of a royal family could be captured and sold as a slave can be explained by the fall of the region to the Tubenan religious revolution in 1677. According to historian Joseph E. Holloway, large numbers of slaves were taken from Senegal, which was then referred to as "Guinea," as a consequence of religious revolts that occurred in that region between 1670 and 1700, and brought to the United States. "Guinea," as a designated region, changed over time, and when Bannaka was kidnapped and enslaved "Guinea" referred to the area extending from modern Ghana to Nigeria. Large numbers of Wolofs were enslaved and transported in the late seventeenth century, a dark period in Senegambian history. Around 1670, Holloway wrote,

> . . . the Wolof, or Jolof, empire broke up into a number of kingdoms owing to a revolt instigated by Mauretanian marabouts [a dervish in Muslim Africa believed to have supernatural power]. The disintegration of this one-time empire caused instability, resulting in prolonged warfare as the Cayor region attempted to sublimate other secessionist states. Each Wolof state tried to fill the power vacuum. The long-term effect of this instability and continual warfare was that large numbers of Wolofs were taken as prisoners of war, sold to slavers, and transported to America. But after the seventeenth century the Wolofs were never again to provide a significant number of Africans to the American slave market.[17]

As well as can be determined, the greatest number of slaves were provided not from the continent's interior but from areas within a radius of two hundred miles of the ports of departure, generally from the west coast of Africa, particularly "the basin of the Senegal River," "the Guinea Coast," and the Niger Delta. The ethnic groups Mandingo, Malinke, Bambara, Wolof and Fula were included in the Senegambia region. This also explains why members of a royal family, or of the family of a tribal chief, would be taken, as has been documented for other Wolofs sold into slavery.[18]

After several years had passed, Molly Welsh gave her two slaves their freedom. In general, manumissions were rare in the province of Maryland, and then usually given because of blood relationships or in recognition of good and faithful service. Slaves might be manumitted by one of three methods during the early history of Maryland: by word of mouth, by last will and testament, or by means of a deed. A formal statute of 1752 abolished the first two methods. Although manumission by deed was rarely employed prior to this date, it became a standard practice by the time of the American Revolution. Molly Welsh's unnamed diligent slave joined the Christian faith, but Bannka held to the beliefs of his African ancestors, as well as his name, which eventually was changed by popular usage to "Banneky."[19]

Soon after Molly's slaves became free, she married Banneky, probably in about 1696. She did so at considerable risk to her own freedom, for Maryland laws governing miscegenation were stringent at that time. The intermarriage of white and black was regarded as a serious problem in several of the British colonies in North America after the middle of the seventeenth century, and legislation regarding its control became increasingly strict and was rigidly enforced. The status of the two classes of servants, the white servant and the Negro slave, varied greatly because the former became free upon the expiration of his term of service, whereas the slave generally remained in servitude all his life. By 1661, Maryland was forced to enact a law which specified:

> And forasmuch as divers freeborn *English* women, forgetful of their free condition, and to the disgrace of our nation, do intermarry with negro slaves, by which also divers suits may arise, touching the issue of such women, and a great damage doth befall the master of such negroes, for preservation whereof for deterring such free-born women from such shameful matches, be it enacted, That whatsoever free-born woman shall intermarry with any slave, and after the last day of the present assembly, shall serve the master of such slave during the life of her husband; and that all the issues of such free-born women, so married, shall be slaves as their fathers were. . . . And be it further enacted, That all the issues of *English,* or other free-born women, that have already married negroes, shall serve the master of their parents, till they be thirty years of age and no longer.[20]

The law was further enforced by a revision in 1681, but miscegenation continued, and new laws later enacted to prevent it only produced a greater problem, the need to provide for the care of illegitimate children resulting from such marriages. By 1681 it had become illegal in Maryland for any minister to join in marriage any Negro and "a white woman servant freeborn." As of 1684 any such woman who married a Negro or bore his child forfeited her freedom and became a servant "to the use of the Minister of the Poor of the same Parish." Laws even more stringent were enacted in 1715 and 1717 in Maryland, providing severe punishment for any white man or woman who cohabited with a Negro, free or slave.[21]

Molly Welsh considered the hazards long and carefully before she undertook marriage, but again, once she had made her decision she proceeded without further hesitation. It was a great risk, but perhaps she concluded that her little farm in the wilderness was too remote to warrant the attention of the law. She changed her name to that of her husband, adopted his people, and thereafter withdrew completely from her white neighbors.

In due time four daughters were added to the Banneky family. The oldest was named Mary, followed by Katherine, Esther, and Jemima. The young family led a peaceful existence in the wilderness, and eventually they prospered. Not for one moment, however, did Molly relax her watchfulness and awareness of the dangers that might threaten her and hers. The unusual circumstances of her family, because of mixed blood, was a subject of unrelenting concern. Official records in that period left much to be desired, and documentary proof of her and her family's freedom, though seemingly essential, may never have existed. In many cases, freedom or manumission papers were never written, and the fact that no evidence of any such papers has been found in Molly's case suggests the possibility that none existed originally, and that her family's security always remained in jeopardy.

Meanwhile the region along the Patapsco River was becoming increasingly settled. Several new river towns had sprung up within a day's ride of Molly's farm, and more and more of the land in that part of the country was being developed into tobacco farms. Prominent among the new settlements was Joppa Town, established in 1707 on the tract of land called Taylor's Choice, northwest of Foster's Neck. Located near the mouth of the Gunpowder River at the intersection of several rolling roads that passed through Baltimore and Harford counties, it replaced the former county seat on the Bush River. Joppa served as the county seat from 1712 to 1768 and rapidly achieved prominence as a major exporting center for the tobacco trade. This was as a consequence of an Act of Assembly of 1724, which specified that planters bringing their tobacco to the port of Joppa for sale and shipment received a 10 per cent credit against any debt they might owe the buyer. This method of paying old debts not only proved to be popular but also had a beneficial effect upon the commercial growth of Joppa. Soon after its establishment as a county seat, Joppa had not only a courthouse, prison and pillory, and tobacco warehouses, but also many town

Panoramic view of Baltimore Town in 1752. Drawn upon stone by J. Bachmann. *Maryland Historical Society.*

houses of imposing size and construction built by affluent officials and merchants. These homes, which formed a social center for the community, were at some distance from the taverns, warehouses, and teeming wharves where English vessels frequently docked to collect tobacco and deliver imported goods. Joppa grew quickly in size and importance, and by 1750 had become a thriving port town with some fifty private residences in addition to warehouses and public buildings. Ships from New England and from the West Indies and Europe made regular calls. The community developed a lively social life as merchants and travelers came to visit friends and attend the local race track.

By 1750 Joppa's fate was already predetermined, however, by the competition that soon developed from Baltimore Town. This new community on the Patapsco River, first settled in 1730, superseded Joppa as a commercial center and became the new county seat in 1768. Contributing to Joppa's decline were the timber cutting along the Gunpowder that had caused the harbor to fill with silt, and a smallpox epidemic that decimated the population. As inhabitants moved to more prosperous Baltimore, storehouses and wharves fell into ruin, the prison and courthouse buildings were sold, and all that remained in the ghost town were a few gravestones.[22]

Another river town of growing importance was Patapsco, later renamed Elkridge Landing. This town, a residential and trading center for farmers, together with the small village of Rag Landing on the Baltimore County side of the river, were the towns most accessible to upper Patapsco Valley residents during the early eighteenth century. Located at the termini of several rolling roads, Elkridge Landing provided an outlet for much of the tobacco produced in Baltimore and northern Anne Arundel counties. Elkridge Landing was established in 1725 by the second Caleb Dorsey of Hockley, who had added to the lands his father had accumulated and opened iron mines, built forges and mills, and developed a port of entry from which he shipped his products to England. He became known as "the rich iron merchant of Elkridge Landing," and in 1738 he built Belmont, an imposing family mansion that still survives. Although the tobacco trade greatly decreased during the Revolutionary War, Dorsey's forges and furnaces busily produced arms for the Continental Army.[23]

The first sadness to strike Molly's family was the death of Banneky, at a relatively early age. Perhaps his constitution had been undermined by the severe winters to which he was unaccustomed, or he may have been a victim of one of several epidemics of yellow fever that raged through the region at the time. Once more Molly found herself alone, with the additional burden of four young children to raise. When the children were old enough, they assisted her with the chores. The years passed quickly, and suddenly Molly realized that her children were grown and soon, one by one, they would marry and leave her. By this time, she had secured her land, and she began to consider the future of her children.

II

HOME AND FAMILY

Chance has often a great share in people's fortunes; why
then should it be thought strange that it sometimes also is
concerned in their reputations?

From "The Commonplace Book of the
Kentucky Philosopher," Banneker's Almanac for 1794

I T IS NOT CERTAIN WHICH ONE OF MOLLY'S BROOD was the first to leave the
family nest. It may have been her oldest daughter, whose name has not
been recorded, or it may have been Mary. The oldest daughter married a man named Henden (also Hendon), and she may have died at an
early age, perhaps in childbirth. Her son, John Henden (1), related that he
had been "raised from a little child" by his grandmother, Molly Welsh. In
1811, his son, also named John Henden, applied for his freedom and that of
his daughter, Alsey, and his application was strongly supported by his
employers, the Ellicott brothers. As certified by the Ellicotts, ". . . we have
known them for more than twenty years, during which most of the time he
has been in our employ, and for several years he and his family have lived
on our land as Tenants — That we have always considered and believed
them to be free persons & the Descendants of the Banneker family." The
court record noted that Henden ". . . is descended from a few men and
women of color of the name of Banneker." The younger Henden was still
living in 1836, when Martha Tyson described him as having ". . . always been
considered a man of strict integrity, and was for a number of years
employed by Ellicott & Co., and had charge of their stables."

In her manuscript of the memoir, Martha Tyson had stated that John
was "the son of Banneker's mother's sister," yet in a later work, *Banneker, the*

21

Afric-American Astronomer, compiled by her daughter from her notes, it was stated that he was "a son of Banneker's older sister." The former is correct, and he was in fact Benjamin's cousin.[1] (Document 48)

The marriages of two of Molly Welsh's daughters were recorded in the registers of St. Paul's Church of Baltimore, the oldest parish on the Patapsco River. Originally known as Patapsco Parish, in 1692 its name was changed to St. Paul's Parish, under the official act of the General Assembly, that gave a church establishment to the province of Maryland and christianized the names of the churches. In 1694, the tax list for the support of the parish numbered 231 persons. In 1702, the original church building was replaced with a new brick building erected on the same site. By 1728, as the city of Baltimore became more settled and had expanded, the center of the community moved, and the church was abandoned and fell into decay. A new church was constructed in 1756 on the present Lexington Street, and the graves were moved to the new burial ground at that time. The burial ground was moved several times thereafter, but no graves of principals relating to Banneker's life have survived, if indeed they had been buried in the churchyard. It is more likely that they were buried in the private burial ground on Banneker's farm.[2]

As already noted, the oldest daughter, whose name has not been recorded, had married a man named Henden. Mary, the second daughter, was born around 1700 and married around 1730. No record of either of these marriages has been found. Several years passed before another member of Molly's family was ready to leave the family. On May 22, 1735, her daughter Katherine was married to James Boston, a young Negro farmer from the same region. Nine years later, On September 22, 1744, Molly's daughter Esther married William Black in St. Paul's Parish.[3]

In about 1730, Mary, now a mature young woman, married a Negro named Robert, a native African from Guinea who had been captured and sold into slavery. He was transported to the tidewater from a slave ship that had docked along the bay ports and was purchased by a tobacco planter who had lived near Molly Welsh. According to surviving records, Robert was in slavery only seven years from the time of his capture and enslavement in Guinea, which may have occurred in about 1720–22. The designation "Guinea" changed with the time period, and during this time the name related to the region that encompassed present-day Ghana to Nigeria. This origin was more than likely due to the decrease of the Wolof slave trade after 1700 and to the tendency of slavers to send slaves of Angolan and other Bantu groups to the southern American colonies, below North Carolina.

Robert was described as having been a most unwilling slave, unruly and extremely violent, who managed to escape his master and found shelter living with the Indians. He was recaptured and escaped again several times, and finally was sold as a slave who had to be chained. It was his good fortune that he was purchased by a wealthy landowner who believed that a man having such dignity as Robert displayed should not be in bondage. Surviving records note that Robert became a willing worker and religiously inclined. He learned about the Christian faith and eventually was converted and became a member of the Church of England. It was when he was baptized that he was given the name of Robert, and at the same time he was granted his freedom by his master. It is not known how or when he met Mary Banneky, but it was sometime thereafter that they were married. Having no surname of is own, he took that of his wife and proudly became Robert Banneky.[4]

When they were first married, Mary and Robert moved in with Molly Welsh temporarily, and assisted Molly with her farm work, carefully putting aside the share of profits in tobacco credits that Robert and Mary earned so that they could eventually purchase their own land. Molly welcomed another pair of strong hands to supplement those of her family, and several years passed in peaceful contentment. Each autumn Robert and Mary totaled their share of the tobacco receipts, as each year brought their dream closer to realization.

Mary and her energetic young husband continued to live and work with Molly. Meanwhile, they had begun a family of their own. Their first child was a son, Benjamin, born on November 9, 1731. The second child was a daughter whose name was not recorded. In the next three years, three more daughters were born to them, Jemima, Minta, and Molly, the latter named after the grandmother. The Welsh farm continued to be the center of active family life, for no sooner were her own young children grown, than a second generation of youngsters arrived to replace them. These were happy times for all of them, and when the aging Molly looked around her at the faces of the several generations of her family, she must have given thought to the strange ways of fate. Possibly she may have wondered what the future might have had in store for her in England had it not been for the pail of spilled milk.

According to the testimony of one of her grandsons, Molly Welsh was not only a white woman, but also had a very fair complexion and blonde hair. Yet every member of her family, including children and grandchildren, were of black complexion, some of the darkest hue. Theirs was an unusual heritage, combining the traditions of English country life which Molly imparted to them in stories about her girlhood in England, with the mystic lore of the African continent, conveyed in the accounts of Bannka and of Robert, intermingled with the customs and conditions of the province they lived in. The one feature of their lives that each of them recognized, from personal experience or from hearsay, was the gift that they cherished above all other aspects of their life together: their freedom.[5]

Molly took particular pleasure in Mary's family. Robert had proven to be not only an excellent and energetic farmer and a good provider, but for Molly, in her aging years, he had also become a veritable pillar of strength. He was becoming impatient, however, because as his own family was developing, he was eager to establish himself independently. He and Mary carefully saved a part of their share of the crop receipts each year, until finally Robert was able to purchase a small tract of land of his own. This consisted of twenty-five acres, situated in that region called Ragland, lying east of the Patapsco Falls, near Molly's farm, above and below the site of Ellicott's Lower Mills, but not farther down than "Relay." It was densely wooded and originally called "Timber Spot"; it was appropriately re-named "Timber Poynt." The tract was located in Baltimore County, and began "at the head of a small gulley which descends into Patapsco Falls" and may have been on the Baltimore County bank of the river somewhere near Elkridge. The land had been acquired by John Howard by means of a warrant granted by His Lordship's Land Office and surveyed for him on February 23, 1729, by Philip Jones, Jr., who changed its name on the certificate to "Timber Poynt." It is not known just when Robert Banneky purchased the land, but it was surveyed for him at the time of its acquisition by J. Gardner.[6]

Robert spent the winter months each year clearing additional sections of his land and preparing it for planting in tobacco, corn, and some wheat when spring arrived. He added a small vegetable garden and from time to time he purchased and planted a few fruit trees. Little by little he was able to establish some security for himself and his family. He continued to assist Molly on her farm as needed, and meanwhile, he and Mary carefully continued to put aside as much as they could of their tobacco receipts each year.

Robert was not satisfied with "Timber Poynt"; he visualized it only as a step to the realization of his dream for a larger farm of his own with which he would be able to fulfill all the family's needs and hopes for their future. He had a specific tract in mind: a piece of land consisting of one hundred acres which had formerly been part of a larger plantation called "Stout." It was located not far from Molly's farm, with the advantages of being situated on high ground, as well as having a useful stream. The day finally came when Robert and Mary had saved enough to pay the price asked for the property, and Robert arranged a meeting with its owner, Richard Gist.

Gist was a man of prominence in Baltimore County. He was the son of the surveyor and land developer Christopher Gist, who had settled on the southern side of the Patapsco as early as 1682. Richard Gist was one of the commissioners responsible for the founding of Baltimore, and was appointed by an Act of the Assembly of July 14, 1729. These commissioners were appointed for life and were regarded as men of consequence. In addition to serving as a justice of the peace, Gist was at this time deputy surveyor of the western shore of the province.[7]

An agreement was reached; Robert tendered his receipts for seven thousand pounds of tobacco in exchange for the land. On March 10, 1737, an indenture was drawn for the conveyance of one hundred acres jointly to Robert Banneky and Benjamin, his son. This deed is an impressive document, even today. It was elaborately written in the decorative hand of the county clerk, J. Wells Stokes, and contained the traditional resounding legal phraseology.[8] (Document 1)

One can well imagine the sense of accomplishment felt by both Mary and Robert Banneky when the deed was signed. Now, they were not only free Negroes, but also landowners of substance. It must also have been impressive for six-year-old Benjamin, who would have been required to be present. The purchase of the land ensured permanent freedom and security for the Banneky children, regardless of any accidents of fate that might yet befall them. A former Negro slave and the daughter of another Negro slave had become landholders—and not owners of merely a small plot, but of a farm of fully one hundred acres—at a time when slavery flourished all around them! This was indeed a most impressive achievement, not only in their eyes, but especially in the view of their friends and neighbors.

The manner in which the indenture was recorded is highly significant. As noted, Robert purchased the land not only in his own name but also in

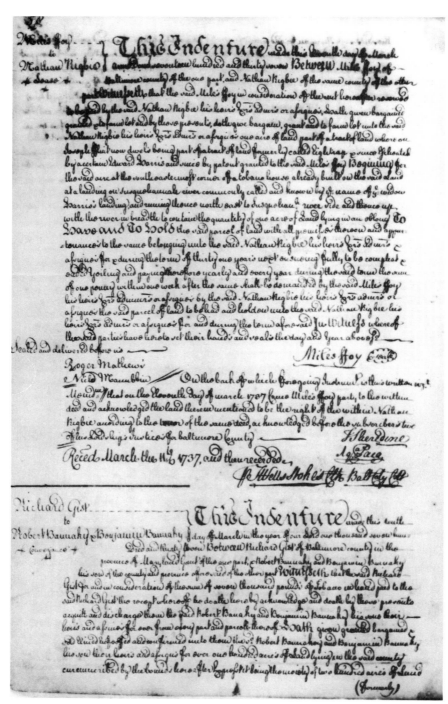

Indenture made between Richard Gist and Robert and Benjamin Banneky for the purchase of Banneker's farm in 1737. *Maryland State Archives.*

that of his son, jointly. When he died, the farm would become the sole property of Benjamin without question and without need of legal involvement. Robert's dreams were vested in his son, and he attempted to make every provision at his command for ensuring Benjamin's independence after Robert was gone.

The Banneky farm had an interesting history, which can be traced back to a land grant made in 1702 by the Lord Proprietor to a certain Captain Thomas Bale (or Beale). The tract named "Stout" consisted of 529 acres, described in the Certificate of Patent as being located "on the north side of the falls of the Patapsco River." This was part of previously unowned land beginning about 600 feet inland from the Baltimore County bank of the Patapsco River. It was just upstream of a branch then called Bales Branch that flows into the river north of the present Dickey mill town, visible in a ravine near Race Road. In 1702 it was surveyed for Captain Bale, at which time he sold 200 acres to John Whipps and described in the rent roll as being: "...on ye N.Side ye falls of Patapsco Begin^g above Bales Branch now so called. Poss.^{r} 200 ac. John Whipps part of this Tract..." Whipps mortgaged 100 acres of his land to a London merchant in 1724, and the remaining 100 acres was sold to Baltimore County merchant Richard Gist in 1733 for £18.03 Sterling. It was this portion that Gist sold to Robert and Benjamin Banneky in 1737.[9]

The Banneky portion of Stout began 284.6 feet north of the present intersection of Oella Avenue and Westchester Avenue running southwesterly to a point just west of the fork of Frederick Turnpike Road and Old Frederick Road, which is believed to have developed from a rolling road that cut through a part of Bannekey's farm. At its northwest corner the property crosses Coopers Branch, and at the southwest corner it dips slightly below Frederick Turnpike Road. No through roads existed in 1702, and Old Frederick Road was probably laid out towards a ford over Jones Falls by a court order of 1720. The Frederick Turnpike dates from 1787, and Oella Avenue, also known as Palmers Lane, which follows the eastern edge of Stout, was laid out in about 1808.

Land travel was relatively rudimentary in the early eighteenth century, and plantations were connected chiefly by means of horse paths, while several rolling roads were developed to transport hogsheads of tobacco to the port towns in the tidal regions. One of these early routes, still known as Rolling Road, was situated less than two miles from the Banneker farm.

Another rolling road which passed within three miles of the Banneker farm followed the approximate route of the present Johnnycake Road. The nearest shipping port was Elkridge Landing, near the tidewater area of the Patapsco River, approximately six miles from the Banneker's farm.

The Maryland rent rolls were records of annual quitrents and alienation fees imposed on the transfer of land in the province by the Lord Proprietor in England. In addition to the record copy maintained in Maryland, a duplicate copy was sent to him in England. Separate rolls were drawn up for each county and there was a further subdivision of each county into hundreds.

Each entry included the name of the tract of land as written in the patent, the acreage, the date of survey, the name of the original grantee, the location of the tract, the amount of annual rent, and the name of the "possessor" of the tract at the time that the rent roll was compiled. Lessees were not included under "possessor," however.

During the seventeenth and eighteenth centuries, Baltimore County consisted of what has since been divided into Harford County, a part of Carroll County, and that section of Anne Arundel County on the south side of the Patapsco River from the bay westward to the highlands beyond Elkridge, in addition to the present Baltimore County. The county at that time was divided into three "hundreds," namely, Spesutia Hundred, Gunpowder Hundred, and Patapsco Hundred. The last named was again subdivided into Patapsco Upper Hundred and Patapsco Lower Hundred. That region now encompassing Ellicott City and Oella was included in Patapsco Upper Hundred. On January 19, 1733, Whipps divided his portion of Stout, retaining a hundred acres and selling the remainder to Richard Gist. It was his moiety of Stout that Gist sold to Robert and Benjamin Banneky four years later. [10]

The remainder of the original grant for Stout formed part of a larger plantation which Anthony Bale had conveyed by deed on November 5, 1717, to Christopher Randall, and part of which was purchased from Roger Randall in 1754 by an ironmonger named William Williams. The Williams land was resurveyed on April 29, 1761, and renamed Mount Gilboa. [11]

Robert had now become a landowner of some consequence. He retained possession of Timber Poynt at the same time that he owned Stout. The Tax List for Upper Patapsco Hundred for the year 1737 listed "James Bannacar [sic] and his wife . . . 2 taxables." The error in the name was inad-

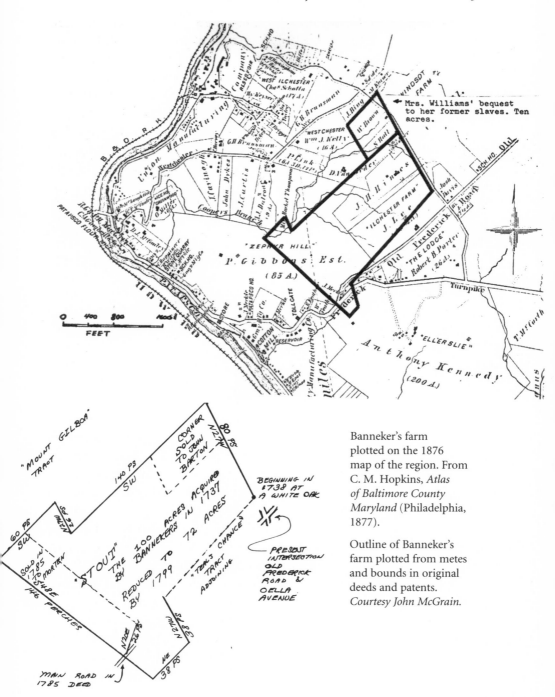

Banneker's farm plotted on the 1876 map of the region. From C. M. Hopkins, *Atlas of Baltimore County Maryland* (Philadelphia, 1877).

Outline of Banneker's farm plotted from metes and bounds in original deeds and patents. *Courtesy John McGrain.*

vertent; the record undoubtedly related to Robert, because the *Baltimore County Debt Book* contains the following entry:

Robert Banniker, D^r.

Pt. Stout	—	100	[acres]	—	0.4.0
Timber Point	—	25	[acres]	—	0.2.0.
					0.5.0.

Although the Provincial Rent Roll records indicate that a Robert Banneky had purchased "Timber Spot" from John Howard, the date of purchase is not indicated, nor is that of the subsequent disposition of the property. If Robert and Mary already owned that tract by 1731, as is probable, Benjamin almost certainly was born there in that year. Since it was part of Ragland, it was in the same general area as Stout.[12]

The annual tax was one shilling for each twenty-five acres owned. The Banneker family had to struggle at first, for the purchase of land absorbed all that they had saved at considerable sacrifice during the seven years of their marriage. They may have continued to live on Molly's farm for a time, or it is possible that by this time Robert had been able to construct a small cabin on Tiber Poynt for his family. Whichever may have been the case, his work was now cut out for him. The first task was to clear one area of the new tract that would be suitable for planting in tobacco and another on which to build their permanent home. He was fortunate in that he had acquired the land sufficiently early in the year to give him enough time to do the preliminary clearing before the spring planting. He worked long hours each day in order to make as much progress as possible.

Even though some part of the Stout tract acquired by Robert may have been cleared or cultivated prior to his acquisition, Robert was faced with a monstrous task of rendering the property suitable for homesteading and tobacco culture. There is no evidence that any structures had existed on the property. Tobacco required a rich soil, and a profitable crop depended on being grown on freshly cleared ground. Robert first removed underbrush from a large area, and then grubbed out the larger roots. He hastily planted a crop of corn and another of tobacco in the midst of the standing timber, so that no time would be lost. Once that had been done, he went on to clear another portion of the property, removing the underbrush and clearing the trees. After the brush had thoroughly dried, he started a great fire on a windy day that destroyed most of the branches and even some of the trunks. He was careful to fell the trees all in one direction, so that he could plow the land with the furrows in the same direction as the felled trees. There was no time to spend on removing the stumps; these were left in the ground to decay and be removed when time was available.

The days passed quickly. In the following spring and summer months, Robert used whatever time he could spare from Molly's farm to continue work on his own. He had lost no time in planting a crop in the first year. Since a newly cleared field could be used for only three or four consecutive tobacco crops before the soil became unproductive, new fields had to be developed to replace exhausted soil that had become fallow. After the initial planting, he started to build a house to accommodate his young family.

It is not known how Robert constructed his log house, but undoubtedly he followed the standard practice of the region. He selected the trunks of the best trees he had felled and trimmed them.

It is unlikely he took them to the sawmill up the river to be sawn into boards and trimmed into logs, as there was a lack of transportation. Wagon roads did not yet exist in the region, and the rolling roads would have been irreparably damaged by dragging heavy timber over them. Furthermore, this would have been a time-consuming procedure, and considerable manual effort would have been required to transport the logs. It is much more likely that Robert constructed the log house with rounded logs or logs having surfaces hewn flat with a broad axe, thus eliminating milling expense and permitting him to drag them only within his own property.

It was a hectic spring and summer, but everyone joined in the spirit of the new enterprise, and even Benjamin provided his share of the work. After the tobacco had been harvested and taken to market, Robert and Mary were free to turn their energies to the interior and exterior needs of their home before winter weather set in. Robert did not share the privilege of white planters in the region who met together from time to time in mutual endeavors such as house raisings, corn huskings, and crop gathering. As free Negroes, they were outcasts from such community activities. During the eighteenth century there was a rising tide of sentiment directed against free Negroes, and the Banneker family was in constant fear of violating statutes or of offending an influential white neighbor.

Robert constructed a one-room log house having a loft; it was not elaborate but it was sturdy. It was roofed with clapboards, and the great logs that formed the walls were chinked with clay on both sides against the cold and the heat. At least one opening for a window was provided. Since he could not afford glass, Robert fashioned heavy wooden shutters that could be closed against the cold and provide protection from the outside. It is likely that Robert had excavated a root cellar, and that accordingly the house was floored in wood, in a rough, puncheon floor—split logs laid lengthwise with the faces smoothed and placed upon floor joists laid upon stone or log piers. The fireplace, which occupied most of one side of the room, was probably constructed with stones dug out of the fields and assembled with sticks, moss, and clay, while the chimney may have been made of wattle and daub, as was the regional practice.

The furniture was sparse but serviceable, made by Robert himself using such simple tools as his ax, an adze, and an auger. The most important piece was the table, upon which many of the family tasks were performed. It consisted of one or more rough-hewn slabs with legs inserted into holes drilled with an auger on the underside. He made stools for each member of the family in the same manner. The beds consisted of wooden slabs laid across poles supported on forked posts. After sundown the cabin was lighted by burning pine knots. Later, as the farm prospered, he acquired a few items of furniture of slightly better quality in exchange for tobacco. The utensils that Mary had for her home were few. An iron pot was essential and greatly treasured. An iron fork and a tin cup probably completed her kitchen equipment, supplemented with pots and utensils made from wood or gourds grown on the farm.

Food for the family consisted largely of small game that Robert and Benjamin hunted and trapped in the nearby woods, and fish they caught in the river not far from their home. These were supplemented with corn bread and porridge, eggs, milk, and poultry, and possibly domestic rabbits that Mary maintained on the farm. Corn bread made from home grown corn was constant fare. In addition to mush and milk, the poor people in the tidewater lived mostly on hominy. Hominy was made by beating the ears of dried maize in a mortar to remove the hull. It was then boiled with a piece of beef or salt pork with some kidney beans. In addition to molasses hominy, there was a less frequent kind called "great hominy," which was made with meat or fowl. It served as the constant basic food, and was supplemented with vegetables such as parsnips, turnips, carrots, potatoes, simmel, (cymling) squashes, and cabbage, as well as beef, bacon, and mutton as available.[13]

When young Benjamin was old enough, Robert took him along when he went hunting and fishing. These were not primarily leisure activities, but required to provide meat and fish for the table and to teach Benjamin the rudiments. They fished in Cooper's Branch, where rockfish, catfish, drum, sheepshead, and eels were to be found, in addition to shad in the month of May. Cockles and oysters were available in abundance and supplemented the family's daily fare. Wild game abounded, including partridges, wild geese and ducks, hares, fox squirrels, flying squirrels, and ground squirrels, wild turkeys, opossums, and raccoons. Robert carefully skinned the hares and other small animals he caught for food, for the skins could be tanned and used for outer winter clothing. He also discovered that there was a market for good pelts; he traded them at the landings for needed commodities.

Early in the spring Robert set out young fruit trees, and after several years he had developed an impressive orchard of apples, pears, plums, and other fruits. After a winter or two, he learned to fence in his trees to keep the young deer from scraping the trunks with their antlers in the winter months. Eventually he added a few hives of bees, and the children had honey as an unbelievable luxury.

Mary Banneky had developed a great interest in herbs, and had become extremely knowledgeable on the subject. Since her early years at home on her mother's farm, she had searched for woodland plants having medicinal value. She collected information about medicinal herbs and remedies not only from her neighbors, but also from the few Indians in the region. She cultivated sassafras, ginseng, and snakeroot and collected the waxy berries from bayberry bushes for making candles. It is likely that she also grew some flax and hemp, and a little cotton, which she could spin and weave for cloth to be used in the house as well as for clothing. She made her own brooms from reeds growing along the banks of the Patapsco. More than likely Mary applied her knowledge of herbs to the brewing of persimmon beer, a great favorite in that part of the country. It was flavored with the leaves of a plant called "cassona," which may have been wintergreen.

Robert continued to improve his home as time went on. Nails were a rarity and were costly, and he had only a few. He learned to fasten his furniture together with pegs in the traditional manner. Mary saved the soft downy feathers from chickens and other fowl that were part of the family menu, and in due time was able to make feather mattresses.

According to provincial land records, much of the tract called Stout and the lands surrounding it remained only sparsely settled as late as the middle of the eighteenth century. Any immediate need for a blacksmith and other trades took Robert to the nearest communities to seek their services, to Joppa and probably Elkridge Landing. Occasionally a traveling journeyman stopped at the farms and plantations on his way through the countryside, enabling the planters to use his talents for resolving other farm needs.

Tobacco culture required constant work and attention, occupying the Bannekers' lives from dawn until dusk, seven days a week, until the arrival of winter. Benjamin accepted it as his lot, and as he grew older he shared to some degree his parents' pride in ownership of the land, exulting with them when the season had been a good one. Despite all their efforts, the annual yield was adequate but not great. History is silent on the subject, but it is likely that due to their status as free Negroes and the relatively small size of their holdings, they were unable to hire labor to share their work on the farm. They did not own slaves, as did some other free Negroes, and consequently operated the farm entirely by themselves. At first Robert and Mary worked alone, but with each passing year they received increasing assistance from their children as each took up his or her share of the farm chores and field work.

Robert had learned how to cultivate tobacco from his former master, to which learning was added the experience of his years working on Molly's farm. Early in the spring, in March or April, depending on the lateness of the frosts each year, he took the tobacco seed he had saved from the previous year's crop and carefully planted it in seedbeds. The seedbeds were laid in the woods in an area of virgin mold that had been cleared of trees and undergrowth, which had then been burned on the site to enrich the soil. The tiny seeds were imbedded in the layer of ash over the virgin mold. The tobacco plants made their first appearance about a month later and by June had become strong enough to handle for replanting. Robert and his family watched over them anxiously until, as tradition required, the new plants "be grown to the Breadth of a Shilling." They were then carefully removed and planted in newly cleared woodland in parallel rows of little hillocks about three feet apart. The transplanting could be accomplished only in wet weather when the ground was soft.[14]

Then followed a period of anxious watching and waiting. Robert and Mary and even Ben spent their time picking insects from the tender shoots and weeding to ensure that the young plants grew strong without obstruction. The soil of their farm was a light sandy loam, so that the plants did not support as many leaves as they would have in soil of a richer quality. When the shoot had put out ten to fifteen leaves the top of the plant was broken or cut off, a process known as "topping," to ensure that the plant grew no higher and that the leaves would receive all of its strength. Meanwhile the plant put out suckers between the leaves, and each week Robert and his family surveyed the rows of hills and plucked off the suckers.

The topping operation required considerable skill and was usually done by Robert. Plants were topped by pressing the stem between the thumb and forefinger, with the thumbnail as the cutting instrument. Topping was done just before the plants came to flower. Robert first went through the fields row by row to select the plants that seemed to be the finest and strongest, to be reserved for seed for the next year's crop. Since the tobacco flower tended to be self-fertilized, it was important to prevent the seed plants from being crossed with those of inferior quality. He covered the flower heads with small cloth bags that he secured to the stems with string after removing the small leaves and branches just below each flower head. This was another chore for the children, for as the flower developed, it was necessary to adjust the bags periodically to leave room for growth. When the seeds were mature, the seed pods turned brown and the flower head became partially dried. Then the seed head was cut off and hung in a cool, dry place to air-dry. Eventually it was shelled out and the seed preserved for the coming year in a place protected from rats and mice.[15]

Like other tobacco planters in the region, Robert fought a constant war with pests. He had to be alert against the small flies and flea beetles that could destroy all the seedlings if they were not quickly removed. Robert made an infusion of sassafras bark which, when sprayed on seedlings, kept them free of the flies. During the first weeks after transplanting he again had to be alert and watch for cutworms and horn worms that developed in the soil and would come out and cut off the shoots. Equally destructive were aphids and slugs. Finally, when the young plants had grown to full size and strength, he was faced with the problem of tobacco caterpillars. These often arrived in great numbers and could rapidly cover the tobacco planting.

It seemed to young Benjamin that there could be no other plant that required as much time and attention as did tobacco, for it was usually his lot to watch for the insects and to get rid of them as they appeared. When he was old enough, he joined his parents with their farmwork in the spring, sharing the chores, grubbing the soil to prepare for the transplantation of the seedlings. There was little pleasure in wielding a mattock or grub hoe; each night he went to bed exhausted. He preferred the hilling hoe rather than the mattock, because that phase of the work was somewhat more interesting although just as exhausting. To prepare the hills he had to stand with his foot advanced, whereas with the hilling hoe he had to throw the soil from all sides around his leg, then withdraw his foot and flatten the top of the hill. Later, when the young shoots began to sprout, he used yet another hoe to chop out the weeds that grew profusely, particularly during the hot spells.

The most active time in the summer was August, when the tobacco plants had grown to perfection, about six weeks or so after topping. Robert waited for a period of dry weather with little wind before cutting the plants. He and his family worked quickly, letting the leaves lie on the ground for not more than half a day until they drooped down on the stalks. Then they collected the stalks and brought them on their shoulders to the tobacco barn. There they split the ends of the stalks and quickly hung them on tobacco sticks as closely together as possible without touching. Here the tobacco remained for five or six weeks. When the stem in the middle of the leaf snapped upon being bent but the leaves were still moist enough that they could be handled without breaking, they were stripped from the stalks, bound into bundles, and packed into hogsheads for shipment.

After the first year or two, Robert was able to estimate the crop yield per acre and per year. One thousand pounds of tobacco yield per acre was considered good in his time, and each acre required from four hundred to five hundred man-hours of work. He probably was able to produce a maximum of two thousand pounds of tobacco in a year, with an equal total amount from Mary, young Benjamin, and later, their daughters. This was in addition to a few barrels of corn.

Estimates of tobacco production per hand in seventeenth- and eighteenth-century Virginia and Maryland vary widely. In 1619, John Pory in Virginia claimed 1,143 pounds per worker, while one Richard Brewster claimed to have produced an average of 700 pounds per man in addition to a crop of corn. Normal production at the beginning of the eighteenth century ranged from 1,000 to 2,700 pounds per man, so that it is reasonable to think that Robert Banneker, with relatively poor soil and few hands, probably produced somewhere between those two amounts.[16]

Like other planters, he shipped his tobacco in hogsheads, which he probably purchased from a cooper at Elkridge Landing or at another river town. The size and details of construction were regulated by law to ensure that the volume of each hogshead was always the same and measurable. A Maryland hogshead was required to be forty-eight inches high by thirty-two inches in diameter at the head with "a bulge proportionable."[17]

Robert delivered the tobacco in hogsheads to tobacco brokers at the landings. The broker weighed it and paid the planter in tobacco notes, then shipped it to the English market on seagoing vessels that came into the bay and up to the landings. Merchants' tobacco notes specified the net weight received, the name of the warehouse, and the type of tobacco, whether it was Oronoko or sweet-scented, stemmed or leaf. These notes were readily negotiable within the same and in adjacent counties and were widely used for the payment of taxes, fees, and other costs.

Young tobacco plants required continuous attention, except during the late autumn and winter when frost prevented any work on the crop. Tobacco also held many hazards that could reduce a planter to poverty in one or two seasons. The threat of crop failure due to the weather was ever present, and it was possible to ruin an entire crop by improper curing or by inadequate prizing into the hogsheads. A depression in prices caused by overproduction affected the value of everyone's crop, and the quality of the cooperage available also could have an important impact on the sale.

Although London or outport merchants generally handled all details of marketing and transportation for larger planters, small farmers like Banneky usually sold their crops outright to a factor or agent at one of the landings. Factors represented large English merchants and resided permanently in the port or landing, working for a salary or a commission. The planter received a lower price for his tobacco, but he avoided most of the risks and delays. Frequently the factor operated a store in his warehouse, in which planters could find goods imported from England and the West Indies.

Young Benjamin did not resist the never-ending chores of a tobacco farm and actually found much in the daily work to interest him. He calculated, for instance, that the entire process of tobacco cultivation included not less than thirty-six separate operations. Even as a small boy he had a great interest in statistics and in any form of mathematical endeavor, which he developed as he grew older.

Tobacco was not the only source of work that had to be done on the Banneker farm. Corn had to be planted, weeded, hilled, and nurtured until the fall, for this was the crop that fed the family. The Bannekers also grew a small amount of wheat, probably not enough to bring to market but enough to satisfy family needs.

Among Benjamin's chores was "cowpenning," which meant moving their several head of stock from one planting area to another and setting up portable fences around them. The purpose of this task was to accumulate manure to enrich the soil. Whenever time permitted, Benjamin and his father took the farm wagon down to the marshes along Cooper Branch or the Patapsco River and shoveled out marsh soil, which consisted of dark, rich loam. This they brought up to the higher meadows and spread on the ground to dry. Later they cleared it of roots and rocks and used it to build the hills for the planting of a new crop of tobacco.

Robert Banneker belonged to the category of small planters having property worth not less than £100 or more that £300. This would have provided no more than a "country living." In addition to his acreage, Robert's holdings included not more than half a dozen cows, two saddle horses, a few swine, some poultry, and a limited assortment of household and farming utensils and tools. It is unlikely that he produced more than six hogsheads of tobacco a year. Occasionally he may have been able to sell a heifer, a pig, or a few bushels of corn to local traders to supplement his income.[18]

The winter months brought a different kind of activity. The farm animals had to be cleaned and fed, and there were other daily requirements. Robert spent some of his time felling trees to clear additional acreage, and, after the branches had dried, burning the brush. Usable wood was sawn into boards or cut into logs and brought back to the barns and stored for future use. Some of it would become riving staves or shingles.

The planter's wife and daughters spent their time spinning and weaving and making clothing for the family and cloth for other needs. Winter was a good time to trap and hunt, and the pelts acquired would be dried and tanned and used for outer clothing. Fine pelts could be sold to local traders or exchanged for other goods. It was also the time for making farm repairs. When the weather was good the planter inspected and repaired walls and fences, pruned his orchards, and cultivated his stand of wild grapes.

Much of Benjamin's free time was spent at his grandmother's farm, where she taught him to read and write. She was particularly concerned that he should have a respect for religion. Partly to practice his reading and partly to learn its contents, on every Sabbath day she had Benjamin read to her from her Bible. She had sent to England for it, and according to one of her grandchildren it was a large volume, one of her few treasures and one that she enjoyed sharing with her young grandson. He soon surpassed her in biblical knowledge, then revealed an interest in the history of the province and its early settlers. Molly was impressed with his agile mind, his ability to learn quickly, and his remarkable memory even as a child. The hours she spent with him were always pleasant for both of them, and as he grew older she looked forward eagerly to his visits.

As young Benjamin learned to read and write he derived much pleasure from it, for it opened up great new worlds for him. His father and mother took pride in his learning and were hopeful for his future. Molly arranged for Benjamin to attend a small country school recently established in the neighborhood. The one-room school, kept open only during the winter months and taught by a Quaker schoolmaster, was attended by several white and two or three black children, who all received instruction together. Jacob Hall, one of Benjamin's classmates, later recalled Benjamin's consuming interest in study even then, saying that as a boy Benjamin was not particularly fond of play or light amusements, and that "all his delight was to dive into his books."[19]

Little is known about Benjamin's other associates as a boy or as a man. The remoteness of his home, the Bannekers' distance from community life, and the needs of the farm limited his number of possible friends. Attendance at the country school was a major event in the boy's life and left a profound impression on him later. Jacob Hall, who remained his life long friend, was, like Benjamin, a free Negro, whose father had been a slave owned by Walter Hall, a wealthy planter in Anne Arundel County. The elder Hall had been given his freedom and a bonus of thirteen acres of land in Baltimore County as a reward for his faithful service. Benjamin and Jacob maintained their childhood friendship for the remainder of their lives. When Jacob was older, he was employed for more than forty years as the keeper of the Ellicott family graveyard in Ellicott's Lower Mills. He and his family held the land given to his father until late in the nineteenth century.[20]

Because school was in session only during the winter months, Banneker's formal education was limited. After he was old enough to work with his father full time, it was no longer possible for him to attend classes. He had especially enjoyed arithmetic and all similar mathematical exercises. Although unable to continue his schooling, Benjamin nevertheless pursued his reading and thus educated himself for the rest of his life. At first he had no books of his own, other than his grandmother's Bible, but it is possible that his former schoolmaster lent him texts to use at home. He later commented that he had "advanced in arithmetic as far as Double Position" by his own efforts. It seems fairly certain that Benjamin was not taught Double Position in the country school but had learned it by himself later.

Double Position is no longer a familiar term, but it was included in school texts as late as the mid-nineteenth century. In Eaton's Treatise "the Method of Double Position" is given for the purpose of obtaining an answer that would now be handled with an equation by any high school freshman algebra student. In Double Position a value is assumed for the number to be derived, which is inserted into given conditions, computed, and then it can be seen how far wrong the result may be. One then repeats, and since by this time the number sought has been bracketed, the correct solution is achieved. The rule or method of Double Position has been known from antiquity, sometimes by other names. In Europe, for instance, it was also known as the Rule of Double False.

False position solutions were widely used in Banneker's time, and known also as "rule of false," "rule of position," "double position," and "scales," which is a type of diagram. The method is summarized in a text by Daniel Adams entitled *The Scholar's Arithmetic* that was written before 1801 and published in 1807. Adams wrote:

> Position is a rule which, by false or supposed numbers, taken at pleasure, discovers the true one required. It is of two kinds, Single and Double. Single Position is the working with one supposed number, as if it were the true one, to find the true number.
>
> RULE 1. Take any number and perform the same operations with it as are described to be performed in the question 2. Then say, as the sum of the errors is the given sum, so is the supposed number to the true one required.

The "Single Position" method was known to the Egyptians and examples are contained in the ancient Egyptian Rhind Mathematical Papyrus copied prior to 1800 B.C.E. by the scribe A'hmosè. The false position method was described in a number of texts on mathematics, including Bonnycastle, Eaton, and Smith.[21]

Robert and Mary Banneker achieved a comfortable living if not actual prosperity by their hard work. They enjoyed their family, their home, and their life together, and in due course the family grew. By the time three daughters had arrived, their log house was no longer adequate, and it became necessary for Robert to construct a larger dwelling.

The years passed quickly for young Benjamin on the farm along the Patapsco, and with each season he learned more and more about the natural wonders around him. He spent his spare time roaming through the cleared fields and venturing into the neighboring forests, sometimes with one or more of his sisters or cousins, but more often alone. His parents encouraged him to explore his surroundings and learn what he could from nature. He soon learned to appreciate the wild beauty of the region.

Not more than a mile from the Banneker house the mighty Patapsco River flowed, enclosed on both sides by chains of uncultivated hills. The water ran with a mighty sound over its bed of broken rocks not yet worn smooth. Some of them projected above the surface and the river dashed angrily against them, creating an unceasing, sepulchral roar. Along the looming hills on either side the trees, stunted by poor soil, bent themselves almost horizontal in an effort to survive, their sparse foliage barely shading the ground. Patches of scrubby undergrowth and yellow, sandy soil were surrounded by great stands of tall trees that rose along the water's edge and covered the hilltops. A short distance from the river was a spring of cool, soft water protected by a grove of trees. According to tradition the area was a camping ground for Indians who came down from the north to fish. Shad and herring were taken in great numbers high up in the Patapsco before the mills and dams were built.

Having been alone much of his boyhood and well into his manhood, Benjamin learned to cherish the solitude. Limited in his travel and association with others by the demands of the farm, he saw few people other than members of his family, none of whom shared his literary and educational interests, although they were impressed with his enthusiasm and evident capabilities. Consequently he became more and more withdrawn, and his senses grew all the more alert to the world around him. His was a keenly developed awareness of nature, and he became unusually observant of the wildlife around him.

Banneker's unusual ability with mathematics was apparent, but he was equally interested and skilled in mechanics, and the farm afforded him many opportunities to apply his mind and hands. Almost to the advent of the American Revolution, tidewater Maryland had no established public craftsmen such as blacksmiths, tinkers, cobblers, or tailors. Men having such skills did exist, but they were few and itinerant, traveling about the province from one plantation or community to another. Large planters employed their own skilled artisans on the premises, but if he could not perform the work himself the owner of a small tobacco farm usually had to wait for repairs until an itinerant craftsman came into the region.

It was while he was still a very young man, in his early twenties, that Banneker created an object that brought him fame in his community and in local literature. This first scientific accomplishment was associated with a theme that preoccupied him during the major part of his life, the concept of time. Those who knew him reported that in all of his young life he had seen but two timepieces. One was a sundial. These were commonly made at home and widely used in the colonial period, often in the form of pewter dials cast in a soapstone mold. Soapstone was available in the region of Ellicott's Lower Mills and was mined commercially in certain parts of Maryland during the nineteenth and twentieth centuries. Such a dial, believed to have been made by or for George Ellicott in 1779 for the latitude of 40°, has survived,[22] but there is no evidence that Banneker ever tried to copy a sundial.

The other timepiece he saw was a pocket watch. According to a statement Banneker made to his neighbors, he borrowed a watch to serve as a model for the clock he subsequently constructed. It is not known whose watch Banneker first saw or from whom he borrowed one. It may have belonged to a merchant at one of the landings to which he brought his tobacco, or to a traveler who passed by the farm. The intricate mechanism of a watch would unquestionably have aroused his curiosity. A most acute observer, he noted everything in detail, and remembered accurately what he had seen. There is no greater evidence of this ability than in the construction of his clock. It is likely that he visualized it as a mathematical puzzle, a collection of varied individual parts, each having its own function that, when all were brought together correctly, produced another entity having yet another function.

Recalling the arrangement of the watch's parts, he approached the project as he would have one of his puzzles, working out the relationship of toothed wheels and gears as components of a mathematical problem. Banneker conveyed his recollection of the watch's wheelwork into drawings, then applied his natural mathematical skill into calculating the relative size and number of teeth required for each of the wheels and pinions. Each wheel and gear was carefully and correctly laid out in a diagram, the balance regulator and the spring barrel, then one by one he converted these into three-dimensional parts. He labored long over the project, carving each item with a knife from selected pieces of hard-grained wood that he had collected and seasoned for the purpose, modifying the parts one by one as needed to fit them together. Unable to produce a spring of sufficient strength to power the timepiece, he substituted a system of falling weights.

At last the movement was finished. Except for a few small parts of iron and brass, Banneker had made a striking clock entirely of wood. For its bell, which struck on the hour, he may have used a piece of resonant metal or more likely, the bottom of a glass bottle. Banneker made a dial plate from a flat wooden panel, inscribed and painted with a chapter ring. He then carved a pair of hands to indicate the hours, and provided a wooden casing for the timepiece. Astoundingly, this miracle of untutored craftsmanship actually worked.

Banneker's own pleasure in it was equaled only by the wonder and astonishment of people who visited the farmhouse and saw it. His fame spread rapidly through the valley. Those who had known nothing about Benjamin Banneker the farmer learned about him as the maker of a fascinating timepiece. He was only twenty-two years old at the time, and his achievement was looked upon as remarkable.

Banneker's clock was by no means the first timepiece in tidewater Maryland during the early eighteenth century, as has occasionally been erroneously claimed. Timepieces were well known and available in the American colonies from the very earliest English settlements, although admittedly they were limited in number. A few watches and clocks had been brought from the mother country and were highly prized. Soon after the colonies were settled, a handful of clockmakers trained in England migrated and established themselves in the larger communities. With increasing affluence among the settlers, clocks and watches were imported and advertised for sale by dealers in the port cities. Often craftsmen trained in England combined the making of clocks and the repair of watches with other skills such as silversmithing or pewtering.

Prosperous Chesapeake planters frequently ordered timepieces from their factors in London. They consigned their tobacco to be shipped, and often requested the factor to purchase items not available in the colonies, such as clothing, tools, and furnishings. Records have survived of numerous such orders. For example, Edward Lloyd of Wye House, the seventh member of his family bearing the name, in correspondence with his London factors, Messrs. Oxley, Hancock & Co., requested the latter to provide him with "...an elegant Watch Clock, proper to fix on a Chimney Piece; also a Sett of fashionable Decorations to set off a Dining or Supper Table that will accomodate 20 People."

Several watch and clockmakers were already established in the colony prior to the time that Banneker made his clock. In Annapolis alone there were at least four such craftsmen prior to 1750. Among these may be mentioned John Batterson, a watchmaker who moved to Annapolis in 1723; James Newberry, a watch and clockmaker who advertised in the *Maryland Gazette* on July 20, 1748; John Powell, a watch and clockmaker believed to have been indentured and to have been working in 1745; and Powell's master, William Roberts.[23]

Completed in 1753, Banneker's clock continued to operate until his death more than fifty years later. After a visit to his home by Mrs. George Ellicott and some friends in 1790, her daughter recalled that

> his clock struck the hour, and at their request he gave them an account of its construction. With his inferior tools, with no other model than a borrowed watch, it had cost him long and patient labor to perfect it. It required much study to produce a concert of correct action between the hour, minute and second machinery, and to cause it to strike the hours. He acknowledged himself amply repaid for all his cares in its construction by the precision with which it marked the passing time.[24]

On July 10, 1759, when Benjamin was twenty-eight years old, Robert Banneker died. Now burdened with the full responsibility for management of the farm and for the care of his mother and sisters, and possibly his grandmother as well, Banneker had little time left for his studies and plea-

Movement of a wooden striking clock, similar to the clock constructed by Banneker in 1759. This one was made by Connecticut clockmaker Benjamin Cheney, circa 1760. Courtesy *National Museum of American History, Smithsonian Institution.*

sures. According to the terms of the original deed, the entire farm became his own, without shares for his mother and sisters. Timber Point, the first tract of land Robert had acquired, was probably divided at his death among his three daughters.[25]

Meanwhile, Jemima, another of Banneker's sisters, had left home at a fairly early age to marry Samuel (Delaney) Lett, a white farmer. It was said that his family name originally was Delaney and that he was of combined English, Irish, and Indian descent. When he was a small boy his widowed mother, a white woman, married again, to an African-American named Zachariah Lett. Samuel, taking his stepfather's name, became known as Samuel Delaney Lett. He and Jemima were married in Baltimore County in 1757, and their oldest son, Aquila, was born in 1758.[26]

Until about 1770 the Letts lived in a log house in the vicinity of what became Ellicott's Lower Mills, and then moved to Frederick in Frederick County, Maryland. It was at about the same time that Zachariah Lett sold his land and moved to Frederick; Samuel and Jemima may have been living on part of Zachariah's land before he sold it. The Maryland Census for Frederick County for the year 1790 listed the Lett household as consisting of Jemima and two of her sons, Aquila and Elijah. The entry specified:

> Jemima Banneker, the daughter of a free black man who had taken the name of Banneker from an unknown source, married a white farmer, Sam Lett of English and Irish descent. They were married in Baltimore County, Maryland, probably in 1757 since her first son, Aquila, was born in 1758..[27]

Jemima was described as a modest person, devoid of all pretense, her complexion reported to have been black or nearly so. She lived a quiet and simple life, exerting a strong influence on her children, eight of her nine living to maturity. All of them were given Biblical names—Aquila, Meshach, Samuel, Elijah, Mary (or "Mollie"), Kesiah (or "Kezzie"), Peter, and Benjamin. Aquila married Christina Cobbler, a white woman of German descent who may have had some Indian antecedents, and they had ten children. Meshach Lett was married four times, and three children were known. In about 1799 the Lett family left Frederick County and moved to Virginia between Leesburg in Loudon County and Winchester in Frederick County. Samuel and Jemima Lett both died in Loudon County, where they were buried.[28]

Benjamin's sister Minta married a young man named Black. Whether Minta's husband was a relative of the William Black who had married her Aunt Esther has not been determined. Minta and her husband settled in the general neighborhood of the Banneker farm and she became well known in the region as a midwife and tailor who also did spinning for hire. These occupations were noted in the business records of one of her clients, Zachariah Maccubbin, a merchant or storekeeper and landowner in Baltimore County. A credit account listing Minta's services during the decade from 1790 to 1800, in which she was occasionally named "Mary Black (Negro)," identified her as having served the Maccubbin family as a "prolific" midwife as well as having provided tailoring and spinning. During this period she delivered six of the Maccubin children as well as three children of their slaves, spun 26 3/4 pounds of "Stocken Yarn" between 1790 and 1792, and made three pairs of men's trousers and four men's shirts.[31] (See Document 2)

Molly, the youngest sister, married Samuel Morten (also Morton), who was employed at Ellicott's Lower Mills. Their son, Greenbury Morten, worked as a cooper and was well known in the region; later he was employed at the Ellicott stables at Ellicott's Lower Mills.

Meanwhile, Molly Welsh Banneky, the family matriarch, had died. No record of her death has been found in any of the surviving documents, nor is the disposition of her farm recorded. Presumably the land passed to her other daughters.

Banneker proved to be a competent farmer well versed in tobacco culture, and after his father's death, and with the help of his mother, he continued to grow tobacco. His contemporaries noted that he owned two horses and several cows, in addition to a number of beehives from which the honey was collected and sold. His mother cultivated a large garden, growing vegetables and other staples for their own use and for sale. Banneker also raised grain, including wheat and corn for his immediate use, but the primary effort of the farm lay in the cultivation of tobacco.

The tax list for Patapsco Upper Hundred for the year 1773 listed Banneker as the single adult member of his household. Although this implied that his mother was no longer living, other records indicate that she was alive at least until mid-1775. Banneker's name has otherwise been found in civil records only in connection with property transfers, with one exception, his registry of a stray animal before Justice Gay at Joppa on October 31, 1761.[32]

A memorable event in Banneker's life was the acquisition of his first book. At the age of thirty-two he bought a quarto edition of the Bible, on the flyleaf of which he proudly inscribed: "I bought this book of Honora Buchanan the 4th day of January 1763. B.B." Two other entries relating to events in his life were made in the Bible at approximately the same time:

> Benjamin Banneker was born November the 9th, in the year of the Lord God, 1731, and Robert Banneker departed this life July the 10th, 1759.

To while away some of his lonely hours, Banneker turned to music. He owned a flute and a violin, and had learned to play both reasonably well. Undoubtedly he visited nearby plantations from time to time, where he acquired the instruments and learned how to play them. He also learned to play the songs of the people. He probably purchased the flute and possibly a music book or two from the stocks imported by one of the larger planters in the area, and he may have traded or purchased the violin from a neighbor at some time in his youth. He made no mention later in life concerning his musical interests, where he had acquired the instruments, nor how he had learned to play them, but music was one of his greatest sources of pleasure. After the day's work was over, he enjoyed sitting outside his house and softly playing one or the other. Sometimes members of his family would join him in the twilight, often singing the words while he played a familiar song. Banneker found utmost satisfaction in the sounds he produced. The pleasure he derived from music, supplemented by his reading, together with his enjoyment of mathematical puzzles, helped to pass the few hours of leisure in the solitude of his farm.

It is conceivable that Banneker's love of music derived from the Senegambian background of his ancestors, perhaps taught by his grandfather. The Wolofs are believed to have been a source of the popular American banjo, the name of which may be a corruption of the word *bania*, a generic name for a similar instrument found in Senegal, and there is also a close connection between the music of the American banjo and that played on the Wolof *halam*, a five-stringed instrument like a guitar, one string of which vibrates openly as a drone and is played in a style called frailing. According to Palmer, Senegambian slaves who played native bowed string instruments would have had little difficulty adapting to the European violin. Flutes were common instruments and made by boys from millet stalks. On some plantations there were slave orchestras made up of various combinations of native instruments including flutes and fifes. These orchestras became a fixture of plantation life.

During the decade or more after his father's death, Banneker lived alone with his mother. He was listed as a taxpayer in St. Paul's Parish among those parishioners whose "taxes as worth £100 and under £300" for the years 1756 through 1762 (records for 1759 are missing) at the rate of twenty shillings annually.[33]

Although Banneker was acquainted with some of the planters in the valley and with the itinerant tradesmen who occasionally passed through the area, he does not appear to have had any close friends, nor did he seek them. The fact that he was a free man of color restricted his activities in the community. He had learned as a small boy that although the industriousness of his family was respected, some barriers could not be hurdled. Banneker seems to have been relatively contented with his lot, and he sought to avoid conflicts arising from the limitations of his station.

With the passage of time, however, Banneker achieved recognition and respect in the region as a man of some learning. Reading and writing were skills rarely found except among the wealthy plantation owners and their families. His neighbors came to him for assistance in making calculations for one purpose or another, for composing the few letters needed, and for help in other simple matters. As a consequence, he became a well-known figure, much admired for his dignity, reticence, and gentlemanly qualities. Many came just to see his striking clock, which had become something of a legend in the valley, and for each visitor Banneker left his fields to display his achievement with modesty and pride.

III

FRIENDS
AND NEIGHBORS

We must think well of that man, who uses his best endeavours to associate with none but virtuous friends.

Banneker's Almanac for 1794

T HE MOST IMPORTANT INFLUENCES upon Benjamin's life were derived
from those individuals who increased his learning. The first of
these had been his grandmother, Molly Welsh. The second was the
unknown Quaker schoolteacher from whom he received the rudiments of
an elementary education. The third was George Ellicott, who became his
neighbor as a young boy and who as a young man befriended him.
Although twenty-nine years his junior, George was to become Banneker's
friend and the one who brought about the major fulfillment in his life.

The history of the Ellicott family in America began with the migra-
tion of Andrew Ellicott [I], a wool manufacturer in England. During a period of business reverses, he came to America with his eldest son, Andrew
[II], for a visit to the community of Buckingham in Bucks County,
Pennsylvania. During this brief sojourn, the younger Andrew fell in love
with Ann Bye, a local girl whom he later married. He and his father
remained in Pennsylvania permanently and never returned to England. In
the course of time Andrew [II] and Ann Ellicott became the parents of five
sons, Joseph, Andrew [III], Nathaniel, Thomas, and John. When Andrew
[II] died in 1741, he left little property, and his family found itself in dire circumstances. A local business associate, Samuel Armitage, came to the res-
cue, undertook the guardianship of the children and found trades for them
as they grew older.

Joseph Ellicott, the eldest of the sons, was placed with the family of a man who wove and combed worsted; Andrew [III] went to live with a house carpenter, and Nathaniel made his home with a blacksmith. Thomas and John were still too young to leave their mother. Armitage noticed that young Joseph had become a good weaver and that he was extremely alert and active. Furthermore, Joseph displayed a preoccupation with mechanics, which led him to seek employment with a millwright named Samuel Bleaker, where he soon developed experience in repairing gristmills. He later married Judith Bleaker, his employer's daughter, and named their infant son Andrew [IV]. Shortly after his marriage, Andrew [III] moved back to his mother's farm, having lost interest in the weaving craft and become unwilling to continue with it. With the reluctant support of Armitage, and utilizing the skills of his four brothers, Joseph built a gristmill before he had reached the age of twenty-one. The mill proved to be eminently successful, and the Ellicott brothers became known throughout Bucks County for their mechanical skills.

In 1766, Joseph was informed that he had inherited property from his late great-grandfather in Cork, Ireland. He journeyed to Great Britain to claim his inheritance, and there he met several important men of science who influenced his later career. He sold the inherited estate for a substantial amount, then returned to Pennsylvania, where he was elected high sheriff. He remained in that office in 1768 and 1769, serving also as a member of the provincial assembly.

Having achieved success in Pennsylvania, the Ellicott brothers sought new regions in which to construct modern gristmills of their own design. The grist mill they had built was owned by Armitage, and now the brothers became impatient to strike out on their own and establish themselves independently. Joseph in particular was restless. The brothers became interested in the nearby province of Maryland and traveled on horseback through a great part of the colony's middle counties, seeking a region in which they concluded cereals and wheat could be grown successfully and for which their mills would be utilized.

They finally selected two tracts of land lying between the Patapsco River and the Blue Ridge Mountains. They purchased approximately seven hundred acres, the major part of which they acquired reputedly at a cost of about three dollars per acre, from William Williams, a wealthy English merchant and iron founder. He owned large tracts of land throughout the region, some of which adjoined the Banneker farm. At the time the Ellicotts first visited the area, Williams was operating a large store that he had maintained for many years. Situated on a lofty hill in what is now Oella, overlooking the span of the river where the Union Manufacturing Company Works was later established, it was the largest store for many miles around. Every spring and fall he sent orders to England and imported goods shipped aboard vessels plying the tobacco trade. Williams announced the arrival of a shipment of fresh goods by firing a cannon installed high on the Patapsco hills, which sent the news reverberating throughout the region. The residents thus notified hurried from miles around, some coming on foot along the old Indian paths, others on horseback along the horse trails and tobacco roads, and still others making their way along the river on barges. In the Williams store the planters found tools, cloth and clothing, books, and many other commodities.

The balance of their land the Ellicott brothers acquired from Emmanuel Teal, who also owned considerable property in the area. The Ellicott holdings now embraced both sides of the river for a distance of four miles and included all the water rights within that span. This was to prove to be of particular value because a Maryland law of 1669 permitted any man who constructed a water mill to take up twenty acres of land on either side of the stream "and hold the same at the valuation of jurors for eighty years." It was on this land that the brothers began the construction of their new community, which became known as Ellicott's Lower Mills. It was on this land, in "The Hollow," that they established a mill site near the falls of the Patapsco about ten miles west of Baltimore.[1]

When the Ellicotts arrived, there were virtually no roads approaching "The Hollow," and the road from Elkridge Landing ended abruptly at the foot of a great barrier of huge rocks and precipices within a mile of the site of the future mills. The plantations in the region all were connected by horseback trails or old Indian trails in addition to the several rolling roads, but the only road worthy of the name was the old Frederick Road that had been built by German settlers of Frederick in about 1760. Communication with the outer world was even less frequent. In 1695 the provincial Assembly had established the post rider as a public official to carry the mail from Potomack (now Georgetown, D.C.) to Philadelphia eight times a year, for an annual salary of fifty pounds. John Larkin was the first such officer appointed. One of his regular stops was Elkridge Landing.

Another important consideration that led the Ellicott brothers to select the site had been its position in relation to the several major river towns or seaports in that region, which would be a major consideration in marketing the mill's products. In addition to being near Elkridge Landing and Joppa on the Patapsco, "The Hollow" was within ten miles of the newly settled Baltimore Town, a growing community in a region that was still virtually a wilderness. It was in 1727 that the Maryland legislature had authorized the layout of the town on the site of what was then the farm of John Flemming, and by 1740 Baltimore was still little more than a fort, with a wooden board fence around it to protect the inhabitants from the Indians. As late as 1754 Baltimore consisted of not more than twenty houses constructed on the east side of Jones' Falls.

By 1768, Baltimore had grown to such proportions, however, that it demanded and obtained the county seat from Joppa. With the removal of its legislative functions, Joppa slowly lost its position as a commercial center and gradually dwindled in importance, until today it is remembered only by a solitary gravestone. The same fate awaited Elkridge Landing, and from the same cause. The growing commercial importance of Baltimore, with its greater accessibility and dependable waterfront closer to the bay, caused the cargoes to veer into the Patapsco. Equally critical was the fact that silt collecting in the Patapsco at Elkridge Landing made it impossible for ships to reach its wharves.

Although Baltimore County was not directly exposed to any major Indian war, nor to the Indian invasions from which other parts of the province suffered between 1749 and 1759, Baltimore Town found it necessary to erect defenses. Braddock's defeat and the advance of the French and Indians created great fear in Maryland. Many inhabitants of western settlements fled to Baltimore and its protective wooden stockade. Rumors of forthcoming raids on interior settlements by the French and Indians periodically led to the mustering of several companies of volunteers recruited from Baltimore and vicinity. In the winter and spring of 1756 raiding parties of Indians occasionally approached to within thirty miles of Baltimore, spreading terror throughout the region. These hostilities, which lasted more than a decade, prevented the establishment of new settlements by the great number of German "Palatines" and other emigrants who came into the area, and they were compelled to take refuge in the larger towns. The population of Baltimore consequently increased, and it developed into an important young city.[2]

The Ellicott brothers considered the proximity of Ellicott's Lower Mills to Baltimore to be advantageous: the town would provide them with a point of export for their flour. The new mill was a cooperative venture, with each of the brothers responsible for a part of the enterprise. Joseph Ellicott was the general superintendent of the project; he spent much time at first commuting between Bucks County and the new installation. John moved to Maryland to live on the premises full time, while Andrew designed the mill buildings that were to be erected. Nathaniel preferred to remain in Pennsylvania, and he subsequently sold his share of the Maryland property to Joseph in exchange for his Buckingham farm.

After the land had been purchased, John and Andrew Ellicott began construction of their new mills along the Patapsco River. In January 1771 they arrived at Croft's Tavern on the old Frederick Road, five miles outside Baltimore, accompanied by some laborers and two strong teams from Pennsylvania. Their project was to hew a path through the heavy wilderness from the road to the river. They made slow progress, but managed to cut a way through the dense woods almost to the water, near the present location of the ninth milestone on the Frederick Turnpike.

The next stretch was extremely difficult, because the most direct route to the river required cutting their way along the side of a hill for a distance of about a mile, a strip later known as the "Devil's Elbow." The descent was too steep to attempt with horses and wagons. Not until the end of February did they complete this seemingly impossible task, but they finally forged a way through the forest to "The Hollow," the bottom land on which the mills were eventually constructed. It was not a pleasant experience, for the work was extremely difficult. Wolves howled in the night a short distance from their camp, and at times they had to fight off wildcats.[3]

The coming of these tall strangers and their determined although painful conquest of their terrain did not go unnoticed by the inhabitants of the region. Word of the sale of the land, and then of the presence of these energetic men as they cut their way into "The Hollow" flew from one farm and plantation to another. Banneker and his mother were among the first to be informed and kept a constant vigil as the adventurers progressed. Why had they come and what did they plan to do with all the equipment they were transporting? Rumors circulated wildly as the neighbors watched and speculated and waited.

Upon their arrival at the site, the newcomers' first concern was shelter. They hastily built a shanty and a stable. The next project was the construction of a sawmill, and at the same time they undertook the building of a dam and mill race which was to supply the power for the machinery of both mills. The sawmill was operated up the stream near the present location of the Oella factory and the hewn lumber was floated down the river to the site they had selected for their gristmill.

After these preliminary structures had been completed, the Ellicott brothers were ready to make the great move, which they had planned in advance in considerable detail. The journey from Philadelphia to New Castle would be by water. They assembled their wagons, carts, wheelbarrows, draft horses, household goods, and mechanical and agricultural implements, including materials and equipment for the new mill, and boarded ship in Philadelphia.

When the vessel landed at New Castle, the long, slow journey across the peninsula by wagon began. They boarded ship again at Head of Elk (now Elkton) for the voyage down the Chesapeake Bay to the head of the Patapsco River, then upriver to Elkridge Landing (still known as Patapsco), where they disembarked for the last time. Wagons and carts were loaded once more for an overland journey. They followed a narrow country road from the Landing until they were within only a mile of their final destination. Here the rugged character of the land forced them to change their method of transportation once more.

The site of their prospective homes and mills, "The Hollow," as already indicated, was a wild valley encompassed on all sides by precipices and great rock structures that made wagon travel impossible. The wagons and carts had to be unloaded and the contents carried by means of hand barrows by parties of men until the final destination was reached. Last of all, the wagons had to be dismantled and carried in detached parts through the rocks, and the horses led separately.

This was an arduous prelude to the beginning of the work itself. Extensive sections of land had to be cleared so that construction could proceed. More temporary shelters had to be provided as more workmen were brought on the scene, and more dams had to be built along the river. Finally, the brothers were ready to begin the construction of the first gristmill, at a carefully selected point on the river. The mill was an impressive structure, with its gable end toward the river, and stretched across what later became the turnpike road.

One hundred feet long and thirty-six feet wide, one and a half stories high, the structure consisted entirely of stone. It contained five pairs of millstones, each five feet in diameter. A wide arch through the center afforded passage for horse-drawn wagons laden with wheat, corn, and rye. The grain was hoisted up through the opening in the arch to the top of the mill, where it was processed, cleaned, and brought to the millstones below. The Ellicotts had not yet constructed an elevator, a conveying screw, or a hopper box. These were added later. Ground flour was carried up manually to the bolting cloths, then passed to the flour chest and packed in sacks and barrels, after which it was lowered through another opening to the mill boys, who placed it in the waiting carts and wagons below. The mill was completed in 1774, having required two years' labor.

The Ellicott brothers did not neglect the problem of transportation. It was essential that they have a good means of connecting their operation with the market at Baltimore Town, and accordingly they improved the rough road they had cut to Croft's Tavern for use by their flour wagons. During the years that Ellicott's Lower Mills were being constructed, there was no way across the Patapsco except by ford. Although this sufficed in good weather, the river became impassable immediately after heavy rains. The Ellicotts accordingly built the first bridge at the point where the present bridge is now found.

Among the more interested spectators who came to watch the work in progress was Banneker, who had always been fascinated by construction, mechanics, and the use of tools of any kind. As the Ellicotts began each new project, he would observe and occasionally remark upon their progress with the other watchers. The newcomers had spread word that they had come to build a series of great gristmills, but Banneker and the other inhabitants were convinced that the story must be in error. Why would these bearded men come such a distance, spending so much money on land and labor to build gristmills, when no one in the region was growing grain?

Meanwhile, a number of small houses had been erected to accommodate the Ellicott brothers and their families. These smaller buildings were made of stone cut from several granite quarries the Ellicotts had developed on the site of their new community. The first dwelling was a large log house erected on the eastern side of the river, in which were housed the mechanics and laborers whom the Ellicotts had brought from Pennsylvania. It was built as a boarding house, with a separate apartment

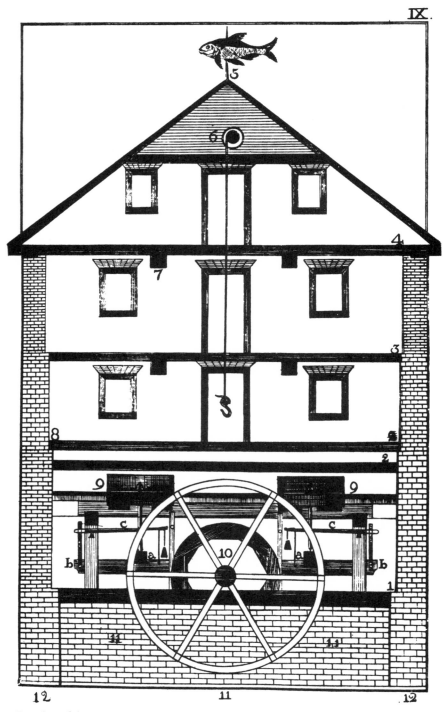

Drawing of the exterior of one of the Ellicott mill houses. Reproduced from Thomas Ellicott, *The Practical Millwright* in Oliver Evans, *The Young Mill-Wright & Miller's Guide* (Philadelphia, 1795).

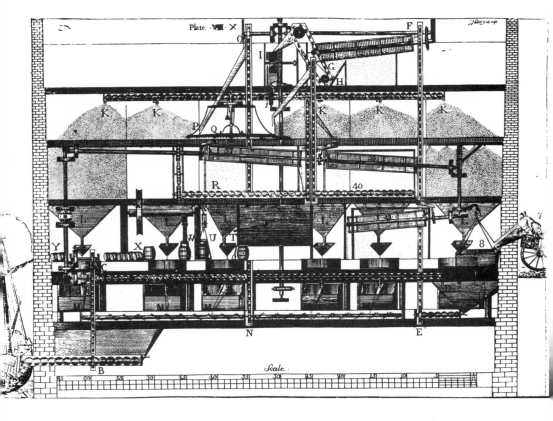

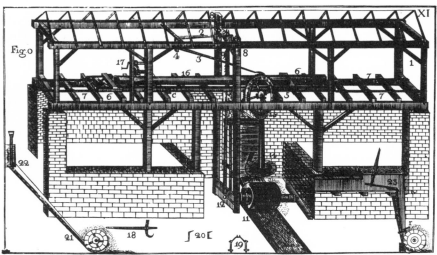

Drawing of the interior of a grist mill similar to those constructed by the Ellicott brothers, showing grain being delivered, ground into flour, and the flour packed into barrels for shipment. Reproduced from Thomas Ellicott, *The Practical Millwright* in Oliver Evans, *The Young Mill-Wright & Miller's Guide* (Philadelphia, 1795).

for each family and designed to serve until individual houses could be constructed. The valley was rich in a variety of trees: oak, hickory, maple, ash, chestnut, and gum, as well as other common varieties. The Ellicotts cleared the valley with great deliberation, leaving stands of trees where it was not essential to remove them.[4]

By the time Ellicott's Lower Mills was ready for production, it had developed into a busy young community. At the last moment, the proprietors' families had become reluctant to leave Bucks County. The first to come was the family of John Ellicott, in 1774, while that of Andrew Ellicott did not make the move until 1797. Joseph Ellicott moved his family in December 1775. In addition to his wife and his own children, he also brought the children of a deceased friend and former neighbor named William Evans. With the arrival of relatives and loved ones, the work of the mills was ready to begin.

Although the purpose of the mills was to produce flour, no wheat had ever been grown in the region except in small quantities for family use. The Ellicotts had anticipated the situation, however, and shortly after their arrival they had cleared large fields and planted them in wheat. As soon as the mills were ready for operation, the brothers utilized their own harvest to produce the first flour, which they then took to Baltimore and sold for export. In a short time, neighboring planters realized the potential of the new market and began growing wheat, which they provided to Ellicott's mills in abundance.

The advent of the Ellicotts and their industrious activity were subjects of considerable interest to the region's inhabitants for many miles around. They came frequently to observe the construction of the buildings as they rose magically one after another where before only a wilderness had existed. The Ellicotts received advice from all sides about their enterprise. Many questioned the wisdom of starting a milling industry in a region where only tobacco was grown. The brothers, members of the Society of Friends, listened politely to dire predictions and friendly cautions and confidently proceeded with their work.

The activity in "The Hollow" continued to hold Banneker's keen interest. After a lifetime of peaceful and quiet existence it was strange to hear the constant muffled sounds of industrial endeavor less than a mile away from his farm. His curiosity frequently brought him to the scene, where he heard and observed the cacophony of organized activity. He visited the scene as often as he could to see what was going on from the seclusion of the hillside, and was intrigued by what he observed.

Occasionally Banneker ventured as far as the mills themselves to watch them in operation. The mechanical integrity of the milling operation enthralled him. The mills were completely automated; bags of grain were taken by machinery from the wagons and raised by means of a hidden mechanism to the highest part of the mill, where they were emptied onto the millstones. The ground meal fell into a bin below, from which it was conducted by more machinery to a loading platform, where it was poured into barrels standing in a production line. The same machinery loaded the barrels into wagons, which were then driven off to market in Baltimore.[5]

The mills erected by the Ellicotts were not the first that Banneker had seen. He had occasionally visited two similar but smaller installations on the river three or four miles from his home. These were of the simplest kind, however, where grain was ground for family use for those who did not have handmills. Hood's mill ground only Indian corn, while the Dismal Mill, located in what is now Ilchester, ground rye, wheat, and corn.

Little by little Banneker became familiar with some of the workmen; eventually he was able to distinguish the proprietors and become acquainted with them. He found them to be fascinating men, who seemed to have the same irresistible attraction to mechanics as he did. At first he kept his distance, but his new neighbors soon learned of him and sought him out.

In the beginning the Ellicotts were faced with the necessity of obtaining food and other provisions for their workmen until such a time as they could grow their own. Baltimore was too far away for practical purposes, so that it was necessary to find a source nearby. The Banneker farm was conveniently located, and there they found Banneker and his mother living in comfortable circumstances and capable of providing most of their needs. Mary Banneker agreed to manage the marketing, and almost every day she brought great quantities of poultry, vegetables, fruit, honey, and other farm products to the boarding house where the laborers were quartered. She was then past seventy, yet surprisingly energetic. Mary and Benjamin became well-known figures in the developing new community, and Benjamin in particular found great fascination and pleasure in the new people who became his neighbors.

After the boarding house, sawmill, flour mill, and a few of the dwellings had been completed, the Ellicotts undertook to build a store to serve the many and varied needs of their community. In fact, such a store was already being operated on a small scale in one of the apartments of the boarding house, where laborers, Ellicott family members, and neighbors could purchase the staples, hardware, and other goods, and within a very short time a post office was added. The Ellicotts succeeded in establishing regular mail service, and the small boarding house store became the place where planters paused to pass the time of day with neighbors and the "mill" people and exchange the latest news and gossip.

It was at this makeshift country store that Banneker occasionally met the new proprietors. Although his mother was the one who customarily delivered the farm commodities to the boarding house, Banneker found frequent opportunity to call at the store, where he enjoyed listening to the bits of conversations going on around him. He was reticent and quiet, and made himself as unobtrusive as possible at first. It was his first real opportunity to enjoy the company of a number of people outside his immediate family, and eventually he made it a habit to spend his leisure time there. Conversation varied in the usual way, from crops and weather to politics and world events. He was especially interested in the men of the Ellicott family and greatly impressed with their goals and achievements. Particularly, he found in these leisure hours much food for his unquenchable thirst for knowledge. Little by little he was drawn out into discussions. His conversational powers were described as being of the first order, and he was encouraged to visit the store frequently.[6]

The Ellicott proprietors in particular enjoyed the retired farmer's company and introduced him to many strangers. His natural modest reserve, particularly with individuals with whom he was not well acquainted, gave him an air of great dignity and remoteness. When prevailed upon to set this reserve aside, however, he joined in enjoyable conversation, sharing his great store of local lore and whatever he had learned from reading. One of his favorite topics was the history of the early settlement of the North American continent and the problems and successes of the settlers as they developed the colonies. During these sessions in the country store, Banneker rarely alluded to himself or to his family, but on occasion he mentioned incidents and situations in his own life, relating to his personal struggle for knowledge.

Banneker was particularly interested in current issues and avidly read newspapers when he could get them. The first newspaper in Maryland was the *Maryland Gazette,* established in 1745 by Jonas Green, printer to the province. Shortly after the Lower Mills was settled, William Goddard began printing the first newspaper in Baltimore. *The Maryland Journal or Baltimore Advertiser* made its initial appearance in 1773, and Banneker read it regularly at the Ellicott & Co. store.

Mary and Benjamin Banneker were among the first clients of the new store. In a large ledger for the years 1774–75, a separate account was maintained for "Mary Baniker." Listed was the acquisition of a pair of shoes on October 4, 1774, for 9s. 6d., for which she paid cash the next spring. The purchase of unlisted sundries on April 11, 1775, for £1 10s. 10d. was charged against a balance due her, presumably for fresh vegetables, fruit, and eggs she furnished the boardinghouse, leaving a balance owed of one pound. The account for "Benjamin Baniker" was more extensive and included a variety of small purchases made at various times from September 1774 to July 1775.

Consistent among the entries was the purchase of rum in quantities of a quart or a half gallon each month during that period. He also bought paper, ink, gunpowder, sugar, molasses, cloth, and other necessities. He made periodic payments, and one of them was made on his behalf by Samuel Morten, the husband of his sister Molly.

An account in the name of Greenbury Morten, Banneker's nephew, revealed that Morten was employed at both the Lower and Upper Mills in clearing land, and that his labors were repaid by purchases at the store. He was paid at a rate of two shillings a day and occasionally at the higher rate of three shillings. In December 1774 his account was charged "To deduction on the Clearing for being unfinished . . . 5 s." Curiously, the account showed charges against Greenbury's account for payments made to others. Among these were payments to Banneker, who was paid 2s. 6d. on Greenbury's account to his father Samuel Morton [sic], and to such others as Henry Hissey, "Yr. brother Joshua," and Betty Matthews.[7] (See Document 50)

The War for Independence touched but lightly on Baltimore County, and on Banneker not at all. Free Negroes were exempted from military service in the Continental Army by the Militia Law of 1777. They became eligible to serve by a revision of the law in 1790, but three years later free Negroes were again exempted from military service by a new law which limited such service to white men.

Baltimore hosted Congress in 1776, when British troops moved toward the Delaware River, after which Congress moved once more to

Ellicott & Company ledger for 1775 showing accounts with Benjamin and Mary Banneker. *Courtesy Emanuel Freeman.*

A panoramic view of part of Ellicott's Lower Mills. The Ellicott & Company store (second from left) has a second-story porch. John Ellicott's house is next to the right, and Jonathan Ellicott's is at far right. From a lithograph by E. Sachse & Co., Baltimore, 1854. *Maryland Historical Society.*

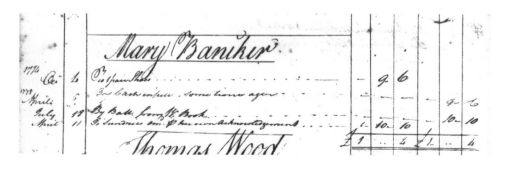

Ellicott & Co. Ledger for 1775. Account with Mary Banneker.

Philadelphia. For the next several years Baltimore became a way station for troops as the war moved southward, but Maryland did not at any time become a scene of conflict. Many of its prominent citizens became important statesmen and soldiers in the war, and Annapolis became a center of political action if not the site of military activity. Among those listed as having taken the oath of fidelity on January 24, 1778 before "the worshipful Charles Ridgely of (William County)" were "Benjamin Baneker," his nephew Greenbury, and the latter's father, Samuel Morten.[8]

Although they were members of the Society of Friends, several of the Ellicott men nonetheless played important military roles in the Revolutionary War. John, who was chiefly responsible for building Lower Mills, lost his right to membership in the Society of Friends because of his involvement in military affairs, although he was reinstated after the war. Jonathan, a son of Andrew Ellicott [III] and George's brother, became a captain of a militia company stationed at Baltimore in 1777, and afterward a manufacturer of the long swords issued to officers of the Maryland line and to dragoons under General Washington's command.

Andrew [IV], who became a professional surveyor after the war, received a commission in 1778 from the governor of Maryland as captain in the Elkridge battalion of the state militia. Before the end of the year he was promoted to major, although he was never in active combat. George Wall Jr., a half-brother of the founding Ellicott brothers, held the title of colonel-lieutenant in Bucks County. Nathaniel Ellicott was so much involved in military action that he permanently forfeited his membership in the Society of Friends.[9]

Another local manifestation of the war was the presence of French troops under command of the Comte de Rochambeau. The French halted in Baltimore in 1781 on their return from Yorktown after the surrender and remained in Baltimore at Sandy Bottom and on Federal Hill until the conclusion of hostilities. The foreign officers, who were much inclined toward field sports, frequently hunted small game in the wooded precincts of the Patapsco River near Ellicott's Lower Mills, and had a favorite spot where day after day they practiced marksmanship. They came often to the Ellicott & Co. store to make purchases, and improved their English by conversing with the clerks and the clients.

The war years were particularly difficult for residents of "The Hollow." Between 1776 and 1783 the Ellicotts barely sustained themselves at the mills. In addition to the vagaries of climate and the elements, the Ellicott enterprise suffered from the lack of a suitable circulating medium. Hitherto the Bank of England had provided the only foundation of currency for half the world, but during the war that was no longer available. The American colonies thereupon issued bills of credit to enable internal commerce, and these soon flooded the country.

In the spring of 1780 a great freshet in the Patapsco River caused the Ellicotts considerable damage and loss. The winter had been severe, water had frozen several feet at the dams, and large masses of ice built up on both sides of the river. The whole countryside was covered in deep snow. In mid-March, when heavy rains followed an abrupt thaw, the Patapsco flooded, carrying away Ellicott property. Undaunted, they resolutely set to work and produced better buildings and facilities than before. They received considerable financial assistance from their neighbors, Caleb Dorsey and Charles Carroll of Carrollton.

Other farms and plantations within the river's reach also suffered violent damage, but Banneker's was among those that were spared. The waters rose in Cooper's Branch, flooding a part of his land but without causing any major destruction. Some of his new tobacco plants were lost, but he had enough land so that he could initiate a new planting elsewhere on the farm.[10]

The peace of 1783 brought about a great change in the economy, and the Ellicotts lost no time in adding new improvements to their original mills and developing a variety of associated enterprises. The mills immediately resumed operations, and the owners added stables that could accommodate eighty horses. They then went on to other projects, among them a school for the children of their community. The Ellicotts hired the best teachers available, paid them well, and controlled the curriculum; the school flourished. Enrollment increased year by year, until the school became one of the most useful projects undertaken by the Ellicotts.

Ellicott's Lower Mills was a community of rapidly changing character, for new projects were being developed annually, and each of these added new buildings, until soon there was little resemblance to the first primitive settlement. A single contemporary illustration of Ellicott's Lower Mills has survived in a crude drawing made in 1782 by George Ellicott when he was twenty-two years old. Prominent in the drawing is the stable for the eighty horses used to haul flour to market at Baltimore. The Ellicotts built no other buildings on that side of the river because of the fear of floods, and occasionally, whenever the river rose to alarming heights, the horses were quickly led out and up the hill behind the stable.[11]

The last major construction at the Lower Mills was a large warehouse completed in 1790 and situated directly opposite the mills on the road from Baltimore to Frederick. Built by the Spicers, a family of Maryland masons from Harford County (all of the other Ellicott buildings were built by Pennsylvanians), it was constructed of triangular blocks of stone from the granite quarries on the premises. This combined store and warehouse had been carefully planned in advance so that it could accommodate a great variety of goods, with special sections assigned to each category. The Ellicotts employed purchasing agents who visited New York and Philadelphia to select items that could be sold at reasonable prices. The goods were then shipped to Elkridge Landing. Included were linens and draperies of both fine and coarse quality, silks, satins, brocades, "India china" dinnerware and tea sets, mirrors, mathematical instruments, iron mongery, foodstuffs, and liquors and wines. Articles of finer quality were stored and displayed on shelves behind sashes of glass and in drawers, so that they were protected from dust while easily visible to the purchaser.

The variety of goods, and the careful attention given to their protection and handling, brought increased patronage from a wide area around the valley. Many of the planters who were accustomed to ordering these same items from their own London agents had been converting gradually from growing tobacco for export to raising wheat and corn, since the latter had a ready market at Ellicott's Mills. Ellicott's store now filled most of their material needs. For a time they even found liquors and wines at the store, until the Society of Friends made it a disownable offense to deal in liquors. When the Revolution ended, the store enlarged its quarters and imported even greater quantities than before. The Ellicotts then dealt with an English agent in London named Samuel Godfrey, who later joined the firm as a partner.

The enlarged Ellicott & Company store provided an improved facility for the post office. Here mail was received and forwarded, and newspapers made available for purchase. The post office became the major center of communication for the entire region. Postal service also brought trade to the new store which achieved even greater importance with the development of the main highway between Baltimore and Frederick. Ladies from Baltimore frequently made the eleven-mile journey to the Mills to shop at the store, where they found many choice materials and other items for their homes. The store flourished until about 1800. It was abandoned and torn down soon afterward.[12]

Banneker and his mother were among the store's most frequent visitors, although most often they came to look but not to buy. News of fresh merchandise spread quickly, and neighbors were often the first to marvel at the goods as they were placed on display, although less frequently did they come to buy. While Mary searched through the selections of fabrics and household materials, Benjamin with equal interest looked over the farm tools, and particularly sought out the books and periodicals.

The major effort of the Ellicott enterprise was the export of flour to England through the port of Baltimore, and in anticipation they purchased a waterfront lot in Baltimore upon which they erected a wharf and a warehouse. The Baltimore operation was assigned to Elias Ellicott, a young son of Andrew Ellicott, who later became the main liaison at Baltimore for the numerous family enterprises as they developed.

Soon after the project was under way, Joseph Ellicott decided to withdraw from the firm and pursue other interests. A division of property was made, and in 1774 he purchased the property and gristmill of James Hood, three miles above the Lower Mills on the Patapsco River. The Hood mill was a small one, built in 1768 to grind Indian corn. Joseph Ellicott had the building torn down and replaced with a larger mill incorporating all of the latest inventions and modifications he and his brothers had developed. He added a storehouse for merchandise, stables, houses for laborers, and a fine mansion for his own family.

This residence was a large two-story building built on the north side of the road and west of Patapsco Falls, with a number of additional rooms in a gabled third floor. At the end of the gable facing the highway, Joseph installed a large round clock he had constructed to tell the time of day to neighbors and passersby. Around the house he planted a large garden, which incorporated useful as well as decorative plantings and which featured a fish pond and a constantly flowing fountain that threw water ten feet into the air. From the same source, a natural spring on the high land west of the house, Joseph supplied the entire garden with water and provided a water supply for the first two floors of the house. His home was tastefully furnished and soon became the conversation piece of the region.[13]

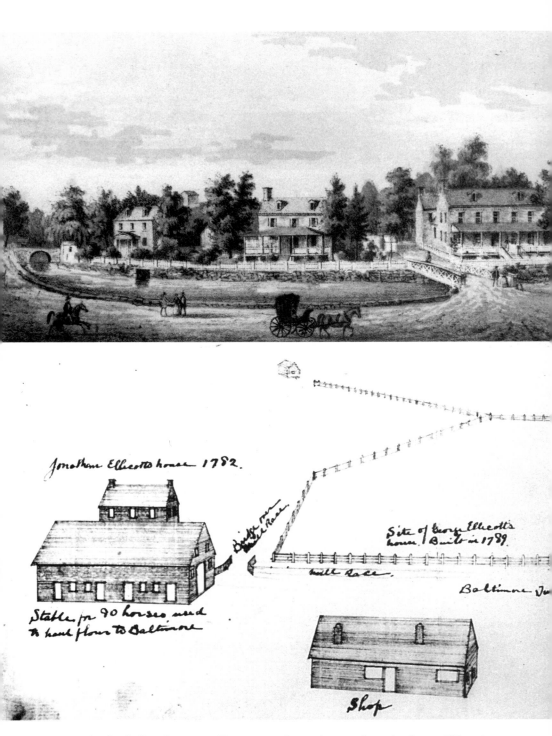

Sketch of Ellicott's Lower Mills ten years after settlement, drawn by George Ellicott in 1782, with later notations. *Maryland Historical Society.*

flour mill & warehouse

John Ellicott's house
built 1772

Saw mill.

Ellicott's Upper Mills as it was in 1781. Engraving by Matthews & Northrup Co., Buffalo, N.Y., 1858.

At the time that Ellicott's Lower Mills was established, there were two rolling roads and two "rolling landings" in the vicinity. One was described in old deeds as "the rolling road from the head of Patapsco to Dogwood Branch" and the other as "the Ragland rolling road." Both followed a direction approximately south and southeast to a landing at the head of tidewater at or near Elkridge Landing. The Baltimore-Frederick Turnpike was at that time a very rough thoroughfare, almost impassable at many points during the winter. The road crossed the Patapsco River about four miles above the level of the Banneker farm, at the point where James Hood had erected his mill, and continued on to Elkridge Landing, the next large community. Many sections of the road were overhung with precipices and great rocks along its sides as it rose out of "The Hollow."

After the Lower Mills had been completed, the founding brothers decided to open a wagon road from their mills to Baltimore, to be built at the expense of their firm, Ellicott & Company. They would follow immediately with another wagon road to connect the mills with Frederick Town in the other direction. This part of the highway would pass by Carroll's Manor, which was the property of Charles Carroll of Carrollton, then the wealthiest capitalist and the most prominent banker in the province of Maryland. The Ellicotts negotiated with him and mortgaged a part of their land for a loan to finance their enterprise. At the same time they obtained his support for the proposed road to Frederick Town.

The survey and laying out of both sections of the road were the responsibility of young George Ellicott, the fourth son of Andrew, second of the founding brothers. George was only twelve years old when the families first arrived in Maryland, but he reached maturity quickly. He had a natural inclination for the sciences and was undoubtedly encouraged in these studies not only by his uncle Joseph, but also by George Wall Jr., who had accompanied his half-brothers to Maryland in their new enterprise and

A "rolling road" for transporting tobacco overland to a port. *Culver Photographic Service.*

who taught George surveying. Wall was well known in his native Bucks County as a professional surveyor, "conveyancer," and as a teacher in a private school. During the first years at the Mills, he trained young George until the latter had become, by the age of sixteen, a fully competent surveyor. Wall returned to Bucks County in 1778 and several years later presented George with his own copy of Gibson's work on surveying.[14]

George's work on the turnpike proved to be most skillful. The section connecting Baltimore with Ellicott's Lower Mills and reaching as far as Carroll's Manor was constructed entirely at the expense of Ellicott & Company. The cost of the section of road from Carroll's Manor to Frederick Town was paid in part by the owners of plantations along its route. Although at first it was only a wagon road, it soon developed into the main thoroughfare between the growing communities which formed its terminals and was three miles shorter than the earlier one. George Ellicott's maps of his road survey, which were executed in his own hand, survived until recent times.[15]

An interesting feature of this highway construction was what may have been the first mobile kitchen. The Ellicotts, faced with providing food and lodging for the laborers, all of whom were from Pennsylvania, constructed a house that could be drawn by horses. In its interior were beds and bedding, and cooking facilities for everything but bread. It moved along the route as the roadbuilding progressed. To eighteenth-century Maryland, this was a new concept in organized efficiency and reflected many of the other innovations introduced in the Mills.

The development of Ellicott's Lower Mills and subsequently of Ellicott's Upper Mills took place rapidly, over a period of five or six years, during which time Banneker had become a familiar spectator and a frequent visitor to the Ellicott & Company store. Because of his mechanical and scientific interests, it is not surprising that in due course he became acquainted with young George Ellicott. The latter had heard a great deal about the unusual tobacco farmer from members of his family and others, and he was curious to meet him.

The first meetings may have taken place in the family store, but thereafter George occasionally visited Banneker's dwelling to talk with him. There he discovered and examined the remarkable striking clock, and looked over Banneker's meager library, finding that they had similar interests. Although Banneker was forty-seven and George only eighteen, shared interests drew them together. Over their subsequent long association, Banneker learned much from George Ellicott but there can be no doubt that young George also profited. The friendship developed without concern for or apparent awareness of the color barrier, which they bridged as easily as they had their differences in age.[16]

Banneker also developed an association with George's uncle, Joseph Ellicott, as a result of their mutual interest in clockmaking. Prior to 1766, Joseph had constructed a repeating watch that he had taken with him on his visit to England. There he met James Ferguson, the popular lecturer on astronomy, and a relative named John Ellicott, who was one of England's foremost clockmakers. It appears that Joseph spent some time with his cousin while in England, and possibly even studied with him briefly before his return to Pennsylvania. At any rate, he brought back with him a wide variety of clockmaker's tools as well as a number of timepieces.

Shortly after he returned, Joseph constructed, with the assistance of his son, Andrew IV, then fifteen, a large tallcase clock housed in a four-sided mahogany pillar almost eight feet high. The clock had four faces. One contained a planetary dial and represented the sun, earth, and moon, and other planets orbiting around the sun. One dial marked the hours, minutes, and seconds as well as the days, months, and years, in addition to the moon phases. The third dial listed the names of twenty-four musical tunes, one of which was played every hour, with a pointer or indicator that when set against any named tune would repeat it. The fourth face consisted of a glass plate through which the wheelwork of the clock movement could be observed.

The clock became a great conversation piece, and Joseph brought it with him to Ellicott's Upper Mills. He designed the great hall of his mansion to accommodate the timepiece so that it could be prominently and proudly displayed to all visitors. The clock was first mentioned in the published account of a French traveler in the United States, Ferdinand-M. Bayard. He visited the mills en route to Virginia in the summer of 1791, eleven years after the death of Joseph Ellicott, and the clock at the late Joseph's residence was shown to him by Joseph Jr.[17]

Joseph Ellicott had also brought with him from his home in Buckingham in Bucks County several other tallcase clocks he had made and which subsequently became the property of various members of the family. He also continued to make tallcase clocks during his later years, although none as elaborate as the four-faced clock. Having learned of Banneker's horological achievement, in due course Joseph Ellicott invited him to visit the Upper Mills, where he demonstrated the other horological mechanisms he had devised, as well as the great clock. Banneker was amazed and intrigued by what he saw, but there is no evidence that there was a continuing relationship between the two men.

Banneker was forty-one years old when the Ellicott families first arrived in "The Hollow," and it was not until approximately eighteen years later that he first undertook his studies of astronomy. Among his early interests in the newcomers must have been the surveying for the turnpike, which Banneker observed with serious attention. Conceivably it was during this early period that young George lent Banneker one of his texts for study.

The advent of the Ellicott brothers and the settlement of Lower Mills and later of Upper Mills greatly changed the tenor of Banneker's life. No longer was he surrounded by only the quiet solitude of nature in the hills and fields around his farm. A teeming new community now bustled within a short walk from his home, the sounds of which reached him frequently and to which he gravitated more and more. The proximity of young George Ellicott and his resources for study provided Banneker with a new fount for his avid thirst for knowledge. George's occasional visits to his home were memorable, for the younger man was interested not only in the sciences but had a great love and knowledge of English literature as well, which they shared. Benjamin also benefitted from the presence of the Ellicott & Company store, where he periodically came to peruse the merchandise imported from overseas, read the newspapers and British magazines, and where he occasionally found inexpensive books for his own small library.

Although he continued his habitual solitary existence as before, and shared his home life only with his mother and with visits to and from other members of his family, there was now a difference in Banneker's life. He was no longer completely alone in his interests, and the mills provided him with his first major link with the outer world. He owed much of his new attitude to George Ellicott, who in the words of his daughter Martha, had with the encouragement of his uncle Joseph and of George Wall, developed into a fine mathematician and competent amateur astronomer.

From time to time George imported, through the store's London agent, a number of technical texts to add to his library, as well as fine scientific instruments from England. The latter included several telescopes, with which he searched the night skies in his hours of leisure. He took particular pride in a pair of globes, one terrestrial and the other celestial, made by one of the popular English makers, probably George Wright, who also issued a treatise on their use. A note by George's daughter Martha pasted inside the cover of the treatise stated:

> This copy of the Use of the Globes was purchased by my father in 1789, to accompany a pair of globes, which he desired to make useful to his friends, and often in fine mild weather, after finding the Planets places on the Celestial Globe, and placing their "signs" upon them, he would have the Globe placed on a table in the front of his house, out of reach of the trees, and deliver a gratuitous lecture on Astronomy. He was the best amateur Astronomer I ever met with, and my remembrance of his kindness in giving gratuitous instruction to enquirers of every class, is still grateful to my memory, now nearly 35 years since he left the earth. 3RD mo. 1ST 1867.
>
> Martha E. Tyson[18]

Quite some time later, while George was having a house built, he courted the attractive young Elizabeth Brooke, daughter of the founder of nearby Sandy Spring. He wished not only to convince her of his own merits but of the pleasures of his hobby as well. In 1786 he presented her with a copy of Ferguson's *Introduction to Astronomy,* a slim volume bound in fine leather. Written in a simple style intended for the instruction of young people, particularly young ladies, the text consisted of a dialogue between a student at Cambridge University named Leander and his sister Eudosia, to whom he attempted to explain the rudiments of astronomy.

History is silent concerning Elizabeth's progress with the science, but her approval of the earnest young man was unquestionable; she married him four years later, in 1790. George's home, which was being erected next door to that of his brother Jonathan, was a large but unpretentious two-story house constructed of granite taken from the Ellicott quarries. In this house, which survives, the young newlyweds began their life together, and George utilized one of the gabled bedrooms on the third floor for his observatory.[19]

In time George's library of astronomy books became fairly comprehensive. He owned copies of Leadbetter's two-volume work on astronomy and of the *Tabulae Motuum Solis et Lunae . . . of Tobias Mayer,* edited by

Presented M. B. Tyson by her Mother E. E.
1832

AN

EASY INTRODUCTION

TO

ASTRONOMY,

FOR

YOUNG GENTLEMEN and LADIES:

DESCRIBING

The Figure, Motions, and Dimensions of the Earth; the different Seasons; Gravity and Light; the Solar System; the Transit of Venus, and its Use in Astronomy; the Moon's Motion and Phases; the Eclipses of the Sun and Moon; the Cause of the Ebbing and Flowing of the Sea, &c.

THE FOURTH EDITION.

ILLUSTRATED WITH COPPER-PLATES.

By JAMES FERGUSON, F.R.S.

LONDON:

PRINTED FOR T. CADELL IN THE STRAND.

MDCCLXXIX.

Title page of the copy of James Ferguson's *An Easy Introduction to Astronomy* that George Ellicott lent to Banneker, with inscription. *Maryland Historical Society.*

Reverend Nevil Maskelyne. Writing about her father's scientific preoccupations, George's daughter Martha again expressed her admiration for his achievements and willingness to share his interests:

> George Ellicott . . . was one of the best mathematicians, and also one of the finest amateur astronomers of the time, and was fond of imparting instruction to every youthful inquirer after knowledge who came to his house. As early as the year 1782, during the fine clear evenings of autumn, he was in the habit of giving gratuitous lessons on astronomy to any of the inhabitants of the village who wished to hear him. To many of these, his celestial globe was an object of great interest and curiosity. He was perfectly at home on a map of the heavens, as far as the telescopes, and writers of his time had given revelations.[20]

Needless to say, among the most devoted of "those inhabitants of the village who wished to hear him" was Banneker, and one can imagine the wonder with which the old farmer first observed the details of the heavens through George's telescope, as the young amateur astronomer identified on his celestial globe on the nearby table each of the stars that Banneker was seeing in the sky. A closer association between the two men was inevitable. To young Ellicott, Banneker demonstrated a natural genius for mathematics and proved to be an eager student who understood and enjoyed his own preoccupations.

To Banneker, young Ellicott was a man of special learning and energy who could excite and satisfy his constant curiosity and thirst for greater knowledge. George's long absences from home on company business meant that a few years would intervene before he provided Banneker with sources for further study. In the meantime, Banneker still had to spend most of his daylight hours in the care of his farm, leaving little time for leisurely pursuits. In the years since Mary Banneky's death, when he was left alone in the world, the tobacco farmer had to learn to do his own cooking. Some of his housecleaning, mending, and laundry chores were probably assumed by one or both of his sisters in the neighborhood, but nevertheless, the household chores must have involved much of his precious leisure. Withal, Banneker had nevertheless found a new direction for his thirst for learning, and he was well on his way to the new avocation that was to change the course of his later years.

IV

WORK AND STUDY

That which we call alternately the morning and the evening
star; as in one part of the orbit she rides foremost in the
procession of night, in the other ushers in and anticipates
the dawn; is a planetary world, which with the four others
that so wonderfully vary their mystic dance, are in
themselves dark bodies, and shine only by reflection; have
fields, and seas and skies of their own. . . .

> *"The Planetary and Terrestrial*
> *Worlds comparatively considered,"*
> *Banneker's Almanac for 1792*

BANNEKER'S STUDIES IN ASTRONOMY developed rapidly, spurred on by his occasional discussions with George Ellicott and the latter's encouragement. Ellicott in turn found in this dignified man, so much older than himself, a kindred spirit and an eager pupil whose remarkable aptitude for mathematical matters was matched only by his consuming desire to learn. Banneker's mind was so agile and his memory so retentive that George found himself hard put to keep them fed. At some time in the autumn of 1788 he offered to lend Banneker several of his own books and instruments. With the increasing burden of his work in the prospering mills, he found himself with little time for his avocation, and he was pleased that someone else could use his materials. He promised Benjamin that as and when he could find the time, he would stop in occasionally to teach him what he knew of the subject and that thereafter Benjamin would be able to progress by himself.

On the very next opportunity George found to ride in that direction, he took along several of his texts and a few of his instruments for Banneker to use. The instruments included a pedestal telescope, a set of drafting instruments, and whatever else Banneker needed for recording observations of the stars on the meridian, their southing, and their rising and setting. He apologized for being unable to stay to give Banneker some preliminary instruction since he was on his way to a business appointment, but he promised to return as soon as he could for a longer visit.[1]

Before departing, however, he paused to take another look at the interior of Banneker's modest abode. The only table was a crude structure that Benjamin's father had constructed many years ago, and it was neither stable nor smooth enough for using a telescope or making calculations. He recalled an old, worn table in his father's house that was being used for potting and other chores, and he made a mental note to send it along.

Banneker could hardly wait for George to leave. He arranged the books and the instruments on his table, then lovingly caressed the long bright brass tube of the telescope and tried to focus it at a point outside his window. He admired the workmanship of the drafting instruments as he removed them from their velvet-lined shagreen case and tested them one by one to determine their function. Last of all he turned to the books, his mind reeling as he perused the complicated diagrams and the impressively unintelligible text. Darkness had fallen without his knowledge by the time he could bring himself to put his new treasures aside. Throughout the evening, as he returned to the books on the table, he asked himself again and again whether he was not presuming too much in the undertaking he had set for himself.

George kept his promise to furnish Banneker with a table. He thought of parting with a fine, modern, oval, cherry drop-leaf table that he had purchased for his new house but decided that it was inappropriate, not only for its cost but because it would possibly embarrass the farmer and make him uncomfortable. The table was too elegant for the rude furnishings of Banneker's dwelling, and he might not accept it either as a gift or a loan. Then George looked about in his father's house and found the old table he had first considered. It was a heavy gate-leg table made of pine and maple that had served the Ellicott family for generations in Bucks County and was now seldom used. It had ample surface and was extremely sturdy.

Several days later George had the table loaded onto a wagon and delivered. Banneker was surprised and touched that George had remembered. The table was massive, as he discovered when he struggled to help

Pedestal telescope made by Dollond of London, owned and used by Andrew Ellicott and probably similar to the one George Ellicott lent to Banneker. *National Museum of American History, Smithsonian Institution.*

the driver remove it from the wagon and carry it into the house. Its many years of hard service were evident in the scars on its surface and the worn stretchers and bottoms of the pad feet. Despite its age and weight, however, it seemed to have been designed exactly for Banneker's needs. He placed it under his window with one of the drop leaves folded down against the wall, leaving the other leaf open to provide the space he required.

The top of the table, which was in a three-board section, and the leaves, which almost reached the floor, were heavy pine; the turned gate-legs and stretchers were of maple. A long drawer traversed the width of the table so that it could be opened from either end. He placed the instruments and the books carefully on its surface, and was delighted with the way his new acquisitions changed the atmosphere of his home.[2]

Realizing that Banneker would be making and recording observations at night, young George had also sent along as a gift a tin candleholder with a broad base that would sit firmly on the table. The old black iron hogscraper candlestick he had seen Banneker using was of uncertain stability at best, and the additional light would make it much easier to work in the evenings. The old farmer forgot about his farm chores as he sat long hours at his table admiring the telescope and tinkering with it and other instruments and looking through the volumes at the impressive diagrams and tables.

The first book Banneker chose to examine was James Ferguson's *An Easy Introduction to Astronomy* because it seemed indeed the easiest. In fact this was the same volume George had given his bride-to-be before they were married, and which he now borrowed from her so that Banneker could use it. There can be no doubt of the high esteem in which he held his friend, nor of the impression of Banneker he must have imparted to Elizabeth Brooke that made her willing to lend it.

The style of Ferguson's work was simple, and Banneker grasped the principles with the promised ease. It provided instructions and illustrations for constructing projections of eclipses using such basic drafting instruments as a pair of compasses and a ruler. Ferguson suggested that the process would be less tedious if a sector were used, because all the measurements could be derived from it and the trouble of dividing could be avoided. Although Benjamin began his studies with compasses and ruler, he subsequently borrowed a sector from Ellicott and eventually purchased one of his own. Ellicott also included a more advanced work of Ferguson's,

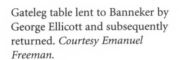

Iron candlestick, candle mold, and tin candleholder believed to have been owned and used by Banneker and later preserved by members of the Ellicott family. *Courtesy Emanuel Freeman.*

Gateleg table lent to Banneker by George Ellicott and subsequently returned. *Courtesy Emanuel Freeman.*

although Banneker surmised that he would not be able to use it until he had mastered the easier one.[3]

The next volume he reviewed was considerably more advanced. It was a copy of the *Tables of Tobias Mayer,* computed on Newtonian principles and sent to the Board of Longitude by Mayer's widow after his death. The *Tables* had been tested at sea in 1757, 1758, and 1759 on behalf of the British Admiralty. The work was edited by the Reverend Nevil Maskelyne and published in England in the original Latin with an English translation. Banneker was certain he would have serious trouble trying to understand this one.[4]

A fourth work lent by Ellicott, which Banneker found particularly useful, was Charles Leadbetter's *A Compleat System of Astronomy* in two volumes. It was one of the most comprehensive works on astronomy of its time and provided much of the advanced data not available in Ferguson's *Easy Introduction to Astronomy.* Although lack of time prevented George from providing the early guidance he had promised, Banneker was undeterred and began work by himself. He plowed through the borrowed books one by one, then turned to the instruments to test what he had learned.[5]

The opportunity to view the stars through a telescope whenever he wished provided the greatest pleasure to Banneker, and the night hours passed swiftly as he kept his eye glued to the eyepiece and studied the structure of the firmament. With only his own thoughts for company, he contemplated the miracle of circumstance that offered him such an unusual opportunity, not shared by anyone he knew except George Ellicott. As he sought out and found the stars and tried to identify them in his books, he remembered also some of the stories he had read about the legendary figures from which their names were derived.

When he had familiarized himself sufficiently with the celestial bodies, Banneker attempted to make a projection of an eclipse of the sun. His books provided all the instruction he required, and he had the simple tools at hand to make the drawing. He had already made great progress in the study of logarithms, which the calculation required, and he eventually completed the projection. He checked over his work carefully, then impatiently awaited George's next visit so that he could show it to him. George's business activities kept him occupied elsewhere, however, and as time passed, Banneker could wait no longer. He forwarded his sketch with a covering letter addressed to George at the Ellicott & Company Store and resumed his studies.

Mayer's *Tabulae Motuum Solis et Lunae* annotated by Martha Tyson in 1864. The book also bears the 1781 signature of George Ellicott. *Courtesy the late Dr. Robert M. Fitzhugh.*

Banneker realized with some concern that his intense preoccupation with astronomy had caused him to neglect his farm, which was beginning to suffer. During the weeks that followed, he tried to make up for the lapse. While he worked in the fields during the day his mind was constantly on his studies. Each evening after work was ended, he reached for his telescope and his books and spent long hours with them. The weeks passed quickly, and then he realized it had been some time since he had seen George. Finally, when Banneker visited the Ellicott store seeking news of him, he discovered that George was away on a prolonged business trip and that it would be some time before he returned. Banneker's life now had taken on new meaning and a new direction, and he found himself again and again postponing work that needed to be done in order to have more leisure for his avocation. He grew increasingly annoyed with himself for his sloth, as he termed it, but found himself powerless to keep his mind fixed on his regular duties.

When George Ellicott received Banneker's letter enclosing his projection, he was speechless with surprise. He suddenly recalled that he had never returned to see Banneker to explain the books he had lent or to provide him with the introductory lessons he had promised. He also realized immediately that such instruction was obviously no longer necessary, as demonstrated by Banneker's work in hand. Carefully reviewing the drawing, he was greatly impressed with his friend's efforts. True, Banneker had made a trifling error in his calculation, but there was no question that he had an unusual affinity for mathematics and had made remarkable progress in mastering the science. George corrected the mistake on the drawing and returned it with a note apologizing for being unable to visit him at that time but promising to do so as soon as he could.

Banneker was both pleased and chagrined by George's comments. He was angry with himself for making such an error and ashamed because it was so apparent, yet he was also pleased by George's surprise and evident pleasure over his accomplishments. He realized the nature of his error and set about trying to find out why he had made it. A close reading of his reference works revealed the source of his miscalculation. He discovered with astonishment and a measure of satisfaction that a disparity existed between two of the sources he had been using. It was hard to believe. Unconvinced at first by his findings, he returned to them again and again until he was certain. When he wrote again to George Ellicott, he happily pointed out the apparent discrepancies in the publications of two of the leading English

authorities on astronomy. He assured George that he had not been offended by the latter's comments and corrections and could explain the reason
for his error:

> I Receiv'd your Letter at the hand of Bell [an Ellicott employee] but found
> nothing Strange to me In the Letter Concerning the Number of Eclipses
> tho according to authors the Edge of the penumber only touches the Suns
> Limb in that Eclips that I left out of the Number — which happens April
> 14th day at 37 minutes past 7 O'Clock in the morning and is the first we
> shall have, but Since you wrote to me I Drew in the Equations of the Node
> which will Cause a Small Solar Defet but as I Did not intend to publish, I
> was not so very peticular as I should have been, but was more intent upon
> the true method of projecting a Solar Eclips — It is an Easy matter for us
> when a Diagram is laid down before us to draw one in resemblance of it,
> but it is a hard matter for young Tyroes in Astronomy when only the
> Elements for the projection is laid down before him to draw his Diagram
> to any degree of Certainty —
>
> Says the Learned Leadbetter the projection that I shall here describe,
> is that mentioned by W^M. Flamsted — When the Sun is in Cancer, Leo,
> Virgo, Libra, Scorpio, or Saggittary, the Axes of the Globe must lie to the
> right hand of the Axes of the Ecliptic, but when the Sun is in Capercorn,
> Aquarious, pisces, Aries, Taurus or Gemini then to the left —
>
> Says that wise Author Ferguson, when the Sun is in Capercorn,
> Aquarius, pisces, Aries, Taurus, and Gemini the Northern half of the Earth
> Axes lies to the right hand of the Axes of the Ecliptic, and to the left hand
> whilst the Sun is in the other Six Signs —
>
> Now Mr. Ellicott two Such learned Gentlemen as the above
> mentioned, one in direct opposition to the other, Stagnates young begin-
> ners, but I hope the Stagnation will not be of long duration for this I
> observe that Leadbetter Count the time on the path of Virtex, 1.2.3. &c.
> from the right to the left hand or from the Consequent to the Antecedent
> But Ferguson on the path of the Vertex Count the time 1.2.3. &c. from the
> left to the right hand according to the order of Numbers, So that that is
> regular Shall Compensate for irregularity
>
> — Now Sir if I can overcome this difficulty I Doubt not being able to
> Calculate a Common Almanack — So no more but remain yr. faithful
> friend Mr. George Ellicott.[6]

Banneker had borrowed the reference "young Tyroes" from the preface to Leadbetter's work, in which the latter had stated, "I have given you all

Sir I Received your Letter at the hand of Bell but found nothing Strange to me In the Letter concerning the Number of Eclipses tho according to authors the Edge of the penumber only touches the Suns Limb in that Eclips that I left out of the Number — which happens April 14th day at 37 minutes past 7 O'Clock in the morning and is the first we Shall have but Since you wrote to me I Drew in the Equations of the Node which will Cause a Small Solar Defect but I Did not intend to publish, I was not so very petticular as I should have been but was more intent upon the true method of projecting a Solar Eclips &c. It is an easy matter for us when a Diagram is laid down before us but it is a hard matter for young Tyroes in Astronomy when only the Elements for the projection is laid down before him to draw his Diagram to any degree of Certainty

Says the Learned LEADBETTER the projection that I shall here describe, is that mentioned by Mr Flamsted — When the Sun is in Cancer, Leo, Virgo, Libra, Scorpio, or Saggitary, the Axes of the Globe must lie to the right hand of the Axes of the Ecliptic, but when the Sun is in Capricorn, Aquarius, pisces, Aries, Taurus or Gemini then to the left

Says that wise Author FERGUSON, when the Sun is in Capricorn, Aquarius, pisces, Aries, Taurus, and Gemini the Northern half of the Earths Axes lies to the right hand of the Axes of the Ecliptic, and to the left hand whilst the Sun is in the other Six Signs —

Now Mr Ellicott two Such learned Gentlemen as the above mentioned, one in direct opposition to the other, Stagnates young beginners, but I hope the Stagnation will not be of long duration from this I observe that Leadbetter Count the time on the path of Virtex, 1. 2. 3. &c from the right to the left hand or from the Consequent to the Antecedent —— But Ferguson on the path of the Vertex, Count the time 1. 2. 3 &c from the left to the right hand according to the order of Numbers, So that, that is regular shall Compensate for irregularity — Now Sir if I can overcome this difficulty I Doubt not being able to Calculate a Common Almanack — So no more but remain your faithfull friend
Mr George Ellicott
Octr 13th 1789

B Banneker

Letter from Banneker to George Ellicott, October 13, 1789, concerning his calculations for the ephemeris for an almanac. *Maryland Historical Society.*

the Terms of Art used in Astronomy; by which the young Tyro is taught to speak properly."

Despite the confusion expressed in his letter to George Ellicott, Banneker had not in fact discovered an error in one or the other of the two authors. The results produced by the procedures described by Ferguson and Leadbetter were actually the same. Banneker's difficulty arose from the fact that he had both of these sources available to him for consultation simultaneously. If he had had either one without the other, the problem would not have arisen. The apparent conflict occurred in the individual statements made by Ferguson and Leadbetter concerning the position of an axis of the earth in relation to the axis of the ecliptic. Ferguson described the geometrical computation of a solar eclipse from a sun-oriented position, and his projection was drawn as viewed by the observer at the sun looking toward the earth. Leadbetter, on the other hand, assumed the opposite position, and viewed the projection as if the observer were behind the earth and looking through it at the sun. Both authors described the procedure in almost exactly the same words, but from entirely different vantage points.

The apparent conflict in the two methods can be easily described in projecting a solar eclipse when the sun is in the first zodiacal constellation, Aries. This is known as the first such constellation because it occupies the position where the ecliptic crosses the celestial equator at the vernal equinox, the first day of spring. Ferguson states that when the sun is in Aries, the axis of the earth appears at the right of the axis of the ecliptic, which is the case only if the earth is viewed from the vantage point of the sun. Leadbetter, on the other hand, specifies that the axis of the earth should appear at the left of the axis of the ecliptic, which is the case when the sun is viewed from the earth. Ferguson's method is the one that is commonly used in current astronomy texts.

Of the two authorities, Ferguson's work was the easier to use because he wrote as he lectured, in a simple flowing style with numerous illustrations. Leadbetter's writing had to be read with extreme concentration, word by word and line by line. Only after one realizes that he was describing the moon moving in a backward direction does his opposite vantage point become apparent. When Banneker tried to make one or more of the several projections of solar eclipses used as examples by both authors he realized that there was in fact no error in either of his sources. He did not encounter the same problem in the projection of lunar eclipses, however, since both

Ferguson and Leadbetter utilized the same approach and vantage point. He came to a realization of the cause of his confusion soon after he had written to Ellicott, and the notes in his manuscript journal made over the next several years indicate that he preferred to work with Ferguson rather than Leadbetter.[7]

It had never occurred to George that Banneker might calculate an ephemeris for an almanac until the latter happened to make a casual reference about it in his letter. After he had thought about it, George could see no reason why Banneker would not be able to produce such a set of calculations. It might even be possible to find a printer for them, and he encouraged his friend to undertake the project. Banneker was both intrigued and fearful of the prospect. The awareness that young Ellicott, who was far more knowledgeable on the subject than he, considered him capable of preparing calculations for an almanac was high praise indeed and an expression of confidence far greater than he had anticipated. Banneker thereupon went on to undertake other more complicated calculations.

Before the end of the summer he had not only mastered the projection of eclipses with accuracy, he was able to produce the various other calculations required to complete an ephemeris. He had also gone through the several works Ellicott had lent him and managed to buy or borrow several more, from which he occasionally copied out important directions and formulas that would be of future use. These he recorded from time to time in the pages of a manuscript journal.

Banneker now applied himself seriously to the preparation of an ephemeris. He hesitated to hope that there was even the slightest possibility of having it published as an almanac, but he realized that it provided the best exercise possible for his new interest. He had probably purchased almanacs for advice on planting and weather during his long career as a farmer, and these would have been among his most prized possessions, inasmuch as they provided virtually the only current reading material available to him. Like many farmers throughout the American colonies, he may have inserted pages in the pamphlets on which he had kept a diary of the important events relating to his farm, such as unusual weather, sale of crops, and related entries. Thus he was able to study the format and content of the common almanac of the period, upon which he could model one of his own. The almanac played an important role in colonial American family life, a role best described by Moses Coit Tyler:

No one who would penetrate to the core of early American literature, and would read in it the secret history of the people in whose mind it took root and from whose minds it grew, may by any means turn away, in lofty literary scorn, from the almanac — most despised, most prolific, most indispensable of books, which every man uses, and no man praises; the very quack, clown, packhorse, and pariah of modern literature, yet the one universal book of modern literature; the supreme and only literary necessity even in households where the Bible and newspaper are still undesired or unattainable luxuries.[8]

From their first appearance in the colonies in 1639 until Banneker's time, almanacs were the only current, secular publications available. Although at first their content was limited to little more than the ephemeris, they gradually expanded to include astrology, chronological tables of scientific data, historical facts, literary items, and occasional poetry. In many regions the almanac was the only printed work other than the Bible that was available to a family. Although newspapers were published weekly, there was no rural circulation until after the middle of the eighteenth century. The daily newspaper was primarily an urban publication infrequently distributed outside of the specific community. The common household calendar, so familiar today, did not come into general use until about 1870, and until that time it was the almanac that served that purpose.

The almanac was of special interest and use to three groups of people. It was useful, first of all, to navigators who sailed to or from American shores, as well as to shipmasters engaged in commerce on the inland and coastal waterways. They consulted it for tide tables and for the times of the rising and setting of the sun, moon, and certain fixed stars, from which they could calculate their true position or at least within seventy miles of it— which was the best that could be done in that period. Next, it was useful to the householder, who referred to its pages for daily information and for the dates of special events. Farmers relied on the almanac for weather forecasts, recommended dates for planting, and information about the moon's eclipses and phases. Finally, it served all who sought entertainment and learning in its pages for lack of other reading matter.

For the common man in a period when timepieces ordinarily consisted of sand glasses and sundials, and clocks and watches were rare luxuries, the times of sunrise, noon, and sunset were of considerable importance, as well as the changes of the moon, eclipses, and conjunctions. Early in the eighteenth century one publisher included a column entitled "Sun fast and slow" which enabled the regulation of clocks and watches at noon by means of sundials. Particularly useful for weather prognostication were the added columns for the positions and declinations of the sun and moon.[9]

Besides such critical data, the pages of the small, cheaply assembled and poorly printed pamphlets were filled with morally elevating scriptural quotations, proverbs, allegorical stories and puritanical essays, all of which contributed to the molding of the national character. The content of the almanac underwent several changes due to time and region. During the seventeenth century it was published chiefly in the New England colonies and consequently reflected the religious influence of that region. Full sermons or parts thereof were often included, and no opportunity was lost to derive moral lessons from astronomical phenomena. Parables, short stories, and essays provided only the slightest sugarcoating for strong exhortations to industriousness, temperance, and frugality; models of virtue and piety were offered as guides for daily living.

By the beginning of the eighteenth century, the almanac changed distinctly in tone from its religious bias to a more practical direction, with emphasis on education. Literary and historical content was the new order. This form of publication achieved its peak with Benjamin Franklin's *Poor Richard's Almanac*. For the first time almanacs were entertaining, and Franklin's homilies, along with homely wisdom cast in contemporary language, brought to the almanac a new popularity. An important philomath of the same period was Nathaniel Ames, who added yet another dimension in the form of verse, imaginative and superior to most of the poetry of his time.

The almanac was a popular seller. Every printer sought to publish one of his own because a successful almanac virtually assured extra income. Some concept of the market for this type of publication may be derived from the fact that Benjamin Franklin reported that he sold as many as ten thousand copies of his issues annually at the modest price of five pence. His chief competitor, Nathaniel Ames, claimed to have sold as many as sixty thousand a year "for five coppers single."[10]

By the final decade of the eighteenth century, the almanac had become the most common printed item in the new American republic. Printers in every state vied with one another in developing a new marketable item, and each printer endeavored to hire a competent philomath to calculate an ephemeris for an almanac that would be exclusively his own.

There were not enough competent astronomers available, however, and the almanac makers compiling ephemerides found such a ready market for their calculations that they frequently sold copies of their ephemeris for each year at the same time to several printers in neighboring cities, and sometimes to several within their own community.

Almanac makers were a rare breed. Few were scholars in the true sense, and most of them were mathematical practitioners who were self-taught in the practical aspects of astronomy. An exception to this general rule must be made for the seventeenth century. Of forty-four almanacs published in the American colonies before 1687, forty-one were compiled by twenty-six Harvard College postgraduate students during the course of their three years of studies for a degree of Master of Arts. In general, however, they hailed from a wide range of other occupations, including statesmen, navigators, surveyors, instrument makers, and such others as developed on their own a competence in the study of astronomy.

At the time Banneker undertook the preparation of an ephemeris, the eighteenth century was drawing to a close, and the content of the almanac was once more beginning to change. The new emphasis would be upon local causes and national events. Because of increased competition, with great numbers of almanacs being published in many states, they were to become more specialized, and many were directed at specific professions.

After Banneker had determined the various types of calculations required for an ephemeris, he set himself to the task of methodically compiling his results one after the other for each month of the coming year. Martha E. Tyson provides a picture of the man at work in her description of a visit her mother, Mrs. George Ellicott, and some of her young friends made to his house in 1790. This was the first year of young Elizabeth's marriage, and she was curious to see the talented farmer about whom her husband had spoken so frequently, and to whom she had lent her own volume on astronomy. Almost half a century later she described the incident to her daughter, who reported the scene as her mother related it to her:

> His door stood wide open, and so closely was his mind engaged that they entered without being seen. Immediately upon observing them he arose and with much courtesy invited them to be seated. The large oval table at which Banneker sat was strewn with works on astronomy and with scientific appurtenances. He alluded to his love of the study of astronomy and

mathematics as quite unsuited to a man of his class, and regretted his slow advancement in them, owing to the laborious nature of his agricultural engagements, which obliged him to spend the greater portion of his time in the fields. . . . His mother had died previous to this, and he was the sole occupant of his dwelling.[11]

With the ticking and striking of his clock the only sounds to keep him company, Banneker found the hours rapidly slipping away as he worked at his table. George Ellicott's occasional visits brought encouragement, and the months passed. By the beginning of autumn the ephemeris was completed at last, and Banneker reviewed his results again and again to ensure their accuracy. He was determined that young George would not find another error in his mathematical work. He copied his results into the customary format of published almanacs, and he may have used as his model one of the almanacs calculated by Major Andrew Ellicott, George's cousin and a professional surveyor who was producing a series of almanacs.

The work was completed at last, and as Banneker looked proudly one more time at the neatly copied sheets for each of the twelve months of 1791 before assembling them, he felt somewhat awed by his own achievement. Convinced that it was publishable and eager to see if it would be accepted, he decided to send it first to a printer in Baltimore. At this time there were three: William Goddard, who was then operating a print shop in partnership with his brother-in-law, James Angell; the recently established Baltimore branch of the Wilmington firm of Samuel and John Adams; and John Hayes, who was then the publisher of the *Maryland Gazette*.[12]

Banneker's first choice probably was Goddard and Angell, the most prominent of the Baltimore printing firms, but they were not interested, and in due course the ephemeris was rejected. Banneker tried again, sending his work to another of the printers and again met with failure; he found the returned ephemeris waiting for him one day in the mail room of the store of Ellicott & Company.

He was determined to make a third attempt. This time he selected John Hayes, reputed to be an excellent printer. Hayes was a well-educated Englishman who had worked first in a printing firm in Philadelphia before moving to Baltimore in 1783 to revive the *Maryland Gazette or Baltimore General Advertiser* as a weekly paper. Hayes continued his paper until the beginning of 1792 and then briefly undertook another career. He returned to printing, however, and late in 1794 tried to revive his newspaper with the name *Maryland Register and General Advertiser,* but without success. He continued to print stationery forms, occasional books, and related materials during the next decade. He was active in the Maryland Society for Promoting the Abolition of Slavery and other charitable causes.

Hayes was already known to Banneker as the publisher of the almanacs calculated by Major Andrew Ellicott. Ellicott had sold his ephemerides for the years 1781 through 1785 to Mary Katherine Goddard, but it is likely that they were printed by John Hayes, since she then did not have her own press. Ellicott's almanac for 1786 was published by the newly organized firm of Goddard and Langworthy, but the association was not continued. On January 1, 1787, Goddard's partnership with Langworthy had been dissolved, and Goddard took as his new partner his brother-in-law, James Angell. Langworthy became the new headmaster of the Baltimore Academy, where he also taught the classics, and at which Ellicott was the instructor of natural philosophy and mathematics.[13]

For the next several years Ellicott sold his ephemerides to John Hayes, Goddard's major rival, probably with an improved financial arrangement. Meanwhile, Goddard felt the loss of Ellicott inasmuch as the almanac was an important source of income, and he sought a replacement. He had arranged with Benjamin Workman, an instructor at the University of Pennsylvania, to calculate the ephemeris for an almanac for the year 1787, which he printed late in 1786, at the same time launching a bitter attack on Hayes. Undoubtedly urged by Hayes, Ellicott compiled an errata list for Goddard's almanac, which Hayes published in his newspaper. This led to an attack on Goddard by a writer using the pseudonym "Juvenal," believed to be Goddard's former partner, Langworthy, in a controversy that continued for some time.[14]

Banneker waited anxiously for a reply from Hayes, and when there was no response, he wrote to him again. Hayes eventually informed him that he had sent the calculations along to Major Ellicott in Philadelphia for a review and that he would inform Banneker when he had received the latter's comments. It was at this point that Banneker decided to communicate directly with Major Ellicott with the intention of expediting his decision. His concerns and reservations about his accomplishment were clearly reflected in a revealing and touching letter to the surveyor, sent in the spring of 1790:

Maryland Baltimore County near Ellicotts Lower Mill
May the 6th: 1790

Sr// I have at the request of Several Gentlemen Calculated an
Ephemeris for the year 1791 which I presented unto Mr. Hayes printer in
Baltimore, and he received it in a very polite manner and told me that he
would gladly print the Same provided the Calculations Came any ways
near the truth, but to Satisfy himself in that he would Send it to philadelphia to be inspected by you and at the reception of an answer from you he
Should know how to proceed and now Sr. I beg that you will not be too
Severe upon me but favourable in giving your approbation as the nature of
the Case will permit, knowing well the difficulty that attends long
Calculations and especially with young beginners in Astronomy, but this I
know that the greater and most useful part of my Ephemeris is so near the
truth that it needs but little Correction, and as to that part that may be
Somewhat deficient, I hope that you will be kind enough to view with any
eye of pitty as the Calculations was made more for the Sake of gratifying
the Curiosity of the public, than for any view of profit, as I suppose it to be
the first attempt of the kind that ever was made in America by a person of
my Complection—
  I find by my Calculation there will be four Eclipses for the ensuing
year but I have not yet Settled their appearance, But am waiting for an
answer from Your HONOUR to Mr. Hayes in Baltimore—
  So no more at present, but am Sr. your very humble and most obedient Serv.

B Banneker[15]

Major Ellicott's reply to Banneker has not survived, nor is there a
record of any report he may have made to Hayes. Ellicott apparently indicated that he did not find the calculations sufficiently complete although
they were reasonably accurate. He may have concluded that too much work
would be required to make the calculations acceptable for publication.
Meanwhile Hayes postponed a reply to Banneker for the next few months,
and finally decided not to publish Banneker's almanac after all, despite his
earlier indication of interest. Hayes had delayed so long that it was no
longer possible for Banneker to submit his work to another printer in time
for its publication for distribution in the following year, much to
Banneker's distress. As his excuse, Hayes used the fact that he had been

Maryland Baltimore County near Ellicott's Lower Mills May the 6: 1790

Sr I have at the request of Several Gentlemen, Calculated an Ephemeris for the Year 1791 which I presented unto Mr. Hayes printer in Baltimore; and he received it in a very polite manner and told me that he would gladly print the Same provided the Calculations Came any ways near the truth, but to Satisfy himself in that he would Send it to philadelphia to be inspected by you and at the reception of an answer from you he Should know how to proceed and now Sr. I beg that you will not be too Severe upon me but as favourable in giving your approbation as the nature of the Case will permit, knowing well the difficulty that attends long Calculations and especially with young beginners in Astronomy, but this I know that the greater and most useful part of my Ephemeris is so near the truth that it need but little Correction, and as to that part that may be Somewhat deficient, I hope that you will be kind enough to view with an eye of pitty as the Calculations was made more for the Sake of gratifying the Curiosity of the public, than for any view of profit, as I Suppose it to be the first attempt of the kind that ever was made in America by a person of my Complection I find by my Calculation there will be four Eclipses for the ensuing year but I have not yet Settled their appearances, But am waiting for an answer from Your Honour to Mr. Hayes in Baltimore So no more at present, but am Sr. your very humble and most obedient Servt

B. Banneker

Letter from Benjamin Banneker to Andrew Ellicott, May 6, 1790, inquiring about his ephemeris for an almanac for 1791. *Historical Society of Pennsylvania.*

printing almanacs containing calculations prepared by Andrew Ellicott and he did not wish to make a change at this time inasmuch "as he was publically known for the name of Ellicott."[16]

This was a great disappointment to Banneker and he turned for assistance once more to his friends at Ellicott's Lower Mills. Meanwhile, by one of the greatest possible coincidences of time and place, Banneker's almanac would serve a much greater purposed than he could ever have contemplated.

The fates had been working on Banneker's behalf without his knowledge. The antislavery movement had been developing not only in Philadelphia but emerging elsewhere throughout the world. The first Continental Congress in 1774 had appointed a committee to develop a plan for effecting non-importation, non-consumption, and non-exportation of foreign goods. Upon their recommendation, a proposal was passed which included the resolution that there would be no importation of slaves or purchase of slaves imported after December 1, 1774. After that date the slave trade was to be completely discontinued.

Despite the legislation's intent, at least thirteen years passed before the resolution could be wholly effected. The onset of war helped to break up the trade in slaves, but at its conclusion the country clearly had suffered from reduction of labor, particularly in the South. Economic forces prompted a revival of the slave trade, which was resumed after the end of hostilities by English traders and in this country reopened in the South. A sharp division of opinion on the subject grew quickly. Under the Articles of Confederation, Congress did not succeed in resolving the problem, although peripheral aspects of the trade were considered.

Meanwhile an antislavery movement was growing on both sides of the Atlantic with increasing impetus, fed by the cooperative efforts of the Society of Friends in New England and the mid-Atlantic states. Not only did the members of the society disown fellow sectarians who persisted in holding slaves, they maintained a large and steady correspondence with Quakers in England over a period of many years. The Society of Friends even managed to convert members of other religious groups to their cause, and a strong sentiment against slavery began to develop even in the states of North Carolina and Virginia.

Correspondence on the slavery question between Quakers in England and the American colonies had continued even during the War of

Independence, and the movement grew rapidly after the close of hostilities. In London, Benjamin Franklin provided assistance to the cause by publishing in the *London Chronicle* an extract of Anthony Benezet's tracts attacking the slave trade. Later he cooperated in Granville Sharp's campaign to eradicate the trade in England. Newspapers and periodicals in London and Edinburgh took up the cause and published strong attacks on the slave trade, spurred by tracts furnished by Quakers in Philadelphia and elsewhere. Members of the British Parliament were being propagandized with copies of these tracts mailed to them from America, and by the decade following 1783 the agitation against the trade became even more strident. Late in 1783 a deputation from the yearly meeting of the Society of Friends in Philadelphia presented a resolution to the Congress, but it had little noticeable effect. Nor did slavery occupy an important place in the resolutions of the Constitutional Convention of 1787, although there was considerable debate over the question. Concessions were made and a bargain was finally achieved in which the Congress resolved that the slave trade would be ended prior to 1808. The clause led to considerable discussion and protest throughout the nation, and many of the state conventions opposed its inclusion.[17]

In Philadelphia, meanwhile, an organization consisting mostly of members of the Society of Friends had been formed in 1775 and taken the name, "The Society for the Relief of Free Negroes unlawfully held in Bondage." Benjamin Franklin was elected its first president, and the founding membership included such other prominent figures as James Pemberton and Benjamin Rush. In 1787 the society was reorganized under a somewhat cumbersome new name, "The Pennsylvania Society for Promoting the Abolition of Slavery, the Relief of Free Negroes Unlawfully Held in Bondage and for Improving the Condition of the African Race," and it became even more active than before. In 1789 the society was incorporated, and individuals from other states were permitted to join. Among them were Elias Ellicott and Joseph Townsend of Baltimore, who were elected to membership on June 5, 1790.[18]

Among the programs of the Pennsylvania society was the development of the antislavery movement in other states, and with its assistance similar satellite societies were formed in New York, New Jersey, Rhode Island, Delaware, Virginia, and Maryland. The first antislavery society formed in Maryland is of particular interest because it played an important role in the publication of Banneker's almanacs. It was modeled closely after the parent Pennsylvania society, even to its name, the "Maryland Society for Promoting the Abolition of Slavery, and the Relief of Free Negroes and Others Unlawfully Held in Bondage." The Maryland society was founded on September 8, 1789, and one of its chief instigators was Baltimore businessman Joseph Townsend, who served as its first secretary.

In his dual capacity as a member of the Pennsylvania society and secretary of the Maryland organization, Townsend was to play an important role in Banneker's future. Born in East Bradford Township in Chester County, Pennsylvania, he remained on his father's farm until the age of twenty-two. He had witnessed the Battle of Brandywine and the passage through the region of the British army under General Howe. In June 1782 he moved to Harford County, Maryland, and settled at the Little Falls of the Gunpowder River. There he taught school for a year, then moved on to Baltimore, where he became deeply involved in civic responsibilities of that growing community.

Shortly after his arrival in Baltimore, Townsend made several attempts to establish himself in trade. In 1792 he advertised that he had for sale eight-day, tall-case clocks, and in 1797 he advertised the sale, at his shop at 18 Baltimore Street, of *A New Introduction to Reading — Or; A Collection of Easy Lessons, Arranged on an Improved Plan.* . . . This was a fourth edition of an English text which he advertised as having published himself. Townsend served on the board of health during the three epidemics of yellow fever in 1794, 1798, and 1800 and was involved in the development of Maryland Hospital in Baltimore. In 1794 he was one of the representatives of the Maryland society sent to the first convention of abolitionist societies held in Philadelphia, and he represented the Maryland society also at the second convention held in 1795.[19]

With the support of significant figures in Baltimore business and political circles, the society dedicated itself to an ambitious program of activities, as described in its constitution:

> The human race, however varied in color or intellects, are all justly entitled to liberty, and it is the duty and interest of nations and individuals, enjoying the blessings of freedom, to remove this dishonor of the Christian character from among them.
>
> From the fullest impression of the truth of these principles; from an

earnest wish to bear our testimony against slavery, in all its forms; to spread it abroad, as far as the sphere of our influence may extend, and to afford our friendly assistance to those who may be engaged in the same undertaking, and in the humble hope of support from that Being, who takes an offering to himself what we do for each other.

We the subscribers, have formed ourselves into the Maryland Society for promoting the abolition of slavery, and for the relief of free negroes and others unlawfully held in bondage.[20]

The first president of the new society was Philip Rogers, and James Carey was elected the first vice president. Other prominent citizens of the community who joined included General Joseph Sterett, William Winchester, Justice James Winchester, Adam Fonerden, William Pinkney, Justice Samuel Chase, and Archibald Robinson. The English philanthropist, Granville Sharp, asked to become a member and was duly elected and served the society as its English correspondent. Gerard Hopkins served on the Electing Committee, and Elisha Tyson and Elias Ellicott were on the Acting Committee. It was the function of the Acting Committee to seek out cases requiring the society's interference, to file petitions for freedom on behalf of individuals held in bondage illegally, and to arrest kidnappers of free Negroes and to bring them to punishment. The committee was responsible also for submitting to the grand jury of the county any known cases of outrageous misconduct of masters in the handling of slaves. In the pursuit of this mission, Elisha Tyson distinguished himself by his dedication to the cause to such a degree that his name became associated with the defense of human rights. The dramatic accounts of his bravery in personally freeing captured Negroes from prison and slave ships became a part of Baltimore history.

One of the society's first endeavors was to petition for a repeal of the law of 1753 prohibiting manumission by last will and testament, and replacing it with more practical legislation. A special committee appointed for the purpose succeeded in introducing in the House of Delegates a bill which led to great controversy throughout the state. The repeal was supported on the floor by William Pinkney, one of the youngest members of the legislative body and a founding member of the society. His impassioned speech had a strong effect on the proposal, which nevertheless lost by a small margin. The society then circulated copies of Pinkney's speech,which was published in newspapers throughout the state. The society kept the proposal for the repeal alive, but it was not until 1796 that they achieved the results they desired. In that year, when the bill came to a vote a second time, it passed.

The Maryland society was more successful in some of its efforts than in others. By the end of 1795 it had effected the release of 138 free Negroes, but efforts to establish a school for black children were unsuccessful.[21]

The Maryland group had the strong support of its sister society in Philadelphia, and there was constant communication between the members. Evidence of this is found in a letter from Joseph Townsend to James Pemberton, in which he reported that the liberation of approximately fifty slaves was contingent upon the rendering of a court decision then pending.[22] (See Document 3)

Pemberton was the first vice-president of the Pennsylvania society and succeeded Franklin as president in 1790. He remained in that office for thirteen years, during which time the society flourished and expanded. Pemberton held many public offices, including membership on the board of overseers of the Philadelphia public schools, and was on the first board of managers of the Pennsylvania Hospital. He was elected to membership in the American Philosophical Society in 1768 and served also in many capacities with the Society of Friends in Philadelphia. He was the author of numerous religious documents and tracts. During the war he had opposed armed resistance to Great Britain and consequently was arrested, imprisoned, and deported to Virginia. After his return he gave up all interest in politics.

The friends of the Negro throughout the country, and in particular the organized antislavery groups, sought to collect evidence to disprove the common claim that the Negro was an inferior being. The most active group was the Pennsylvania Society for the Promotion of the Abolition of Slavery, which in addition to its own positive efforts provided inspiration to such similar organizations as the Maryland society and its English counterpart. Anthony Benezet in Philadelphia collected whatever materials he could find and sent them to the English abolitionists. One of his American-born former pupils, William Dillwyn, organized a small group in London that became a center for propaganda. The students at a school for Negroes that had been established in Philadelphia were described to English sympathizers as examples of blacks' capacity for learning when given the opportunity. English periodicals sympathetic to the cause sought to publish Negro contributions in any field, but with little success. Consequently, the discovery of a free Negro in Baltimore County who had become a self-taught amateur astronomer, and who had calculated an ephemeris for an almanac, was an important event.

It was James Pemberton who first associated this unusual achievement with its value as propaganda. Banneker's letter to Major Andrew Ellicott arrived in late spring, at a time when Ellicott was involved with the survey of the lands ceded by the State of New York at Lake Erie. The rest of the summer and autumn he spent in the field at Presque Isle. Upon returning to his home in Philadelphia in mid-October, he turned over to James Pemberton the letter from Banneker that he had received earlier in the year. He suggested that Banneker's almanac might be a subject of possible interest to the Pennsylvania abolition society. Pemberton realized the potential immediately and made several copies of the letter. One of these he returned to Ellicott for his letter file on or about October 30, with the inscription at the bottom: "Literal Copy from the Original."[23] At the same time Pemberton forwarded another copy to Townsend at Baltimore, asking him to provide any further information he could find about this man of unusual talent, Banneker. Townsend replied in mid-November, advising Pemberton that "I have not as yet procured the necessary information respecting the Black man's Calculations of the Almanack but shall attend to it & comply with thy request accordingly."[24]

Townsend grasped the significance of the assignment at once and lost no time in conferring with his associates in the Maryland society. He was fortunate in discovering that several of his fellow members were acquainted personally with Banneker, including Elias Ellicott, George's brother, and the printer, John Hayes. By the time he received his next communication from Pemberton, he was in a position to provide some new data.[25]

Pemberton had written to Townsend on November 21st, to which the latter replied:

> I have made inquiry respecting the Negro Man mentioned in my two last — Elias Ellicott informs that the Calculation of the Almanack was nearly brought to perfection but is refer'd to next season — John Hayes says that the author presented it to him in due time for publication, but as he had for years past been in the practice of printing Ellicotts he did not like to Change as his was publickly known by the name of Ellicotts, on which account he objected, not as he had any reason to doubt its exactness — If I can discover anything further respecting him or his performance I shall convey it accordingly—[26]

Pemberton had foreseen the potential appeal of an almanac for the general public having an ephemeris calculated by a free Negro, and he visualized that it could in fact be used as an illustration of the mental capability of the Negro when given sufficient opportunity. Under his leadership, other members of the antislavery movements in Philadelphia and in Baltimore directed their efforts in a cooperative endeavor to publish Banneker's almanac.

By this time it was already too late to undertake the printing in time to distribute it in the year the almanac was calculated, and the project had to be postponed. Townsend and Pemberton and others had done all they could and felt greatly frustrated, but there was no alternative. They would attempt to issue an almanac in the following year. Meanwhile, Banneker was about to be offered another unique opportunity, which was to take him away from his farm for the first and only time in his life.

V

THE GREAT ADVENTURE

We but view the scene before us
Strangers to each future stage;
Greater strangers to the glories
Blooming thro' th' eternal age.

"On a Cloud," *Banneker's
Almanac for 1794*

ARLY IN 1791, Banneker became involved in what he considered the greatest adventure in his life—the survey for a federal city which was to serve as the capital of the new republic, on a site chosen by President Washington. Curiously enough, until recently the record of Banneker's involvement rested on extremely meager documentation, consisting of a statement in a letter written by Thomas Jefferson and two statements reported to have been made by Banneker himself. Biographers and scholars assumed that other supporting records existed, but they were not found. Recently, however, new documentation has come to light that positively confirms his participation beyond all doubt.

Plans for a national capital had been in progress for a long time. The need to establish a capital arose out of the growing inconvenience posed to Congress by its constant movement from city to city. Congress had met in eight different cities during the War of Independence and the following period of Confederation. Various sites had been offered for the new capital, and final selection was predicated upon the resolution of two major questions: geographical location and jurisdiction. Most agreed that the new capital should be centrally located along the Atlantic seaboard, and a site at

Georgetown, Maryland, near the Potomac's lower falls, was finally selected. It was further agreed that Congress should have exclusive jurisdiction over the seat of government.

Congressional discussions concerning a national capital had begun in 1779, but not until 1783 was a site selected. A proposal to establish a national capital city under congressional jurisdiction was included in the draft of the Constitution of the United States, which was ratified by the states in 1789. When the first Congress under the federal Constitution met in 1789, members deliberated over the site. In 1790 they reached an agreement, which took the form of a bill that became law that year. The states of Maryland and Virginia ceded portions of their respective territories to form what was to be known as a new District of Columbia. President Washington launched the project with a proclamation on January 24, 1791, in which he directed that a survey be made of a ten-mile square. Two days before the proclamation, the president appointed three commissioners to oversee the survey and design of the city—Daniel Carroll and Thomas Johnson of Maryland, and Dr. David Stuart of Virginia.

The ten-mile square was to be situated between Georgetown and the Eastern Branch and included two unincorporated "paper" towns known as Hamburgh and Carrollsburgh. Hamburgh consisted of 130 acres fronting on the Potomac River just above the mouth of Tiber Creek (also known as Goose Creek). It was a platted town laid out by Jacob Funk in October 1771 from land purchased from Thomas Johns in 1765. Carrollsburgh consisted of about 160 acres lying between the north bank of the Eastern Branch and James Creek and consisted of land sold by Charles Carroll Jr., to three purchasers.

The only settled community within the region was Georgetown, an active trading center that had been laid out as a town in 1751. Its economic roots were the mercantile houses of Scottish agents of English merchants. Vessels docking at its wharves brought dry goods, wines, and hardware and returned to England with tobacco and furs. Georgetown also served coastal commerce; brigs and schooners traded with New York, Boston, and other New England ports as well as the West Indies, returning with sugar and molasses. Conestoga wagons rumbled along the dusty streets, as farmers brought wheat and corn from Maryland and central Pennsylvania to barter for groceries, dry goods, and fish. The Potomac served as the route for flat-bottomed boats transporting pork, flour, corn, and iron to other ports from Georgetown. Eight miles farther down the Potomac was the port town of Alexandria, Virginia, then one of the three most important seaports in the country.

The site chosen for the new capital city was not only centrally located along the seaboard but would occupy a strategic position in the commercial life of the new republic. Following Washington's proclamation and the appointment of the commissioners, the next step was to define the area and then design the city itself. The choice of the individual to undertake the survey was an obvious one: Major Andrew Ellicott.

Ellicott was by this time regarded as a seasoned professional surveyor who had achieved distinction in his work. Born in Bucks County, Pennsylvania, the son of Joseph Ellicott of Ellicott's Lower Mills had attended had a Quaker school and a new academy established by the Scottish-Irish immigrant, Robert Patterson. There he had received training in mathematics, astronomy, and other sciences. He moved to Maryland in 1772 with his father and brought his own family soon after his father had established Ellicott's Upper Mills. He had assisted his father in the operation of the mills and clockmaking endeavors until the advent of the American Revolution. Despite the fact that he was a member of the Society of Friends, in May 1778 Andrew was commissioned first a captain and later promoted to major in the Elkridge Battalion of Militia for Anne Arundel County. Following his father's unexpected death in 1780, he assumed supervision of Ellicott's Upper Mills, while continuing his activities as a surveyor.

In September 1784, Andrew Ellicott was appointed to be one of the commissioners to represent Virginia in running the boundary lines between that state and Pennsylvania through an untraveled wilderness. In the course of this work he met David Rittenhouse, a fellow surveyor, and they became lifelong friends. Upon his return to the Upper Mills in November of that year, Elicott found his family in poor health; one of his sons was seriously ill and finally died in March 1785. Bitterly blaming the climate for his son's death, Ellicott leased the mills and moved his family to Baltimore. There he represented the city in the General Assembly for one term and refused a second when offered. It was during this period, November and December 1784, that he constructed a number of his own surveying instruments for use in the field. He had been trained in clockmaking and instrument-making by his father, and among the items he produced were a portable quadrant and a transit and equal altitude instrument, as well as his field regulator clock.[1]

Thereafter Andrew Ellicott frequently left home for long periods to undertake surveys. When in early 1786 the Commonwealth of Pennsylvania and the State of New York agreed to ascertain their adjoining boundaries by a survey the following summer, the only instrument then known having sufficient accuracy to trace a parallel of latitude was the zenith sector. The one used by Mason and Dixon for surveying the Pennsylvania-Maryland border in 1763 to 1768 was not available, and accordingly Rittenhouse and Ellicott undertook the task of constructing one for Pennsylvania that was to be five and one-half feet in radius.

Ellicott was summoned away to the Upper Mills and Rittenhouse completed the principal part of the work. The instrument required an achromatic lens of sufficient focus to enable the surveyor to observe stars of the second and third magnitude as they passed near the zenith at any time of day. Lenses were not yet produced in the United States and generally were imported from England. Rittenhouse and Ellicott borrowed a suitable lens from a Philadelphia instrument-maker, and the sector was used successfully for the survey and again used by Ellicott for the survey of the islands of the Allegheny and Ohio rivers within the boundaries of Pennsylvania, which he completed in 1788.

In the following year Ellicott moved his family from Baltimore to Philadelphia, which provided him with a better base of operations because of the federal government's presence there. Having become interested in new surveys that were being proposed, he asked an influential friend, Benjamin Franklin, to submit a recommendation to the government on his behalf. Whether his appointment derived directly from Franklin's support or not, Ellicott was commissioned to run the western boundary of the State of New York. He took as his assistants his brothers, Joseph and Benjamin, whom he had trained in surveying. They began the project in September 1789, but winter weather made it difficult to continue work in the field, and Ellicott customarily closed his camp and returned to his family until spring. He managed to complete the survey of the western boundary late in 1790 and retired to Philadelphia for several months of rest and relaxation.

It was during this period that he was commissioned to undertake the survey of the ten-mile square for the new Federal City. After the preliminaries had been dispensed with, the commissioners were informed of Ellicott's appointment in a letter from Secretary of State Thomas Jefferson conveying the wishes of the president.[2] Washington expressed himself to

Miniature portrait on ivory of Major Andrew Ellicott "done by a Spanish Lady in New Orleans" in 1799. *National Museum of American History, Smithsonian Institution.*

Jefferson as being extremely anxious to proceed with the project now that the various problems with the landowners appeared to be resolved, and he so informed Jefferson, urging him to have Ellicott proceed as soon as it could be arranged.[3] (Document 4)

Ellicott received his formal notification from the Secretary of State in a letter written the following day, February 2, 1791. Washington's instructions conveyed by Jefferson to Ellicott were carefully delineated, as was to be expected from a former surveyor. Ellicott was advised that he was to run the first two lines as mentioned in the president's proclamation, to fix the beginning point, and from that to establish the four "lines of experiment" for the ten-mile square. Furthermore, he was to find the true meridian and determine the latitude and map the course of the rivers within the segment surveyed.[4] (Document 5)

Ellicott was pleased and excited by the assignment, and he lost no time in making preparations for a long absence from home. His first concern was for skilled assistance. His two younger brothers were still completing the survey in New York and it would be several months before they could join him. In addition to the field hands he needed, he required someone with a knowledge of astronomy who was capable of using scientific instruments and making the daily observations. Few men possessed such knowledge and ability, and none were available. He then considered his young cousin, George Ellicott, who was both an amateur astronomer and a competent surveyor, as he had so ably demonstrated in laying out the Baltimore-Frederick Turnpike. Although he did not have the field experience he would serve the purpose. Major Ellicott wrote to George, offering him the position of scientific assistant.

George was interested but explained that business pressures would not permit such a prolonged absence. Along with operating the grain mills in partnership with his brothers, he was responsible for several new enterprises that they had developed in the Lower Mills. However, he reminded Andrew about his neighbor Banneker and his mathematical skill, and described the remarkable progress he had made in the study of astronomy. Banneker was sixty years of age, however, and might not be able to cope with the hardships of working in the field.

Whether Andrew Ellicott communicated with Banneker from Philadelphia before meeting with him is not known. He recalled having received a communication from Banneker concerning the latter's ephemeris for an almanac for 1790, so he already was familiar with Banneker's knowledge of astronomy. Andrew also was aware that Banneker had acquired a local reputation for drinking. Ellicott probably wrote to George and asked him to speak to Banneker to determine whether he would consider the opportunity.

In subsequent conversations with Secretary of State Jefferson, Ellicott mentioned his need for trained assistance and discussed the scarcity of competent persons, none of whom was available for the project on such short notice. Jefferson encouraged Ellicott to employ Banneker for the preliminary survey and suggested that he would be useful until such a time as Andrew's younger brothers could join him. Confirmation of this discussion is to be found in Jefferson's letter to the Marquis de Condorcet, written in the following year. "I procured him to be employed under one of our chief directors in laying out the new Federal City on the Potomac." Although there is no further indication of Jefferson's role in hiring Banneker, and Banneker did not acknowledge that role when communicating with Jefferson in the following year, there can be no doubt that Jefferson approved of Ellicott's choice.[5]

After making the final preparations for his sojourn, Andrew left Philadelphia on horseback. He planned to break his journey so that he could visit his widowed mother at Ellicott's Upper Mills and at the same time meet with Banneker to complete his arrangements for travel. The recommendation of Banneker by other members of Andrew's family who knew him, Andrew's own familiarity with Banneker's calculations of an ephemeris for 1791, and the lack of other qualified candidates for the position of a scientific assistant were all factors favoring Banneker's employment on the historic survey. Despite his demonstrated knowledge of practical astronomy and its related instruments, however, Banneker had only a passing familiarity with surveying and no field experience. Among the books that George Ellicott had lent him was Robert Gibson's famous treatise on surveying, which Banneker may have perused. Yet his lack of field experience and his age and increasing infirmity would limit his role in the survey. Obviously that role was not that of a laborer hired to fell trees to clear the lines of the square, or a supervisory one directing others in these chores. He was not capable of serving as a chain man, which required wearying hours of tramping through the underbrush and patiently holding the rod or chain for the surveyor.

Instead, the temporary position being offered was ideal, serving as Ellicott's assistant, maintaining notes of observations, making calculations as required, and using the astronomical instruments for establishing base points. Once the square had been laid out and markers established, Ellicott would have been able to proceed with the finer details of the survey aided by the assistant surveyors hired for that purpose some months later.

Banneker was indeed excited by the prospect offered, and responded with enthusiasm. He immediately began to make preparations for the trip while Andrew visited for several days with his mother at Ellicott's Upper Mills. Banneker asked his two sisters, who lived in the neighborhood, to care for his livestock during his absence and to keep an eye on the house. Meanwhile Banneker, never having been away from home, was uncertain about his needs during his absence and kept collecting and discarding possessions in considerable confusion until the final moment of departure. Touching evidence of the great esteem for Banneker that Elizabeth Ellicott shared with her husband is a statement written by her daughter concerning the preparations made for Banneker's sojourn. "Under the impression that Banneker would fall under the notice of the most eminent men of the country, whilst thus engaged, . . . [she] was careful to direct the appointments of his wardrobe, in order that he might appear in respectable guise, before the distinguished personages likely to be assembled there."[6] Banneker's sister Minta Black was an experienced tailor and seamstress, and under the guidance of George Ellicott's wife, she took charge of outfitting her brother, sewing new shirts and trousers for him.

In a short time all was in readiness to proceed to the new Federal Territory. Just before the day of departure, Banneker rode to the Lower Mills to bid good-bye to his friend George. The latter was almost as excited by the assignment as was Banneker himself. They discussed the nature of the work and the possibilities for the use of astronomical instruments which would not otherwise have been available. Andrew was equipped with what were probably the finest astronomical instruments in the country at that time. Banneker would have been content merely to watch Major Ellicott use them, to say nothing of handling them himself. He could hardly believe that he, a farmer sixty years of age, having no education other than what he had painfully gleaned from borrowed books, would have the opportunity to participate in what was unquestionably the most important surveying project of the new republic. One resolution he had made privately when Major Ellicott offered him the work was that during the course of the project he would do no drinking.

Major Ellicott was eager to begin work and finally the day of departure arrived. Shortly after dawn, the two men set off on horseback, with their equipment and luggage packed behind their saddles. They appeared as an unusual pair to the few they encountered along the highway. Major Ellicott was tall and big-boned, and despite his youth—he was thirty-eight—he looked much older, possibly owing to his graying hair and portliness. He wore sturdy garments against the winter cold, a snug vest, and a tricorn hat. Riding along beside him, Banneker made a pronounced contrast. He was considerably shorter than his companion, with a heavy frame. Farm work had made him muscular, but the advancing years had also rendered him somewhat corpulent. He had a rather short neck, and with his shock of white hair it was said that he most resembled Major Ellicott's eminent friend, Benjamin Franklin.

Banneker was not as accustomed to riding long distances as was his companion, and his age and rheumatism or arthritis contributed to his weariness. They followed the turnpike, stopping for a meal and a short rest en route before continuing on their way. Ellicott had decided to make his first base at Alexandria, in preference to Georgetown. The survey would begin at Hunting Creek, and it would be more convenient to operate from a spot nearby until the survey was more advanced.

The two travelers arrived at Alexandria on the evening of February 7 and obtained lodging at Wise's Fountain Tavern on Cameron Street. When they drew up before the tavern, they were directed around the corner to the stables on Pitt Street, where they left their horses. Banneker was impressed by his surroundings; he had never before seen a city of this size, so much larger and busier than Joppa or even Baltimore. The tavern itself fronted on three streets and was one of the busiest centers in town, with merchants, gentlemen, sailors, and others constantly coming and going.

Despite the excitement of finding himself in new surroundings, Banneker welcomed the opportunity to rest. They had traveled the last part of the journey through a constant rain. The skies remained overcast, and Ellicott worried that the weather might delay the beginning of the survey. His predictions were justified: they were beset with bad weather, causing them to remain indoors during the next several days. Banneker was curious about his new surroundings, and after he had rested he ignored the drizzle and wandered around the seaport town by himself, observing the people and the activity.

He found the place exciting, for Alexandria was then one of the country's largest commercial centers. It had become a rendezvous for merchants, soldiers, and travelers of all kinds. The wharves teemed with activity as all sorts of cargoes were loaded and unloaded on the ships at anchor in the harbor. As he walked along the streets, he was enthralled by the sounds of the busy city and the voices that spoke in many languages. The city brought to life the magic world of history which he had found in his books, and his eyes and ears and mind were filled with a multitude of exciting impressions.[7]

Meanwhile, Major Ellicott went about the city busily making arrangements for the purchase of equipment for his field camp, hiring laborers and woodcutters, purchasing horses, and completing the many other necessary preparations. He grumbled about the weather and the overcast sky that prevented him from making astronomical observations. The first step was to set up a surveyor's camp near the apex of the proposed square, somewhere near Jones's Point on the upper cape of Hunting Creek near Alexandria. As soon as weather permitted, Ellicott assembled his surveying party at the site, and they set to work organizing a camp.

Ellicott preferred to establish his main encampment on the top of the highest available elevation in the region to be surveyed, and when possible he customarily sought a grove of trees or the edge of a forest for additional protection. The focal point of his operation was the observatory tent, which Ellicott located by tracing a meridian and then laying off an angle from it. It had to be on a fairly level area having at least one large tree within its confines. He had the tree cut down, leaving only a stump projecting slightly above the ground. After this had been leveled, it served as a shelf upon which the regulator clock was placed. When a tree of suitable size was not available, he had a strong pole driven deep into the soil to which he lashed the clock several feet above ground.

The clock was critical to all his astronomical observations and the single piece of equipment that habitually presented the most problems. It was a precision timekeeper, liable to derangement from any one of many causes. Vibrations caused by movements upon the ground nearby, changes in temperature, and any contact with it might cause inaccuracy. After the clock had been accomodated, he installed the large zenith sector nearby and then erected his observatory tent over these and his other instruments.

Other tents for sleeping and for meals were then set up in the vicinity, and an area was provided nearby for tethering the horses.

The larger of two zenith sectors was by far the most important of Ellicott's instruments, and probably the most accurate scientific instrument in America at that time. It was five and one-half feet in length, its object lens projecting through an opening at the top of the tent. It was an achromatic lens of five and one-half feet focus by means of which it was possible to observe stars of the second and third magnitudes as they passed near the zenith any time of the day. The sector was used for determining the latitude by observation of stars near the zenith. Observations would be made of six or seven stars as they crossed the meridian at different times of the night, and the observations would be repeated a number of nights over a period of time. Ellicott had a particular interest in this instrument which he and David Rittenhouse had made by their joint efforts early in 1786 and used for surveying the boundary between Pennsylvania and New York.[8]

Ellicott had remarked in some of his writings that when the stars were so near the zenith they were affected by the different refractive powers of the atmosphere derived from the varying degrees of density. He found that the error of the visual axis could be reduced to a reasonable minimum by taking zenith distances of the stars with the plane, or face, of the sector alternately facing east or west. The figures derived in this manner were averaged and corrected for refraction, after which aberration and nutation were applied, and then a comparison was made with the data in published star catalogues. Determination of the latitude was accomplished from this comparison, based on each of the stars observed.

Another important instrument used extensively by Ellicott in the field was his transit and equal altitude instrument, which he had constructed himself in 1789 based upon the design illustrated and described by Pierre Charles Le Monnier in his *Histoire Celeste*. Ellicott had already made good use of it in running the western boundary of New York State, and in his opinion it was an almost perfect instrument, particularly adapted for running straight lines. Banneker also used it, for taking equal altitudes of the sun by means of which the regulator clock could be rated and checked for accuracy at intervals throughout each day.

Included in Ellicott's field equipment was a zenith sector made by David Rittenhouse with a radius of nineteen inches. It was much smaller than its counterpart, and consequently less accurate. Its advantage was in its portability, which made it possible to use it in the field in areas to which the large sector could not be transported and installed.

For taking horizontal angles Ellicott used a brass circumferentor with an eight-inch radius, made by the prominent London instrument-maker George Adams. A fine plain surveying compass of brass made expressly for him by Benjamin Rittenhouse served for running the lines. Ellicott customarily had with him several sextants as well, one having a radius of seven inches, made by Jesse Ramsden of London, which served him in taking lunar distances.

Three telescopes were usually on hand, the largest of which was an achromatic instrument with pedestal produced by Dollond of London and equipped with a terrestrial eyepiece having a magnification of about sixty times, as well as several eyepieces which magnified from 120 to 300 times for celestial observation. His two other telescopes were smaller, having sliding tubes for taking signals and used primarily for making observations of the occultations and eclipses of the satellites of Jupiter for determining the longitude. Ellicott determined the longitude by two methods. He recorded the time of the appearance or eclipse of one of Jupiter's satellites with the time that the same event had been observed at Greenwich Observatory, then converted the differences into the appropriate degrees of longitude. The second method he employed was the observation of lunar distances for the same purpose.

Among Ellicott's smaller surveying instruments were an artificial horizon, several thermometers, two stopwatches having seconds hands, two sets of cased drafting instruments, and two copper lanterns of his own design that had special slits for tracing meridians and giving the direction of the lines when he determined them at night by means of celestial observation. Finally, two two-pole chains completed his field scientific equipment.

Banneker soon found that his assignment was not as simple as he had envisioned. He was to assist Ellicott in the observatory tent and possibly participate in making observations in the field as well. His most important responsibility was the maintenance of the regulator clock, which proved to be far more complicated a chore than he had imagined. The clock had been constructed by Ellicott himself, who had been trained in clockmaking by his father. He had produced it between 1785 and 1789 in his own clock and instrument-making shop while he was living in Baltimore and awaiting field assignments.

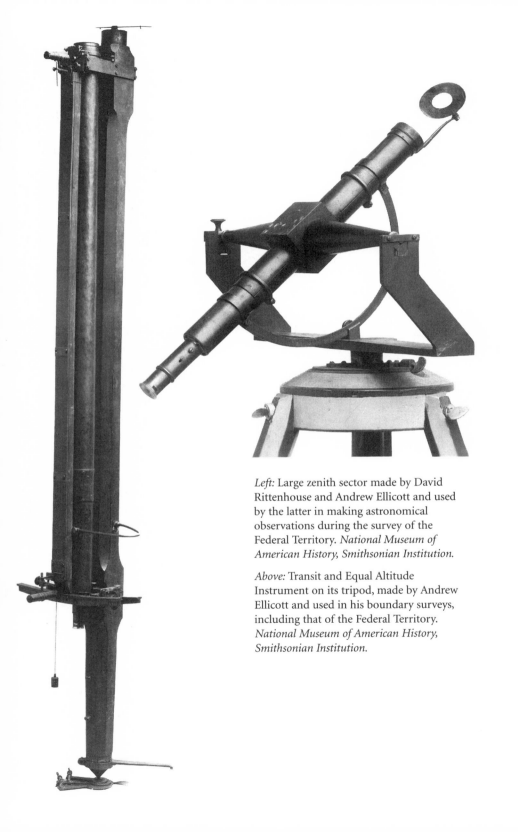

Left: Large zenith sector made by David Rittenhouse and Andrew Ellicott and used by the latter in making astronomical observations during the survey of the Federal Territory. *National Museum of American History, Smithsonian Institution.*

Above: Transit and Equal Altitude Instrument on its tripod, made by Andrew Ellicott and used in his boundary surveys, including that of the Federal Territory. *National Museum of American History, Smithsonian Institution.*

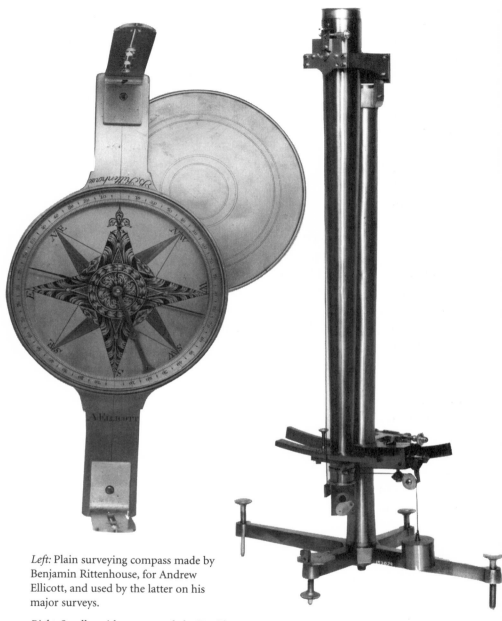

Left: Plain surveying compass made by Benjamin Rittenhouse, for Andrew Ellicott, and used by the latter on his major surveys.

Right: Small zenith sector made by David Rittenhouse for Andrew Ellicott and used in areas where limitation of space made use of the larger sector impractical.

It was an extremely well-made timepiece designed for the maximum precision that could be achieved in that period, and sturdily made for field use. The movement was equipped with bolt and shutter maintaining power. The square dial was made of sheet iron painted white and was mounted directly to the movement without a false plate, confirming that it was made locally and not imported. The clock had an eight-day time train with, a deadbeat escapement with adjustable steel pallets, and a seconds-beating pendulum supported by a conventional fixed clock-driving escapement through a steel open-fork crutch.

Ellicott housed the clock movement and dial in a simply made tall-case of pine without adornment. Remembering his own wooden clock, Banneker admired the mechanism in this one, the finest that he had ever seen. It was his duty to keep it wound, to check its rate by means of equal altitudes taken of the sun at periodic intervals with the transit and equal altitude instrument, and to keep the temperature in its vicinity constant. For this purpose he had several thermometers placed at appropriate points from which he recorded the readings several times each day.

The regulator clock was a particular cause for concern. Ellicott's experience in previous surveys had made him aware of the constant problems in keeping the timepiece accurate. Minor accidents were liable to occur in its vicinity that would affect its rate. Banneker was constantly on the alert in fulfilling his responsibility, and began to understand why Ellicott seemed to be so fretful about its operation.[9]

On other surveys, Ellicott's two younger brothers worked in the field running the lines while Ellicott himself spent part of his time in the observatory tent. Now he was required to change his methods. Since Banneker was neither physically capable nor trained to run the lines and was much more useful with the astronomical instruments, Ellicott supervised work in the field, where he keenly felt the absence of experienced assistants. He customarily worked with a crew of twenty men, but he had been able to recruit only six men for this survey, none having any previous field experience.

Ellicott was finally able to make the first of his astronomical observations on the evening of Friday, February 11. In a letter written exactly one week after his arrival at Alexandria, he forwarded his first report to Jefferson, describing the conditions he had found and what he had been able to accomplish. He explained how cloudy weather had hampered him from making observations earlier in the week, but he had used the interim

Dial plate of Andrew Ellicott's field regulator clock inscribed "ELLICOTT/ BALTIMORE," and it's movement. This is the timepiece that Banneker maintained in the survey tent. *National Museum of American History, Smithsonian Institution.*

profitably by buying needed equipment, hiring woodcutters to cut down trees and to work in the field, and in establishing his camp. The first major difficulty he encountered was that his instructions had specified that the wharves and harbor of Alexandria were to be included within his square. Since from his point of view this was not desirable, he had adjusted his lines accordingly and planned to submit them for approval.[10] (Document 6) On the same evening he wrote to his wife to advise her that he had been well received in Alexandria and that he had been able to begin work at last.[11] (Document 7)

Ellicott's procedure for laying out the ten-mile square was a simple one. Before undertaking the definition of the square, Ellicott traced a meridian at Jones's Point on the west side of the Potomac River and then laid off an angle of 45 per cent from this meridian, continuing it in a straight line for ten miles to the northwest. At the termination of this line he made a right angle, a straight line he carried ten miles in a northeasterly direction. From the termination of this second line he carried a third line for the same distance at a right angle to it, to the southeast. Finally he carried a line from Jones Point to meet the termination of the third line. He measured these lines by means of a surveying chain that he examined each day to ensure that the links had not stretched or opened and that nothing affected its accuracy. He plumbed the line wherever the ground proved to be uneven, and traced it with his transit and equal altitude instrument.[12]

Ellicott knew that President Washington was impatiently awaiting a report of his results, but he encountered one frustration after another. "I have met with many difficulties for want of my old hands," he wrote to his wife. The lack of experienced assistants meant he was immersed in the countless details of day-to-day operation, and that the work was slowed. Adding to his troubles was "a most severe attack of influenza," from which he did not fully recover until the middle of March. "The President will be here next Monday," he told her after his recovery, "and after I receive his future orders, you shall hear from me.[13]

Ellicott had found it expedient to stabilize a base for himself with accommodations in Georgetown, and he moved from Alexandria to new lodgings at an inn with an office in the home of William Prout. It is possible that he stayed at Prout's inn as well, or he may have kept a room at Suter's Tavern. In 1791 the latter was one of only two inns in Georgetown. Built in 1761, it was kept by several landlords before John Suter acquired it in 1783. Situated on High Street (now Wisconsin Avenue) between Bridge and Water Streets (M Street and the Canal Bridge), this long wooden building of one and a half stories with a projecting roof over a long veranda served as the community center. Although formally named The Fountain Inn, it became locally known by the name of the innkeeper, and was particularly favored by gentlemen over the neighboring Sailor's Tavern. It was at Suter's that President Washington had his accommodations during his visits to supervise the survey.[14]

Banneker meanwhile remained at the survey camp. While the other men slept in the tents, Banneker decided to sleep in the observatory tent, since he spent so much of his time there. He was not accustomed to exposure and cold, but he made the best of it, consoling himself with the uniqueness of his opportunity to work with one of the country's foremost scientists and to use his fine astronomical instruments. Ellicott may have taken Banneker with him on occasion to the meetings with the commissioners; there were also other occasions when Banneker was able to leave the confines of the camp. He was learning a great deal about astronomy in the course of his work, and he used every spare moment to familiarize himself with the instruments and the few scientific texts Ellicott had brought along. He realized how relatively simple his own work in calculating ephemerides had been when compared with the project on which he was now involved.

The old farmer kept returning periodically to working on his almanac calculations, drafting and refining an outline for an ephemeris for the following year because he planned to make another attempt to have one published. He utilized what little free time he had for the purpose, taking advantage of Ellicott's texts and other materials available to him. This was not a simple matter, for he was required to work long hours, and he was usually exhausted by the time he was able to rest.

Banneker's greatest problem stemmed from the erratic schedule he was forced to follow, owing to the nature of his assignment. His day and night hours were broken up so that he was able to rest only during those brief periods when his presence was not needed elsewhere. The kind of astronomical observations required for the survey made night the most important working time for him, so that he could not retire until the morning. As the night ended and he was ready to go to bed, Major Ellicott customarily arrived in camp from his Georgetown lodgings, riding up to the observatory tent just at sun up. It was his habit to look over Banneker's notes and review the night's observations before proceeding with the field work. As the other men were beginning their working day, Banneker was finishing his own and preparing to retire to rest.

But not always without interruption. There were specific times during which he had to be awake to take observations of the sun with the transit and equal altitude instrument to establish the correct time for the regulator clock. The last of these daytime chores took place at mid-afternoon, so that he was able to sleep for the remainder of the afternoon, unless in the meantime one of the men had need to come into the tent. This schedule, combined with the extreme cold and humidity, aggravated Banneker's aches and pains, often causing him considerable distress.

The problems encountered by Ellicott and his men while working in the field were magnified for the older man, but since he was required to spend little of his time in the field, he consoled himself with the fact that he was gaining new experience with instruments. A review of his opportunities was enough to ease his discomfort. Nevertheless, he eagerly awaited the arrival of spring.

Banneker came to realize that Major Ellicott was a hard taskmaster. Each morning he rose while it was still dark, and by first light he had completed his breakfast and ridden to the camp to begin work. He worked his men seven days a week, never leaving the field until late evening. With the end of winter, conditions improved, although the thaw made the ground underfoot less favorable for the field work.

The project's slow but certain progress was being observed with interest by the citizens of Georgetown. On February 23 the *Gazette* noted: "Mr. Ellicott, we learned, finished the first line of his survey of the Federal territory in Virginia yesterday, and crossed below the Little Falls, the river Potowmack, on the second line."[15]

When Ellicott had the boundary survey well underway, Jefferson notified Major Pierre Charles L'Enfant, in a letter dated early in March. Jefferson's instructions were as precise with L'Enfant as they had been with Ellicott. L'Enfant was to prepare drawings of the grounds best suited to the site for the Federal city and for the specific government buildings to be erected thereon. He was to note roads, streams, and other topographical data, within the area that Ellicott was surveying.[16] (Document 8)

Contrary to popular notion, Ellicott was the first to receive an appointment to undertake the survey, and L'Enfant's appointment was made at least one month later. L'Enfant was a French officer and engineer who had fought with the Continental Army and later remodeled the temporary quarters for the federal government in New York. He arrived at the scene of the survey on March 9, 1791, a month after Ellicott had begun work on the project. President Washington had neglected to emphasize to L'Enfant that he was to be subordinate to the District Commissioners, so that L'Enfant was led to believe that he was responsible only to the president himself. It was this notion that later caused friction between the commissioners and the engineer and subsequently led to his dismissal.

Historians have occasionally erroneously reported that Andrew Ellicott and Banneker were L'Enfant's assistants. Such was not the case. Ellicott was never appointed as assistant or subordinate of L'Enfant; he worked independently under the jurisdiction of the commissioners. Banneker was an assistant to Ellicott and worked only under his direction and was not involved with other aspects of the project. During the summer of 1791, however, Benjamin Ellicott, Andrew's younger brother and assistant surveyor, was delegated to assist L'Enfant in drawing up the sketch of the city. It is probably from this assignment that the confusion of given names may have developed.

An interesting commentary on this matter was made by John Saurin Norris in a written statement prepared for Martha E. Tyson, perhaps to provide clarification of a point in her paper which he had read before the Maryland Historical Society in 1854. After describing the legislation for creating the Federal Territory, the appointment of commissioners, the survey of the ten-mile square, and the design of the city itself, Norris made some interesting comments as to whether Banneker was employed to lay out the "District," so called, or whether he worked with L'Enfant in laying out the city. He pointed out that the former required knowledge of astronomy and the use of scientific instruments, whereas the latter could be accomplished merely with a knowledge of engineering, so that it was his conclusion that Banneker was involved only with the former. Norris went on to assume that during his sojourn Banneker had met Jefferson, but obviously he was in error, inasmuch as Jefferson is not reported to have visited the site during the period in question.[17] (Document 9)

The arrival of L'Enfant at the Federal Territory was announced in the *Georgetown Weekly Ledger*, which also reported the presence of Banneker attending Ellicott, on the one and only occasion in which his participation was publicly noted:

> Some time last month arrived in this town Mr. *Andrew Ellicot,* a gentleman of superior astronomical abilities. He was employed by the President of the United States of America, to lay off a tract of land, ten miles square, on the Potowmack, for the use of Congress; — is now engaged in this business, and hopes soon to accomplish the object of his mission. He is attended by *Benjamin Banniker,* an Ethiopian, whose abilities, as a surveyor, and an astronomer, clearly prove that Mr. Jefferson's concluding that race of men were void of mental endowments, was without foundation.
>
> Wednesday evening arrived in this town, Major *Longfont,* a French gentleman, employed by the President of the United States to survey the lands contiguous to George-Town, where the federal city is to be built. His skill in matters of this nature is justly extolled by all disposed to give merit its proper tribute of praise. He is earnest in the business, and hopes to be able to lay a plat, of that parcel of land, before the President, upon his arrival in this town.[18]

This newspaper article has been quoted widely in subsequent historical accounts of the survey, and it has in fact served as evidence in the litigation of the Potomac Flats Case in the late nineteenth century relating to the scandal over the allocation of lots laid out during the development of Washington.[19] Curiously enough, not a single copy of this issue of the *Ledger* is known to have survived. The same account was published verbatim with a Georgetown byline and the date of March 12 in newspapers in other areas, including the *Maryland Gazette.*[20] It was also the basis for an abbreviated news item which appeared in the Philadelphia press a week later: "Mr. Ellicot and Major L'Enfant, are now engaged in laying out the ground on the Patowmac, on which the Federal buildings are to be erected."[21]

On March 28, President Washington arrived at Georgetown to inspect the area and to reach an agreement with the thirteen original proprietors for the conveyance of such parts of their farms as was required for laying out the streets without compensation, and such land as was needed for buildings and public reservations at a specified amount. Washington met with the three commissioners in the morning, then proceeded to dinner with the principal citizens at Suter's Tavern.[22]

There Washington "examined the Surveys of Mr. Ellicott who had been sent on to lay out the district of ten miles square for the Federal seat; and also the works of Maj. L'Enfant who had been engaged to examine & make a draught of the grds. in the vicinity of George Town and Carrollsburg on the Eastern Branch." The next day he personally visited the grounds and the following day departed from Georgetown.[23]

On March 31 the commissioners directed Ellicott to proceed with the survey of the ten-mile square as soon as possible, and he immediately undertook the preliminary work. Within two weeks he was able to inform them that he had run a line from the courthouse in Alexandria due southwest one half mile and thence southeast course to Hunting Creek to locate the beginning of "the four lines of experiment."

On April 15, 1791, the commissioners, in company with the city officials, Ellicott and many spectators, took part in a ceremony to install the first of the stone markers at Jones's Point. The accounts noted that on Friday, April 15, after Daniel Carroll and "Dr. David Steward [Stuart]" arrived in Alexandria to supervise the fixing of the Federal District, the mayor, other town officials, and the townspeople turned out to participate in the event. The marker was placed after Ellicott had ascertained the precise point for its installation, and a ceremony followed which was performed according to the rites with the ancient implements of Freemasonry. The level, as an emblem of equality, the plumb, as the emblem of rectitude of life, and the square, which represents virtue, were all applied in setting the stone. After the stone was in place it was consecrated with corn for nourishment as a symbol of goodness and plenty, wine for refreshment as a symbol of joy and gladness, and oil as a symbol of peace and harmony. The event was reported not only in the Alexandria press but in Baltimore, Boston, and other cities. Although the notice did not mention Banneker's presence, he undoubtedly would have participated as a spectator.[24] (Document 10)

With the installation of the foundation stone as the first marker, the formal survey of the new national capital city had begun. Several years later, on June 21, 1794, the temporary marker was replaced by Thomas Freeman, an assistant surveyor, upon instructions from the commissioners, with a more formal monument inscribed: "The beginning of the Territory of Columbia." The area surveyed for the district was generally described as a square, yet it was in fact more in the nature of a trapezoid. The northern point is not situated exactly north of the southern point, but bears 5' 19.7" west of north of it. It is 116 feet west of the meridian through the southern corner. The sides, intended to be exactly ten miles in length, vary in length as follows:

Southwestern side is 10 miles plus 230.6 feet long;
Northeastern side is 10 miles plus 263.1 feet long;
Southeastern side is 10 miles plus 70.5 feet long;
Northwestern side is 10 miles plus 63.0 feet long.[25]

When the boundary survey was completed, the line was carefully and thoroughly cleared for a distance of twenty feet on either side, making a clear lane forty feet wide through the woods for each ten-mile distance. In this lane stone posts were placed at every mile, and only the fourteen stones set on the Virginia line were completed before the end of the year. They each bear the date 1791; the twenty-six stones on the Maryland side are marked 1792. Each stone also had the distance from the preceding corner. Occasionally Ellicott's men discovered that the exact number of miles from one of the corners ended in a point ill-suited for a monument, such as a marsh or a stream bed. In such instances they measured back and forth from that point to firm ground and there placed the monument. Since the commissioners had not as yet reached an agreement on the name of the new city, which was finally resolved to be the City of Washington in the Territory of Columbia, the monuments do not bear the chosen name, having been installed earlier.

Although Ellicott had planned to make periodic visits to his family in Philadelphia, the first occasion on which he was able to make the journey home was in the last two weeks of April, at which time he called upon Tobias Lear, President Washington's secretary.[26] During this period his letters to his wife expressed the loneliness he felt during his absence from home. "We have a most eligant Camp and things are in fine order but where you are not there are no charms," he wrote her in June. There followed the usual complaints. The weather was "extremely hot," and dry. The countryside was also poor. "I think for near seven miles, . . . there is not one house that has any floor except the earth, and what is more strange it is in the neighborhood of Alexandria and Georgetown. We find but little fruit, except huckleberries, and live in our Camp as retired as we used to do on Lake Erie." There were dangers as well. "One of our Hands was killed last

Topographical map of "The Territory of
Columbia," now the District of Columbia,
compiled by Andrew Elliott 1791–93. *Library
of Congress, Geography and Map Division.*

One of the boundary stones of the ten-mile
square of the District of Columbia surveyed
and installed by Andrew Ellicott. *Courtesy,
U.S. Geological Survey.*

week by the falling of a Tree." This was not in fact an unusual incident. "I have had a number of men killed this summer," he wrote, "one of whom was a worthy, ingenious, and truly valuable character, he has left a wife and three small children to lament his untimely fate."[27]

Ellicott was now ready to undertake the next phase of the project. The boundary survey in New York had been completed by his brothers, and Benjamin, the younger one, had arrived at the Federal Territory in early April. His other brother, Joseph, was due to join him a month or two later. As in earlier surveys, both brothers were employed by Andrew as his assistants in the field. For some time Banneker had been ready to return to his farm, for he had fulfilled Ellicott's immediate needs and Benjamin Ellicott was now available to replace him in the observatory tent.[28]

Banneker was also becoming increasingly concerned for his health. The winter months had been cold and difficult, and his working schedule had been a stressful one, although the major had been as cooperative as the nature of the work permitted. He thought longingly of his hearth and home where he would have some rest, and even more, he was eager to complete the calculation of an ephemeris for another almanac that he had begun. He had learned much about practical astronomy from using Ellicott's books and astronomical instruments, and he was anxious to apply it to his own work. He also worried about his farm, which he could not leave in other hands much longer. It was thus with mingled regret and relief that he reported to Major Ellicott in mid or late April 1791 that on the latter's next journey to Philadelphia he wished to return home. Although now impatient to leave, Banneker waited until Ellicott made his next journey to Philadelphia, and then he accompanied him as far as the Lower Mills.

An exhaustive search of government repositories, including the Public Buildings and Grounds files in the National Archives, and varied collections in the Library of Congress, failed to turn up Banneker's name on any of the contemporary documents or records relating to the selection, planning, and survey of the City of Washington. Nor was he mentioned in any of the known surviving correspondence and papers of Andrew Ellicott and of Pierre Charles L'Enfant.

Not until recently did conclusive evidence of his participation in the project finally come to light, in an entry in Ellicott's report of expenditures. Entitled "Expences Incured in Surveying the Experimental and Permanent Lines of the District of Columbia" it revealed that the cost from February 4,

1791 through the month of December 1792 totaled $2,986.25. The first section listed expenses for the first twenty-three days of work laying out the experimental lines of the Federal Territory, from February 4 to March 1, 1791. In addition to noting salaries due to Ellicott and his assistant Isaac Roberdeau, it noted supplementary costs for which Ellicott had laid out personal cash and for which he required reimbursement. Ellicott's salary was $5 per day exclusive of room and board, while Roberdeau received $2 per day. Among the items for which Ellicott had advanced personal cash were $74 in payment to his chainmen and laborers for marking the lines. Provisions furnished to the camp included food and sundries costing $70. Traveling expenses for Ellicott from Philadelphia to Alexandria and return to Georgetown came to $24. Ellicott also advanced cash

> To Ditto
> pd. Benj.n Banneker Expences from & }
> to Geo.Town & whilst at Geo. Town . . } 60.0 -

Other expenses included $6 for portage of provisions and instruments to the "Lines" (campsite) and for hiring a boat to cross the Potomac and "freighting sundrys up & down the River" at a cost of $4.50. The total expenditure for establishing the experimental lines was $413.

The second section of the account listed expenses incurred for establishing the "permanent lines" from June 4 to July 18, 1791. Ellicott's salary remained the same as for the first period, and that of his assistants at $2 a day, for Roberdeau and Joseph and Benjamin Ellicott, who had joined him on June 10 after completing the survey in western New York, a combined total of $264. Payment of chainmen, axemen, and laborers for clearing the lines totaled $225, and the cost of provisions for the camp in this period was $277.33. To the cost of cartage for movement of provisions and instruments was added the additional cost of $97.66 for moving "Milestones to their respective places on the Lines." The third section of the account listed expenditures for the period July 18 to December 23, 1792, during which Ellicott spent sixteen days plotting the lines of the Territory of Columbia and preparing a report on the same. The total cost of establishing the permanent lines was $1,504.32. The report terminated with an attestation of the commissioners.[29]

This expense account had not come to notice earlier because it had been filed among Jefferson's papers in the Manuscripts Division of the

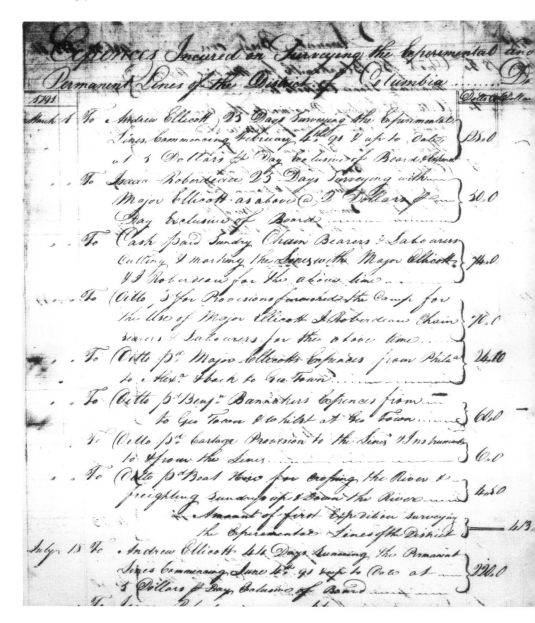

First page of Andrew Ellicott's accounting of "Expences Incured on Surveying the Experimental and Permanent Lines of the District of Columbia," listing payment to Banneker for his participation. *Library of Congress, Manuscripts Division.*

Portable quadrant made by Andrew Ellicott on the Ramsden design and used on his surveys. *Smithsonian Institution National Museum of American History.*

Library of Congress instead of in the files of the city commissioners. The commissioners had attempted to separate the expenses for surveying the experimental and permanent lines from the expenses incurred in surveying the city streets and lots, on which Ellicott was also engaged in 1791. The commissioners attempted to save money by having the costs for surveying the lines of the District assumed by the State Department, inasmuch as Jefferson, nominally in charge of the project, was secretary of state. Thus, Ellicott's report may have been deliberately misfiled.

Although the exact date of Banneker's departure from the survey is not specified in Ellicott's report of expenditures, it occurred at some time late in the month of April 1791, following the arrival of one of Ellicott's brothers. It was not until some ten months after Banneker's departure from the scene that L'Enfant was dismissed, by means of a letter from Jefferson dated February 27, 1792. This conclusively dispels any basis for the legend that after L'Enfant's dismissal and his refusal to make available his plan of the city, Banneker recollected the plan in detail from which Ellicott was able to reconstruct it. Equally untrue and in fact impossible is the legend that Thomas Jefferson as secretary of state invited Banneker to luncheon at the White House. Jefferson during this period was in Philadelphia, the national capital in Washington had not yet been built, and there was no White House (Document 9).

It is possible and even probable that Banneker was mentioned in Ellicott's field notes, journals, and diaries of his survey, papers that have not been found. Some of them were stolen from Ellicott's premises and others removed from Ellicott's surveyor's office by order of the commissioners in 1793. They have not been consulted or quoted by any of the writers on the history of the Federal Territory. Banneker's involvement in the survey, although not mentioned in Latrobe's memoir, was described in the biographical sketch by Martha Tyson from notes assembled in 1836:

> Banneker was but once absent, at any distance, from his domicil. An appointment having been made after the adoption of the Constitution, in 1789, of commissioners, to run the lines of the District of Columbia — then called the "Federal Territory," they wished to avail themselves of his talents, induced him to accompany them in the work and retained him with them until the service was completed.[30]

Tyson elaborated her report of the incident in her later writings but without any major change in the substance of her account.[31] (Document 11) She also commented on Banneker's deportment during his sojourn, and his relationship to the other principals involved in the project. She noted that he had won the respect of those with whom he worked to such a degree that they overlooked his color, and that he was able to discourse with them on a variety of topics.[32] (Document 12)

This episode has been the subject of some attention by later writers, many of whom have claimed that it was the commissioners who invited Banneker to join them at their table during meals. In actual fact, the commissioners were in the field only rarely, and there would have been only infrequent opportunities for issuing such an invitation if at all. In her later account, Tyson clarified the situation, and explained that it was the members of "the engineer corps" who invited Banneker to dine. "He was invited to sit at table with the engineer corps, but, as his characteristic modesty induced him to decline this, a separate table was prepared for him in their dining-room; his meals being served at the same time with theirs."[33]

Among the few surviving mentions of Banneker's participation in the survey in his own words was the reference in a letter he wrote to Thomas Jefferson as secretary of state after his return from the Federal Territory:

> And altho I had almost declined to make my calculation [of an almanac] for the ensuing year, in consequence of that time which I had allotted therefor being taken up at the Federal Territory, by the request of Mr. Andrew Ellicott, yet finding myself under Several engagements to printers of this state, to whom I had communicated my design, on my return to my place of residence I industriously applyed my Self thereto.[34]

There is a single entry in Banneker's manuscript journal that may relate to his sojourn in the Territory. This can be compared with two observations of the annular eclipse made by Ellicott at the Federal Territory at the same time, and which were subsequently published.[35] Finally, Banneker's presence at the survey was described by Jefferson in his letter to the Marquis de Condorcet on August 31, 1791, which has already been noted.[36]

Martha Tyson reported Banneker's return to Baltimore County by recalling the account rendered by her parents:

> On his return home, he called at the house of his friend George Ellicott to

give an account of his engagements. He arrived on horseback, dressed in his usual costume, a full suit of drab cloth, surmounted by a large beaver hat. He was in fine spirits, seeming to have been reanimated by the kindness of the distinguished men with whom he had mingled. With his usual humility he estimated his own services at a low rate.[37]

After Banneker's departure from the survey camp and Ellicott's return from Philadelphia, the latter was recalled from his work on the ten-mile square to join his efforts with those of L'Enfant in order to hasten the survey of the city lines. Conflicts developed with some of the proprietors early in May, and President Washington and the commissioners were eager to proceed with a sale of lots as quickly as possible. The progress achieved through the combined efforts of the surveyor and engineer made it possible to render a plan of the city to the president and to report substantial accomplishment.[38]

A month later, on June 4, it was reported in the press that on the previous Saturday, Ellicott, "the geographer general of the United States," had completed the six main lines of the federal city, and was engaged in clearing and bounding the lines of the district or ten-mile square.[39]

Ellicott's participation in the design of the city at this time is confirmed by a notice issued by the commissioners to property holders on June 30, requesting them to submit any information they had about the lines of their land to "Major L'Enfant and Major Ellicott" for inclusion on the general plat. By this time it had become necessary to establish a surveyor's office in Georgetown from which Ellicott and L'Enfant operated and directed the several aspects of their work. Tradition claims that it was located in the two-story structure at 3049 M Street.[40]

After establishing the boundary of the ten-mile square, Ellicott drew a north-south straight line through the area which was specified by L'Enfant to be occupied by the Capitol, and then crossed it at this point with another line drawn at right angles through the rear door of the President's House. He then continued both lines to the outer boundaries of the new city. He attempted to lay off the parallels with a chain, but encountered difficulties because of the cold weather. He was concerned with the degree of expansion and contraction of the links of the iron survey chain as a consequence of temperature change and the errors resulting from attempts to bend and straighten the links. Finally, Ellicott laid his chain aside and instead used a set of wooden rods accurately divided with graduations like a carpenter's square. They were accommodated with plummets and sliders to permit the measurements to be made horizontally, and the devices worked successfully. (Document 13)

Ellicott found that one source of error remained, namely, the human element. His line men occasionally made errors in returning the tallies, and Ellicott discovered that the intersections of the major avenues, which established the locations of other streets, were sometimes moved, leading to much confusion. He suspected that this was being done deliberately. It worried him and required constant vigilance and re-examination of each point before going on. He used this method to establish all the main avenues as well as the parallel streets with the transit and equal altitude instrument.

The work progressed on both projects until the beginning of September, when a series of incidents brought L'Enfant into disfavor with the commission and with the president. The first was when the commissioners requested ten thousand copies of the map to be distributed in October for use in the sale of lots in the new city. L'Enfant had arranged with a French printer to produce them. They were never delivered, and the first land sale was done without maps. It was a great disappointment to all concerned, but Washington was convinced that it was not L'Enfant's fault. However, he was provoked when L'Enfant refused to permit the original of his general plan to be displayed at the sale.

Then in November L'Enfant discovered that one of the commissioners was having a house built on the line of Jersey Avenue at E Street which would project out about seven feet into the street. L'Enfant ordered the house destroyed, an action that outraged Carroll, who was one of the most influential men assisting in the development of the new city. Washington was greatly annoyed, and reprimanded L'Enfant and told him that in the future he would have to submit to the orders of the commission. L'Enfant refused to subordinate himself to the commissioners, and on March 6, 1792, Jefferson wrote to them that it was impracticable to keep L'Enfant on the project.

Overleaf:
Topographical map of "The City of Washington," now the District of Columbia, compiled by Andrew Ellicott 1791–93. *Library of Congress, Geography and Map Division.*

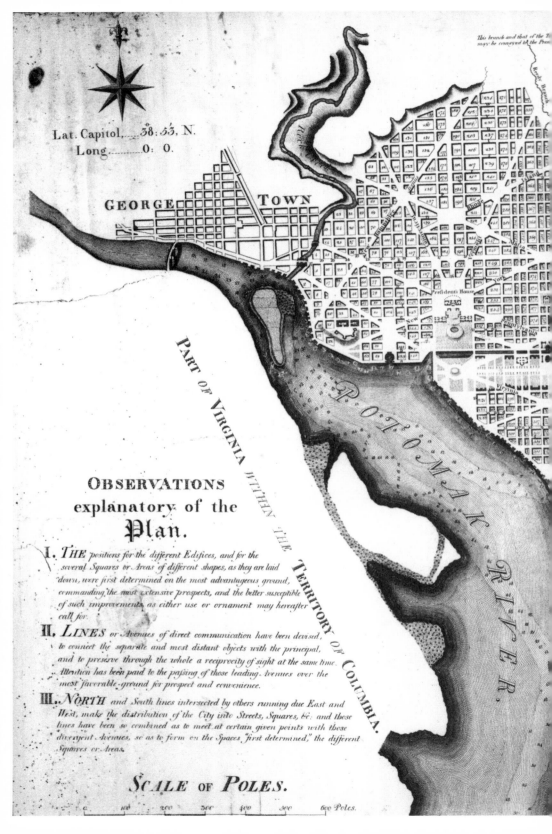

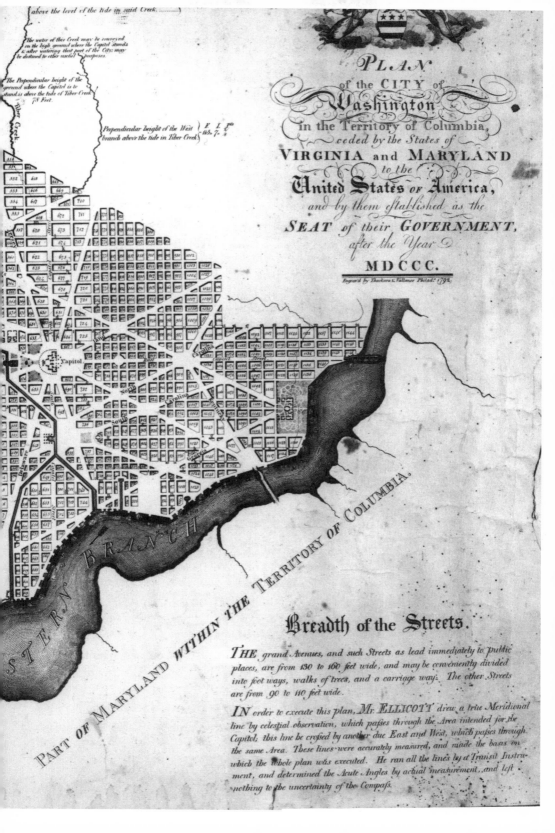

above the level of the tide in said Creek.

The water of this Creek may be conveyed on the high ground where the Capitol stands & after watering that part of the City may be distined to other useful purposes.

The Perpendicular height of the ground where the Capitol is to stand is above the tide of Tiber Creek 78 Feet.

Perpendicular height of the West branch above the tide in Tiber Creek

PLAN
of the CITY of
Washington
in the Territory of Columbia,
ceded by the States of
VIRGINIA and MARYLAND
to the
United States of America,
and by them established as the
SEAT of their GOVERNMENT,
after the Year
MDCCC.

Engraved by Thackara & Vallance Philadt 1792.

Capitol

STERN BRANCH

PART OF MARYLAND WITHIN THE TERRITORY OF COLUMBIA.

Tiber Creek

Breadth of the Streets.

THE grand Avenues, and such Streets as lead immediately to public places, are from 130 to 160 feet wide, and may be conveniently divided into foot ways, walks of trees, and a carriage way. The other Streets are from 90 to 110 feet wide.

IN order to execute this plan, Mr. ELLICOTT drew a true Meridional line by celestial observation, which passes through the Area intended for the Capitol; this line he crossed by another due East and West, which passes through the same Area. These lines were accurately measured, and made the basis on which the whole plan was executed. He ran all the lines by a Transit Instrument, and determined the Acute Angles by actual measurement, and left nothing to the uncertainty of the Compass.

Meanwhile the winter weather made it impossible to continue work in the field, and in December Ellicott closed down his camp and returned to his family in Philadelphia for the rest of the winter. By the beginning of March, as the weather improved, he became concerned about the program of work for the following season. Despite his communications, he had received no reply from the commissioners, and he wrote to them once more in desperation. He pointed out the scarcity of qualified surveyors and scientific assistants, noted the problems that had developed with L'Enfant, and justified the expenses he had incurred with the project.[41] (Document 14)

This letter is of particular importance because it described the nature of Banneker's role in the survey prior to the arrival of Ellicott's brothers. Ellicott did not receive a satisfactory reply to his letter, and in the interim L'Enfant was discharged. An assistant surveyor named James Dermott had been hired without Ellicott's knowledge or approval because he had come to the favorable attention of Dr. David Stuart, one of the commissioners. Dermott, a young Irish emigrant had taught mathematics at the Alexandria Academy.

The commissioners placed Ellicott in charge of the overall project on March 14, 1792, and in the following August a young surveyor named George Fenwick was added to his staff. During the remainder of the year Ellicott and his party laid out and divided the squares of the city at the same time they were completing the boundary survey. It was an unpleasant period for Major Ellicott, because he succumbed again to influenza which also disabled both of his brothers and Fenwick.[42]

Inevitably problems continued to arise between Ellicott and the commissioners with increasing frequency. Pressures developed from proprietors who complained that the project was proceeding too slowly. Ellicott in disgust offered to yield the project to someone else if the commissioners wished, but he was asked to continue. He submitted his formal report on the completion of the boundary survey on January 1, 1793.[43]

A week later, Ellicott felt constrained by the increasing number of proprietors' complaints to announce that he planned to resign from the project the following May. Continued harassment from the proprietors as well as the press led Ellicott at the end of the month to demand that the commissioners undertake an investigation of the Surveyor's Office. At the same time he brought to light his dispute with Dermott, whom he claimed had removed some of the important papers relating to that office, presumably for the purpose of discrediting him. Ellicott's exasperation and the continuing friction in his relations with the commissioners led to an open controversy, with the result that on March 12, 1793, the commissioners discharged Major Ellicott and his assistants.[44]

It was only through the intercession of President Washington, during his visit to the site a week later, that Ellicott and his assistants were returned to service on April 3, after a reorganization of the Surveyor's Office. In the course of this development, the commissioners ordered the confiscation of all of Ellicott's papers from that office, an action that led to another eruption between them and Ellicott. He angrily described the incident in a letter to his wife. With a certain measure of satisfaction, however, he reported that he had succeeded in having all of his men reinstated after a month's suspension of work. Inasmuch as his papers had been seized by the commissioners' order after his return from Philadelphia, his contest with them continued, although his files were later restored to him.[45] (Document 15)

Ellicott departed for Philadelphia on July 19, 1793, informing the commissioners that his services would not be required for the time being and that surveyors Isaac Briggs and his brother Benjamin would remain in charge during his absence. These two assistants carried on through the summer and the autumn, during which time their relationship with Dermott worsened. It led to a confrontation between Briggs and Dermott before the commissioners in October, and Briggs was dismissed. Joseph Ellicott and Fenwick then assumed charge of the project. Andrew returned on December 9 and the commissioners lost no time in informing him that during his absence the work had progressed satisfactorily and suggested that they had no real need of him during the winter. Andrew thereupon incited his brothers to rebellion, and Benjamin Ellicott, half in fun and half in earnest, advertised in the press the theft of the L'Enfant map by Dermott. At this point the controversy grew even more heated.

The president drew the attention of the commissioners to letters that had been addressed to Washington by Andrew and Benjamin Ellicott and by Isaac Briggs dated June 29, 1793, and February 28, 1794, which described in detail the complaints of the writers against Dermott and the commissioners. The commissioners' response to the president came in a long letter dated March 23, 1794, which fully detailed the incidents that had occurred, expressed their dissatisfaction with Ellicott's performance, and described their consequent actions.[46]

They admitted the seizure of the surveyor's papers in connection with his accusations against Dermott. The matter of the confiscation and the restoration of the papers, as well as the eventual loss of some of them, is intimately connected with the problem of documenting Banneker's presence at the Territory, and for that reason has been given in some detail. Meanwhile, Ellicott had received an appointment from the governor of Pennsylvania to survey a road from Reading to Waterford. He undertook the project upon his departure from Washington and spent the following two years in its completion. The commissioners placed Dermott in charge of dividing the Federal Territory's squares into lots, and the work progressed. (Document 16)

The second incident in which Ellicott's papers were seized is of particular significance, for it may explain the total absence to the present time of his field notes, journals, and diaries. Ellicott made reference to the loss in a communication to Robert Patterson published several years later, in which he commented: "A number of the eclipses of the first Satellite of Jupiter together with a great proportion of my notes relative to the city of Washington, were privately taken from my lodgings in Georgetown, otherwise they should have appeared in this paper."[47]

Ellicott planned to prepare a paper for presentation and publication by the American Philosophical Society in which he would mention the survey of the City of Washington and "the method pursued in executing that part of the plan in which I have been concerned will be explained," as he wrote to Dr. William Thornton some time later. He registered his objections to the changes made in the plan after his departure, and his conflicts with the Commissioners during the course of the project. Particularly he commented on the pillaging of his office during which the notes of his observations for determining the longitude were lost or destroyed.[48] (Document 7)

Ellicott's strong statements were a severe indictment of Dermott's intentions and actions, and the statement that he had pilfered Ellicott's papers would explain their mysterious absence from the records of this important survey. Ellicott further commented on the incident in a communication to Jefferson some years later:

> Whilst I was engaged in the City of Washington some years ago I made a
> number of observations to determine its longitude but all those observa-

tions with some others relative to the plan of the City were lost when the office was pillaged; — but fortunately two very important observations which I had communicated to our late worthy friend Mr. Rittenhouse have been saved and published in the fourth volume of the transactions of our Society.[49] (Document 17)

The late Julian P. Boyd, editor of the Princeton edition of the papers of Thomas Jefferson, in reporting the survey of the Federal Territory and the laying out of the national capital, commented on the mention of Banneker's presence on the survey as reported in the press. He pointed out that the basis for the claim of Banneker's involvement in the project was based on extremely meager documentation chiefly derived from the recollections of members of the Ellicott family "who were prompted by Quaker inclinations to justice and equality." Dr. Boyd was unaware, it is true, of the later discovery of documentary evidence of Banneker's participation in the preliminary survey, but nevertheless, his conclusions appear to be somewhat biased.[50]

VI

HIS
FIRST ALMANAC

View yon majestic concave of the sky!
Contemplate well, those glorious orbs on high—
There Constellations shine, and Comets blaze;
Each glitt'ring world the Godhead's pow'r displays!

Banneker's Almanac for 1794

A S SOON AS BANNEKER HAD SETTLED DOWN ONCE MORE to the homely routine of his farm, he turned his full attention to astronomical observations. His first attempts with publishers had been greatly discouraging, but he now had hopes of achieving his dream. His surveying work with Major Ellicott had taught him much about the use of instruments for making astronomical observations, and with renewed vigor he set about producing an ephemeris for 1792.

He had completed the preliminary work during his occasional leisure moments in the field camp, and he now undertook the projections for the eclipses. Within a short time he had outlined each of the months, and had completed the tedious task of inserting his calculations in the columns for each segment of the project. The arduous months on the survey had tired him, and he had little energy to do more than work on the ephemeris after his return. Yet the solitary spring and early summer nights at the telescope were enjoyable and let him sleep through the hottest part of the day.

One lesson he had learned in particular from his brief employment with Major Ellicott was the need for orderliness and accuracy in the making and maintenance of mathematical calculations. If the results were to be useful, they must be readily available and identifiable. Accordingly, he came to the conclusion that he needed a special volume in which to keep his astronomical records together. He found just what he needed in the Ellicott & Company Store, a handsome volume of folio size bound as a journal. It proved to be an expensive purchase, but since astronomy was to be his new work he considered it to be a justified investment. Still, he took the time to study how the journal could best be arranged before making any use of it.

Banneker now devoted a part of each day, as well as the major part of his evening, to astronomical studies. He worked alone, with only the company of his own thoughts and the comfortable sound of the ticking clock against the wall near the fireplace. The hours passed quickly, punctuated periodically by the striking of the clock, and time seemed to have become an endless sea with no shore in sight.

The new manuscript journal occupied an honored place upon the oval table next to his text books, which he kept in a neat stack to one side, and his telescope and drafting instruments. It was a splendid volume, three hundred pages of fine handmade paper measuring nine by almost fifteen inches, with a sewn binding and parchment covers; its pages fairly beckoned him to begin his work. Each page bore a watermark of a hunting horn and the cipher "G R." The paper itself appeared to have been made in the American colonies, possibly by one of the two new paper mills that had been established near Baltimore after 1778, or perhaps by a mill in nearby Pennsylvania, but the cipher is not known to have been used by colonial American papermakers. On the other hand, the horn and shield watermark with the "G R" cipher was quite common in England in the period from just prior to 1750 until a little after 1800.[1]

Banneker began to copy his final calculations for each month from his work sheets onto the recto pages of the journal, reserving the verso side for miscellaneous notes. He had made a careful study of the general format of several published almanacs and adapted them for his results. Leaving the first several pages blank, he then inscribing his finished calculations from his notes:

1792

January First Month hath 31 Days . . .

As was his wont, he wrote carefully, forming his letters with precision in the beautiful style that his grandmother had taught him and of which he was inordinately proud. At the top of the facing page he inscribed the formula for the use of the Dominical Letter, with a reference to his source, Ferguson's *Astronomy Based on Sir Isaac Newton's Principles,* citing chapter and page.[2]

This entry was followed by "Common Notes and Movable Feasts for the Year 1792," and then a quotation that was probably also taken from Ferguson's volume:

> It is to be observed that the Moon and the five primary planets has the Same Declination as the Sun has, when in the Same Sign and Degree that the Moon or planet is in at the given time.[3]

Banneker made the first drawing for a projection of an eclipse of the sun on the page facing the calculations for May 1792. It includes the following notation:

> This projection I laid down for April the third 1791 when the Sun rose Centrally eclipsed at the City of Washington this is a back tryal to See how present method would agree with the former.

> N. B. Ferguson's Tables make the new abotit [orbit?] 30 minutes to Soon Viz

	d	L	M	
April	3	10	30	
I say	3	11	2	A.M.
			32	

On one of the first leaves in his manuscript journal, Banneker had made a notation relating to one of his reference works, but it is not completely comprehensible because part of the page has been torn or cut away:

> . . . Astronomy Explain'd on S[R] Isaac Newton's principles says . . . Stands in the Same line as Easter Sunday . . . must Serve for the given year.

In his *Astronomy Based on Sir Isaac Newton's Principles,* Ferguson repeatedly referred the reader for more specific information to one of his lesser known works, *Tables and Tracts...,* which Banneker subsequently acquired for his own library, although his copy has not survived. (Document 18) He extracted useful passages from this text and occasionally added them to his manuscript journal as reminders of procedures to be followed.[4]

By the beginning of June, Banneker had completed a draft of his manuscript ephemeris and promptly mailed a copy of it to a printer in Georgetown. Whether he had had previous contact with the printer cannot be ascertained, but apparently he received some assurance that his work would be accepted. The Georgetown printer may have been either Charles Fierer, the printer and publisher *of* the *Times and the Potowmack Packet,* or one of the partners—Matthias Day or William Hancock—who published the *Georgetown Weekly Ledger.*[5]

Banneker decided at the outset that it would be desirable to obtain the greatest possible public distribution for his work, and accordingly he sought printers in both Baltimore and Philadelphia. He had already heard of William Goddard, the patriot and enterprising publisher in Baltimore who printed the *Maryland Journal.* As soon as Banneker was strong enough to travel, he made another copy of his ephemeris and brought it on horseback to Baltimore.

Goddard was to become a significant figure in Banneker's life as well as in the history of American printing. Born in New London, Connecticut, in 1740, into a prominent New England family, Goddard from an early age worked with newspapers in Connecticut. In 1762 he moved first to Providence, Rhode Island, then went on to New York and later Philadelphia, where in early 1767 he began to publish the *Pennsylvania Chronicle.* The newspaper continued until 1773, when its Tory leanings brought about its demise.

Early in 1773, Goddard visited Baltimore at the urging of some of its citizens who wished him to establish the first newspaper in that city. He arrived in June and opened a printing shop on Market Street. The first issue of his new weekly paper, the *Maryland Journal or Baltimore Advertiser,* appeared in August. In October he made a visit to "the northern provinces" (New England), leaving the paper in the care of his sister, Mary Katherine Goddard.

Goddard made a second trip north the following year for the purpose of developing a proposal for an American postal system. His plan for a Continental Post Office proved so successful that it forced the discontinuation of the British postal system and was taken over by the Continental Congress in 1775. He received no compensation and subsequently returned to Baltimore to assist his sister with the newspaper he had founded.

Goddard's articles brought him much censure, first from the Loyalists —leading to his banishment to Annapolis—and then from the patriots. As wartime supplies of paper became increasingly scarce, Goddard became involved with the operation of a paper mill at Elk Ridge and with a book-binding business. After a short partnership with his sister in the publication of the *Maryland Journal,* he entered a short-lived partnership with the printer Edward Langworthy, which ended in 1787.

In 1786 Goddard was married to Abigail Angell, and in 1789 he took as his partner her brother, James Angell. The partnership continued until August 1792, during the period that Banneker's almanac was being considered for publication. Goddard then sold his interest to Angell although his name remained on the shop's imprint until February 1793. Angell continued the printing business alone, including the *Maryland Journal,* until November 1, 1793. In the summer of 1792 Goddard moved permanently to Rhode Island, and Angell took another partner into the firm for a brief period before selling the printing business to Francis Brumfield in October 1794; he died three years later.[6]

Banneker was impressed with Goddard at their first meeting and perhaps for that reason failed to obtain a definite decision concerning his work. Goddard, who had published almanacs in the past was interested in issuing another, primarily to compete with local printers, and thought that an almanac with an ephemeris calculated by a Negro philomath might be advantageous for marketing. Banneker explained that he planned to sell copies of his calculations to one or two printers in other cities and that he believed that such distribution would not affect Goddard's sales. The printer did not comment but offered Banneker a small sum for his work, with the promise that if the almanac proved successful a bonus might follow.

Banneker was quite well satisfied with himself, for he had found two printers who expressed interest in his work and who probably would publish it. His satisfaction soon gave way to doubt, though, and he wondered whether he might find a printer in Philadelphia, where he believed the almanac would receive the greatest exposure of all, particularly if it were supported by the Pennsylvania Society for the Abolition of Slavery. The society had already expressed some interest in his work. At the first opportunity he consulted with George Ellicott, who suggested he make the effort. Banneker provided him with another manuscript copy of his ephemeris which George sent to his brother Elias in Baltimore. During the previous summer, Elias Ellicott and his friend and business associate Joseph Townsend had been elected to membership in the society and had become increasingly active in its activities.[7]

Elias Ellicott saw in Banneker's achievement an opportunity to serve the antislavery cause and was eager to be of assistance. During the previous year he had learned from Townsend that James Pemberton had expressed an interest in Banneker's first ephemeris, and now he lost no time in writing to Pemberton directly to advise him that Banneker had completed the calculations for an ephemeris for 1792 and that he was seeking an interested printer in Philadelphia:

> Understanding that thee wrote to Joseph Townsend expressing a desire to be informed particularly respecting Benjamin Banaker, I take the Freedom to inform Thee that I am personally Acquainted with him. He is a Black Man about 56 Years of Age. His Father was a Guinea Negroe. He is a man of strong Natural parts and by his own Study hath made himself well Acquainted with the Mathematicks. About three Years Ago he began to study Astronomy by the Assistance of some Authors which he with much difficulty procured soon became so far a proficient as to Calculate an Almanac, he calculated one for the Year 1791 and Intended to have had it Published but could not. He hath a Copy now ready for the Press for the Year 1792 — and is very desirous of having it Published in Philadelphia. Now if Thee thinks it Worthy thy notice it might be well to make inquiry of the different Printers to know whether any one of them will undertake to Print it. He is a Poor man & Would be Pleased With having something for the Copy but if the Printer is not Willing to give any thing He would rather let him have it for nothing than not to have it Published. He thinks as it is the first performance of the kind ever done by One of his Complection that it might be a means of Promoting the Cause of Humanity as many are of Opinion that the Blacks are Void of Mental endowments. If thee can find any one that will take the Copy of the Almanac please to inform me by the Post and I will have the Copy Forwarded.

Elias then added a postscript:

> Said Banaker lives about 10 miles from Baltimore near Ellicotts Lower Mills, it may be depended upon that he never had any assistance from any Person in respect to his Knowledge of Astronomy.[8]

Pemberton replied promptly with an expression of interest and an assurance that a suitable printer could be found, if upon examination the ephemeris proved to have been competently calculated. He urged Elias to forward it as quickly as possible, because the year was already half over and there was relatively little time left to have the calculations reviewed and to negotiate with a printer.

Elias informed his brother of the results, and George visited Benjamin to obtain a copy of the ephemeris to be forwarded to Philadelphia. He found instead that Banneker had been seriously ill in bed for a number of days and had not been able to complete the required copy. The elderly man was more concerned about the delay of his project than about his pain and discomfort, for it seemed that once again fate might keep his work from publication. As soon as he was able, Benjamin returned to his work table and completed a clean copy of his work, which he sent by one of his young relatives to George Ellicott's home. The latter immediately forwarded it to Elias in Baltimore. John Todd, a Philadelphia businessman and fellow member of the society was visiting in Baltimore at the time, and since the post left much to be desired, Elias made arrangements with Todd to deliver by hand to Pemberton the manuscript ephemeris together with his own covering letter explaining the causes of the delay.[9]

Meanwhile, an event had taken place in Baltimore that helped to cement Banneker's importance as a man of science and as a free Negro. On the occasion of the July 4 celebration in Baltimore, the Maryland Society for Promoting the Abolition of Slavery held a public meeting at which the speaker was Dr. George Buchanan, a distinguished local practicing physician and a member of the American Philosophical Society.[10] A large crowd gathered to hear Buchanan's declaim on the achievements of distinguished Negroes, a daring subject, to say the least, particularly in Maryland and only four years after the adoption of the Constitution. Among those he mentioned was Banneker:

> Many instances are recorded of men of eminence among them. Witness Ignacio Sancho, whose letters are admired by all men of taste; Phillis Wheatley, who distinguished herself as a poetess; the Physician of New Orleans; the Virginia Calculator; Banneker, the Maryland Astronomer, and many others. . . .

The oration was subsequently published in a pamphlet of twenty pages with a dedication to Thomas Jefferson, Secretary of State.[11]

That Buchanan had named Banneker made the publication of his almanac all the more appealing to Pemberton and his associates, but he considered it necessary to have the work reviewed by competent scientists, and so he forwarded a copy to David Rittenhouse. Unquestionably the foremost scientist in the country at that time, Rittenhouse had recently been appointed president of the American Philosophical Society to succeed Benjamin Franklin, who had died in the previous year.

Rittenhouse, ill and nearing the end of his active career, was burdened with many responsibilities. In addition to his appointments as a trustee of the University of Pennsylvania and as the new president of the American Philosophical Society, he had recently embarked upon a program undertaken by the State of Pennsylvania relating to the improvement of roads and rivers and the construction of a network of canals. Despite all these other commitments, Rittenhouse also reviewed and reported on many of the proposals submitted to the American Philosophical Society in this period.[12] He nevertheless took the time to examine Banneker's ephemeris, checked a number of calculations, and reported promptly and favorably. "I think the papers I herewith return to you a very extraordinary performance, considering the Colour of the Author," he replied to Pemberton, claiming that Banneker's calculations were "sufficiently accurate for the purposes of a common Almanac." He added, "Every Instance of Genius amongst the Negroes is worthy of attention, because their oppressors seem to lay great stress on their supposed inferior mental abilities."[13]

Despite this accolade from the country's foremost astronomer, Pemberton submitted Banneker's ephemeris to a second authority for review, and finally selected William Waring, who was conveniently in Philadelphia. Although his name has not survived prominently in the annals of science, Waring was a popular figure in Philadelphia's scientific circles. He was a teacher of mathematics at the Friends' public school on Pear Street and author of a journal published in 1791 for the use of seamen in making lunar observations for calculating the longitude. A few years later he co-authored *The American Tutor's Assistant* in cooperation with John Todd, Zachariah Jess, and Jeremiah Paul. Waring was also concerned with mill construction, and several of his papers on aspects of the subject were read before the American Philosophical Society, to which he was elected in 1793. Each year after 1787, Waring calculated the ephemerides for *Poor Will's Almanack* which had been published in Philadelphia by Joseph

Crukshank. He was acknowledged to be a competent astronomer and his professionally calculated almanacs were popular. He was associated with Pemberton as a fellow member of the Pennsylvania Society for the Abolition of Slavery, to which he was elected on April 4, 1790, and both were engaged in a cooperative enterprise in which Banneker's work could be useful. He was undoubtedly one of the most competent astronomers available at that time to evaluate Banneker's work.[14] Waring made his report in the form of a general statement of approval that could be published in the almanac if desired, and which he submitted to Pemberton.[15]

Pemberton, meanwhile, had been occupied in other quarters, and sent word back to Banneker through the Ellicotts, that he had aroused the interest of Joseph Crukshank in the almanac, and that although the printer had not reached a final decision, the prospects seemed favorable. Banneker was delighted, for Crukshank was one of the foremost printers in Philadelphia.

A member of the Society of Friends and one of the founding members of the Pennsylvania Society for the Abolition of Slavery, Crukshank utilized his press freely on behalf of the Friends as well as in support of the antislavery movement, and he published a number of Negro writings in which he had an interest. In 1786 he produced the first American edition of the poems of Phillis Wheatley, and in 1790 he published a work of his own authorship entitled, *A Poetical Epistle to the Enslaved Africans in the Character of an Ancient Negro Born a Slave.*

Banneker now was waiting impatiently on three fronts—Georgetown, Baltimore, and Philadelphia—and he found it difficult to believe his good fortune, and that a work produced by his own efforts would possibly be published and distributed over such a large part of the country. As he ruminated over this prospect, an idea began to form in his mind. From his conversations with the Ellicotts and their reports of the interest in his work expressed by other members of the Society of Friends in Philadelphia, he became aware that it was the subject of his race that actually generated the greatest response. He was at first somewhat put out by this attitude, for in his own opinion, the proposed almanac was of interest and value primarily because of the competence of his astronomical calculations and not because of his color. Now he began to realize that he and his work were being used for other purposes.

It was at this juncture that Banneker came to the decision to write a letter to Thomas Jefferson, submitting also a manuscript copy of his almanac calculations. Banneker's letter to Jefferson has been generally construed as evidence that he was aware of how he could be useful to the cause of antislavery by having himself cited as an example of the Negro's mental capacity, in refutation of Jefferson's statements in his *Notes on the State of Virginia*. But there is reason to doubt that such was just what he had in mind. Certainly he was aware of his achievements, that they challenged "the almost general prejudice and prepossession which is so prevalent in the world against those of my complexion." Taking up Jefferson's claim that all men are created equal, Banneker pointed out that natural rights do not permit of exception. His was a simple logic derived from his scientific interests.

A careful study of Banneker's life, and a review of his correspondence, the notes in his journal, and his general attitude as related by those who knew him, reveal him to have been an amateur in the arts and sciences, but also a man of considerable dignity and industry, and deeply religious although not a member of any sect. He appreciated his many opportunities, and he never aimed beyond his reach. At no time was he known to have displayed resentment of his station or that of his race. Because of the relative remoteness of his home and his solitary work, Banneker appears to have had little if any personal experience of oppression and cruelty to Negroes. On the other hand, he could not have avoided some knowledge of slavery, certainly from his own family's circumstances as well as from the presence of slaves working on neighboring farms and properties along the Patapsco River.

During his boyhood a plantation adjacent to his father's farm was owned by Roger Randall, who kept two slaves. Beyond Randall was the farm of Emmanuel Teale, who owned one slave. Some distance away was John Owings' farm with two slaves, and Thomas Floyd kept a single slave to help with his work. There would have been little communication between the Banneker family and the slaves on these other farms, however, so that the matter of slavery apparently remained relatively remote during Banneker's boyhood.[16]

Nowhere in his surviving letters and papers did Banneker express any real concern for the subjugation his race or a willingness to champion the antislavery cause. Now he suddenly found himself faced with a unique opportunity to address the subject directly to the author of no less than the famous *Notes on the State of Virginia*. Before proceeding with his letter, he undoubtedly discussed it with George Ellicott and possibly other members of the local abolitionist society, and received their encouragement and perhaps their assistance in formulating it. It provided the opportunity to advertise and popularize not only Banneker's almanacs but also the abolitionist movement.

Whether others proposed the idea or he initiated it by himself, Banneker surely approached the prospect of writing to Jefferson with caution. He readily understood that publication of an exchange of letters with the secretary of state would benefit the advertising and sale of his almanac, but he also realized that a letter from an unknown, amateur almanac-maker might be offensive to the statesman. He gave his letter careful thought. It was important to identify himself with Jefferson's interests, and this he could do with reference to the survey of the Federal Territory.

Doubtless he recalled the account in the *Georgetown Weekly Ledger* that described his arrival in the new national district ". . . as an Ethiopian whose abilities as surveyor and astronomer already prove that Mr. Jefferson's concluding that that race of men were void of mental endowment was without foundation." That statement may have led him to emphasize Jefferson's own involvement in having him appointed as Ellicott's assistant. He would also, of course, note his subsequent achievement in calculating an ephemeris for an almanac that was about to be published. He gave no indication that he was otherwise informed of Jefferson's expressed opinions or writings on the subject of the Negro, and he did not refer to the *Notes on the State of Virginia*. Instead he likened the slavery of Negroes to the enslavement of the American colonies by the British Crown and proposed justifying the correction of one state of oppression on the basis of the other. He drafted the letter carefully, describing his involvement with the sciences, his participation in the survey, and his calculation of an ephemeris, as a way of appealing to Jefferson's own avid interest in the sciences and in American scientific achievement. Still, it is too much to believe that Banneker, who had distinguished himself by a lifetime of modesty, prudence, and dignity, could have conceived, without the guidance and encouragement of others, a letter so deliberately planned to evoke a statement of position from the statesman who had whenever possible avoided a public committment on the subject of slavery.

Maryland, Baltimore County, Near Ellicott's Lower Mills
August 19TH 1791.

Thomas Jefferson Secretary of State.

Sir, I am fully sensible of the greatness of that freedom which I take with you on the present occasion; a liberty which Seemed to me Scarcely allowable, when I reflected on that distinguished, and dignifyed station in which you Stand; and the almost general prejudice and prepossession which is so previlent in the world against those of my complexion.

I suppose it is a truth too well attested to you, to need a proof here, that we are a race of Beings who have long laboured under the abuse and censure of the world, that we have long been looked upon with an eye of contempt, and that we have long been considered rather as brutish than human, and Scarcely capable of mental endowments.

Sir, I hope I may Safely admit, in consequence of that report which hath reached me, that you are a man far less inflexible in Sentiments of this nature, than many others; that you are measurably friendly and well disposed towards us, and that you are willing and ready to Lend your aid and assistance to our relief from those many distresses and numerous calamities to which we are reduced.

Now, Sir, if this is founded in truth, I apprehend you will readily embrace every opportunity to eradicate that train of absurd and false ideas and oppinions which so generally prevail with respect to us, and that your Sentiments are concurrent with mine, which are that one universal Father hath given being to us all, and that he hath not only made us all of one flesh, but that he hath also without partiality afforded us all the Same Sensations, and endued us all with the same faculties, and that however variable we may be in Society or religion, however diversified in Situation or colour, we are all of the Same Family, and Stand in the Same relation to him.

Sir, if these are Sentiments of which you are fully persuaded, I hope you cannot but acknowledge, that it is the indispensible duty of those who maintain for themselves the rights of human nature, and who profess the obligations of Christianity, to extend their power and influence to the relief of every part of the human race, from whatever burthen or oppression they may unjustly labour under; and this I apprehend a full conviction of the truth and obligation of these principles should lead all to.

Opposite and overleaf:
First and second pages of Banneker's letter to Thomas Jefferson dated August 19, 1791. *Library of Congress, Manuscripts Division.*

Maryland. Baltimore County. Near Ellicotts Lower Mills August 19th 1791

Thomas Jefferson Secretary of State.

Sir

I am fully sensible of the greatness of that freedom which I take with you on the present occasion; a liberty which seemed to me scarcely allowable, when I reflected on that distinguished, and dignifyed station in which you stand; and the almost general prejudice and prepossession which is so prevalent in the world against those of my complexion.

I suppose it is a truth too well attested to you, to need a proof here, that we are a race of Beings who have long laboured under the abuse and censure of the world; that we have long been looked upon with an eye of contempt; and that we have long been considered rather as brutish than human, and scarcely capable of mental endowments.

Sir I hope I may safely admit, in consequence of that report which hath reached me, that you are a man far less inflexible in Sentiments of this nature, than many others, that you are measurably friendly, and well disposed toward us; and that you are willing and ready to lend your aid and assistance to our relief from those many distresses and numerous calamities to which we are reduced.

Now Sir if this is founded in truth, I apprehend you will readily embrace every opportunity to eradicate that train of absurd and false ideas and oppinions which so generally prevails with respect to us; and that your Sentiments are concurrent with mine, which are that one universal Father hath given being to us all, and that he hath not only made us all of one flesh, but that he hath also without partiality afforded us all the same Sensations, and endued us all with the same faculties, and that however variable we may be in Society or religion, however diversifyed in Situation or colour, we are all of the Same Family, and Stand in the Same relation to him.

Sir, if these are Sentiments of which you are fully persuaded, I hope you cannot but acknowledge, that it is the indispensible duty of those who maintain for themselves the rights of human nature, and who possess the obligations of Christianity, to extend their power and influence to the relief of every part of the human race, from whatever burthen or oppression they may unjustly labour under, and this I apprehend a full conviction of the truth and obligation of these principles should lead all to.

Sir, I have long been convinced, that if your love for your Selves and for those inestimable laws which preserve to you the rights of human nature, was founded in Sincerity, you could not but be Solicitous, that every Individual of whatsoever rank or distinction, might with you equally enjoy the blessings thereof, neither could you rest Satisfyed, short of the most active diffusion of your exertions, in order to their promotion from any State of degradation, to which the unjustifyable cruelty and barbarism of men may have reduced them.

Sir I freely and Chearfully acknowledge, that I am of the African race, and in that colour which is natural to them of the deepest dye; and it is under a Sense of the most profound gratitude to the Supreme Ruler of the universe, that I now confess to you, that I am not under that State of tyrannical thraldom, and inhuman captivity, to which too many of my brethren are doomed; but that I have abundantly tasted of the fruition of those blessings which proceed from that free and unequalled liberty with which you are favoured and which I hope you will willingly allow you have received from the immediate Hand of that Being from whom proceedeth every good and perfect gift.

Sir, Suffer me to recall to your mind that time in which the Arms and tyranny of the British Crown were exerted with every powerful effort in order to reduce you to a State of Servitude; look back I intreat you on the variety of dangers to which you were exposed, reflect on that time in which every human aid appeared unavailable; and in which even hope and fortitude wore the aspect of inability to the Conflict, and you cannot but be led to a Serious and grateful Sense of your miraculous and providential preservation; you cannot but acknowledge, that the present freedom and tranquility which you enjoy you have mercifully received, and that it is the peculiar blessing of Heaven.

This Sir, was a time in which you clearly saw into the injustice of a State of Slavery, and in which you had just apprehensions of the horrors of its condition, it was now Sir, that your abhorrence thereof was so excited, that you publickly held forth this true and invaluable doctrine, which is worthy to be recorded and remembered in all Succeeding ages. "We hold these truths to be Self evident, that all men are created equal, and that they are endowed by their creator with certain unalienable rights, that among these are life, liberty, and the persuit of happyness".

Here Sir, was a time in which your tender feelings for your Selves had engaged you thus to declare

✗ my Father was brought here a Slave from Africa

declare, you were then impressed with proper ideas of the great valuation of liberty, and the free possession of those blessings to which you were entitled by nature; but Sir how pitiable is it to reflect, that altho' you were so fully convinced of the benevolence of the Father of mankind, and of his equal and impartial distribution of those rights and privileges which he had conferred upon them, that you should at the same time counteract his mercies, in detaining by fraud and violence so numerous a part of my brethren under groaning captivity and cruel oppression; that you should at the same time be found guilty of that most criminal act, which you ~~~~~~~~~ professedly detested in others, with respect to yourselves.

Sir, I suppose that your knowledge of the situation of my brethren is too extensive to need a recital here; neither shall I presume to prescribe methods by which they may be relieved; otherwise than by recommending to you and all others, to wean yourselves from those narrow prejudices which you have imbibed with respect to them, and as Job proposed to his friends " Put your Souls in their Souls Stead," thus shall your hearts be enlarged with kindness ~~~~~~~~~~~~~~~~~~ towards them, and thus shall you need neither the direction of myself or others in what manner to proceed herein.

And now, Sir, altho' my sympathy and affection for my brethren hath caused my enlargement thus far, I ardently hope that your candour and generosity will plead with you in my behalf, when I make known to you, that it was not originally my design; but that having taken up my pen in order to direct to you as a present, a copy of an Almanack which I have calculated for the succeeding year, I was unexpectedly and unavoidably ~~ led thereto.

This calculation, Sir, is the production of my arduous study in this my advanced stage of life; for having long had unbounded desires to become acquainted with the secrets of nature, I have had to gratify my curiosity herein thro' my own assiduous application to Astronomical Study, in which I need not to recount to you the many difficulties and disadvantages which I have had to encounter.

And altho' I had almost declined to make my calculation for the ensuing year, in consequence of that time which I had allotted therefor being taking up at the Federal Territory by the request of Mr. Andrew Ellicott, yet finding myself under several engagements to printers of this state to whom I had communicated my design, on my return to my place of residence, I industriously applyd myself thereto, which I hope I have accomplished with correctness and accuracy, a copy of which I have taken the liberty to direct to you, and which I humbly request you will favourably receive, and altho' you may have the opportunity of perusing it after its publication, yet I chose to send it to you in manuscript previous thereto, that thereby you might not only have an earlier inspection, but that you might also view it in my own hand writing.

And now Sir, I shall conclude
and Subscribe my Self with the most profound respect
your most Obedient humble Servant

Benjamin Banneker

NB. any communication to me
may be had by a direction to
Mr. Elias Ellicott, merchant
in Baltimore Town
BB

As an Essay of my calculation is put into the hand of
Mr. Cruckshank of Philadelphia, for publication I
would wish that you might neither have this ~~~~~~~~~
Almanack copy published nor give any printer an opportunity
thereof, as it might tend to disappoint Mr. Joseph Cruckshank
in his sale
BB

Sir, I have long been convinced, that if your love for your Selves and for those inesteemable laws which preserve to you the rights of human nature, was founded on Sincerity, you could not but be Solicitous, that every Individual of whatsoever rank or distinction, might with you equally enjoy the blessings thereof, neither could you rest Satisfyed, short of the most active diffusion of your exertions, in order to their promotion from any State of degradation, to which the unjustifyable cruelty and barbarism of men may have reduced them.

Sir, I freely and Chearfully acknowledge, that I am of the African race, and, in that colour which is natural to them of the deepest dye*; and it is under a Sense of the most profound gratitude to the Supreme Ruler of the universe, that I now confess to you, that I am not under that State of tyrannical thraldom, and inhuman captivity, to which too many of my brethren are doomed; but that I have abundantly tasted of the fruition of those blessings which proceed from that free and unequalled liberty with which you are favoured and which I hope you will willingly allow you have received from the immediate Hand of that Being from whom proceedeth every good and perfect gift.

Sir, Suffer me to recall to your mind that time in which the Arms and tyranny of the British Crown were exerted with every powerful effort, in order to reduce you to a State of Servitude; look back I intreat you on the variety of dangers to which you were exposed, reflect on that time in which every human aid appeared unavailable, and in which even hope and fortitude wore the aspect of inability to the Conflict, and you cannot but be led to a Serious and grateful Sense of your miraculous and providential preservation; You cannot but acknowledge, that the present freedom and tranquillity which you enjoy you have mercifully received, and that it is the peculiar blessing of Heaven.

This, Sir, was a time in which you clearly saw into the injustice of a State of Slavery, and in which you had Just apprehensions of the horrors of its condition, it was now Sir, that your abhorrence thereof was so excited, that you publickly held forth this true and invaluable doctrine, which is worthy to be recorded and remembered in all Succeeding ages. "We hold these truths to be Self evident, that all men are created equal, and that they are endowed by their creator with certain inalienable rights, that amongst these are life, liberty, and the persuit of happiness."

Here, Sir, was a time in which your tender feelings for your selves engaged you thus to declare, you were then impressed with proper ideas of the great valuation of liberty, and the free possession of those blessings to

---

*My Father was brought here a Slave from Africa.

which you were entitled by nature; but Sir how pitiable is it to reflect, that altho you were so fully convinced of the benevolence of the Father of mankind, and of his equal and impartial distribution of those rights and privileges which he had conferred upon them, that you should at the Same time counteract his mercies, in detaining by fraud and violence so numerous a part of my brethren under groaning captivity and cruel oppression, that you should at the Same time be found guilty of that most criminal act, which you professedly detested in others, with respect to yourselves.

Sir, I suppose that your knowledge of the situation of my brethren is too extensive to need a recital here; neither shall I presume to prescribe methods by which they may be relieved, otherwise than by recommending to you, and all others, to wean yourselves from those narrow prejudices which you have imbibed with respect to them, and as Job proposed to his friends "Put your Souls in their Souls' stead," thus shall your hearts be enlarged with kindness and benevolence towards them, and thus shall you need neither the direction of myself or others in what manner to proceed herein.

And now, Sir, altho my Sympathy and affection for my brethren hath caused my enlargement thus far, I ardently hope that your candour and generosity will plead with you in my behalf, when I make known to you, that it was not originally my design; but that having taken up my pen in order to direct to you as a present, a copy of an Almanack which I have calculated for the Succeeding year, I was unexpectedly and unavoidably led thereto.

This calculation, Sir, is the production of my arduous study, in this my advanced Stage of life; for having long had unbounded desires to become Acquainted with the Secrets of nature, I have had to gratify my curiosity herein thro my own assiduous application to Astronomical Study, in which I need not to recount to you the many difficulties and disadvantages which I have had to encounter.

And altho I had almost declined to make my calculation for the ensuing year, in consequence of that time which I had allotted therefor being taking up at the Federal Territory by the request of Mr. Andrew Ellicott, yet finding myself under Several engagements to printers of this state to whom I had communicated my design, on my return to my place of residence, I industriously apply'd myself thereto, which I hope I have accomplished with correctness and accuracy, a copy of which I have taken the liberty to direct to you, and which I humbly request you will favourably receive, and altho you may have the opportunity of perusing it after its publication, yet

I chose to send it to you in manuscript previous thereto, that thereby you might not only have an earlier inspection, but that you might also view it in my own hand writing.

And now Sir, I Shall conclude and Subscribe my Self with the most profound respect,

Your most Obedient humble Servant
Benjamin Banneker.

N.B. any communication to me may be had by a direction to M[R]. Elias Ellicott merchant in Baltimore Town.

B.B.

Hopeful of some reply, Banneker then added a second postscript. It provides some insight into his concern relating to publication of his calculations, a concern that he found himself forced to express without wishing to offend his correspondent:

As an Essay of my calculation is put into the hand of M[R]. Cruckshank of Philadelphia, for publication I would wish that you might neither have this Almanack copy published nor give any printer an opportunity thereof, as it might tend to disappoint M[R]. Joseph Cruckshank in his sale.

B.B.[17]

Banneker thus confirmed in his postcript that the almanac already had been given to Crukshank for publication, and that he was the Philadelphia printer with whom Pemberton had made arrangements.

The letter and manuscript copy of the almanac was forwarded to Philadelphia, still the seat of government. Jefferson received it exactly a week later, on August 26, and within four days' time the statesman replied. He acknowledged Banneker's plea for the improvement of the state of the Negro and expressed his own hope that a system would be initiated which would make that improvement possible as soon as circumstances would permit. Jefferson then added that he had forwarded the manuscript copy of the ephemeris to his friend, the Marquis de Condorcet, who was Secretary of the Royal Academy of Sciences at Paris, as evidence of the equal talents of the Negro race. Jefferson's letter was relatively short but nonetheless provided Banneker with immense satisfaction:

Philadelphia, Aug. 30. 1791.

Sir,

I Thank you sincerely for your letter of the 19th instant and for the Almanac it contained. No body wishes more than I do to see such proofs as you exhibit, that nature has given to our black brethren, talents equal to those of the other colors of men, and that the appearance of a want of them is owing merely to the degraded condition of their existence, both in Africa & America. I can add with truth, that no body wishes more ardently to see a good system commenced for raising the condition both of their body & mind to what it ought to be, as fast as the imbecility of their present existence, and other circumstances which cannot be neglected, will admit.

I have taken the liberty of sending your Almanac to Monsieur de Condorcet, Secretary of the Academy of Sciences at Paris, and member of the Philanthropic society, because I considered it as a document to which your whole colour had a right for their justification against the doubts which have been entertained of them.

I am with great esteem, Sir your most obedt humble servt.

Thomas Jefferson.

Mr. Benjamin Banneker,
Near Ellicott's Lower Mills, Baltimore Co.[18]

That Banneker had written with deliberate intent after all became clear shortly after he received Jefferson's reply. The Ellicott brothers and other abolitionists were involved, too, for the two letters were published as a pamphlet by a Philadelphia printer, Daniel Lawrence, and widely distributed shortly after the appearance of the almanac for 1792.[19] The letters were also published the following year in at least one popular periodical, the *Universal Asylum and Columbian Magazine.*[20]

Jefferson forwarded the manuscript ephemeris with a covering letter to Condorcet as he had promised. After acknowledging receipt of materials relating to the adoption of a unit of measure by France, of which Jefferson admitted he did not approve because of its liability to error, Jefferson went on to mention his enclosure and the circumstances that had brought it to his attention:

Sir   Philadelphia Aug. 30. 1791.

I thank you sincerely for your letter of the 19th. instant and for the Almanac it contained. no body wishes more than I do. to see such proofs as you exhibit, that nature has given to our black brethren, talents equal to those of the other colours of men, & that the appearance of a want of them is owing merely to the degraded condition of their existence both in Africa & America. I can add with truth that no body wishes more ardently, to see a good system commenced for raising the condition both of their body & mind to what it ought to be, as fast as the imbecillity of their present existence, and other circumstances which cannot be neglected, will admit. I have taken the liberty of sending your almanac to Monsieur de Condorcet, Secretary of the Academy of sciences at Paris, and member of the Philanthropic society, because I considered it as a document to which your whole colour had a right for their justification against the doubts which have been entertained of them. I am with great esteem, Sir

Your most obed:t humble serv:t

Th: Jefferson

M:r Benjamin Banneker
near Elliot's, lower mills. Baltimore coun:t

File copy of Thomas Jefferson's response of August 30, 1791, to the letter written by Banneker, August 19, 1791. *Library of Congress, Manuscripts Division.*

I am happy to be able to inform you that we have now in the United States a negro, the son of a black man born in Africa, and a black woman born in the United States, who is a very respectable mathematician. I procured him to be employed under one of our chief directors in laying out the new federal city on the Potowmac, & in the intervals of his leisure, while on that work, he made an Almanac for the next year, which he sent me in his own hand writing, & which I inclose to you. I have seen very elegant solutions of Geometrical problems by him. Add to this that he is a very worthy & respectable member of society. He is a free man. I shall be delighted to see these instances of moral eminence so multiplied as to prove that the want of talents observed in them is merely the effect of their degraded condition, and not proceeding from any difference in the structure of the parts on which intellect depends.[21]

Jefferson's letter to Condorcet reflected a marked mellowing of attitude toward the Negro from that written some years earlier in his *Notes on the State of Virginia*. In that work he had expressed his hatred of the system of slavery in America despite the fact that his own livelihood as a planter depended upon the system. He noted that he hoped to change the status of his slaves to that of tenants, but his financial status never enabled him to do so except in token instances. Although most of his writings on slavery had been more academic than practical, he admitted the system to be an evil as well as an injustice, but he believed that slavery was evil primarily because of how it affected the masters by appealing to their baser instincts, rather than because of its effect on the slaves themselves.

Much of Jefferson's feeling about slavery derived from his fear of a slave rebellion. It was only with the greatest reluctance that he had permitted his *Notes on the State of Virginia* to be published, and then only several years after he had written it. During his years as Minister to France he had refused to become a part of the antislavery movement in the United States or in France because of his honest concern that as a public figure his involvement might be detrimental to the movement. When invited to become a member of the French Société des Amis des Noirs, Jefferson replied to Jean Pierre Brissot de Warville:

. . . You know that nobody wishes more ardently to see an abolition not only of the trade but of the condition of slavery: and certainly nobody will be more willing to encounter every sacrifice for that object. But the influence & information of the friends to this proposition will be far above the need for my association. I am here as a public servant; and those whom I serve having never yet been able to give their voice against this practice, it is decent for me to avoid too public a demonstration of my wishes to see it abolished. Without serving the cause here, it might render me less able to serve it beyond the water.[22]

The letter to Condorcet is of particular interest for another reason. Obviously Jefferson had received information about Banneker other than those facts derived from the latter's letter. The reference to the secretary's involvement in Banneker's employment confirms the previously unsupported supposition that Major Ellicott had consulted with the statesman before he had accepted Banneker as his assistant. Undoubtedly Ellicott mentioned Banneker's fondness for mathematical puzzles, of which his cousins had told him. Furthermore, during the previous year, in the spring of 1790, Ellicott already knew about Banneker, having been asked by the Baltimore printer John Hayes to review Banneker's calculations for an almanac for 1791 and concerning which Banneker later had written to him.[23]

Jefferson's decision to send Banneker's manuscript ephemeris to Condorcet demonstrated his intention to provide Banneker with the best possible exposure if his work deserved it. In writing to Condorcet about him he was paying Banneker great honor. Not only was the Académie the foremost body of scientific learning in France, but Marie Jean Antoine Nicholas Caritat, Marquis de Condorcet (1743–94), was one of that country's foremost scholars.

A noted mathematician, philosopher, statesman, and more recently a revolutionary, Condorcet was a descendant of an ancient aristocratic family. In 1777 he became perpetual secretary of the Académie Royal des Sciences, in 1782 he was elected a member of the French Academy, and in the same year he published an important work on the doctrine of probability. During this period he served as inspector-general of the mint. He subsequently opposed the arrest of the Girondists, which led to his own condemnation.

In September 1791 Condorcet became secretary of the Legislative Assembly, and during the political ferment that followed, he was among the first to support the proposal for a republic. It was he who drew up the memorandum that led to the suspension of the king and summoned the national convention. Just at the time he would have received the letter from Jefferson with its enclosure, Condorcet went into hiding, during which time he produced some of his most important philosophical works. Believing that he was being watched, he tried to escape from his refuge but was captured and imprisoned. On the following morning, March 28, 1794, he was found dead, whether from exhaustion or poison was never determined.

It had been Jefferson's intention to have Banneker's work reviewed by one of the Académie's committees, probably with the thought that if the report was favorable it would shed honor not only on Banneker but upon the scientific work of the New World, which was one of Jefferson's ongoing concerns. Although Jefferson mailed his letter with the enclosed manuscript at the end of August 1791, it is fairly certain that either Condorcet never received it, or that if it did reach the marquis, he did not present it to the Académie. There are several reasons for this conclusion.

First of all, a letter from Jefferson, as a prominent American figure in science and as secretary of state, would not have gone unanswered. No reply from Condorcet or from the Académie has been found among the Jefferson papers, nor does a draft of such a reply survive among Condorcet's voluminous papers which are preserved in the Bibliothèque de l'Institut de France in Paris.[24] Furthermore, a careful search of the manuscript proceedings of the Académie for the period revealed that Banneker's ephemeris had not been presented to that body nor, as revealed by a search of the surviving records, was it presented to the sister body, the Académie des Inscriptions et Belles-Lettres.[25]

The fact that Banneker's work was not presented to the Académie by Condorcet is not surprising in view of the events already described. Since the French statesman was also greatly concerned with the French antislavery movement and, together with Jean Pierre Brissot de Warville and the Marquis de Lafayette, was among the founders of the Société des Amis des Noirs, the possibility that the Banneker ephemeris might have been submitted to that society was also explored, with negative results.[26]

Had Banneker's achievement been presented to the Académie it would have created a sensation in France at that time, and particularly in pro-Negro circles. The Société des Amis des Noirs would have welcomed this fresh and impressive example of Negro accomplishment, and it would have been widely publicized. That no mention is to be found in any of the

French literature of the period confirms the conclusion that while Condorcet may have received it, he probably did not have the opportunity to present it himself or to have someone else do so.

Banneker was nonetheless greatly pleased with Jefferson's reply and with the latter's decision to forward the manuscript to the great French body of learning. A few problems were developing in the plans for publishing the almanac, however. Pemberton and his friends were seeking a leading popular figure to write an introduction to the new almanac, someone publicly recognized whose name would help to promote it. They finally selected Senator James McHenry (1753–1816) from Maryland, who agreed to write a preface or introduction. There were several advantages in having McHenry's name associated with the publication. He was popularly recognized as a southerner, and he was well known throughout the country for having served prominently in the American Revolution and for his standing as a statesman of importance. (Document 20)

Having emigrated from his native Ireland in 1771, McHenry studied medicine under Dr. Benjamin Rush in Philadelphia and later served on the medical staff of the Continental Army. He worked as General Washington's private secretary for more than two years and subsequently filled the same position with the Marquis de Lafayette. McHenry was a member of the Continental Congress for three years from 1783, after which he was elected delegate from Maryland to the Constitutional Convention in 1787. At the time in question he was a senator from Maryland in the U.S. Congress. From 1796 until 1800 he was to serve as secretary of war in the cabinet of President John Adams.

Despite McHenry's promise, his introduction was not forthcoming, and there was some question whether it would be made available in time for a printer to include it. George Ellicott expressed this concern to Pemberton late in August, when Elias's prolonged absence from Baltimore forced him to take action. "I am fearfull there will be a disapointment in respect the preface for Banakers Allmanacke," he wrote the publisher. "Inclosed is a Coppy of a Letter which Benjamin Banaker wrote to Thos. Jefferson Secretary of State which he . . . desired Me to send to thee . . . to have it put into the Allmanacke if its thought proper or in to the publick papers. . . . Their is a small piece of poetry inclosed of Banaker's composing which he desires may be put under the Letter if its published."[27]

Banneker's suggestion that his letter to Jefferson be published as part of the almanac "or in to the publick papers" confirms the supposition expressed earlier that the letter was a deliberate attempt to use the almanac as propaganda for the abolitionist movement, and to involve Jefferson because his published opinions on slavery made him a natural target for any timely expression on the subject. The "small piece of poetry . . . of Banaker's composing" did not survive in the same repository, but it probably can be identified as the poem which formed one of the exhibits at the anniversary meeting of the Banneker Institute held in 1860, and which a newspaper account of the event described as a "curiosity." A copy made at that time bears the date "October 19, 1791" and the following verses:

Behold ye Christians! and in pity see
Those Afric sons which Nature formed free;
Behold them in a fruitful country blest,
Of Nature's bounties see them rich possest,
Behold them herefrom torn by cruel force,
And doomed to slavery without remorse,
This act, America, thy sons have known;
This cruel act, relentless they have done.

B. Banneker[28]

While arrangements were being made with haste and concern in Baltimore and Philadelphia for the almanac's publication, a new obstacle suddenly presented itself. When Banneker had given a copy of his calculations to William Goddard, it was with the expressed intent that in order to ensure its widest possible distribution, the almanac could be published by several printers simultaneously in Baltimore and Philadelphia without conflict of interest. Goddard did not agree with such an arrangement, and chose to understand that in submitting the manuscript to him, Banneker had given him exclusive rights. He had meanwhile managed to obtain the manuscript of Senator McHenry's introduction, and he planned to proceed with an exclusive publication.

Goddard, who was then one of the most prominent printers in the country, had distinguished himself by the high quality of his work and because he was always in conflict with almost everyone he dealt with. "William Goddard it seems is really printing Bannakers Allmanack. . . . he Nevertheless thinks or affects to think himself intitled to an exclusive right in it and Refuses to give a Coppy of the introduction Written by Dr.

McHenry," Elias Ellicott reported to Pemberton. He suggested that Crukshank could compensate for the loss of the McHenry introduction by including a copy of Banaker's letter to Jefferson or any other introduction that explained Banaker's situation and achievements. "This disappointment, I am Sorry for and doe not think Godard hath Acted a Generous part."[29]

Goddard's behavior in this situation did not surprise those who knew him, although it proved to be a disappointment to the Ellicott brothers, and Goddard's response to McHenry himself showed that he would not retreat from his position. However, the inclusion of McHenry's introduction was not critical to a publication of the almanac if other suitable material—particularly Banneker's letter to Jefferson—could be found to replace it.

Elias Ellicott wrote to Banneker and suggested that it might be useful if he would prepare a statement describing the details of his negotiations with Goddard, which could be used to inform Pemberton and the others involved. Banneker was appalled by the situation he had unwittingly created, and he was concerned that his friends the Ellicotts should not be embarrassed by any of his actions. He was perturbed by the impression his mishandling may have given to the members of the Abolitionist Society, and he set about writing an account of the circumstances as he had understood them. He had just received Jefferson's reply to his letter, which had impressed him deeply, and it seemed feasible to consider publication of both letters together in the first issue of the almanac in lieu of the McHenry introduction. He copied Jefferson's reply and the letter he had sent and forwarded them to Elias with a covering letter from the mail room at the store of Ellicott & Company. He wrote:

> After an inspection of a Letter by you directed to Mr. Elias or George Ellicott, respecting the sale of my essay of an Almanack to Mr. William Goddard, I find myself desirous to reply thereto. It appears that you are apprehensive that Mr. Goddard has purchas'd the Copy Right to my Calculations, of which I can inform you, that he has purchased a Copy, which I have Sufficient reason to believe he will publish; but that I have not an Idea that he has purchased to himself the Sole and exclusive right to the publication, this would be unreasonable in him to expect, after reflecting on my indigence, as also my labour and loss of time in the Calculation, and his compensation to me therefor the Sum of £3, and which in case he is Successful in the sale he will increase to 3 Guineas, but he has lately in-

formed me that there is a probability of my Still being further rewarded
and I can Scarcely think that Mr. Goddard considers the Sole right to the
Copy to be in himself, for I have in my Conversation with him intimated,
that the publication of another Copy in Philadelphia would not be injuri-
ous to him with which he expressed neither unwillingness nor dissatisfaction, and as the disposing of the same Copy to different printers is not
unprecedented, I have thought it was allowable in me when I had not
bound myself by any contract to the contrary, and it was under this Idea
that I not only Sold a Copy to Mr. Goddard, But also previous thereto disposed of one to a printer in George Town on Patowmac, and interceded
with my friends Messrs. Ellicotts to assist me in endeavoring to have one
published in Philadelphia, which anxiety proceeded not so much from a
lucrative view as a certainty of its publication, which in the preceding year
my utmost exertions were ineffectual to obtain, for having prepared a
Copy, I offered it to three printers of this State two of which refused its
acceptance, and the third after detaining it in his possession under a
promise to publish it until a period to far advanced therefor, when he
informed me that he could not. And now Sir, I hope that these
Circumstances are Sufficient to Justify my conduct, under which I shall
conclude with assuring you, no person can wish more sincerely to regard
truth and adhere to reputation than Sir,

Your most obedient humble Serv^T
Benjamin Banneker
Sept. 3d, 1791

N. B. I send inclosed the Copy of a Letter which I received from the
Secretary of State, in answer to one I sent him, the Copy of which Mr.
George Ellicott sent you Some time Since, both of which, if you See proper
I have no objection to have published.

N. B. The introduction that Dr. M'Henry wrote, was intended for the
Almanac that was to be published in Philadelphia, as also the one that Mr.
Goddard was to publish, Mr. Elias Ellicott informs me that Mr. Goddard
hath it in his possession and will not give a copy of it, now I have a great
desire to have an Allmanack published in Philadelphia as I think it would
tend greatly to increase the circulation as I do no expect that Mr. Goddard
will circulate his into Pennsylvania. I think that the certificate which Mr.

Elias Ellicott will forward, and my letter to Mr. Jefferson and his answer to me, will answer in place of a preface.[30]

Banneker's letter was revealing and informative; it described a financial arrangement with Goddard that is of particular interest. The payment of three pounds for the ephemeris was modest, and the printer's promise of an increase to three guineas if it proved to be successful was hardly a substantial bonus. Banneker's letter indicated that there had been further communication with Goddard on the subject by personal contact; this probably required a second visit to Baltimore prior to this date.

The letter clarifies yet another point. Banneker's decision to have his ephemeris published in an almanac had not developed as much from the urgings of George Ellicott as has popularly been supposed, but as an independent idea of his own. He had offered his work to several printers before informing George of his desire for assistance in finding a printer in Philadelphia for the purpose of obtaining wider distribution. George was willing to assist, and in doing so, brought the elderly philomath to the attention of his brother Elias and his friends, who recognized in this request an unforeseen opportunity to also serve the antislavery movement.

When Banneker's report reached him, Elias Ellicott read it with considerable annoyance. Exasperated by Goddard's action, and determined that the best solution would be to publish an affidavit of Banneker's authorship, he drafted an appropriate statement and circulated it with the request for signatures to interested members of his family and to prominent citizens of Ellicott's Lower Mills and Baltimore. The "Certificate" was an unusual and impressive document, addressed simply, "To the Public . . . to clear up any doubt that may Arise as to Benjamin Banneker (a Black man whose Father came from Africa) being the Author of the Prefixed Almanac" and to "Certify that we for several Years have been Acquainted with him and that his knowledge in Astronomy and the Mathematicks was of his own Acquiring Assisted only by Astronomical Tables which he with much Difficulty procured." It was signed by a list of distinguished men, impressively headed by none other than the Geographer General of the United States, Major Andrew Ellicott. In addition to the Ellicott brothers, other signers included Joseph Evans, a millwright married to Joseph Ellicott's daughter Ann, and James Carey, a Baltimore merchant married to John Ellicott's daughter Martha. Gerard Hopkins was a minister of the Society of

Friends whose wife was a cousin of Elizabeth Brooke Ellicott. Daniel Carroll was a merchant in Baltimore; James Gillingham, later a respected elder in the Society of Friends, was a blacksmith who had lived for a time at the Lower Mills. Dr. Michael Pue was a physician in Baltimore, and William Dillworth was a long-time customer of Ellicott & Company who later served as a witness for the Ellicott brothers in a lawsuit.[31]

Elias assembled Banneker's report and and forwarded it with a certificate of authenticity to Pemberton. In a covering letter, Elias explained that he had asked Banneker to send Pemberton the details of his contract with Goddard and copies of his letter to Jefferson and Jefferson's reply, which Banneker had done. "I think You need not hesitate in Respect to the propriety of Publishing the Allmanack," he told Pemberton, "as it is clear that Goddard hath not the Least Shadow of right to the Exclusive privilege of printing his Allmanack — We Shold have discouraged Benjamin's having a copy Printed in Your City had we not good reason to believe that it wold not interfere with any Contracts which he had made." He added, "If You Shold think proper to form an introduction or preface Your Selves we can furnish You with Something of Baneker's Life & Situation in Life. We Shold be glad to hear your determination."[32]

Upon receipt of Banneker's letter and that of Elias Ellicott, Pemberton realized he had no more time to lose if the almanac was to be published in a Philadelphia edition. Since the major obstacle appeared to be William Goddard, the matter had to be settled with him as soon as possible— whether Goddard planned to publish it and what he would do if others issued the almanac. Pemberton then wrote tactfully to Goddard:

> Towards the close of last year, I first Recd. information of the Astronomical Genius of Benj. Banniker a Black man in the neighbourhood of Baltimore and that he had made calculations for an Almanac for the pres.ᵗ year but he was disappointed in the publication of it which induced me to make enquiry concerning him, and receiving satisfactory information on the Subject from some of his friends one of them Sent me a few weeks past a Copy of his Calculations for the ensuing Year, which I communicated to David Rittenhouse, who after inspection as fully as his leisure would permit Returned the copy with a letter expressing his approbation of the Calculations. I then laid them before another Astronomer who also after an examination Certified in writing to the same effect; I then engaged a printer to publish 4000 Copies on terms very advantageous to Banniker & had

To the Public

In Order to clear up any doubt that may Arise as to Benjamin Banneker (a Black man whose Father came from Africa) being the author of the Prefixed Alma=nac We whose Names are hereunto annexed do Certify that we for Several Years have been Acquainted with him and that his knowledge in Astronomy and the Mathematicks was of his own Acquiring Afsisted only by Astronomical Tables which he with much Difficulty procured

~ Andrew Ellicott

James Gillingham

Daniel Carroll

Elias Ellicott

Wm. Dillworth

Joseph Evans

Michael Pue M.D.

George Ellicott

Jesse Hopkins

Jonathan Ellicott

James Carey

Statement "To the Public" signed by responsible citizens attesting that Banneker personally calculated ephemerides for his almanacs without assistance. *Historical Society of Pennsylvania.*

made a Collection of some instructive essays to be published as usual in an
Almanac expecting it to be prefaced by some account of the Author, which
was to be sent up in time, and understanding Dr. McHenry had made such
an Essay, I applied to him just before his leaving the city last week when he
informed me that he had left the Essay in thy hands, and that thou had
undertaken to publish the Almanac, upon which I conjectured Banneker
had sold thee the Copy Right, & therefore thought it improper to proceed
in the Publication here, and altho' I do not find that is altogether the case, I
have judged it best to decline any further progress in the business, and to
inform thee of it, that thou may publish a larger number of Copies than
thou might otherwise conclude to be necessary, and being informed of thy
attachment to the Cause of humanity, and kindly disposition towards the
poor degraded Blacks, whom the prejudices of some men & the Avarice of
others have held in estimation equal or inferior to the Brute Creation,
while the most extensive Proclamation is made of the uninterrupted enjoyment of Liberty & the Rights of Man under the Constitution of in the
United States of America.

Having no interest of my own in this, I now only Sollicit thy attentive
benevolence to poor Banniker to make further Compensation as thou may
Judge to make up in some measure for the disappointment he will be sub-
jected by the publication of his performance being laid aside here — And I
further request thee to send me up a dozen Copies of the Almanac as soon
as it is published, the members of our Abolition Society intended to have
interested themselves in the sale of the Almanac had it been published, & I
have reason to believe a considerable number of Copies will still be taken of
by them.[33]

Goddard lost no time in responding to Pemberton, assuring his full
cooperation in the project:

Your highly acceptable Letter, rec.[D] this Day, merits greater Attention and a
more explicit Answer than I am, at present, able to give it, being suddenly
called from Home to visit a dear Friend in a House of Mourning. I cannot,
however, delay informing you that B. Banniker's Almanack will be
published in a few Days, and that I Shall not only send the Copies you
desire, but will, most cheerfully, cooperate with you in giving Success to
your benevolent wishes & endeavours — Tho' I had engaged to send a
Number to W. D. Humphreys, yet as M[R]. Crukshank hath been at some
Trouble and Expense, I shall consider it an Act of Justice & Civility to give
him the Advantage of selling the Work, & will, therefore, send him a

Number of the first Impression. I am heartily disposed not only to be just, but generous to poor Benjamin, and as I Sincerely respect your Character, your Principles & Profession, I shall be governed by your Advice and Opinion as to what would be a liberal ample Compensation to the Sable Astronomer, — I shall give you an honest Account of my Sales, in which I hope for the Assistance of the Benevolent, and flatter myself the Issue will prove advantageous to the ingenious Man you aim to patronize, and pleasing to yourself and Fellow Labourers in the same glorious Cause. In great Haste,[34]

Goddard's unexpected cooperation reflected Pemberton's importance as a leading figure of his time. The apparent conflict among several printers was resolved to the satisfaction of each, although Goddard profited most, and Banneker's almanac was assured a wide distribution. This was to be something of a new venture for Goddard for he had not recently produced any almanacs. In December 1790 he had acquired a stock of an almanac produced by another and made them available with a brief advertisement in his newspaper.[35] Now, although he had assured Pemberton that Banneker's almanac would be printed within a matter of days, it was late December before he first announced publication of "BENJAMIN BANNEKER'S highly approved ALMANACK, for 1792."[36]

Significantly, although the almanac featured Banneker's race, the advance announcement made no mention of it. Pemberton's note that he had selected "instructive essays" to include in the almanac is revealing. It confirms that, contrary to popular belief, the almanac maker who calculated the ephemeris generally was not responsible for the literary content of the publication. That portion of most eighteenth-century almanacs was in fact assembled by the printer, who gathered prose and poetry from available periodicals, chose appropriate allegories, proverbs, and recipes, and copied remedies from standard works. To these he added useful information such as would be desired by the reader: a listing of the more important positions in the federal government, including members of the cabinet, Senate, and federal courts; a calendar of the courts of law holding sessions in areas where the almanac would be distributed; a calendar of meetings of the Society of Friends; measurements of roads and distances of cities from the place of publication; and miscellaneous tables of general use, such as the weights and values of sundry coins, interest rates and a scale of depreciation.

In general the contents of Banneker's almanac resembled those of his contemporaries. His ephemeris was supplemented by such other of his own contributions as a list of movable feasts, followed by a calendar of the eclipses for the year, with a page devoted to the Anatomy, or "The Moon's Man." The ephemeris for each of the twelve months was complemented at the foot of each page with a single item of useful information. A short essay on "The Planetary and Terrestrial Worlds comparatively considered" may have been submitted by Banneker but could have been taken from another unidentified publication.

Goddard and Angell used quotation marks at the beginning and end of many of their essays and other literary contents to indicate that the material was not original and had been taken from a published source. "The Planetary and Terrestrial Worlds" was followed by a two-page essay of "Remarks on the Swiftness of Time," and then by a letter to the editor of *The London Magazine* on the "Origin of the Gray's Mare being the Better Horse." Miscellaneous short subjects included an allegory on "The Two Bees," an item "On Health," and another item purporting to be "Extracts from the Common-Place Book of the Kentucky Philosopher." Other brevities, designed to be amusing, instructive or elevating or both, included "Extracts from the Writings of the Ancients of distinguished fame," "The stings of Poverty, Disease and Violence . . . ," "The Balance of Happiness equal," and a treatise on curing the defects and diseases of trees presented in an address to the House of Commons by the well-known British botanist and gardener William Forsyth (1737–1804). Buried among the poems and remedies was a short excerpt from *The Columbian Magazine* entitled "On Negro Slavery, and the Slave Trade" which quoted a statement on skin pigmentation by none other than David Rittenhouse.

When the arrangements between the respective printers had at last been completed, the almanac finally went to press at Goddard and Angell's establishment on Market Street in Baltimore. As indicated in the notice of imprint, it was made available for distribution in Philadelphia separately by Joseph Crukshank and Daniel Humphreys, and in Alexandria at the shop of Hanson and Bond.

Humphreys was a prominent printer of the period. The son of Joshua Humphreys, he served an apprenticeship as a printer with William Bradford. In 1775 he opened a printing office in partnership with Enoch Story the elder in Norris Alley near Front Street. They undertook to produce a newspaper, but a few months later a fire destroyed their shop and its contents, and the partnership was dissolved. Humphreys opened another printing shop of his own, and from 1783 to 1784 was a partner with Ebenezer Oswald in the publication of the *Independent Gazetteer*. Later he established another newspaper of his own.

The first issue of Banneker's almanac bore an impressive title which promised a wide range of useful materials to the prospective purchaser:

BENJAMIN BANNEKER'S
PENNSYLVANIA, DELAWARE, MARYLAND, AND
VIRGINIA
ALMANAC
AND EPHEMERIS
FOR THE YEAR OF OUR LORD,
1792.

Being Bissextile or Leap Year, and the sixteenth year of American Independence, which commenced July 4th, 1776. Containing the Motions of the Sun and Moon, the true places and aspects of the Planets, the Rising and Setting of the Sun, and the Rising, Setting, and Southing Place and Age of the Moon, etc., the Lunations, Conjunctions, Eclipses, Judgments of the Weather, Festivals, and other remarkable days. Days for holding the Supreme and Circuit courts of the United States, as also the usual courts in Pennsylvania, Delaware, Maryland, and Virginia; also several useful Tables and valuable Recipes; various selections from the Commonplace Book of the Kentucky Philosopher, an American sage; with interesting and entertaining Essays in Prose and Verse, the whole comprising a greater, more pleasing and useful variety than any work of the kind and price in North America.

The introduction of a new almanac featuring the calculations made by an African American provided the distributors with an unusual opportunity for promotion, and they made every use of the materials available to them. Not only would the cooperation and promotion of the abolitionist societies assure the success of the project, but they had in hand the best evidence yet available that Negro capability was equal to that of other races. Goddard and Angell took every advantage of the opportunity, as evidenced in the introduction, which appeared on the reverse of the title page:

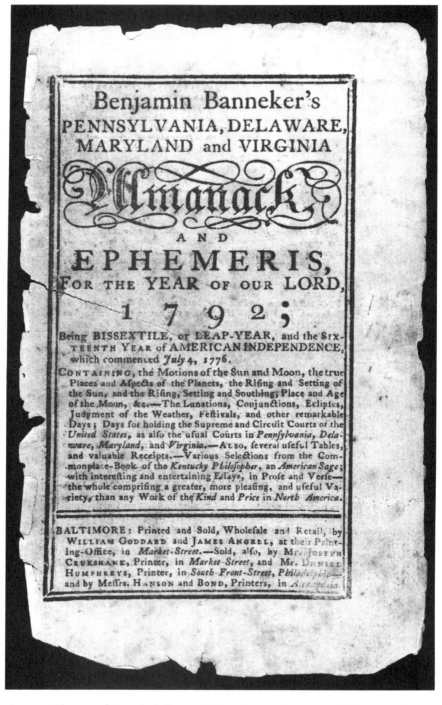

Benjamin Banneker's
PENNSYLVANIA, DELAWARE,
MARYLAND and VIRGINIA

Almanack

AND

EPHEMERIS,
FOR THE YEAR OF OUR LORD,

1792;

Being BISSEXTILE, or LEAP-YEAR, and the SIX-
TEENTH YEAR of AMERICAN INDEPENDENCE,
which commenced *July* 4, 1776.

CONTAINING, the Motions of the Sun and Moon, the true
Places and Aspects of the Planets, the Rising and Setting of
the Sun, and the Rising, Setting and Southing, Place and Age
of the Moon, &c.—The Lunations, Conjunctions, Eclipses,
Judgment of the Weather, Festivals, and other remarkable
Days; Days for holding the Supreme and Circuit Courts of the
United States, as also the usual Courts in *Pennsylvania, Delaware, Maryland*, and *Virginia*.—Also, several useful Tables,
and valuable Receipts.—Various Selections from the Commonplace-Book of the *Kentucky Philosopher*, an *American Sage*;
with interesting and entertaining Essays, in Prose and Verse—
the whole comprising a greater, more pleasing, and useful Variety, than any Work of the *Kind* and *Price* in *North America*.

BALTIMORE: Printed and Sold, Wholesale and Retail, by
WILLIAM GODDARD and JAMES ANGELL, at their Print-
ing-Office, in *Market-Street*.—Sold, also, by Mr. JOSEPH
CRUKSHANK, Printer, in *Market-Street*, and Mr. DANIEL
HUMPHREYS, Printer, in *South-Front-Street*, *Philadelphia—*
and by Messrs. HANSON and BOND, Printers, in *Alexandria*.

Cover or title page of Banneker's first published almanac, for the year 1792, printed in
Baltimore by Goddard & Angell. *Maryland Historical Society.*

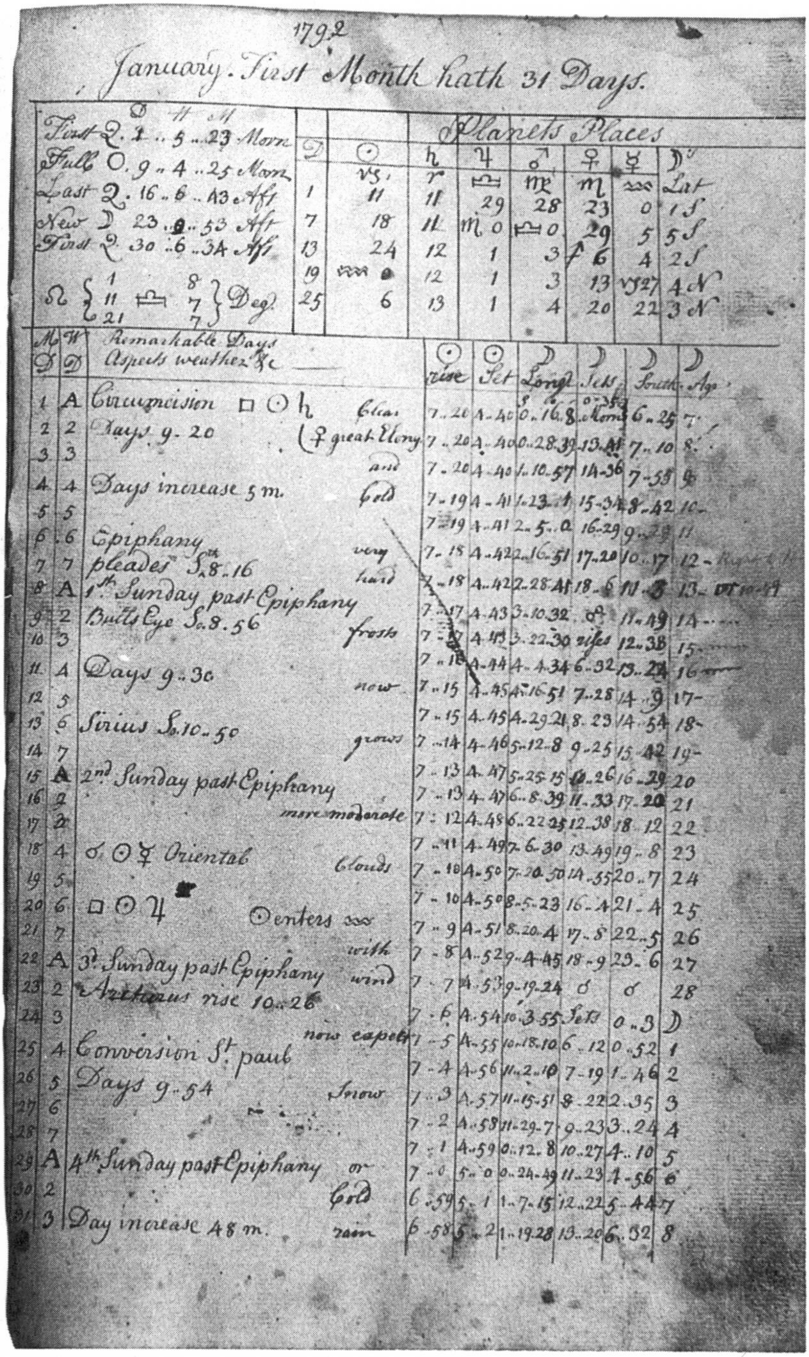

1792

January. First Month hath 31 Days.

	D	H	M	
First ☾.	1	5	23	Morn
Full ○.	9	4	25	Morn
Last ☾.	16	6	43	Aft
New ☽	23	[illegible]	53	Aft
First ☾.	30	6	34	Aft

☊ {1, 11, 21} ♎ {8, 7, 7} Deg.

Planets Places

D	☉	♄	♃	♂	♀	☿	☽
	♑	♈	♎	♍	♏	♒	Lat
1	11	11	29	28	23	0	1 S
7	18	11	♏ 0	♎ 0	29	5	5 S
13	24	12	1	3	♐ 6	4	2 S
19	♒ 0	12	1	3	13	♑ 27	4 N
25	6	13	1	4	20	22	3 N

M D	W D	Remarkable Days Aspects weather &c		☉ rise	☉ Set	☽ Long	☽ Sets	☽ South	☽ Age
1	A	Circumcision □ ☉ ♄	Clear	7..20	4..40	0..16..8	0..35 Morn	6..25	7
2	2	Days 9..20	(♀ great Elong	7..20	4..40	0..28..39	13..41	7..10	8
3	3		and	7..20	4..40	1..10..57	14..36	7..55	9
4	4	Days increase 5 m.	Cold	7..19	4..41	1..23..1	15..34	8..42	10
5	5			7..19	4..41	2..5..0	16..29	9..29	11
6	6	Epiphany		7..18	4..42	2..16..51	17..20	10..17	12
7	7	pleades S. 8..16	very	7..18	4..42	2..28..41	18..6	11..3	13
8	A	1st Sunday past Epiphany	hard	7..17	4..43	3..10..32	☌	11..49	14
9	2	Bulls Eye So. 8..56		7..17	4..43	3..22..30	rises	12..38	15
10	3		frosts	7..16	4..44	4..4..34	6..32	13..24	16
11	4	Days 9..30		7..15	4..45	4..16..51	7..28	14..9	17
12	5		now	7..15	4..45	4..29..21	8..23	14..54	18
13	6	Sirius So. 10..50		7..14	4..46	5..12..8	9..25	15..42	19
14	7		grows	7..13	4..47	5..25..15	10..26	16..29	20
15	A	2nd Sunday past Epiphany		7..13	4..47	6..8..39	11..33	17..20	21
16	2			7..12	4..48	6..22..25	12..38	18..12	22
17	3		more moderate	7..11	4..49	7..6..30	13..49	19..8	23
18	4	☌ ☉ ☿ Oriental		7..10	4..50	7..20..50	14..55	20..7	24
19	5		Clouds	7..10	4..50	8..5..23	16..4	21..4	25
20	6	□ ☉ ♃	☉ enters ♒	7..9	4..51	8..20..4	17..8	22..5	26
21	7		with	7..8	4..52	9..4..45	18..9	23..6	27
22	A	3d Sunday past Epiphany	wind	7..7	4..53	9..19..24	☌	☌	28
23	2	Arcturus rise 10..26		7..6	4..54	10..3..55	Sets	0..3	☽
24	3		now expect	7..5	4..55	10..18..10	6..12	0..52	1
25	4	Conversion St. paul		7..4	4..56	11..2..10	7..19	1..46	2
26	5	Days 9..54	Snow	7..3	4..57	11..15..51	8..22	2..35	3
27	6			7..2	4..58	11..29..7	9..23	3..24	4
28	7			7..1	4..59	0..12..8	10..27	4..10	5
29	A	4th Sunday past Epiphany	or	7..0	5..0	0..24..49	11..23	4..56	6
30	2		Cold	6..59	5..1	1..7..15	12..22	5..44	7
31	3	Day increase 48 m.	rain	6..58	5..2	1..19..28	13..20	6..32	8

First page of Banneker's manuscript original, with calculations for the month of January 1792 for his first almanac. From the manuscript of his ephemeris for 1792 that he had submitted to Goddard & Angell in 1791. Found among the papers of William Goddard. *American Antiquarian Society.*

The Editors of the PENNSYLVANIA, DELAWARE, MARYLAND, AND VIRGINIA ALMANACK, feel themselves gratified in the Opportunity of presenting to the Public, through the Medium of their Press, what must be considered an extraordinary Effort of Genius — a COMPLETE and ACCURATE EPHEMERIS for the Year 1792, calculated by a sable Descendant of Africa, who, by this Specimen of Ingenuity, evinces, to Demonstration, that mental Powers and Endowments are not the exclusive Excellence of white People, but that the Rays of Science may alike illumine the Minds of Men of every Clime, (however they may differ in the Colour of their Skin) particularly those whom Tyrant-Custom hath too long taught us to depreciate as a Race inferior in intellectual Capacity—They flatter themselves that a philanthropic Public, in this enlightened Era, will be induced to give their Patronage and Support to this Work, not only on Account of its intrinsic Merit, (it having met the Approbation of several of the most distinguished Astronomers in America, particularly the celebrated Mr. Rittenhouse) but from similar Motives to those which induced the Editors to give this Calculation the Preference, the ardent Desire of drawing modest Merit from Obscurity, and controverting the long-established illiberal Prejudice against the Blacks. Though it becomes the Editors to speak with less Confidence of the miscellaneous Part of this Work, they yet flatter themselves, from their Attention to the variegated Selections in Prose and Verse, that their Readers will find it both USEFUL and ENTERTAINING, and not undeserving of that Approbation which they have had the Happiness of experiencing for a Series of Years — an Approbation they are still ambitious of meriting, and which, they hope, will crown their present Wishes and Labours with Success.

The publishers included the letter from James McHenry, "containing Particulars respecting Benjamin," an important addition, supporting with its new evidence the arguments against slavery. It not only described Banneker and his career but left no doubt concerning the purpose of the publication:

BENJAMIN BANNEKER, a free Negro, has calculated an ALMANACK, for the ensuing year, 1792, which being desirous to dispose of, to the best advantage he has requested me to aid his application to you for that purpose. Having fully satisfied myself, with respect to his title to this kind of authorship, if you can agree with him for the price of his work, I may venture to assure you it will do you credit, as Editors, while it will afford you the opportunity to encourage talents that have thus far surmounted the most discouraging circumstances and prejudices.

This Man is about fifty-nine years of age; he was born in *Baltimore County;* his father was an *African,* and his mother the offspring of *African* parents — His father and mother having obtained their freedom, were enabled to send him to an obscure school, where he learned, when a boy, reading, writing, and arithmetic as far as double position; and to leave him, at their deaths, a few acres of land, upon which he has supported himself ever since by means of economy and constant labour, and preserved a fair reputation. To struggle incessantly against want is no ways favourable to improvement:

What he had learned, however, he did not forget; for as some hours of leisure will occur in the most toilsome life, he availed himself of these, not to read and acquire knowledge from writings of genius and discovery, for of such he had none, but to digest and apply, as occasions presented, the few principles of the few rules of arithmetic he had been taught at school. This kind of mental exercise formed his chief amusement, and soon gave him a facility in calculation that was often serviceable to his neighbours, and at length attracted the attention of the Messrs. Ellicotts, a family remarkable for their ingenuity and turn to the useful mechanics. It is about three years since Mr. George Ellicott lent him Mayer's Tables, Ferguson's Astronomy, Leadbeater's Lunar-Table, and some astronomic instruments, but without accompanying them with either hint or instruction, that might further his studies, or lead him to apply them to any useful result. These books and instruments, the first of the kind he had ever seen, opened a new world to Benjamin, and from thenceforward he employed his leisure in astronomical researches. He now took up the idea of the calculations for an ALMANACK, and actually completed an entire set for the last year, upon his original stock of arithmetic. Encouraged by this first attempt, he entered upon his calculation for 1792, which, as well as the former, he began and finished without the least information, or alliance, from any person, or other books than those I have mentioned; so that, whatever merit is attached to his present performance, is exclusively and peculiarly his own.

I have been the more careful to investigate these particulars, and to ascertain their reality, as they form an interesting fact in the History of Man; and as you may want them to gratify curiosity, I have no objection to your selecting them for your account of *Benjamin.*

I consider this Negro as a fresh proof that the powers of the mind are disconnected with the colour of the skin, or, in other words, a striking contradiction to Mr. *Hume's* doctrine, that "Negroes are naturally inferior to the whites and unsusceptible of attainments in arts and sciences." In every civilized country we shall find thousands of whites, liberally educated, and who have enjoyed greater opportunities of instruction than this Negro, his inferior in those intellectual acquirements and capacities that form the most characteristic feature in the human race. But the system that would assign to these degraded blacks an origin different from the whites, if it is not ready to be deserted by philosophers, must be relinquished as similar instances multiply; and that such must frequently happen cannot well be doubted, should no check impede the progress of humanity, which, meliorating the condition of slavery, necessarily leads to its final extinction.— Let, however, the issue be what it will, I cannot but wish, on this occasion, to see the Public patronage keep pace with my black friend's merit.

I am, Gentlemen, your most obedient servant,

JAMES McHENRY.

With the best intentions in the world, McHenry's account was not entirely accurate in all details relating to Banneker's life, but it was nonetheless an impressive statement. Inasmuch as Goddard utilized McHenry's introduction in this, his exclusive publication of Banneker's work, Pemberton and his associates reserved the exchange of letters with Jefferson for a later issue of the almanac. For some reason, Banneker's poem on slavery was not published in this or any other of the almanac issues which were to follow, nor was it deemed necessary after all to include the certification of Banneker's authorship which Elias Ellicott had so carefully prepared.

Banneker's almanac went on sale at the end of 1791 and immediately sold in great numbers. Large inventories were furnished by Goddard to the three other distributors, and it was not long before the first printing was exhausted, requiring Goddard and Angell to produce a second printing. One of these editions bore the title "Benjamin Banniker's Pennsylvania, Delaware, Maryland and Virginia Almanac and Ephemeris." That the author's name was misspelled was apparently no reason for recalling the issue, and there is no way of knowing whether this error was also in the first of Goddard & Angell's editions.

The unidentified printer in Georgetown whom Banneker had contacted did not publish the almanac after all. If the firm involved was Hancock and Day, it may have abandoned the project because they had decided to sell out their printing business during the following months.

A separate edition of Banneker's first almanac was issued by another of Philadelphia's prominent printers, William Young (1755–1829). His firm was one of the most important in Philadelphia during the late eighteenth and early nineteenth centuries. Young was born in Scotland and migrated with his family to the United States in 1784. He settled at Philadelphia and established a printing and stationery shop at the southwest corner of Chestnut and Second streets, where he printed and sold books. The business prospered and in 1793 he established a paper mill at Wilmington, Delaware, which he continued as a second business. Young's edition of Banneker's almanac was not a reprint of the Goddard & Angell edition but a distinctly separate issue. It was somewhat smaller in appearance and reduced in content from twenty-four to eighteen pages.

An impressive advertisement appeared in the *Maryland Journal* or *Baltimore Advertiser* on December 2, 1791, describing "A Complete and Accurate Ephemeris, calculated by the ingenious Mr. BENJAMIN BANNEKER, *a free black man*, (a Native of this County, born of *African Parents*), whose Calculations, now offered to the Public, have met the Approbation of several of the most distinguished Astronomers in America." After listing the contents in some detail, the announcement reported that "At a meeting of the Maryland Society for promoting the gradual Abolition of Slavery, and the Relief of Free Negroes and others, unlawfully held in Bondage," held in Baltimore, the fifth day of October, 1791," the society considered the almanac "a Work of Merit, worthy their Attention as a Body," and agreed "to patronize the same, and use Endeavours to promote the Sale thereof."

Banneker was stunned by the degree of unexpected fame that came to him so quickly. The almanac proved to be an unusual success, although in his own mind the amateur astronomer attributed this to the determination and organized efforts of the Pennsylvania and Maryland Societies for the Promotion of the Abolition of Slavery rather than to the significance of his achievement. The fact that so many individuals prominent in public affairs and in business had devoted so much of their time and effort to publishing his work led him to a deeper examination of their purpose and of the anti-slavery movement.

Banneker found that his life was changing almost overnight. Neighbors and occasional travelers through the region called at his home to see him and speak to him, marveling at the evidence of accomplishment attained through self-teaching and undertaken so late in life. Banneker was hospitable and courteous to all who came. He invited them into his house,

Advertisement appearing in the December 2, 1791, issue of the *Maryland Journal or Baltimore Advertiser* announcing Banneker's almanac for 1792. *Maryland Historical Society.*

Opposite: Calculations for the month of June 1792. *Maryland Historical Society.*

Baltimore, November 14, 1791.

Juſt publiſhed, and to be SOLD by the Printers here-of, WHOLESALE *and* RETAIL, *with large Allowance to thoſe who purchaſe Quantities,*

THE
PENNSYLVANIA, DELAWARE, MARYLAND, AND VIRGINIA
ALMANACK,
FOR THE YEAR 1792:

A COMPLETE and ACCURATE EPHEMERIS, calculated by the ingenious Mr. BENJAMIN BANNEKER, a *free black Man,* (a Native of this County, born of *African Parents*) whoſe Calculations, now offered the Public, have met the Approbation of ſeveral of the moſt diſtinguiſhed Aſtronomers in America.

CONTAINING, intereſting Particulars of the virtuous Life and laudable Purſuits of BENJAMIN BANNEKER, and his Progreſs to ASTRONOMIC FAME.—The Motions of the Sun and Moon, the true Places and Aſpects of the Planets, the Riſing and Setting of the Sun, and the Riſing, Setting and Southing, Place and Age of the Moon, &c.—The Lunations, Conjunctions, Eclipſes, Judgment of the Weather, Feſtivals, and other remarkable Days ; Days for holding the Supreme and Circuit Courts of the *United States,* as alſo the uſual Courts in *Pennſylvania, Delaware, Maryland,* and *Virginia.*—Various Selections from the Commonplace-Book of the *Kentucky Philoſopher,* an *American Sage* ; with intereſting and entertaining Eſſays, in Proſe and Verſe—the whole compriſing a greater, more pleaſing, and uſeful Variety, than any Work of the *Kind* and *Price* in *North-America.*

N. B. The above Work, amongſt other Particulars, contains the following Eſſays, which will be found highly pleaſing and inſtructive:—The Planetary and Terreſtrial Worlds, comparatively conſidered—Remarks on the Swiftneſs of Time—Origin of the Gray Mare being the better Horſe—The Two Bees—On Health—Origin of the Proverb, " *Lay hold of the Tail if you can, and be ſure to keep it faſt*"—Extracts from the Writings of the Ancients of diſtinguiſhed Fame—The Stings of Poverty, Diſeaſe and Violence, leſs pungent than thoſe of guilty Paſſions—The Balance of Happineſs equal—Effuſions on a Town and Country Life—On Negro Slavery and the Slave-Trade—Alſo, a Liſt of the Legiſlature and principal Officers of the General Government.

⁂ *Orders, from our Country and diſtant Cuſtomers, will be duly attended to.*

At a Meeting of the " *Maryland Society for promoting the gradual Abolition of Slavery, and the Relief of free Negroes and others, unlawfully held in Bondage,*" *held in Baltimore, the firſt Day of October,* 1791,

MESSRS. GODDARD and ANGELL preſented to the Society an ALMANACK for the Year 1792, the *Aſtronomical Calculations* thereof performed by BENJAMIN BANNEKER, a *black Man,* a *Deſcendant* of *African Parents*—The Calculations appear to be atteſted by a Number of reſpectable Characters, as very accurate.

The Society conſidering the Performance a Work of Merit, worthy their Attention as a Body, agree to patroniſe the ſame, and uſe Endeavours to promote the Sale thereof.

Whereupon Reſolved, That the Secretary furniſh Meſſrs. Goddard and Angell with a Copy of the foregoing Determination, to be made public.

Copied, by Direction, and ſigned,
JOSEPH TOWNSEND, Secretary.

Baltimore : Printed by William Goddard, and James Angell, in Market-Street.

VIth Month, JUNE, hath 30 Days.

D.H.M.			
Full ○	4	7 55	aft.
Last Q.	11	1 10	aft.
New ●	19	7 49	mo.
First Q.	27	5 10	mo.

☊ { 1 30, 11 ♍ 29, 21 29 } deg.

PLANETS Places.

D.	☉	♄	♃	♂	♀	☿	☽'s L.
	♊	♈	♎	♍	♉	♉	
1	11	28	22	24	24	19	N. 2
7	17	29	2	26	♊ 1	25	N. 5
13	23	♉ 0	22	29	8	♊ 0	S. 2
19	29	1	22	♎ 0	16	9	S. 5
25	♋ 4	1	22	2	24	17	S. 1

M D	W D	Remarkable days, aspects, weather, &c.	☉ rises.	☉ sets.	☽'s Pla.	☽ sets.	☽ south	☽ A
1	6	△ ♂ ♀ *Sultry*	4 43	7 17	♎ 27	2 23	9 28	12
2	7	*and*	4 42	7 18	♏ 11	2 57	10 20	13
3	G	Trinity Sund. *dry,*	4 42	7 18	25	3 39	11 17	14
4	2	*close*	4 41	7 19	♐ 9	rises.	Morn.	15
5	3	Spica ♍ sets 1, 47.	4 41	7 19	24	8 18	0 16	16
6	4	*weather,*	4 41	7 19	♑ 9	9 17	1 15	17
7	5	*followed by*	4 40	7 20	23	10 12	2 14	18
8	6	△ ♂ ☿ *thunder*	4 40	7 20	♒ 8	10 56	3 12	19
9	7	*and rain.*	4 40	7 20	23	11 40	4 8	20
10	G	1st Sun. aft. Trin.	4 39	7 21	♓ 7	Morn.	5 2	21
11	2	St. Barnabas. *Cool*	4 39	7 21	21	0 18	5 54	22
12	3	△ ☉ ♃ *breezes,*	4 39	7 21	♈ 4	0 49	6 42	23
13	4	☿ gr. elong. *with*	4 39	7 21	17	1 23	7 30	24
14	5	*flying*	4 39	7 21	♉ 0	2 1	8 18	25
15	6	Pegasi M. r. 10, 32.	4 38	7 22	13	2 35	9 6	26
16	7	[Alban.	4 38	7 22	25	3 8	9 53	27
17	G	2d S. aft. Trin. St.	4 38	7 22	♊ 8	3 48	10 40	28
18	2	*clouds.*	4 38	7 22	20	4 27	11 27	29
19	3	Day's l. 14h. 44m.	4 38	7 22	♋ 1	sets.	Af. 14	●
20	4	☉ en. ♋ *Clear and*	4 38	7 22	13	7 58	0 55	1
21	5	Longest day. *warm.*	4 38	7 22	25	8 40	1 44	2
22	6	*Very*	4 38	7 22	♌ 7	9 30	2 38	3
23	7	△ ♃ ♀ [John Bap.	4 38	7 22	19	10 6	3 25	4
24	G	3d S. aft. Trin. St.	4 38	7 22	♍ 1	10 36	4 5	5
25	2	*sultry.*	4 38	7 22	14	11 7	4 50	6
26	3	*Clear*	4 38	7 22	26	11 41	5 34	7
27	4	♃ sets 1, 2. *and hot*	4 38	7 22	♎ 9	Morn.	6 22	8
28	5	*weather.*	4 38	7 22	23	0 12	7 12	9
29	6	St. Peter and Paul.	4 39	7 21	♏ 6	0 48	8 3	10
30	7	Day's de. 2m. *Rain.*	3 39	7 21	20	1 22	8 58	11

New-Jersey relinquished by the Dutch, and granted to the Duke of York, 1647; settled, 1682; proprietary-government surrendered, 1702.

where they wished especially to see his clock and the work table with his calculations. Although he had to abandon tobacco growing because of his infirmities, he continued to cultivate a small garden just for his own needs, and to provide attention to his beehives and his fruit orchard. He enjoyed the visits of neighbors and strangers and did not feel that his had been a meager lot, as some suggested, for life had indeed been good to him, and he intended to make the most of the years that remained.

As he whiled away the hours at his work table or in his garden, Banneker had much time for thinking, and in his solitude his mind turned to the cause in which he had become involved. He often reflected on his correspondence with Jefferson. As he reviewed his letter to the statesman—he had carefully copied both letters into his journal—he may have been dissatisfied with his own, wishing he had expressed himself differently. In retrospect, many of his statements may now have sounded stultified and pompous as he reread them, and he wondered what Jefferson had felt upon first seeing them. That such sentiments from an unknown Negro farmer could have been expressed directly to one of the leading American statesmen of his time and elicited a reply was particularly impressive. Looking over his draft of his letter, Banneker tried to remember the exact wording in some instances, since he recalled having made some last-minute revisions in the copy he had forwarded.[37]

The more his mind returned to the exchange of letters, however, the more Banneker gave serious consideration to the suggestions being made by his friends, the Ellicott brothers, and by Pemberton, to publish them in the almanac. The addition of McHenry's introduction had eliminated the material unnecessary in the 1792 issue, but Goddard & Angell and Pemberton were already planning the next year's almanac and were pressing to publish the letters. After long consideration, Banneker finally decided the letters should be published, if indeed they would serve the antislavery movement, and he began his preparations for the next year's almanac.

VII

THE YEARS
OF FULFILLMENT

The expanded spheres, amazing to the sight,
Magnificent with stars and globes of light,
The glorious orbs which heaven's bright host compose,
The imprison'd sea that restless ebbs and flows,
The fluctuating field of liquid air,
With all the curious meteors hovering there,
And the wide regions of the land, proclaim
The Power Divine that rais'd the mighty frame.

Benjamin Banneker's Almanac for 1792

NOW THAT THE SUCCESS OF HIS FIRST ALMANAC WAS ASSURED, Banneker lost no time in preparing an ephemeris for the following year. There would be no further reluctance of printers to publish his work—in fact he found himself faced with having to choose among several. Two separate editions of his almanac for 1793 appeared, one by his former publishing firm in Baltimore, Goddard & Angell, and another by Joseph Crukshank in Philadelphia.

Although it had agreed to publish the almanac for 1793, the Goddard & Angell firm was in the midst of an upheaval. The partnership which had been formed in 1789 dissolved in August 1792, and thereafter Angell continued the business alone. Goddard's name was retained on the imprint of the shop until February 1793, but Banneker negotiated solely with Angell.[1]

Banneker's ephemeris for the year 1793 followed the same format that he had established the previous year. Angell made some changes in the contents of the almanac, including more long stories and essays. He organized the contents in a more orderly fashion and improved both the appearance and literary quality of the publication. The publisher enthusiastically introduced the almanac, touting the "rapid Sale and extensive Circulation" of the 1792 edition and claiming the new version by "the same ingenious self-taught Astronomer" was just as accurate. Banneker's work, he asserted, had impressed Europe. British antislavery advocates "Pitt, Fox, and Wilberforce" had introduced the work in the House of Commons "as an Argument in favour of the Cause of Humanity . . . , and with a View of putting a Period to the diabolical Traffic in human Flesh on the Coast of AFRICA, in which we are happy to observe, they were, in a great Degree, successful."[2]

Banneker's friends and printers had wisely reserved the correspondence with Jefferson for inclusion in this second issue so that it could be given greater prominence. Banneker's letter to Jefferson and Jefferson's reply followed the introduction without editorial comment.

Another important item included in the 1793 almanac was "A Plan of a Peace Office for the United States," which aroused considerable comment at the time. Many believed it to have been Banneker's own work. Even recently its authorship has been debated, but in 1947 it was identified beyond question as the work of Dr. Benjamin Rush, in a volume of his writings published that year.[3] (Document 19)

Nevertheless, the publication of Rush's "Plan" for the first time, in Banneker's almanac, added prestige and contributed greatly to the almanac's impact on behalf of the antislavery movement. For some unexplained reason, it was published without identifying the author. Not until 1798, five years later, did Rush himself publish the "Plan" in a collection of essays, with substantial additions to the text. Rush's introduction to that volume, *Essays Literary and Moral,* stated that most of the essays had been previously published in *The Museum, and Columbian Magazine* in Philadelphia soon after the end of the War of Independence, and that a few of them had first appeared in pamphlets.[4] A careful survey of the contents of *The Museum, and Columbian Magazine* has failed to locate the "Plan," though it may have appeared as a separate pamphlet, from which it was reprinted in abridged form by Angell. The "Plan" presented Rush's strong philosophical opposition to war, which he had not expressed during the course of the American Revolution nor during the War of 1812. He did assume a clearly stated pacifist position in his later writings.[5]

The contents of Joseph Crukshank's Philadelphia edition of Banneker's almanac were particularly directed to the interests of the anti-slavery movement and included materials not contained in the Goddard & Angell issue. This was a deliberate choice, based upon the prospective distribution of the several editions. Besides the McHenry biographical sketch, Crukshank's edition contained Rush's "Plan," extracts from British Parliamentary debates in 1792, speeches of William Pitt, M. Montague, and Charles James Fox, an extract from "Wilkinson's appeal to England on Behalf of the Abused Africans," and a passage on slavery from Jefferson's *Notes on the State of Virginia*.

Banneker's letter to Jefferson and the latter's reply received additional distribution shortly after the appearance of the almanac for 1793. The letters were published late in 1792 in a widely circulated, fifteen-page pamphlet by Daniel Lawrence, a Philadelphia printer. Later that same year, after the first edition sold out, Lawrence reprinted the pamphlet in a twelve-page format. It proved to be particularly useful for circulation by the abolitionist societies in support of claims for Negro equality.

Banneker derived great satisfaction and pleasure from the fact that during these first two years of his endeavors, his almanacs competed with those calculated by Major Andrew Ellicott and published in Baltimore by John Hayes, Goddard's great rival. He also gained a certain amount of satisfaction from the knowledge that his own publication was now vastly outselling its competitor, particularly since Hayes had refused to purchase his first ephemeris.

As a consequence of its special contents—the Banneker-Jefferson correspondence and the first printing of Rush's "Plan"—Banneker's almanac for 1793 was one of the most important publications of its time. It was distributed in great numbers and became the subject of widespread discussion at all levels. The Pennsylvania Society for the Promotion of the Abolition of Slavery took advantage of this new medium for propaganda purposes and made careful plans for producing the Banneker almanac the following year. William Young of Philadelphia made arrangements to publish a separate edition of his own.

Inasmuch as the first issues of his almanac had now achieved national importance, Banneker was assured there was no further question about producing almanacs for the following years. Fairly early in the spring he began to make his projections of eclipses and to compile the monthly calculations of an ephemeris for 1794. The printers, as well as his patrons, planned to start work early on putting this issue together. Unfortunately, the winter proved to be a difficult one for Banneker. He worked on the ephemeris as well as he could between repeated bouts of illness, but it was the middle of May before he was able to make substantial progress. Joseph Townsend had become increasingly concerned, meanwhile, whether the materials would be ready in time for the printers' schedule, and he wrote to Banneker early in May to inquire.[6]

Banneker's reply reflected his ill health and poor spirits. His letter was not written in the precise script and with the careful attention to form that distinguished most of his handwriting, and it was obvious that it had cost him some effort. Evidence of the prolonged illness from which Banneker suffered at this time is to be found in his manuscript journal. Under the date of May 15, 1793, he recorded payment to be made to a Doctor Hulse for £5 16s. 8d., of which he noted having made a partial payment of £3 18s. 9d. He forwarded his reply to Townsend through Elias Ellicott:

> I received your favour of the 8th instant and can give two reasons that I did not answer till now, the first is I have been very unwell scarce able to Set up. the Second I have been calculated the rising and Setting of the Sun for every Sixth day of the year for the Latitude of London, which I have inclosed Sent unto M^R. Pemberton requesting him to have it inspected by some Judicious person and if the work proves erroneous, I will confess there is many errors in my calculations for London—if otherwise I shall think european printers no better than those of America.
>
> I wrote M^R. Pemberton to remind M^R. Cruckshank of the ballance due me and Send it to you —
>
> I am busy when circumstances permit, making ready copies to put into your hands.
>
> I am your Humble Serv^T.
B. Banneker.[7]

That Banneker took the time to calculate an ephemeris for the latitude of London at a time when he was so far behind schedule with his next ephemeris for a local almanac is surprising. It could have been due to only one reason, that Pemberton had suggested or requested that he produce an ephemeris for an almanac to be published in England, presumably to be distributed by the English abolitionist society. During this period the

English abolitionists had grown into a large and strong body, and had become very active, nourished by the enthusiasm and assistance provided by the American abolitionist societies. Undoubtedly they had become aware of the substantial propaganda value to be derived from a British almanac featuring the abolitionist cause, as had been so clearly demonstrated by the first two issues of Banneker's almanac in the United States. Consequently, a similar publication was being planned in Great Britain. Such a work required an ephemeris calculated specifically for the latitude of London or another of the major British cities.

If no astronomer was available to the English abolitionists, it was conceivable that Banneker's assistance would have been sought through the Pennsylvania Society. Copies of his American almanacs had been sent to England for the purpose of demonstrating achievement of a member of the Negro race, and had been distributed not only in England but elsewhere in the United Kingdom. Banneker's almanacs had already been presented in the House of Commons as tangible evidence by such great proponents of the movement as William Pitt the Younger, Charles James Fox, and William Wilberforce, and consequently the potential successful sale of an English edition could readily be foreseen.

That Banneker was involved in producing an ephemeris for England is supported by a drawing of a projection included in his manuscript journal, with the statement, "This projection is for an eclipse of the Sun for the Vortex of London, June the 24th, 1797." To this he had added the notation, "I find by this Diagram this Eclips at London . . ." followed by data relating to its beginning, greatest obscuration, end, and duration.[8]

The additional burden imposed upon Banneker's time by having to produce an ephemeris for England, in addition to the one he had promised to the Philadelphia printers, proved to be too much for him with his poor health. He continued to work hard, and during the next few weeks completed his calculations for the Philadelphia publication. He forwarded them to William Young in Philadelphia by the usual circuitous route from Ellicott's Lower Mills to Townsend at Baltimore to Pemberton in Philadelphia. He had delayed in preparing the tide tables, however, as reported in the following communication from Townsend to Pemberton. The same letter indicated that Banneker had not yet received the balance of payment from Crukshank due him.

This is to acknowledge the receipt of thy favor by Jos. Thornburgh, as also the receipt of G. Sharp's Letter, &c. Our Committee has since concluded to recommend the publication of said Letter to the Society at their next Meeting which will be on 7th day next—I have wrote to Benj^N. Banneker for the Tide Table for Wm. Young but have not rec^D. his Answer yet—I am owing Owen Jones Ju^R. a balance please pay him £5.5 for the Calculation, & I will pay Benj^N. that sum by first conveyance.—We are preparing to meet this Morning at 9 O'Clock to hear an Oration on the Institution of the Society by James Winchester—I shall write thee soon.[9]

On the reverse side of the letter Pemberton had noted that it had been received from Joseph Townsend in Baltimore on July 4, 1793, forwarded via Jacob Myers, received on July 6, and "Answered the 18th & sent him Owen Jones, Jun^R. Rect. for £5.5—paid him as desired." Neither Pemberton's reply nor evidence of any assistance he may have provided to Banneker is recorded.

Joseph Thornburgh, who served as Townsend's messenger, was a native of Carlisle, Pennsylvania, who moved to Baltimore and became a wealthy merchant with a dry goods business. In 1800 he married Cassandra Hopkins Ellicott, the attractive young widow of John Ellicott (1739–95), one of the founding brothers of Ellicott's Lower Mills. The several editions of Banneker's almanac for 1794 went to press simultaneously. A large sale was anticipated and James Angell took the opportunity to include a suitable preface in his edition, in which he related Banneker's work to that of another outstanding American Negro, the poet Phillis Wheatley, as further evidence that "Africans and their Descendants are capable of attaining a Degree of Eminence in the Liberal Sciences."[10] (Document 20)

The popularity of the new issue exceeded the printer's wildest expectations. It sold rapidly and widely, and Banneker was delighted with the growing success of his venture. He may have considered having future editions of his work published by other printers as well. There is some evidence that he did in a letter he wrote to James Pemberton at Philadelphia on March 22, 1794. Hoping that Pemberton was well despite "the raging of the pestilential disorder in your City," he told Pemberton that "the rapidity of the Sale of my Almanac for this present Year," had encouraged him to make another for 1795. "I flatter my Self that the work are as correct as any of the kind in common use among us." He hoped, too, that Pemberton would continue their friendship, and that "if it be not too burdensome unto you to mention me to your printers and if any of them has an inclination to take a copy of mine, by giving timely notice I can Supply them."[11]

From time to time Banneker received fan mail from admirers. A Miss Sally Lane of Philadelphia wrote to him about his calculations in his almanac for 1794, sending along a "Religious Book" and a pocket almanac, whose calculations Banneker compared to his own. On January 8, 1795, he graciously responded that he could find no important discrepancy "save in the case of the Rising and Setting of the Moon[.] There I find some trifling variation which I imagine arises from the difference between the ancient and the modern Tables[.] Those I make use of are Fergusons and Leadbetters, which were calculated many years since, and I doubt not but that your calculator has new Tables and perhaps more correct that those of mine." He assured her that if he ever got to Philadelphia "I shall make bold to do my self the pleasure to call upon you, and altho it seems unlikely it may not be impossible for it to be in my power to be serviceable unto you in some respect or other."[12]

The almanac for the year 1795 enjoyed a substantially increased circulation. Angell produced one edition shortly before he sold his firm to Francis Brumfield, and two other editions appeared in Baltimore, one printed for John Fisher and another issued by the Wilmington printers, S. & J. Adams, who had recently established a printing firm in Baltimore. Five other separate editions were produced by the Adams firm at their Wilmington press, one of which was printed exclusively for Frederick Craig for distribution from his stationery store.

Samuel and John Adams were sons of the Wilmington, Delaware, printer James Adams, who had established himself in Philadelphia in 1753 and worked for a time with Benjamin Franklin. The Adams brothers opened a printing office in partnership in Wilmington in about 1761 and then late in 1789 added a branch shop in Baltimore in which they featured the printing of almanacs and religious books. Following their father's death, the brothers removed their operation entirely to Wilmington, and thereafter their Baltimore printing office was continued by others.

Meanwhile, editions of Banneker's almanac for 1795 were also produced separately by three other Philadelphia printers, William Young, William Gibbons, and Jacob Johnson & Company. Yet another edition was published by Matthias Day of Trenton, New Jersey. The total of at least nine known editions of Banneker's almanac for the same year was remarkable,

Bal. County near Ellicotts mills January 8th. 1795

Dear Miss.   I Received your kind letter of the 9th ult.
and with it a Religious Book and a pocket Almanac, and I
compared the calculation therof with that of my own, and they
seem to agree so well that I can find no considerable defference
save in the case of the Rising and Setting of the Moon, there I
find some trifling variation which I imagine arifs from the
difference between the anccient and the modern Tables, those I make
use of are Fergusons and Leadbetters, which were calculated many
years since, and I doubt not but that your calculator has new
Tables and perhaps more correct than those of mine, but be
that as it may I humbly thank you for your present, for
your letter, and for your well wishes toward me, and if I
should ever come to philadelphia, I shall make bold to do
my self the pleasure to call upon you, and altho it seems unlikely it may not be impossible for it to be in my power to be
serviceable unto you in some respect or other and if it should
ever be the case, then your reasonable requests shall be armed
with the obedience of

                        yr loving friend and most obedient Sevt.

Miss Sally Lane ————   B B Banneker

Letter from Banneker to Sally Lane, 1795. *Courtesy, the Banneker-Douglass Museum, Annapolis.*

and brought the amateur astronomer not only considerable renown but substantial income as well.

The notable feature of the 1795 issue was a purported portrait of Banneker on the cover or title page of several editions. The clearest of the likenesses was that appearing on the cover of the edition printed for John Fisher of Baltimore, a woodcut representing the portrait bust of a young Negro wearing the typical Quaker garb of the period. (See Frontispiece). The edition published by S. & J. Adams at Baltimore attempted to reproduce the woodcut portrait without success. The same strong lines of the woodcut were used in what was unquestionably a copy of the portrait on the Fisher edition, but without delineation of the features or other major details. The artist who produced the portrait is not identified.

The literary and miscellaneous contents assembled by the respective printers of the several editions varied considerably. Fisher prefaced his version with a page quoting from McHenry's letter about Banneker's life. The Adams brothers, on the other hand, introduced theirs with a short original preface touting "the Accuracy of the astronomical Calculations; the pleasing Variety of Essays, of moral Excellence and genuine Humour; and the numerous useful Receipts, Tables, &c. contained in this Year's Almanac," and the following bit of verse:

> The wisest Men that ever writ
> To please each Taste could never yet;
> What some disdain, others commend;
> Come buy our Book, and there's an End.[13]

Joseph Crukshank's edition of the almanac contained extracts from several publications and speeches on the subject of slavery and the slave trade; an abstract of the debates in the last session of the British Parliament in April 1792; and William Pitt's speech on the motion proposing the abolition of the slave trade. Among those quoted were an "Extract from Wilkinson's Appeal to England on Behalf of the Abused Africans," and an extract concerning slavery from Thomas Jefferson's *Notes on the State of Virginia*.

William Young's edition differed from the others in that it featured "An Account of the MALIGNANT FEVER which prevailed in Philadelphia, 1793." The only other notable literary content was a poem "Addressed to Benjamin Banneker" by an unidentified writer who signed the work "G.H." The poem extolled the amateur astronomer's accomplishments despite the color of his skin and compared his achievements with those of Isaac Newton. It reads in part:

> But what are *colours*? do *complexions change*
> The *human intellects*? Ah! doctrine *strange*!
> Banneker is an argument 'gainst *those*
> Whose *prejudices* thus themselves expose.
> Banneker shews in demonstrative light,
> Tho' *black* his skin, his talents yet are *bright*,
> He e'en may dare in *competition* place
> His talents *rare*, with those who thus *disgrace*
> His sable brethren; yea, and clearly shew
> Talents to *such*, perhaps *superior* too.
> Great Genius! tho' arriv'd to life's *last stage*!
> Tho' hoary hairs thy earthly *end* presage!
> Yet may kind heaven multiply thy days,
> With many years, 'till nature quite *decays*!
> Long may thou live an evidence to shew,
> That A*fric's* sable race have *talents* too.
> And may thy genius bright its *strength* retain,
> Tho' nature to decline may still remain;
> And may thou favour us to thy *latest* years
> With thy *Ephemeris* call'd BANNEKER's.
> A work which ages yet *unborn* shall name,
> And be the *monument* of lasting *fame*;
> A work which after ages shall *adore*,
> When BANNEKER, alas! shall be *no more*![14]

The almanac for 1796 for which Banneker provided an ephemeris had a much more limited distribution. Only two editions are known to have been printed, both issued by the firm of Philip Edwards, James Keddie, and Thomas, Andrews, and Butler of Baltimore. Of the numerous partners of this firm, Edwards was the best known. A native of Baltimore, he opened a printing office in 1792 and two months later undertook publication of the *Baltimore Evening Post,* the name of which was later changed to *Edwards' Baltimore Daily Advertiser.* He also printed broadsides, sermons, and the first magazine to have a Baltimore imprint. He was the printer of George Buchanan's *Oration* in 1793, and in 1795 he acquired the *Maryland Journal,* which he combined with his own newspaper until it became defunct two years later. Neither of the two editions of Banneker's almanac for 1796 included any material of particular note, but a preface provided another opportunity to the publishers to speak on behalf of the antislavery movement with some clever use of language.[15]

The almanac emphasized the fact that the work was the achievement of a man of color and that a basic lesson could be learned from it. "Although the God of Nature has marked the face of the African with a darker shade than his brethren, he has given him a soul equally capable of refinement." (See Document 21.) Unfortunately, it did not sell well. It was Banneker's first association with this printing firm. Perhaps his change of publishers was due to the vagaries of the printing business, but whatever the reason, the 1796 almanac had the smallest distribution. The production of this issue is the only record of Banneker's negotiations with his printers that has survived. He made the following entry of the transaction in his commonplace book: "Sold on the 2nd of April, 1795, to Buttler, Edwards & Kiddy, the right of an Almanac, for the year 1796, for the sum of 80 dollars, equal to £30."[16]

The last issue of Banneker's almanac known to have been published was that for the year 1797. In Baltimore, Christopher Jackson produced two editions, and separate editions were produced in Petersburg and Richmond, Virginia. Jackson printed one edition for distribution by George Keatinge's Book Store. Jackson's second issue of Banneker's almanac was for wider distribution, in Pennsylvania, Delaware, Maryland and Kentucky.[17]

The Petersburg imprint, issued by William Prentis and William T. Murray, was distributed only in Virginia and North Carolina, while the Richmond edition, published by Simon Pleasants Jr., was issued "[by privelege]" for Pennsylvania, Delaware, Maryland, and Kentucky. The size of the almanacs in these editions ranged from sixteen leaves for the Baltimore and Petersburg versions to twenty-two leaves for the Richmond edition. Arrangements for publication by a Petersburg printer probably were made through members of the Ellicott family, who maintained business interests in that community.

Two items of more than usual interest were contained in the almanac for 1797. One was a caution to gentlemen smokers:

Looking over a few old papers the other day, I found the following anecdote, which seems to concern your employment, and as it affords the first, and I believe the last *royal* opinion ever given on the subject of smoaking, I hope you will receive it with all due respect.

Although in this age we see every school boy strut along with his segar and puffing it was most ridiculed in the court of James the 1st. and the courtiers affected to reject it, with horror. The king said that "tobacco was the lively image and pattern of Hell, for that it had in it, by allusion, all the parts and vices of the world whereby hell may be gained, viz.

1st. It was smoak; so are all the vanities of this world.

2nd. It delighteth them who take it; so do all the pleasures of the world delight the men of the world.

3rd. It maketh men drunken, and light in the head; so do all the vanities of the world, men are drunken therewith.

4th. He that taketh tobacco, saith he cannot leave it, it doth bewitch him; even so the pleasures of the world make men loath to leave them, they are for the most part, enchanted with them.

And farther, besides all this, it is like hell in the very substance of it, for it is a stinking loathsome thing; and so is hell."

And farther, his majesty professed that were he to invite the Devil to a dinner, he should have three dishes: first, — a pig; second, a pot of ling and mustard; and, third, a pipe of tobacco for digesture.

Having perused this, gentlemen, I hope you will profit by it, as coming from *the Solomon* of his age; and when you fill your pipes, or illumine with your segars, most gratefully remember the kindness of your affectionate brother.

TOM WHIFF.

Segar Manufactory, Baltimore, 1796.[18]

The second item, entitled "Epitaph on a Watchmaker," appeared in all the four editions:

EPITAPH ON A WATCH-MAKER

———

HERE lies, in a *horizontal* position,
The *outside case* of
Peter Pendulum, Watch-Maker
Whose abilities in that line were an honour
To his profession.

Integrity was the *main spring,*
And prudence the *regulator*
Of all the actions of his life,
Humane, generous and liberal,
His *hand* never *stopped*
Till he had relieved distress,
So nicely *regulated* were all his *motions,*
That he never *went wrong,*
Except when set a *going,*
By people
Who did not know
His key:
Even then he was easily
Set right again
He had the art of disposing his time
So well,
That his hours glided away
In one continual round
Of pleasure and delight,
Till an unlucky *minute* put a period to
His existence.
He departed this life
Wound up
In hope, of being *taken in hand*
By his *Maker,*
And of being thoroughly *cleaned, repaired,*
And set a *going*
In the World to come.[19]

This epitaph, which might have served admirably for Banneker's own gravestone, had he been honored with one, presents a literary mystery that still remains unsolved. It is noteworthy that it was included in each of the four issues of the 1797 Banneker almanac, published by three different printers, indicating that it was not part of the usual varied miscellany customarily compiled by each printer from various resources and repositories. Undoubtedly Banneker had selected and provided it together with his ephemeris to each of the printers, but it is unlikely that he composed it, for the terminology suggests considerably more familiarity with the technical aspects of the craft of watch and clockmaking than he possessed. The most

Tombstone of George Routleigh. Overall view of the tomb and detail view of the inscribed gravestone. *Rector, Lydford Parish Church, Lydford near Okehampton, Devon.*

logical explanation is that Banneker copied it from one of the English periodicals imported by the Ellicott & Company store, though that periodical has not been found.

The epitaph actually exists, beautifully carved upon a gravestone covering the tomb of George Routleigh, a watchmaker of Devonshire, England. Routleigh died in 1802, six years after the epitaph appeared in print in Banneker's almanac. The epitaph is inscribed upon the large slate stone with the text exactly as it was printed in the almanac, except that throughout the name of "Peter Pendulum" is replaced by that of "George Routleigh," and to the line "He departed this life" was added Routleigh's date of death and his age, "November 14, 1802, Aged 57, wound up," followed by the remainder of the text.

George Routleigh (also spelled Routledge), born in 1745, was a watchmaker in the ancient Saxon town of Lydford in Devon, England. Although his name appears in both the Devon and Cornwall lists of clockmakers, he was never a member of the clockmakers' guild. He maintained a shop in Launceston and employed an assistant named William Coryndon, who later established himself as a clockmaker on his own in the region. The cases for Routleigh's tallcase clocks were made for him by his friend, a cabinetmaker or carpenter named Ernest Petherick, who lived not far from the local church. A clock made by Routleigh with a case constructed by Pettrick is currently owned by a Petherick descendant in Tavistock.

Little is known about Routleigh or his family, perhaps because there is little to be known. In 1794 a certain Edward Routleigh, who may have been the watchmaker's brother, was the church warden in Lydford and lived in the Parsonage House. He served as a witness of the marriages held in the church until 1816. The church register records not only the burial of George Routleigh in 1802 but also that of Susannah Routleigh, age eighty-nine, in 1836. Edward Routleigh probably arranged for the watchmaker's burial and the installation of his tombstone; Edward died in 1821.

Routleigh's tomb stands upon a slight bank in the graveyard just to the east of the main Porch of the thirteenth-century St. Petrock's Church in Lydford. Constructed of blocks of stone bound together with mortar, the tomb is raised above ground and covered by a large slab of smooth slate, the upper surface of which bears the whimsical inscription. The carving has suffered from weathering through the years, and the slab eventually may have to be removed to the interior of the church to preserve it. Because of the tomb's position, the slab could be photographed only from a position on the church roof.[20]

It has always been assumed in Lydford that the inscription was original with Routleigh's tomb and that it had been composed locally, but the curious circumstances surrounding this gravestone inscription suggest several possibilities. The source of the inscription was probably older and discovered by Banneker in an English journal, the identity and date of which are not known. Routleigh or a member of his family may have read it in its original source, the proposed journal, or Routleigh or one of his survivors read it in fact in a copy of Banneker's almanac for 1797. His almanacs circulated widely in England as well as in the United States. Whoever saw it may have recalled it and decided to use it for Routleigh's gravestone five years later. The epitaph has become well known and the gravestone itself has become an object of curiosity beyond the community, often quoted in

Overleaf:
Two facing pages from the manuscript journal showing the projection for a lunar eclipse for February 1793 on the left and calculations for the month of July 1793 on the right. *Maryland Historical Society.*

July Seventh Month hath 31 Days

	D	H	M	
New ☽	8	0	3	Morn
First Q.	16	2	0	Morn
Full ○	23	2	47	Morn
Last Q.	29	6	51	Aft

☊ {1, 11, 21} ♍ {9, 8, 8} Deg.

Planets Places							
D	☉	♄	♃	♂	♀	☿	☽
	♋	♉	♏	♊	♊	♋	Lat.
1	10	13	23	27	3	18	4 S
7	16	14	23	♋ 1	6	29	4 S
13	22	14	23	5	9	♌ 9	1 N
19	27	14	23	9	14	19	5 N
25	♌ 3	14	23	13	19	28	0 N

M D	W D	Remarkable Days Aspects weather &c.	☉ rise	☉ Set	☽ Long	☽ rise	☽ South	☽ Age
1	2	Days Decrease 2 m.	4..39	7..21	0-23-0	12..59	19-28	23
2	3	Visitation of V. Mary	4-40	7..20	1-6-50	13..32	20-19	24
3	4		4-40	7-20	1-20-19	14..10	21-12	25
4	5	St. Martin	4..40	7-20	2-3-29	14-51	22-1	26
5	6	*☉♄	4-41	7-19	2-16-21	15-39	22-56	27
6	7		4-41	7-19	2-28-53	16-24	23-41	28
7	F	6th Sund. past Trin.	4-42	7-18	3-11-13			29
8	2		4-42	7-18	3-23-18	Sets	☌ 27	☽
9	3	Lyra South 11-15	4..43	7-17	4-5-17	8-27	1-17	1
10	4		4..43	7..17	4-17-10	9-2	2..1	2
11	5	Days 14..32	4..44	7-16	4-29-0	9-36	2-45	3
12	6	♃ Stationary	4..44	7..16	5-10-50	10..6	3-30	4
13	7	*♀☿	4..45	7-15	5-22-46	10..37	4..12	5
14	F	7th Sund. past Trin	4-45	7-15	6-4-50	11..8	4..48	6
15	2		4-46	7-14	6-17-5	11-39	5..34	7
16	3	Spica ♍ set 10-58	4..47	7..13	6-29-29	12..12	6..25	8
17	4		4..47	7-13	7-12-20	12..46	7..12	9
18	5	Arcturus Sets 1-25	4-48	7..12	7-25-24	13..26	8-4	10
19	6		4-49	7-11	8-8-48	14..10	8..57	11
20	7	Margaret	4-49	7-11	8-22-31	14-56	9..52	12
21	F	8th Sund. past Trin	4..50	7..10	9-6-35	15-44	10-51	13
22	2	Magdalene	4-51	7-9	9-20-55		11..49	14
23	3	☉ enters ♌	4-52	7..8	10-5-26	rise	12-45	15
24	4	~~Dog Days begin~~	4..53	7..7	10-20..7	8..20	13..45	16
25	5	St. James	4-54	7-6	11-4-48	9-4	14-40	17
26	6	St. Anne	4..54	7-6	11-19-32	9-39	15-33	18
27	7		4-55	7-5	0-4-0	10..14	16-26	19
28	F	9th Sund past Trin	4..56	7-4	0-18-18	10-49	17-14	20
29	2	Days 14..0	4 57	7-3	1-2-17	11..27	18..9	21
30	3	~~Days 14..4~~ Dog Days begins	4-58	7-2	1-15-58	12..5	18-55	22
31	4	Days Decrease 42 m.	4..59	7..1	1-29-18	12..44	19..50	23

July 30 is the true time the Dog Days begins
for that morning that Star rises with the Sun
Sept. 5 the Dog Days end

horological literature and visited by clock-collecting tourists. Novelist Elizabeth Goudge featured the inscription in its entirety with Routleigh's name at the beginning of her popular novel, *The Dean's Watch*, although she made no reference to it in the text.[21]

Banneker's almanac for the year 1797 was the last of his almanacs to be published. He may have completed and submitted ephemerides for almanacs for one or two of the succeeding years after 1797, but if so they were not rendered into print. His increasing infirmities deterred him, and an examination of his manuscript journal reveals a progressively increasing deterioration in his handwriting during these final years. Nevertheless, Banneker continued his astronomical observations and calculations until he had reached the age of seventy-one, and recorded ephemerides for each succeeding year through 1802 in his manuscript journal. He went on to make and record several calculations for the years from 1802 to 1805, but thereafter he was no longer able to continue the work he cherished.

The manner in which Banneker's almanacs appeared so suddenly and then were as abruptly terminated has invited speculation. The series was unquestionably popular, for at least twenty-eight known editions were published within a period of six short years, examples of all of which survive. It may be assumed that the series was abandoned when Banneker was no longer able to continue his astronomical studies. His manuscript journal proves beyond doubt, however, that he continued to calculate complete ephemerides for each year from 1798 through 1802.

Another factor has to be considered: the increasing competition among printers in the publication of almanacs. In New England, the almanac was particularly popular. In Massachusetts, between eleven and fifteen different almanacs were published each year from 1791 through 1797. In Connecticut during the same period, between ten and thirteen almanacs appeared annually, and comparable statistics can be derived for Pennsylvania, Maryland, and other states.

A much more likely explanation of why Banneker's almanacs suddenly disappeared is that the times had changed. Whereas almanacs throughout the eighteenth century had been primarily educational and instructive, they adopted a new direction during the last decade of the century and became dedicated to national events and local causes. Banneker's almanacs were among the first to reflect that new emphasis. They were the first to popularize the theme of antislavery, and they contributed substantially to the abolitionist cause. As the scientific effort of a free Negro, the almanacs provided tangible proof of the mental equality of the races, a topic that was central to the antislavery movement. By the second half of the final decade of the century, however, a strong reaction to the cause of abolition had set in. This turn in the tide was to persist for a short span of years but long enough to preclude a possible revival of Banneker's almanacs.

The reign of Banneker's almanacs perfectly coincided with the origin and demise of the Maryland Society for the Abolition of Slavery. By the latter half of the decade, the antislavery movement had begun to lose its impact. With the end of the American Revolution and the emergence of the new republic, the ideological basis for the war, which had included antislavery, had begun to recede in importance against the press of many new national endeavors and concerns, particularly an economic depression and uncertain national politics.[22]

The Maryland society declined as the popularity of its mission waned. In 1797 it had a respectable 231 members and was the third largest such organization in the United States. Among its most important achievements were legislation on manumission and the publication of Banneker's almanacs. Although there is no ready evidence that Banneker's almanacs owed their publication directly to the society, the correspondence among Joseph Townsend, Elias Ellicott, and James Pemberton leaves little doubt that the society and its officers played a significant role in their production.[23] The society itself did not boast of that role. In a report made to the Pennsylvania Society for the Promotion of the Abolition of Slavery, the Maryland society listed the events of its short history and achievements without mentioning the name of Banneker. Still, not to be overlooked is the fact that the first of Banneker's almanacs appeared shortly after the Maryland society was founded, and his last issue was published on the eve of the society's demise.[24]

VIII

✦❦✦

SCIENTIFIC
CONSIDERATIONS

The most sensible of those who make scientific researches,
is he who believes himself the farthest from the goal, & who
whatever advances he has made in his road, studies as if he
yet knew nothing and marches as if he were only yet
beginning to make his first advance.

From "A Scrap,"
Banneker's Almanac for 1795

A STUDY OF BANNEKER'S MANUSCRIPT journal and a comparison of his
notes with his published almanacs provide a most revealing documentation of how he taught himself astronomy. It is possible to
follow, step by step, many of his attempts to calculate eclipses and the
numerous computations required to prepare an ephemeris. It is possible
also to detect his occasional errors, and to see how in the laborious process
of self-instruction he was able to correct them. His notes survive as a monument to his love of astronomy and to his unflagging determination to
master every aspect of the task he had set himself. An adequate evaluation
of Banneker's scientific attainments cannot be made without reviewing his
astronomical notes and almanacs.

An ephemeris is calculated from a series of basic computations
required to establish the positions of the sun, moon, and planets each year,
from which other calculations may be made: the solar and lunar eclipses,
the times the sun and moon rise and set, identification of remarkable
days, weather forecasting on a daily basis, tide tables for the region, and
similar data.

The page format for the monthly ephemerides selected by the publisher was, as previously noted, similar to that of the almanacs calculated by Andrew Ellicott and printed by John Hayes of Baltimore. Although the printing style and layout of content otherwise varied considerably in the editions produced by different printers, the ephemerides remained constant in form. The one minor difference is Banneker's use of Arabic numbers for months and days instead of Roman numerals at the top of each page.

A comparison of the ephemerides Banneker recorded in his manuscript journal with the published versions in his almanacs reveals his method. First, he had to make a reckoning of the calendar, which was one of the major preoccupations of the almanac-maker. He then entered the times of sunrise and sunset and listed the important religious and noteworthy days of each month in an outline he had previously prepared. These figures could be entered long in advance, once the pattern of the page had been established. Remarkable days included the most important religious and saints' days, and important dates in American history. Weather prognostications were noted in addition to miscellaneous astronomical information.

Before proceeding with the remainder of the calculations, Banneker customarily awaited the arrival of the new edition of the *Nautical Almanac,* from which he extracted some of the preliminary data. This reference work probably was ordered from England for him by the Ellicott & Company store. He then listed the figures of reference and the necessary notes for calculating the ephemerides for each year. These "Common Notes," as he called them, he placed within a separate box on his page, wherein he included the Dominical Letter, the golden number, the epact and the cycle of the sun.

He also recorded the longitude and anomaly of the sun for every sixth day of each month, together with the logarithms of the sun's distance from the earth, the longitude and anomaly of the moon at the beginning of each year, and the position of the moon's node for the first month of each year. The word "anomaly," which is used frequently, is the distance that the sun or the moon has traveled from its apogee, or farthest point from the earth. It is reckoned by the twelve zodiacal constellations, each of which is allocated thirty degrees along the ecliptic.[1]

Certain mathematical computations had to be made before the calculations of the eclipses for that year could be undertaken. These were required to establish the positions of the sun and the moon. In order to do so it was necessary to determine the times of the new and full moon for each of the twelve months and list them in a column. When that had been done, he calculated the sun's position for each of these times during the year and compared them to determine in which months an eclipse might occur. After he had identified the months, Banneker made detailed calculations and prepared a projection or geometrical diagram of the eclipse on the nearest page of the journal that remained blank. The column of "New and Full Moons" was used also as the basis for the date and time of the new, first quarter, full, and last quarter moons, information usually found at the top of each page of an almanac.

A vast amount of work was required to calculate a single eclipse, which makes Banneker's accomplishment in this field all the more impressive. He had to make at least sixty-eight mathematical calculations to produce the ten elements required to construct a single eclipse diagram. The results of his calculations, each of which was computed to the nearest second, were entered on a blank journal page, including the semi-diameter of the earth, and of the sun's and moon's disks. Also included were the sun's distance from the nearest solstice, the declination of the sun and the moon, and the moon's latitude.[2]

After Banneker had derived the results of these preliminary calculations, he then utilized them to project the eclipse, which he customarily drew on the next blank page using a sector and dividers. The illustration drawn, he labeled it with a brief statement describing the eclipse. After all the eclipses for the year had been projected, he combined the descriptive statements into a single text to be entered in the space provided for notes for the coming year. This statement, in addition to a listing of the times of the eclipses, would be inserted in the published almanac. Sometimes Banneker was uncertain of his results, so he reconstructed a given eclipse a second time, which would be found elsewhere in the pages of the journal.

In columns following those listing the times of sunrise and sunset, he entered the position of the moon with respect to the constellations for each day of the month, the times of the rising or setting of the moon, and a particularly interesting designation for "Moon's Southing," which indicated the time that the moon crossed the meridian each day. The last column listed the "age" of the moon with relation to the days of the month.

Banneker's ephemeris included the changing length of the days, the times of the rising and setting of bright stars, and other astronomical phenomena. He modeled his monthly tables upon those published in the

Nautical Almanac, and his completed data, with the exception of his times for the principal phase of the moon, were generally in agreement with the British publication. In most instances where discrepancies occurred, the error or difference was seldom more than for one day. However, for the year 1793 Banneker predicted that Jupiter would be stationary on March 15, whereas the *Nautical Almanac* indicated that this occurred on March 17, two days later.

Although the British publication provided the longitude and latitude of the moon and information on the planets, Banneker had to work out the times of moonrise, moonset, sunrise, and sunset for the region in which the almanac would be sold. Likewise, the *Nautical Almanac* listed the times for the eclipses of the sun and moon when they occurred for the latitude and longitude of London, and Banneker had to compute all the data for each eclipse—including time of beginning, total, and end—for the region of his ephemeris.

Banneker's published almanacs included certain phenomena and data not available to him in the *Nautical Almanac,* Moore's *Practical Navigator,* or other published sources. Such data could only be derived from his own mathematical calculations and by use of his instruments, and included the southings, risings, and settings of the bright stars, and the changing length of days. The calculations for the moon were somewhat less accurate than those for the sun, suggesting that Banneker probably used an incorrect eccentricity of the moon's orbit or possibly applied the change of eccentricity incorrectly. The moon's ascension varied by as much as three degrees, plus or minus, from the correct position in some of his calculations for 1794.

The entries in his manuscript journal show that for the first several years, Banneker computed the moon's position by assigning the numbers from zero through eleven to each of the twelve zodiacal constellations. For the table of the moon's longitude for January 1, 1792, for example, the figures were inscribed as 0-16-8, the 0 representing the first of the constellations, Aries, and the other figures the moon's position as sixteen degrees and eight minutes; as each constellation was allocated thirty degrees along the ecliptic, this placed the moon near the center of the constellation. In the published version astronomical symbols replaced the numbers. The manuscript journal reveals that by 1795 Banneker had become sufficiently familiar with the process so that he inscribed the symbols directly instead of the numbers assigned.

During the first years of his astronomical endeavors, Banneker attempted to calculate and project eclipses by several different methods, until he finally selected one that suited him best. He occasionally tested one method against another, as seen in an example he drafted in the pages of his journal for 1792. This was the projection for the solar eclipse of April 3, 1791, which he performed by means of Ferguson's method and termed a "back tryal." His previous calculation for the same eclipse may have been done by using Leadbetter's method. He noted in a short text near the projection that he was performing the test to determine whether "this present method will agree with the former."[3]

After completing the drawing, Banneker recorded a mathematical calculation in the margin as a comparison of his conclusions with those published in Ferguson—and noted that his results differed by thirty-two minutes! He attempted to make a "back tryal" on other occasions as well, in order to compare construction techniques during some of the later years. For example, he projected an eclipse of the moon for May 8, 1762, an event that had taken place twenty-nine years before he calculated his first ephemeris.[4]

As he worked with his texts, the amateur astronomer occasionally inserted an annotated illustration in his journal of a problem he might encounter again and for which he needed some means to help him remember, particularly when the astronomical relationships required for calculations of future eclipses were involved. In preparing his ephemeris for 1793, for example, Banneker drew an unusual diagram of the several possible positions of the axis of the moon's orbit to the axis of the earth that might be encountered when plotting a lunar eclipse during the course of a lunar cycle. Without realizing it, Banneker inscribed the terms incorrectly. Where he should have written "North Ascending" he wrote "North Descending" in the upper part of the drawing, and he also inadvertently exchanged the proper places for "South Ascending" and "South Descending." Since he used the terms correctly in his individual predictions of eclipses in later pages, he must have become aware of his error in the interim.[5]

At first Banneker found the task somewhat confusing and made projections for eclipses that were not always useful to his purpose. After the first few years, however, he had learned to conserve his efforts and thereafter made few constructions for eclipses that were not for the latitude of London or visible in the Baltimore-Washington area in which his almanacs would be sold. He had obviously become sufficiently adept at making an analysis of his initial calculations so that it was no longer necessary to waste his efforts on projections that were not essential for the published almanacs.

In the standard works by Ferguson and Leadbetter, the calendar was reckoned in the Old Style, by means of the Julian calendar, while in Banneker's time the New Style, or Gregorian calendar, had come into use. In the latter system, only those century years which are divisible by the number 400 may be considered as leap years. By the year 1800 a discrepancy of nearly two weeks had developed between the two calendars, a situation that had been anticipated by Ferguson.[6]

The calendrical problems caused Banneker exasperation from time to time, and occasionally he was forced to select one form of calendar over the other. In 1796 he noted:

> According to the Nautical Ephemeris, if the moon changes in the morning of any given day, the succeeding day is the third day of her age because it begins the day at noon, but according to the common way of reckoning, if the moon changes in the morning of any given day, the succeeding day is the second day of her age but if in the afternoon it is allowed to be the first day of her age.[7]

In that year Banneker recorded a decision he had made in reckoning the calendar:

> In 1800 This Year in obtaining the planets places I shall keep by the old Stile with the addition of 12 days according to the method prescribed by Doc[R]. Ferguson, but I had like to forgot the Sun and Moon had only 11 days added to the old Stile.[8]

Banneker occasionally noted how he had derived his results on the blank pages opposite the entries for the monthly calculations. One example is the following:

> To obtain the Latitude of the above places [that is, Baltimore] I took the point where the path of the penumbral center intersected the Earth's axes and the center of the projection. In my compasses from the line of Sines, the Sector being first set to the radius of the disc that subtracts from

the Sun's declination being of contrary names, leaves the Latitude of the place where the Sun is centrally eclipsed and the declination greatest.[9]

Before venturing to make calculations of his own, a competent philomath must have mastered a substantial part of the text by an authoritative writer on the subject, such as Ferguson or Leadbetter. Banneker had both texts available to him. He not only studied them thoroughly but compared the procedures described by each author. It turned out that he had an embarrassment of riches, for he became confused by the apparently conflicting instructions occasionally presented by the two authors for the same type of computation. At first he convinced himself that one or the other must be at fault. After further study he discovered that the results achieved were in fact the same, although their methods differed.

The methods used by Ferguson and Leadbetter to construct the diagrams for the solar eclipse differed substantially. A reader who undertook to construct a diagram for a solar eclipse according to the method described by Ferguson would draw the axis of the earth to the right of the axis of the ecliptic. Leadbetter's instruction for the same eclipse, on the other hand, specified that the earth's axis should be placed to the left of the axis of the ecliptic. Banneker described his confusion resulting from this diversity of procedure in a letter to George Ellicott dated October 13, 1789.

Again and again during the years that followed, he experienced the same problem of encountering apparently conflicting instructions not only from Ferguson and Leadbetter, but from the *Nautical Almanac* as well.[10] This important work had been first conceived by the Reverend Nevil Maskelyne in 1765, and the first issue was published in 1766 for the year 1767. At the same time Maskelyne published his *Tables Requisite to be Used with the Astronomical and Nautical Ephemeris* which served as a handbook to be used with the *Almanac*. The latter included the lunar tables of Tobias Mayer for determining longitude at sea in addition to compilations of other astronomical data useful to sailors. The work was published annually with relatively little change until 1834, when it underwent major revision with the replacement of the apparent time with mean time as the argument of the ephemerides.

The conflict in the methods used by the various authors repeatedly forced Banneker to make a decision in favor of one over the other. Frequently he was uncertain and went on to attempt the computation with the other method prescribed as a check upon his results. He occasionally found apparent discrepancies in the works and noted them in his journal if he could not resolve them immediately. In 1796, for example, he wrote:

> It appears to me that the wisest of men may at certain times be in error, for instance Doctor Ferguson informs that when the Sun is within 12° of either Node at the time of full, that moon will be eclipsed, but I find according to the method of his projecting a Lunar Eclipse there will be none by the above Elements, and yet the Sun is within 11° . 4'6" . 11" of the Moon's Ascending Node — But Moon's being in her Apogee prevents the appearance of this Eclipse.[11]

Ferguson explained this presumed mistake in a footnote added to his published description, in which he indicated that if the full moon is in apogee, the eclipse will not occur if the sun is more than ten degrees and thirty minutes from the node.[12]

    Elsewhere in his journal Banneker made another notation for his own guidance in future calculations, again based on errors he had discovered in the published sources he was using.

> Errors that ought to be corrected in my Astronomical Tables are these 2 Vol Leadbetter, page 204, when ♄ Anomaly is 4^s 30°, the equation 3° 38' 41" which ought to have been 3° 28^s 41". In ♂ equation page 155, the Logarithm of his distance from ☉ ought to have been as thus, in the 2nd place from the Index, instead of 7, that is from the time that his Annomally is 3^s 24° until it is 4^s 0°.

> In ☿ Node Novemb. 30th where 66" read 46".[13]

Another example of the confusion Banneker experienced is to be found in his notations relating to the times of the moon for the year 1795.

> In the year 1795, according to the Nautical Almanac
> the Moon was full that year in the month of
> February . . . . 3 . 12 . 32.
> But according to Doc. Leadbetter the moon
> was full . . . . 3. 9 . 44.
> By the Nautical Almanac New Moon in
> February . . . . 19. 1 . 5.

By Leadbetter's method full Moon
February .... 19. 3 . 16.
1795 By the Nautical Almanac Full Moon
in March........................... 5. 5. 6.
By Leadbetter's method full Moon
in March........................ 5. 2. 44.
1795 By the Nautical Almanac New Moon
in March....................... 20. 11 . 42.
    By Leadbetter's method New Moon
    in March................. 20. 13. 40.[14]

Still another interesting entry is the following:

It is Said and generally believed that when the Moon is changing that she is
in conjunction with the Sun, viz, in the Same Sign, the Same degree and
minute with him, likewise when the Moon is full that she is in direct opposition to the Sun, being in the opposite Sign, degree and minute to him, but
it will not be the case, Calculations tho' made by the best of Calculators —
I have taken all the fulls and new Moons from the Nautical Almanac for the
year 1781 and have given the difference at each time in motion.[15]

Banneker then added a table of differences in the positions of the sun
and moon for the twelve months. This was followed on a later page by a listing, "New and Full moons for the year 1781 by the Nautical Almanac and by
a method prescribed by Mr. Leadbetter"[16] which showed substantial variation in every single example listed for the twelve-month period. Banneker
studied his texts with considerable care, as is evident in some of the notations he made from them. In one instance he noted, "For discovering how
many Luminarian Eclipses may happen in any year, See a Compleat System
of Astronomy Vol. I page 413 precept 14."[17] A note that followed on the same
page, "To find the time the Moons Southing See Doctrine of the Sphere
page 264," related to the same work by Leadbetter.[18]

An almanac-maker was required to commit to memory a considerable amount of information derived from his texts in order to develop the
necessary calculations. Such a question as the direction to which the axis of
the earth would point in relation to the axis of the ecliptic would have to be
kept constantly in mind while preparing a projection for a solar eclipse.
Ferguson noted that "If the Sun's declination had been south, the diurnal
path of London would have been on the upper side of the line VI-K-VI [of

his diagram included] and would have touched the line DL-E in L." No less important were the small subsequent changes required, depending on whether his calculations revealed the sun's declination to be north or south.[19]

Occasionally, when published astronomical tables suggested the possible occurrence of an eclipse, Banneker made a detailed projection just to ascertain whether the prediction was accurate. He did not wish to leave the matter to a hasty judgment. Published tables, regardless of their sources, sometimes provided data so close that a decision unsupported by calculations could not be made, and a projection was required. As an example, he figured that for 1797 there would be a solar eclipse visible at Baltimore on November 18, beginning at 7:44 A.M. Later he made new calculations, found that he was in error, and noted in his journal that "This diagram is corrupt — Moons Lat[itude] thr[ough] mistake is too great North." He then crossed out the description of this eclipse in the appropriate section for that year, reducing the number of eclipses to four. Specific information concerning the incorrect prediction was deleted from the published ephemeris, but an error remained in the text. "ECLIPSES for the year 1797 are five in number, to wit, three of the Sun and two of the Moon, although the listing actually included only four eclipses."[20]

Banneker occasionally encountered similar problems in the ensuing years. He calculated and projected a solar eclipse for April 23, 1800, then came to the conclusion that it would be "invisible at the City of Washington." Later he crossed out this statement and wrote instead that it would be "partly visible in the United States."[21] Still unsatisfied, he reconstructed the diagram for the eclipse, to which he added the note: ". . . by projection it begins some minutes before the true conjunction and Sun sets before the general observation so it is partly visible in the United States."[22]

A similar difficulty arose with the second solar eclipse for that year, which occurred on October 18. He plotted this eclipse three separate times, and after looking in vain for confirmation in Ferguson's *Astronomy* remarked with some dismay, ". . . Ferguson speaking of all visible eclipses at London says nothing of this so that the mistake may be in me."

Ferguson indeed cautioned would-be almanac-makers that theirs was not an exact science. "These suppositions do not exactly agree with the truth," he warned his readers, "and therefore, supposing the Elements given by the Tables to be accurate, yet the times and places of the Eclipse, deduced from its construction, will not answer exactly to what passeth in the Heavens; but may be at least two or three minutes wrong, though done with the greatest care." It may be assumed from this statement that an error of two or three minutes, which was inherent in the construction of an eclipse, could lead to a difference as great as five or six minutes for any single eclipse which was being predicted by two different almanac-makers, even though they employed the identical method. Ferguson compared his tables with those prepared by others and commented, "According to Mayer's *Tables*, this eclipse [April 1764] will be about a quarter of an hour sooner than either these Tables, or Mr. Flamstead's or Dr. Halley's makes it; and Mayer's *Tables* does not make it annular at London."[23] Consequently, if Banneker relied on Mayer's *Tables* instead of employing Ferguson's, he could have introduced an appreciable discrepancy into the time of the eclipse. In general, he preferred to use Ferguson's tables instead of those of Leadbetter or Mayer.

Banneker's problems derived from more than variances in his sources. In calculating the lunar eclipse for February 25, 1793, for example, he plotted it incorrectly. A mistake in the setting of his drafting compass resulted in his placing the moon at mid-eclipse in the wrong portion of the earth's shadow, though he had correctly plotted the moon's path at the beginning and end of the eclipse. Later he recalculated the same eclipse and arrived at a time difference of approximately one minute.

Banneker's great concern for the accuracy of his work is apparent in his notes. Having made calculations for the first five months for his ephemeris for 1795, he came to the realization, perhaps after having studied almanacs produced by others, that his method for calculating the "rising," "setting," and "southing" of the moon was erroneous. In his notes for January of that year, which he evidently extracted from a published source, he observed that, as it related to the meridian of Baltimore, "As the Moons Diurnal motion in Degrees and minutes is to that motion turned into time, So is 2° 44' the Moons obit motion between the Meridian of Greenwich and that of Baltimore to a fourth proportional number which must be added to the moon's apparent Southing to reduce it to the mean time of Southing." With a *note bene*, he added: "The above must be farther examined before I can pass it for the truth."[24] On reexamination he discovered that the statement was correct, and he then rewrote the equation for the longitude of Baltimore in addition to a list of figures to be added to the moon's monthly calculations:

As the Moons Diurnal motion turned into time is to 24 hours so is 5 hours, the difference between the meridian of Greenwich and that of Baltimore, to a fourth proportional number which must be added to the moon Southing on the Meridian of Greenwich to reduce it to meridian of Baltimore

When the Moons Diurnal motion	Min.
is 11°, add to her Southing	9
When 12°, add	10
When 13°, add	11
When 14°, add	12
When 15°, add	13[25]

Banneker then crossed out all of his figures relating to the moon for the first five months, with the statement that they were "Corrupt," and added corrected figures in the margin.

Some of the pages of Banneker's journal reveal other minor errors which led in turn to yet a number of others. An example is his work on the lunar eclipse for July 31, 1795, which he had to calculate twice. In his preliminary eclipse data, he had provided information required for the solar eclipse for July 16 and the lunar eclipse for July 31, and for both of these he had calculated the moon's motion as being "South Ascending." That is to say, at the time of the eclipse the moon would be crossing the ecliptic (the path of the sun) traveling from south to north. This was an obvious error because if the moon is ascending in one node, it must be descending when it reaches the opposite node two weeks later. The first time that he constructed the projection, he plotted the moon's path as "South Ascending" as he had just done for the solar eclipse. Although he had already mathematically determined that the eclipse would be about two and a half digits eclipsed (one digit is one-twelfth the diameter of the orb of the moon or sun), he proceeded to construct a diagram which showed the moon to be about three-fourths eclipsed. When he became aware of his mistake sometime later, he reconstructed the figure and recalculated it with the moon's path now "South Descending" and the eclipse plotted for Greenwich time, the moon shown properly eclipsed about two and a half digits. This was Banneker's first attempt to calculate an eclipse as seen from Greenwich rather than from Baltimore.

It was during this year that Banneker changed his method for presenting information on solar eclipses. Instead of merely stating that the eclipse was visible or invisible from Baltimore, as before, he now provided the precise latitude and longitude of the location from which an eclipse could be most centrally observed. This broadened geographically the scope of his almanacs, greatly enhanced their utility, and led to his production of simultaneous calculations of eclipses not only for the United States but for England as well.

Other mistakes that he made and corrected are recorded in the manuscript journal. For an eclipse that was to occur on January 10, 1796, he indicated variously that the time of occurrence would be 10:15 A.M. and elsewhere on the same diagram 11:15 A.M. Seeing his error, he crossed out the projection, labeled it "corrupt," and then proceeded anew. His new computation indicated that the correct time for eclipse was 1:15 A.M., which later appeared in the published ephemeris.

In addition to his other texts, Banneker also used John Hamilton Moore's *Practical Navigator,* a world-renowned basic and encyclopedic work, containing detailed descriptions of the principal navigational instruments and practices. Moore, a native of Edinburgh and educated in Ireland, established an academy at Brentford in which he taught navigation to young men. Later, with his sons and son-in-law, he opened a shop at Little Tower Hill in London, where he sold charts and instruments and advertised himself as a hydrographer. His *Navigator* went into more than nineteen editions and continued to be published long after his death. It appeared in the United States in an edition revised by Nathaniel Bowditch.[26]

"Wind may be Culled, by the explosion of a vigorous Cannonade," Banneker copied into his journal. "See Hamilton Moore's practical Navigator, p. 241." He copied other things as well. On the first pages of his journal one can read from Moore:

To Find the Moon's Rising

We must Subtract the Sun's Right Ascension from the Moon's Oblique Ascension then Enter the Table Shewing the time of the planets Setting when they have North Declination, and their rising when they have South Declination. Enter this Table I say with the Moon's Declination at the head and your Latitude in the Side Column and in the Common Angle is the hours and minutes that is to be added to the difference of the Sun's and Moon's Ascensions if it be less than Six Hours but Subtracted if more — the Sum or Difference is the time of rising — Practical Navigator.

And on the same page:

> In Calculating the Moon's place, we must observe to add 2° 44" to the
> Longitude that is given by the Table, to compensate for the Difference in
> the Meridians, as the Tables was calculated to the Meridian of Greenwich.

In an adjoining table, he noted that in order to "To find the Mean Changes
of the Moon, See practical Navigator, p. 150."

Comparing Banneker's calculations to the ephemerides for the same
months prepared by his mentor, Major Andrew Ellicott, and published by
John Hayes in 1792 is a helpful means of evaluating his accuracy. Generally,
Ellicott listed several more entries of remarkable events for each month in
his almanacs than did Banneker. A comparison for each of the twelve
months of the two almanacs for 1792 shows that Ellicott included twenty-
two entries each month whereas Banneker had no more than twenty. The
only tables that agreed were the ones for sunrise and sunset. These were
computed from the apparent instead of the mean sun time. The differences
in time of the various phases of the moon for each month varied by as
much as three hours and as little as fifteen minutes. Banneker calculated the
moon's first quarter for April 29, 1792, would occur at 1:37 A.M. Ellicott indicated that it would occur at 4:57 A.M., a difference of three hours and twenty minutes.

The figures presented in the *Nautical Almanac* and those that
appeared in Banneker's ephemeris for that year suggest that Banneker
probably did not have published tables available for comparison, and that
he was forced to compute his own times for the phases of the moon in that
year. In contrast, Ellicott's figures for Baltimore are consistently six hours
and fifty-four minutes later than those published in the British publication,
suggesting that he merely applied a calculated correction factor.

Differences of several minutes also occur in the time given for the
moon's "southing," or its highest elevation for that day, when the moon is
on the observer's meridian. The moon's position among the constellations,
or "moon's place," never varied more than one whole degree between the
two almanacs, which leads one to the conclusion that both philomaths
derived their figures from the same source, which may have been a printed
book of tables. The error of one degree may have resulted from the round-
ing off of numbers.

In Banneker's almanac the positions of the planets frequently differ by as much as one and two degrees from those noted in the *Nautical Almanac*. He may have derived his data from other tables, inasmuch as the planets come to a stationary point at the same time but not at exactly the same place. The same error occurred in the tables for the moon's position, in which the error could have become greater.

A variation of several minutes occurred in virtually every other astronomical entry included in the two series of almanacs. For instance, although Banneker and Ellicott both indicated that winter and summer would begin on the twentieth day of the appropriate month of that year, they differed by one day for the beginning of spring and autumn. Banneker indicated that spring would begin on March 20 and autumn would commence on September 23, while Ellicott listed March 19 as the beginning of spring and September 22 as the first day of fall. Ellicott indicated that Jupiter would be 90 degrees from the sun on July 14; Banneker indicated that it would occur on July 16. There were numerous other disparities in the two ephemerides. Banneker stated that the bright star Arcturus would be on the meridian on April 17 at the twelfth hour and twenty-third minute, while Ellicott listed the same time but on April 16. Banneker noted the hour 8:48 P.M. as the time of the rising of the bright star Sirius on December 4, while Ellicott gave the time as 8:42 P.M. on the same day.

A major discrepancy in the times for the solar eclipse for March 22 exists in the calculations for the almanacs for 1792. Banneker calculated that it would begin at 1:22 P.M., twenty-nine minutes later than predicted by Ellicott. Banneker went on to calculate that some of the other phases of the eclipse would lag behind Ellicott's prediction by as much as thirty-two minutes. Similar comparisons can be made with the calculations published by William Waring in his "Poor Will's Almanac" for the same year:

	BANNEKER	ELLICOTT	WARING
Beginning time	1:22 P.M.	0:54 P.M.	1:01 P.M.
Greatest eclipse	2:15	1:51	1:58
End	3:15	2:43	2:49

The reason for identifying Banneker's mistakes in this work is not to demonstrate that he was a poor mathematician or to compare his work unfavorably with that of other astronomers of his day who also produced ephemerides for almanacs. Instead, these errors demonstrate the laborious process by which he was forced to teach himself, without guidance from

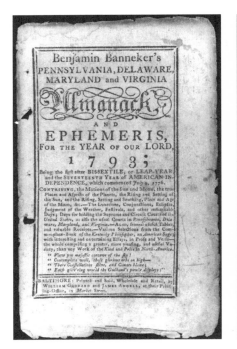

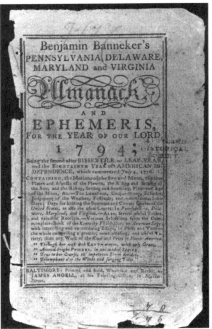

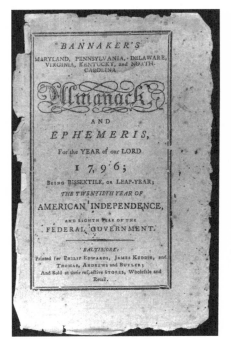

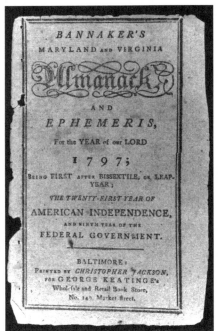

Covers or title pages of Banneker's almanacs for the years 1793, 1794, 1796, 1797. *Maryland Historical Society.*

others—actually by trial and error. Again and again Banneker must have faltered in his work, wondering if he had assumed a project beyond his capabilities. These pages prove beyond doubt that by his method of self-instruction he emerged as a most competent mathematician and amateur astronomer and that his published results were of equal caliber with those of most of his contemporaries.

There is no way to know what basis Banneker used to make weather predictions, since none of his working notes or clues relating to them have survived. Nor has a survey of the literature of the almanac-makers of England and America revealed standard formulae for making such prognostications, although it has been presumed that many were based on astrological sources. According to the preface of a work published in England at the end of the eighteenth century:

> Many ingenious gentlemen in different and distant places, at home and abroad, have kept journals of the weather, air and its temperature, and their monthly and yearly quantities of rain; several abstracts of all which I have perused and computed at monthly mediums between the highest and lowest of mercury, or spirits in their tubes, or rain in its receiver; but these being fitter for speculation and amusement than any other useful purpose yet known, though if collected, compared and improved, might afford some not contemptible hints, therefore such journals should be deposited in some public museums where the curious might have access to them.[27]

Such a source may indeed have served Banneker for making his forecasts; having been a farmer most of his life, long before he engaged in making astronomical observations of his own, he would have purchased or consulted an almanac each year to guide him in his farming and tobacco planting schedules, as was then the custom. If he had not been able to purchase them previously, he would have found almanacs available for sale after the Ellicott & Company store had been established. Because of the dearth of available reading matter, he undoubtedly followed common practice and carefully preserved his copies of old almanacs through the years and consulted them from time to time for the literary content.

When he undertook to produce his own almanacs, he may have referred to this collection once more and made a comparative study of the weather predictions for each day of the year. If, for example, he discovered that for eight of twelve years a cold spell of several days had been predicted for the second week of January, or rain for the fourth of July, it was reasonably safe, he may have assumed, that the same weather conditions would prevail on those dates in the following year. Certainly such predictions would have been quite as legitimate as those produced by other almanacmakers during and before his own time.

Prior to the mid-nineteenth century, not only were there no methods, instruments, or institutions for weather forecasting, there was little actual knowledge of the laws that governed the weather. An accumulation of miscellaneous information on specific aspects of the subject existed, however. It was known, for instance, that northerly winds in the Northern Hemisphere were ordinarily attended by low temperatures and southerly winds were usually followed by rising temperatures, and that in the middle latitudes snow or rain followed easterly winds, and that clearing or fair weather followed westerly winds. Observations of clouds produced the information that specific cloud formations and movements were usually indications of certain types of weather, and that changes of atmospheric moisture could be used to predict anticipated weather changes. But no compilations of weather observations were available in published form in the eighteenth century in the United States.

Several records of the climate in the Chesapeake region had been made and published in England, though it is doubtful that Banneker had access to them, and if he did they probably would not have served any useful purpose in the day-to-day compilation of forecasts required for his almanacs. The earliest account of weather on the American continent was in fact that recorded by Captain John Smith and published in his *History of Virginia* early in the seventeenth century. He described the climate of the Chesapeake Bay area as reported by the first English settlers during the winters of 1606 and 1607.[28] Similar records were maintained by John Campanius from 1644 through 1645 at Wilmington and Philadelphia and reported early in the eighteenth century by his grandson, Thomas Campanius Holm.[29] In 1667, Thomas Glover reported on storms in Virginia and the lower Chesapeake Bay.[30] His work was followed by a much more detailed account of observations made in about 1685 by the English botanist John Clayton and reported to the Royal Society. This account of the climate around Jamestown and the lower Potomac region was the first scientific report that included details of weather conditions.[31]

Eighteenth-century published records of weather phenomena were slightly more useful. Benjamin Franklin made observations in 1747 relating to northeast storms, as did Lewis Evans in his *Map of Pensilvania, New Jersey, New York and the three Delaware Counties,* published in 1749. The map included "Several Useful Remarks in Physicks & Commerce" which were probably derived from Franklin's observations.[32]

Undoubtedly the most useful records of weather were those maintained in the field notes and journals of such professional surveyors as Charles Mason, Jeremiah Dixon, David Rittenhouse, and Andrew Ellicott. These were not published or made available to almanac-makers except in those instances where the surveyors were themselves almanac-makers, such as Rittenhouse and Ellicott. Also of interest were the weather observations made by Dr. Richard Brooke between 1753 and 1757, probably the first made by means of meteorological instruments. Dr. Brooke was born near Nottingham in Prince George's County, and lived at Brookfield, the family estate, where presumably he made his observations. These studies were communicated to the Royal Society and published in its *Transactions* over a period of several years. They might have been available to Banneker but it is doubtful whether he used them.[33]

Another method Banneker could have used, and one that almost certainly he would have attempted, was the traditional belief that the moon was the weather breeder, and that prognostications could be made from astronomical analysis of the moon's positions. Although the concept of lunar control of weather has been discarded in modern times, it prevailed in the eighteenth century. The concept is simply stated. The appearance of the moon to a terrestrial observer is determined by its relative position to the sun in relation to the earth. As the moon progresses from a new moon to a full moon, the orb gradually develops in appearance from a slim crescent to a full circle, and then reduces gradually from a full circle back to a slim crescent. It is visible because it reflects the light of the sun back to the earth. The time of day in which it can be seen changes, in accordance with the moon's progress in its monthly journey around the earth.

Numerous traditions concerning the moon and the weather have developed over the centuries, the most prevalent of which relate to the positions of the "horns" or cusps of the new moon. When the moon is in such a position that an invisible line connecting the cusps is nearly horizontal, it is considered to be a "wet moon," presaging rainy weather. When such a line is nearly vertical, it predicts a "dry moon" and dry weather. Doubtless these and other traditions arose from a natural and frequent coincidence between selected moon phases and specific weather changes. For instance, the moon enters a new phase every seventh day, and in the middle latitudes the weather normally changes once or twice within the same period. This led to many coincidences and formed the basis for a system of prediction in which only the agreements are considered and the disagreements are ignored.

This system could be further refined by consideration of the time of day that the moon enters into any one of its four phases. Presuming that the moon entered a new phase between 12 midnight and 2 A.M., it indicated fair weather if it occurred during the summer, and presaged fair weather with hard frost if it occurred in winter. If the moon entered a new phase between 12 noon and 2 P.M. in summer, it indicated rain; or rain and snow in winter. Such a system was developed and produced in tabular form by John Gruber in *The Hagerstown Almanac.* Gruber, of Lancaster County, Pennsylvania, worked as an apprentice with Carl Cist in Philadelphia and in 1795 moved to Hagerstown, where he established several newspapers, all of them short-lived. He published several books and then in 1797 printed the first issue of *Neuer Hagerstauner Kalendar,* an almanac in the German language, which he continued to publish for a quarter of a century. In 1822 he added an English edition. Gruber published reference tables for all the hours to indicate the affinities of the sun and moon, a feature begun in the almanac published in 1797 and continuing to the present. The tables were said to have been compiled by Friedrich Wilhelm Herschel (1738–1822), although the astronomer later repudiated them. The system in fact was developed by Gruber's assistant, Charles Flack, for making the annual weather prognostications for *The Hagerstown Almanac.*

Other considerations have been applied in predicting weather. Generally a full moon is associated with clear and cold weather, perhaps because it is more noticeable when the skies are clear, and the nights are generally cooler when there are no clouds due to the more rapid radiation of the earth's heat. Furthermore, in winter the moon's path, which is inclined to the ecliptic, is elevated higher above the southern horizon and therefore to the observer is rising earlier and setting later than in other seasons.[34]

Long-term weather forecasts were a traditional component of the almanacs in the American colonies. They were first instituted by John

Tulley (ca. 1639–1701) in the almanacs he produced late in the seventeenth century. Tulley was a teacher of astronomy and navigation and had reasonably good training in these subjects for his time. His prognostications were deliberately vague, hardly useful by modern standards. As an example, he advised in his forecast that during the week of December 26–31, 1692, there would be "Perhaps more wet weather, after which cold winds and frosty weather may conclude the year." In general, however, Tulley's astrological and meteorological prognostications were considered to be extremely skillful in comparison with the absurd predictions generally found in English almanacs of his time. His forecasts became such a successful feature of his almanacs that his method was adopted by his successors and became standard procedure. Owners of almanacs frequently interleaved the pages and added a record of events for the year, including daily weather reports, a record of political and national events, and family data. These written comments may have been noted and assimilated by other almanac-makers for future reference.

In planetary meteorology as applied by long-range weather forecasters, the moon was given the primary responsibility for weather changes. A nineteen-year lunar cycle, during which the new and full moons were repeated on corresponding days of the month, was believed to form the basis of the rotations of certain types of weather. The daily change of the moon's aspect was correlated with the daily changing weather, and the weekly change of the lunar phases was also related to the prevalence of storms.

The weather and seasonal conditions, as well as the results of human endeavors, have been foretold from ancient times from the relative positions of the planets, and the practice of astrology for this purpose was continued by almanac-makers into the nineteenth century.[35]

Although it may not be related to Banneker's weather forecasts, an intriguing entry in Banneker's journal describes an unusual relationship between the moon and the weather he observed and recorded on March 8, 1796:

A Chronological Observation

1796 March 8 Snow Moon in ♓ her Latitude South
March 14th Thunder and rain Moon in ♊ her Lat. South
16th High wind ☽ in d°————— [36]

In this notation Banneker seemed to have explored the possible existence of yet another connection between the moon and the weather,
depending on whether the moon's latitude was north or south of the ecliptic. No system presently known can be identified as the one Banneker used
for his weather prognostications, but it is certain that he did not use the
table employed by Gruber. A comparison of a compilation of the weather
conditions described in his almanacs for a period of several years with the
phases of the moon indicates that the phases did not provide a basis for the
forecasts. The same is true of Ellicott's almanac for 1792, in which there is
no correlation between the prognostications and the moon's phases. Nor
does there appear to be any similarity between the weather data shown in
the almanacs of Ellicott and Banneker for the same year, 1792.

Furthermore, Banneker's manuscript and published prognostications
are not the same in any of the months for the years 1792 through 1795. This
suggests that he attempted to develop his own system of forecasting as an
experiment but that his printers had a prepared system or systems of their
own which they preferred.

The basis of another system was that the occurrence of certain weather phenomena on particular days indicated the weather for specific subsequent days. A common saying, for instance, is that if it rains on the first
Sunday of a month, it will rain on every Sunday of that month. The six-day
or seven-day period of recurring weather is usually based on the supposed
influence of the moon.

A great body of proverbs has been created over the centuries providing formulas for forecasting weather based on the behavior of clouds,
winds, temperature, and humidity. Often there is some basis for such conclusions, but in general they are not reliable. Yet another ancient system of
prediction was derived from the supposed effect of sun spots upon meteorological conditions.[37]

Observations of the habits and conditions of animals, birds, and
plants, particularly undomesticated animals, have traditionally been used
as another basis. Several of the systems described were embodied in an
interesting compilation of "Prognosticks of the Weather" included by the
Adams brothers in their issue of Banneker's Almanac for 1795:

> Those who look after cattle observe when they go together in troops or
> herds; or whether the swine grub the earth with their heads turned to the

north; and if they find it so, let them take care to provide store of fuel, for it generally proves a hard and long winter.

Take notice of the 24th of November, and as the day is, so the winter is like to prove; and as you find the 25th of the same month, so will the month of January be.

You may easily know what sort of a winter it will be, by observing the last days of the moon between November and December; for as they prove, so will the winter.

And to know what sort of a summer you will have, those who are nice observers of the seasons say, that the three last days of the moon between April and May, are infallible presages how it is like to prove. A great plenty of acorns are a certain presage of a severe winter.[38]

It had been scientifically established that the moon has no significant effect on the weather, but until a system of systematic weather records could be compiled, and means for observing weather throughout the world could be established, the almanac provided the only source of information. The predictions were cast in flexible language, safeguarded by words most frequently encountered, including "moderate," "changeable," "variable," and "unsettled," which left room for much variation from the prediction.

In 1830 and in fact earlier, skeptics who made a study of the weather forecasts in almanacs concluded that one correct guess in every ten was a reasonably good record for the almanac-maker. The bits of evidence that have survived seem to support the conviction that in general almanac-makers merely guessed the daily weather conditions for the forthcoming year, with no other basis except possibly reference to guesses made during the previous year by other almanac-makers. As already suggested, some almanac-makers used data from previous almanacs for predicting weather conditions.

Among the most desirable and useful features of Banneker's almanacs was a tide table for the Chesapeake Bay, which made the almanac particularly useful for river pilots, fishermen, and others who lived and made their living on the water. The form and content of the tide table were identical in the first three issues of Banneker's almanacs. It listed times for high water or high tide at Cape Charles, Point Lookout, Annapolis, and Baltimore. Why his competitors ignored this feature is a mystery, for it was simple enough to calculate: the high tide at Annapolis was two hours later than at Point Lookout, and at Baltimore and Head-of-the-Bay the high tide was five hours later than at Point Lookout. The almanac cautioned that:

The times of High-Water in Chesapeake-Bay are very uncertain, and
depend much upon the circumstances — the distance between Cape-
Charles and Cape-Henry being small, in comparison to the extent of the
Bay, and therefore not capable of admitting a sufficiency of water during
the time of flood at Cape-Charles, to make any considerable tide toward
the Head of the Bay, without being assisted by a smart S.S.E. wind; and in
time of a N.N.E. wind, the tides from Patuxent, upwards, will be very small.

The tide table was simplified considerably in Banneker's almanacs for
1795 and 1796, which also provided data for determining tides in ports as far
north as Halifax and Boston. It was entitled *"Rule to find the Time of HIGH
WATER at the following Places"* and consisted simply of an additive for each
of the places listed to be combined with the day of the moon's age.

Banneker changed the format once again in 1796 and utilized that
same form in the following and last issue of the series. This was entitled
*"TABLE Shewing how much should be added to, or subtracted, from the
moon's southing, for the time of high water at the several places following; this
mark * directing to add and this symbol + to subtract."* Twenty-five ports
ranging as far north as Quebec and Plymouth were listed alphabetically,
from Albany to Wilmington.

Banneker himself, and not his printer, compiled the tide tables for his
almanac. The data were simple to acquire, and no mathematical achievement was involved. The changing of the tides had been associated with the
motions of the moon for centuries; the earliest surviving tide tables were
compiled in the thirteenth century by the monks of St. Albans in England.
Once the time of the highest tide or spring tide was known at a particular
point at the age of the full and new moon, it was a simple matter to derive
a table for each day of the month at the same place. Banneker applied the
standard daily retardation of forty-eight minutes or 4/5 of an hour. This
determination of the highest tide waters or spring tides on the days of the
full and new moon were known as "the establishment of the port" and was
generally marked on the charts for the port in question.[39]

As Banneker undoubtedly knew from having spent his life on the
Patapsco River, the tides of Chesapeake Bay were considerably less than
those at other points along the Atlantic coast. They were relatively small in
the bay, and considerably affected by wind direction. The tides were particularly high with a southerly wind. As the tidal current began to flood, water
flowed into the bay through the opening between the Virginia Capes. Only

a small amount of water passed these points before the sea tide began its ebb because the opening between the capes was relatively small in proportion to the size of the bay itself. As the sea tide began its flood, the water spread itself over the wide span of the bay and its many rivers, so that the flood was dispersed and the rise of the tide within the bay area was relatively small. The same was true of the ebbing tide. As the waters of the bay slowly receded through the opening between the capes, the sea tide was again rising so that there was comparatively little change.

Tidal waters were swept up into the river openings by strong tidal currents, until they reached their fall lines. A river's width generally decreased in proportion to the distance from its mouth, which had the effect of making the tide change at the fall line higher than that at the mouth. Rivers emptying into the Chesapeake also had the curious characteristic of half tides, which ran opposite the main current on either side. Some of them were relatively strong and provided an advantage to pilots when the channel current was adverse.

Banneker occasionally recorded in the pages of his manuscript journal unusual atmospheric phenomena he had observed. On the very first page, under the date of December 23, 1790, he noted: "About 3 o'clock, A.M. I heard a Sound and felt the Shock like unto heavy thunder. I went out but could not observe any Cloud about the Horizon. I therefore Conclude it must be a great Earth Quake in some part of the Globe."[40] Such notations were few and interspersed apparently at random throughout the journal, frequently inserted between mathematical calculations. Two years later he recorded another observation. "May the 4th 1792. In a Squall from the N.W. I observed the Lower regions of the Clouds to move Swiftly before the wind, and the upper region Slowly against it."[41] Six years later, on a November evening in 1798, Banneker looked skyward and found "a bur or some Condensed particles of the Atmosphere, of divers colours gather round the moon, and that which was first and nearest to her center appeared white, the Second of an orange, the third blue, and the fourth red, nearly coloured like unto the rain bow, this small circle was in breadth, about seven times the moons apparent Diameter."[42] Even in his later years the weather continued to interest him.

> 1803, Februr 2nd in the morning part of the day, there arose a very dark Cloud, followed by Snow and haile a flash of lightning and loud thunder

crack, and then the Storm abated untill after noon, when another cloud arose the Same point, viz, Northwest, with a beautiful Shower of Snow, but what beautyfyed the Snow was the brightness of the Sun, which was near Setting at the time. I looked for the rain bow or rather Snow bow, but I think the snow was of too dense a nature to exhibit the representation of the bow in the Cloud.

N.B. The above was followed by very cold weather a few days.[43]

Banneker also recorded in his journal several observations relating to the meridian of Baltimore, to which he added a carefully drawn projection for a solar eclipse, with its description.[44] He then noted the following reference to the Federal Territory in his manuscript journal:

1793 January the first day at noon, we find the Sun's Longitude at the Meridian of Greenwich to be 9-11° 39' and as his mean motion is 59' 8", and the Difference between the Meridian of Greenwich and that of the Federal District is about 5 hours west Longitude, we must say by Trigonometry As 24 hours in time is to 59' 8" motion, so is 5 hours time to 12-7/24ths minutes motion which must be added to the Greenwich Longitude, to make it right at the Federal District.[45]

From data in his published almanacs, it is evident that Banneker made his observations from a point at latitude 39° 30' north and a longitude of 4 hrs. 59 minutes west. In addition to recording the ephemerides for each of the years that he calculated them, the pages of Banneker's journal served as the repository for numerous miscellaneous exercises in mathematics and astronomy. Among these was an unfinished table of "The days of year returned from the beginning of January" which was completed only through the month of July, and may have been compiled in 1802.[46] Of interest, too, is a table of the moon's longitude and anomaly compiled for the years 1806 through 1820. This table, which appears on a separate sheet of paper folded four times and bearing Banneker's signature in pencil at the top, was probably one of the last compilations he undertook before his death.

The journal also provides ample evidence that Banneker's ability to pursue his astronomical endeavors diminished in his final years. The last ephemeris for which he completed and entered all the required calculations was for 1800. He managed to finish the outlines of the ephemerides for the next two years, 1801 and 1802. He completed all the calculations and entered them for the twelve months of 1801 but did not add the important days or the weather prognostications for that year. In 1802 he successfully calculated all the eclipses as well as the times for sunrise and sunset and moonrise and moonset, and he entered a few of the remarkable days in the outline. Presumably he was unable to complete the remaining data.

In 1987, Dr. Charles W. Koontz compared the astronomical calculations in Banneker's almanacs with ephemerides of almanacs for the same periods compiled by Andrew Ellicott, M. K. Goddard, and William Waring, whose almanacs were popular in the region, and other contemporary almanac-makers. The results were compiled in an unpublished manuscript entitled, *A Comparison of Benjamin Banneker's Astronomical Data with Other 18th Century Almanacs.* In "A Table of Gross Errors" Koontz made the following comparison:

Author	Years	Calculation Errors	Typographical Errors	Totals
Goddard	1	1	0	1
Ellicott	7	4	4	8
Banneker	6	1	4	5

He reported:

An error analysis of the astronomical data in Benjamin Banneker's published almanacs (1792–1797) shows that his data compared very favorably with that published by his contemporaries. There was no significant difference (at the .05 level) between Banneker's star data and that of Andrew Elicott or that published by M. K. Goddard. While his planetary data were somewhat less accurate that either Ellicott's or Goddard's, it was still quite usable to the ordinary purchaser of an almanac.

Considering the length and complexity of the calculations involved in determining the the rising and setting of certain stars and planets and realizing this was only a small segment of the mathematics required for one year's almanac, one can only have the greatest respect for this self-taught man of science.[47]

Banneker's manuscript journal and his commonplace book are unique records of an eighteenth-century almanac-maker. Their contents give us invaluable information about his way of life and about events of major and minor importance. We have in them a clear exposition of the method by which almanacs were calculated during this period of American scientific history. In Banneker's work we can follow his progress from the beginning of his self-instruction, through his computations, to the published product, year after year, for the entire period of his scientific involvement. Few, if indeed any, similar sources, in which the entire evolution of a philomath can be traced, have survived.

IX

THE FINAL YEARS

Presumption should never make us neglect that which
appears easy to us, nor despair make us lose courage at the
sight of difficulties.

Banneker's Almanac for 1794

HE LAST DECADE and a half of Banneker's life, from the time he calculated his first ephemeris, saw a marked change. Following the
death of his mother some years earlier, he had become accustomed
to living alone on his farm. Two of his sisters, who lived with their own families a short distance away, visited him regularly and took turns attending to
his needs. He generally prepared his own meals, but his sisters assisted with
the laundry and the other household chores his mother had performed.

With each advancing year, Banneker's health deteriorated, and it
became increasingly difficult for him to pursue his accustomed activities as
much as he wished. He discontinued tobacco growing with a sense of great
relief and limited his labors to the cultivation of a garden, to his beekeeping, and to the maintenance of his fruit orchard, all chores of which he was
fond. The almanacs provided a modest source of income that enabled him
to purchase whatever he needed and could not produce on his land, but his
requirements were few. He reorganized his life on this new modest scale
and managed an orderly daily existence.

Banneker remained a bachelor all his life. No evidence exists of a love
interest, which may be explained by the solitary nature of his life. As a
young man, he lived and worked on the farm with his parents and his sisters. The only others with whom he associated were his grandmother and
his aunts and their families. The peculiar circumstances of his family would
have separated them from their neighbors, and Banneker never spoke of

close friends in his childhood or adult life. His father's death, when Banneker was twenty-eight—an age when he would have been seeking a wife—left him with the full responsibility for the care of his mother and the farm, all of which he assumed with his accustomed seriousness. By then his sisters had already married and left the farm one by one. Later, his mother developed an independent source of income from sales of farm produce and other staples to Ellicott's Lower Mills.

Several factors may have influenced his decision to remain single. His grandmother and mother had shown themselves to be women of considerable presence, perhaps dominating, and Banneker seemed to have always lived within the shadow of matriarchal supervision. His increasingly casual existence, as well as his reported weakness for liquor, undoubtedly became deterrents to thoughts of having a family of his own. His consuming interest in reading and the pursuit of mathematical studies, and his inclination to jealously preserve the little leisure he had for pursuing them, discouraged matrimony at an advanced age.

As he grew older, his reliance upon the Bible and its teachings as a guide to daily living made itself more and more manifest, and perhaps in itself was a deterrent to marriage. Among the few pieces published in his first almanac without quotation marks to indicate that it came from another source, was a short essay, perhaps of his own composition, containing the passage: "Assemble all the evils which poverty, disease, or violence can inflict, and their stings will be found, by far, less pungent than those which guilty passions dart into the heart."[1] Discovering the whole new field of astronomy had been like the beginning of a new life for Benjamin. He regretted that the opportunity had come so late, but now that he had it in hand he was determined to make the most of it.

It was at this point in his career that he paused to take stock of himself and his prospects for the future. He was sixty years of age when the first almanac was finally published; he lived alone, with no responsibilities to anyone or anything other than himself.[2] His mother, Mary Banneker, had made her home with him until her death, which occurred some time after July 1775. Curiously enough, the tax list for 1773 listed Banneker as the single adult on his property, yet there is no evidence that his mother was living elsewhere at the time. Possibly she had become ill and was being cared for at the home of one of her daughters during her final illness.[3] Banneker's nephews and nieces who lived nearby had reached adulthood, and he felt reasonably reassured that their families were in comfortable circumstances. It is probable that Banneker's sisters had inherited shares in Molly Banneky's farm and shared the acreage at Timber Point as well, or that their husbands pursued some sort of trade in the neighborhood.

A dedicated farmer all his life, he was distressed at first to see his land lie fallow and unused. When some of his neighbors asked to use it, he divided part of his acreage into several small holdings and rented to them. This promising arrangement proved to be less than successful. He repeatedly encountered problems collecting the rents. Occasionally he forgot the time for collections, and at other times his tenants were unable or unwilling to pay the small amounts due. Often they deliberately quarrelled with him to avoid payment. This unpleasantness was disturbing and distracting, for he had lived a lifetime of cooperative endeavor, always at peace with everyone he knew, and he concluded that it was too late in life to suffer these new annoyances. If he insisted on payment, which he did infrequently, his tenants annoyed or threatened him so that he was not inclined to return to collect from them. To add insult to injury, they sometimes prevailed upon him to lend them small sums, then refused to repay him.

The unpleasant incidents increased. On December 18, 1790, Banneker noted on the first page of his manuscript journal, "————— ————— informed me that ————— Stole my horse and Great Coat, and that the said ————— intended to murder me when opportunity presented, and further gave me Caution to let no person in my house after Dark."[4] Some time after writing these words, he carefully went over them and obliterated the names of the individuals. Finally, he crossed out the entire entry, concerned that its discovery might bring further trouble.

His solitude was periodically jarred by further attempts to annoy him. On August 27, 1797, he wrote in his journal, "Standing by my door, I heard the discharge of a gun, and in 4 or 5 Seconds of time after the discharge, the Small Shot came rattling about me, one or two of which Struck the house." Always of a scientifically inquiring mind he added, "which plainly demonstrates that the Velocity of Sound as [sic] much greater than that of a Cannon-Bullet."[5] He did not indicate whether this was another attempt to annoy him or whether the shots that flew about his house might have come from a careless hunter. The persecution, however, did not cease. Less than a year later, on April 29, 1798, he recorded: "Came two Black men with a gun in my inclose and discharged it a few perches from door, I being very unwell

I could not persue them to find out who they were."[6] A few years later he wrote: "On the night of the 27th November 1802 my house was violent broke open and Several articles taken out."[7]

These distressing incidents may have originated from any one of several sources. There were, of course, the disgruntled tenants who resented his insistence on collecting their rent. Also, the publication of his almanacs had rendered him a person of more than local distinction, and there were those who assumed that his fame also had brought him fortune. Some suspected that probably he had money hidden away in his log house. He was held in high esteem not only by his neighbors and friends at Ellicott's Lower Mills, but also by travelers who had heard of him and wished to meet this unusual man of achievement. As a consequence, there may have been those of both races who were envious and resentful of his accomplishments and fame. Banneker, who had devoted a lifetime to living according to the best Christian principles, was made uneasy again and again because of these disturbances during his final years.

Annoyances came from all directions. The orchard adjacent to his house, which he loved and maintained with such tender care, was well known and admired in the neighborhood. The fruit trees became a favored target of youngsters who cherished his pears and cherries. As the local population grew, Banneker's orchard increasingly became the target of boys of varying ages. Several would call at his door and with utmost respect and politeness, and the full appearance of innocence, ask permission to pick some of the fruit. Banneker always graciously agreed before returning to the books and papers on his table. Later, the boys would return and quietly strip the trees bare. He frequently scolded them and even attempted to negotiate with them. If they would leave him half of his crop, he suggested, they could take all the rest, but this had no effect. To a friend who called upon him once during the summer, he apologized that he had no fruit to offer, adding: "I have no influence with the rising generation. All my arguments have failed to induce them to set bounds to their wants."[8]

As routine matters again and again interrupted his work, Banneker longed more than ever for solitude so that he could pursue his studies undisturbed. He wasted many hours puzzling over how this could be achieved and finally concluded that his problems derived chiefly from his only valuable possession—his land. Perhaps if he disposed of it his troubles would disappear. Since his father's death in 1759, he had become the sole owner of more than a hundred acres. The prospect of having to sell any of it saddened him, as he recalled his parents' fierce joy at having acquired the property and their strenuous work developing the farm. Benjamin recalled the loving care with which his father had planted and nurtured the orchard, erected the tobacco sheds, and built his log house. He had been a small six-year-old boy when the land was purchased, but he could bring back to mind the many walks he had taken with his father during leisure hours on Sunday afternoons, during which Robert Banneky revealed his pride of possession. Again and again he had reminded young Benjamin that it was the land that made the difference between independence and slavery. Benjamin had been so impressed by his father's words, that he made every effort during the major part of his life to develop and improve what his father had created.

Now came the time to resolve his dilemma. Should he sell the land or convey it by deed to his nephews and nieces? It was a hard decision, and he considered it long and seriously before making up his mind. Some years earlier, in 1781, he had given thought to the nature of his obligations to his sisters and their families in the event of his own demise, and particularly his obligations to his favored young nephew, Greenbury Morten.

Young Morten had reached manhood and was employed as a cooper by Ellicott & Company producing barrels for storing and transporting flour at the Lower Mills. His account with the Ellicott store noted that in addition to cooperage he earned part of his income as a wage laborer occasionally clearing land for the proprietors. He had demonstrated a determination to develop a farm of his own, and accordingly Banneker had sold him a tract of twenty acres for twenty-five pounds in common currency. The price was modest and designed to meet Greenbury's circumstances. It gave Banneker pleasure to help assure his future.[9]

But all did not continue to go well between uncle and nephew. Within two years of having obtained a bond from his uncle for the purchase of a piece of Banneker's land, Greenbury had fallen into arrears in his payments, and the invariably kindly Banneker must have had other cause as well to insert an advertisement in the pages of the *Maryland Journal* on July 19, 1783:

> Whereas Greenbury Morten obtained a Bond of me, bearing date November 19, 1781 for the Conveyance of a lot or parcel of Land, lying in the above County, but as the said Morten has not complied with his agree-

ment, this may serve to forewarn any person or persons of taking an assignment of the said bond, as I am determined not to convey the land until he makes reasonable satisfaction.[10]

Whether Greenbury subsequently fulfilled his obligation to his uncle is not known. Several years after Banneker's death, Greenbury came to public attention again in a somewhat unusual manner. Although the Constitution of 1776 had granted the right of suffrage to all freemen of Maryland if they owned a certain amount of property, a law enacted in 1783 specified that "no colored person freed thereafter, nor the issue of such, should be allowed to vote, or to hold any office, or to give evidence against any white, or to enjoy any other rights of a freeman than the possession of property and redress at law or equity for injury to person or property."

An amendment to the Constitution was adopted in 1810 which further limited the right of suffrage to white men. Greenbury Morten had voted regularly and was not aware of the new law. When he reported to the polls in Baltimore County in that year, his vote was rejected. He became greatly incensed, and "in a state of excitement took his stand upon a doorstep, and was immediately surrounded by the crowd, whom he addressed in a strain of passionate and prophetic eloquence which bore all hearts and minds with him." He warned them that the new law was a step backward from the standard which their fathers had raised in the Declaration, and which they had hoped would be realized in universal freedom; that that step, unless retraced, would end in bitter and remorseless revolutions. The crowd was held in breathless attention, and none were found to favor the new law.[11]

Banneker had given careful consideration also to the other children of his sisters and finally reached a conclusion. Any attempt to partition the farm among them would serve no purpose; the portions would be inadequate due to the quality and nature of the land. Presumably none of the other nephews, the number and identity of whom are not presently known, was in a position to purchase the land as Morten had done. If Banneker conveyed his land to several of them, such a decision might engender envy and ill feeling in his immediate family.

In addition to the full one hundred acres of the original farm called "Stout," Banneker owned another tract of approximately ten acres adjoining the main farm. This may have been his share of Timber Poynt or his mother's share of Molly Welsh's land. No records of its acquisition can be found, and it is not mentioned as a separate parcel, but its existence came to light in compiling a total of the land sold by Banneker during the next decade.

It was at this time, probably about 1790, that he divided his land. He set aside certain portions that he planned to sell individually in the next few years as needed and kept intact the largest segment consisting of seventy-two acres. The Ellicott brothers had expressed an interest in acquiring this tract, since it would supplement their own holdings in the area, and when Banneker broached the subject again they suggested that he sell them the land and retain life residence on the premises. They offered him £180 for the land, or £2-1/2 per acre. This seemed to be a practical solution, to which he agreed. An arrangement appears to have been made that the sum was to be paid to him in annual increments to insure that Banneker would not invest the money foolishly and that he would be assured of having a constant income. Banneker could not resist the opportunity to apply his mathematical skills to such an intriguing arrangement, and he set about to calculate his life expectancy, and to determine the amounts of the annual payments accordingly. The results of his computations were recorded as part of his agreement with the Ellicott family. "I believe I shall live fifteen years, and consider my land worth £180 Maryland Currency; by receiving £12 a year, for fifteen years I shall in the contemplated time, receive its full value; if on the contrary I die before that day, you will be at liberty to take possession."[12]

The sale was made by verbal arrangement, and not formalized with a deed until October 23, 1799. There is some confusion about the date of the transaction, because Tyson as well as Latrobe stated that for once in his career Banneker erred, and that he lived beyond the period that he had estimated. Banneker frequently expressed concern over his error, but the Ellicott firm continued to pay his annuity without question, dismissing his worry with the reassurance that in the interim his land had increased in value and that his continued use of it was no burden to them. (See Document 51)

The sale of his land to Ellicott & Company provided Banneker with security for the rest of his days, but there still remained five small parcels of land, which he eventually sold. The income provided him with those extra luxuries that he could not otherwise enjoy, such as books and other needs for his studies. The first of these sales was to John Barton, a neighbor, of ten acres "including all the Improvements thereon and appertainances thereto

belonging, effected in April 1792, for the sum of thirty pounds."[13] Later that
year Banneker disposed of a second parcel, consisting of sixty-four perches, or 2 1/2 acres, of the original farm, to John Nimiy, a cooper of Baltimore
County and presumably a near neighbor. The sum paid by Nimiy was two
pounds and ten shillings. It is interesting to note that, in the indenture of
this sale, the seller is identified as "Benjamin Banneker of Baltimore County
in the State of Maryland astronomer." John Nimiy may have been one of
Benjamin's relatives, possibly a cousin or nephew.[14]

Two years later, in December 1794, he once again agreed to sell part of
his patrimony to a certain Edward Shugar, this time a small parcel of two
acres, for the sum of five pounds.[15] Benjamin sold two more portions of land
during the next several years, both of them to the same purchaser, a cooper
of Baltimore County named Thomas Gibbons. The first tract consisted of a
parcel of undetermined size described as "parts of tracts" which were
approximately two acres and sold for the sum of ten dollars in June 1797.[16]
The second parcel of one acre was sold in October 1799 for the sum of five
pounds.[17] Greenbury Morten also appeared in Baltimore to formalize the
sale of land he had acquired from his uncle, to the self-same cooper, Thomas
Gibbons.[18] It was at this time that Banneker finally transferred his remaining land to Ellicott & Company. By means of an indenture dated October 23,
1799, he conveyed his remaining seventy-two acres of land in equal shares to
Jonathan, Elias, George, and John Ellicott. The conveyance was made for the
sum of 180 pounds which he stated he had received to his full satisfaction.[19]

It is to be assumed from this transaction that Banneker had already
received a number of payments in either cash or goods purchased from the
Ellicott brothers in annual amounts of £12 or equivalent, leaving a balance
of some £70, or that he had received varying amounts totaling the entire
price specified of £180. Whichever may have been the case, after the for-
malization of the sale by indenture, a new procedure for payment was instituted. Thereafter Banneker was provided with a charge account at the
Ellicott & Company store by means of which a record could be kept of his
purchases during the year. In mid-November of each year his indebtedness
would be totaled, subtracted from the £12 due him annually, and the balance rendered to him in cash by one of the Ellicott brothers.

Banneker maintained a running account of his expenditures recorded on blank pages of his manuscript journal. The contents of this volume
were well organized in that each right-hand page was carefully inscribed

with the calculations for the ephemeris for each month, set down as it would appear in a printed almanac, and constituted Banneker's master copy. The left-hand page was used for various other purposes, not always in chronological order. Many of the left-hand pages were filled with projections for eclipses with related notes. Occasionally they were used for tables and records of observations and for noting a formula or set of directions for making calculations, often copied from one or another of the published sources he used. He also used the blank pages for noting personal notations, records of dreams, proverbs, and quotations.

The listing of expenditures for each year was headed "Articles Received of Ellicott & Co." and variously "for the fourth payment [1802]," or "for the fifth payment [1803]," and so on. There may have been several reasons for such an arrangement, one being that Banneker was not required to keep substantial amounts of cash on hand. Possibly his drinking might tempt him to spend his money. On the other hand, the anxiety he expressed concerning incidents which ranged from threats on his life to thefts from his home increased his uneasiness when he kept money on hand.

The first recorded payment made to Banneker by Ellicott & Company was for the year from November 1798 to November 1799, which he identified as "Second Payment," probably in error. The second payment began with three entries—two of them dated December 29, 1798:

By Cash received of them in
part pay[t]. £0.1.10-1/2
~~To Cash paid for Signed a~~
~~Deed~~————————£[illegible]
1799 January 12 by an Almanac . . . . . . 0.0.11[20]

The almanac, as indicated by the price he paid for it, probably was a common one of the region, and not the current issue of the *Nautical Almanac*. Although of no great historical importance, these accounting records are useful in providing some indication of how Banneker lived. The most frequent store purchase he made was of pork; he bought between seven and ten pounds each month. He averaged two pairs of shoes every year at a cost of 11s. 3d. each. He bought corn on a monthly basis, a half bushel at a time, and molasses and candles.

He occasionally indulged in the purchase of clothing. On December 23, 1801, two days before Christmas, he paid a tailor for making him a new pair of breeches, and on the following April 15 he recorded the purchase of "A fine hat for 4 dollars (£1.10s.0d)." On June 25 he bought 3 1/4 yards of Irish linen, in addition to 3 1/2 yards of other linen as well as thread and buttons. Presumably the cloth was for shirts and handkerchiefs which his sister Minta may have sewn for him. During the course of the year he listed other purchases of cloth including sheeting, nankeen, muslin, as well as thread. One entry recorded payment to a tailor (probably not his sister) for making a jacket for him. He purchased stockings separately.

Purchases of unusual items were "a paper of ink powder, one quarter pound of gunpowder, as well as some shot." The balance due him for the year was four dollars or £1.10s.0d. There were several unusual expenses as well. On May 20, 1802, he purchased a gunlock for 9s.4-1/2d., and on August 4 he invested two shillings for a padlock and 1/4 pound powder (probably gunpowder) as well as two pounds of lead shot. Each year he recorded his payment of taxes to the sheriff in the amount of 4s.6d. Several purchases were recorded for scholarly materials. On July 8, 1802, he listed "cash payd for a Book 3 Dollars (1£ 2s.6d.)" and in November 1803 he purchased an ink stand for three shillings.

At the end of each November, when Banneker's account was totaled, any unexpended balance was rendered to him in cash. On November 16, 1802, for example, he received the amount of £1.18s.8d. For some reason not apparent, a departure from this procedure was made in 1803. On November 14, George Ellicott paid him £5 17s.4d. in cash, leaving a balance of £6 2s.8d. An unexplained item is Banneker's payment of 6s.3d. in June 1803 to Nanny Hall. She was a neighbor and may have served as a part-time housekeeper who came in occasionally to help with household chores.

In 1795, Banneker began to keep a separate set of accounts in a small book that he called his "Commonplace Book." This little volume was one he had constructed, utilizing materials he had at hand. He folded, trimmed and sewed sheets of paper he had saved from discarded astronomical observations. These were bound within protective covers made from those of a salvaged old account book consisting of heavy boards with blue marbled lining. A piece of leather, possibly from an old shoe or boot covering, part of which is lacking, protected the whole. This little record book measures three and one-half by six inches. It contained thirteen sheets and there is evidence that other sheets were removed. Eleven of the twenty-six pages were filled with ephemerides in draft form; six pages were left blank.

Certain of the minor entries made in Banneker's journal and in his commonplace book yield valuable insight into how he lived during his final years. One purchase, which he recorded and later crossed out because he wished to use that page of his journal for drawing a lunar projection, was the following:

1796. John Barton D[R]
July 3 To 1 Candles.[21]

On a separate sheet of paper that he had inserted in his journal he had drawn two horizontal lines intersected by five vertical lines. The whole was part of a notation of his purchases of cider, for it was labeled "The long marks are barrels Cyder for B.B." and below the diagram were the words "for (or per) Barton & Samson." The entries relate primarily to miscellaneous purchases and loans he made of small sums of money. The first item on the first page, which was later crossed out, is the following:

April 30th, 1795
Cash lent John Ford
Five Dollars £1.17.6

This was followed by

1797 Dec.[R] 12th
bought a pound of candles
at 1/8 p.———

An undated notation lists several names followed by a calculation:

Henry Ball
Sam[L] Harlan
Rowan Hugh
John Lyons

d h m   d h m
4 8 11 twenty times added together give 19 1 50
thirty times added gives   4 6 0

The second page contains a draft of significant days for an unidentified month, and the following entries appear on the third page:

1795) Received of John Henderson
June 1) - £0.2.0

Cover and page from Banneker's Commonplace Book containing entries relating to household expenditures and related matters, containing notations of astronomical observations. *Courtesy the late Mrs. Henry M. Fitzhugh III.*

1803
April 13th planted Beans and Sowed Cabbage Seed.

On the eleventh page is written in a shaking hand the name "Harriet Ministry," and on the seventeenth page there is the following item:

1799 Harriet Ducket D.^R
Nov.1 17 To 1/2 pint honey £0.0.7-1/2

Banneker used the pages from both ends of the volume at the same time instead of in a continuous manner from front to back. On the last page is the following:

1795) Sold Butler, Edwards and Kiddy the right of
Ap 2) a copy of an almanac for the year 1796, for
        the Sum of 80 dol. equal to 30£

1795) June 5, answered James
Marr £0-1-6

On the 26th day of March 1798 came Joshua Sank with 3 or 4 Bushels turnips to feed the Cows. B. Banneker

One page contained calculations for the moon's longitude for the month of January 1804, as well as the following entries made in 1795:

William Hubbard D^R.
April 30 [1795] Cash lent him £0.0.10
R 2 b 2 C 1   C 1 b 1 2   D^R.

1795   )
) Cash lent her £0.7.6
May 23)
June 22   Cash of her £0.1.6
Aug. 27   Cash lent her—0.4.2-1/2

Both entries were later crossed out, indicating that they had been settled. Another page stated:

1796 Thos Finton D^R.
May 4 To a watch 4 dol. £1.10.0

The last entry deserves particular attention. The purchase of a pocket watch was a notable event in Banneker's life and marked a milestone in his career. During the many decades since he had constructed a wooden clock, he undoubtedly had occasion to see and examine a number of other clocks and watches, but he never had sufficient funds to buy one. Now, in the sunset of his life, such a purchase would still have constituted a major luxury but one that he felt he could afford and which would be particularly useful for the precision timekeeping required for making astronomical observations. The old wooden clock would have sufficed for measuring the mere passage of time but lacked precision.

Banneker's income from the sales of several parcels of property and the payments he received for the various editions of his almanacs provided him with sufficient funds for an occasional unusual expenditure during this period, and the investment was relatively modest. The watch was not noted among the memorabilia that survived his death some years later. There can be no doubt, however, that it was a new addition to the cherished materials that occupied the place of honor on his oval gateleg table, which served as his observatory. The watch entry was canceled at a later date with a line drawn through it. On the same page were the following:

1799 Contra C^r.
Sept. 18 Reced of John Collins
at Sundry times £1.15.11
Receded fodder 0.11. 3

                                2. 7. 2
                          _____

Nov. 23 Cash of wife 0.11. 6
~~Nov^R.2~~

1799 John Collins D^R.
To house and Grounds Rent £3. 0. 0
June 24 lent yr. wife 0. 2. 6
Sep^t. 7 Cash lent you 0. 0. 11
Cyder at Sundry times 0. 4. 9
2 Quarts dry peaches 0. 0. 6

~~Nov. 27 To 1/2 peck Apples . . . . 0. 0. 11-1/2~~

Dec. 31 To a Quart mead 0. 0. 4

1800)
) Cash lent y^r. wife. 0. 1.10-1/2
Jan. 2)

Banneker equivocated about the disposition of his land, probably concerned about how his decision would appear to his family, his neighbors, and others. For a time at least, he felt the need to justify his actions, which may not in actuality have been required. As he grew older, his health began to fail, and he lacked the strength and tenacity for work which had marked his younger years. Should his land no longer be adequately cultivated and fall into disuse, he undoubtedly feared probable censure from his family and his neighbors perhaps more than he was willing to admit. Bad enough that he drank—a weakness from which he had suffered since his youth but which his mother had kept under control while she lived. After her death, Banneker's willpower occasionally failed, but it must be stated that in this respect he was no different from any man of his time, white or black, wealthy or poor. Nonetheless, his addiction, together with what seemed like his increasingly slothful existence, was noticed and caused him concern. To himself he justified his retirement from farming and the sale of his land on the basis of his desire to develop his scientific knowledge; previously he had neither the time nor the means.

Despite the anticipated criticism from others of his apparent laziness, he was greatly relieved when he could stop field work. At last he was able to spend the night hours, as late as he wished, contemplating the celestial wonders through his telescope. Often he wrapped himself in his cloak and lay upon the ground as he observed the stars, experiencing the greatest pleasure in the nocturnal solitude, drinking in the beauty which in the past he had been too preoccupied or tired to notice or appreciate.

Banneker now customarily retired at dawn and spent part of each day sleeping and resting indoors. He did not need very much sleep as he became older. Later in the day he would work around his house and yard. Passing neighbors often observed him at domestic chores, hoeing his corn, pruning fruit trees in his orchard, or weeding his garden. With all the leisure now at his command, he took the time to observe also Nature's terrestrial wonders that were close at hand. He would sit for hours and watch his bees, for instance, as they departed and returned to their hives.

At the end of each day Banneker customarily relaxed with music. He brought out his violin and flute and alternated in playing them, which he did with a certain degree of skill. His favorite place was under the large chestnut tree near his doorway, where he often sat playing until sunset passed into twilight before resuming his nightly astronomical observations. Passersby sometimes observed his figure silhouetted against the tree and heard the soft sounds of his music.

There were few other diversions for the elderly farmer besides his studies and his music, and relatively no social activities. He still hunted occasionally, in search of small game for the table, and fished in the nearby streams. He was very much at home in the woods, and from the time he was a young boy he was able to identify every shrub and tree in the region: prickly ash, spice wood, alder, red bud, tulip tree, elder, and dogwood, as well as the great chestnuts, oaks, ash hickories, maple, and gums. He was familiar with the small game, and he frequently startled herds of deer and flocks of wild turkeys as he wandered among the trees. He went after larger game only when an occasional wildcat ventured from its haven to plunder his farmyard of a young pig or some of his poultry. He made no mention of hunting in his writings, but in his later years his accounts with the Ellicott & Company store now and then included purchases of gunpowder and shot.

Banneker took pleasure in smoking; it was one of his few diversions. Tobacco had been widely used as snuff and smoked in clay pipes from the earliest days of the province. The cigar did not come into popularity until late in the eighteenth century, and cigarettes did not follow until much later. He smoked the common clay or kaolin pipe, which he purchased in some numbers from the Ellicott & Company store; his store accounts also listed periodic purchases of tobacco by the half pound. On July 13, 1803, for example, he purchased one pound of tobacco and another half pound on November 11 of the same year.

Except for the common ills of the aged, Banneker appears to have enjoyed reasonably good health throughout most of his life until his final years. The earliest record of illness occurred in the spring of 1793 while he was in the midst of preparing an ephemeris for the printers and had to delay submitting his manuscript. He recorded payment of his account with his doctor in his manuscript journal. The amount due—more than £5— suggests that he had been ill for some time.[22]

Approximately six years later, Banneker was stricken with a serious illness that brought him close to death. The nature or name of his ailment was not recorded, but it was extremely serious and incapacitated him for a long time. It was in this period that he reviewed his estate and decided its disposition. Tyson reported the illness as having occurred some years prior to Banneker's death. Convinced that he would not recover, he instructed his family in the specific disposition to be made of each of his personal possessions, particularly the borrowed scientific material that was to be returned to George Ellicott, but he did not put these instructions in writing.[23]

The illness probably occurred in about 1799. The general concern for his health led the Ellicott brothers to complete a transfer of his land after his recovery in October of that year. Banneker's weakness for liquor undoubtedly had undermined his health. This was remarked upon by several writers, among them Martha Tyson. Concerning Banneker's mother, she wrote:

> Being much attached to her son, she had watched over his best interests with prudent care; a care, which we regret to record, became necessary, from one great weakness that occasionally appeared in this, in other respects fair character. Inebriety was the ruling vice of the day, and he had sometimes been the victim of its influence.[24]

Elsewhere Tyson again referred to his excesses, mentioning that he

> had not always refrained with prudence from intoxicating liquors. No one appeared to be more sensible of their debasing effect, than the subject of our notice; and, as to "know ourselves diseased is half a cure," he lamented his weakness, and gradually relieved himself of its fetters, not, however, until excess had impaired his strength, given him the appearance of premature old age, and produced the diseases which shortened his days.[25]

Another reference to this problem is mentioned in connection with Banneker's sojourn in the Federal Territory:

> One matter, personal to himself, gave him great pleasure in the retrospect. He had not, during his absence, tasted either wine or spiritous liquors. He had experienced the fact that it was unwise for him to indulge, ever so slightly, in stimulating drinks. On this occasion he said, "I feared to trust myself even with wine, lest it steal away the little sense I have." He was a noble example of what may be accomplished by a firm resolve.[26]

A contemporary reference to the same problem is found in an unpub-

lished manuscript journal maintained by the Reverend William Colbert, a
Methodist Episcopalian minister who rode the Chester and Strassburg circuit in September 1799.[27] An entry for Sunday, September 22, recording a
burial service at the Banneker homestead, reads as follows:

> I preached at John Hagerty Paper Mill on Acts 3rd 19. Bro. Neel gave an
> exhortation. It appears to me, that if there was proper attention paid to the
> people in this place some might be brought to the knowledge of the truth.
> In the afternoon brother Neel preached at Benjamin Banneker's, this black
> man has acquired so much knowledge in the science of Astronomy as to
> attract the public notice in the calculation of several Almanacs but has
> become a great drunkard, for while bro. Neel was preaching on Rom. 6 &
> 23rd he was so drunk that he could hardly stand. I spoke a little at the grave
> as it was a funeral sermon.[28]

This account reveals several facts that are useful in reconstructing
Banneker's life. First, the presence of the Reverend Colbert and Brother
Neel at his home to officiate at a burial indicates that the deceased was a
member of Banneker's immediate family, perhaps a nephew or niece, and
was a member of the Methodist Episcopal faith. Banneker's instability may
have been due to one of several reasons, having been overcome with emo-
tion over the loss of a member of his family, for example, or it may have
been grief rather than overindulgence that can have accounted for his inebriated state at the graveside.

Perhaps too much of an issue has been made by past writers about
Banneker's weakness for liquor. One possibility not previously suggested is
that his occasional inebriated appearance may have been a symptom of the
unidentified illness which eventually led to his death, or to its medication,
rather than of a weakness for liquor. Furthermore, if drinking to excess was
indeed his failing, it was one he shared with many at every level of society.

One of Banneker's nephews, Meshach Lett, son of his sister Jemima,
remembered his uncle Benjamin quite well and recalled how as a boy he
had occasionally visited him in Baltimore County. As later reported by
Meshach Simpson, Lett's grandson, "Gran Dad had seen Banneker quite
often — he was bookkeeper for the Ellicots." "Gran Dad used often to laugh
when he would hear the Letts dilating [sic] upon the Dollars of Uncle Ben,"
he went on. "'Humpf,' Gran Dad would say, 'The ground was too poor to
raise beans. He evidently had no high opinion of his uncle's reputed great

wealth. Gran Dad Mesh used to tell of visiting his uncle Ben who always wanted him or one of his brothers to stay with him and help him with his work. But the boys thought that the work was too monotonous for them. Gran Dad Mesh used to tell with great pride of how Uncle Ben showed him a keg with silver [coins] telling him he could keep all he could pick out with his fingers. He blistered his fingers trying, but to no purpose. The old man would laugh at him, reach into his pocket and toss him a [silver] dollar or two. Gran Dad Mesch was not aware of the fact that the money [coins] had been wedged into the cask."[29]

Another who recalled Banneker was James Guy Jr., maternal great-grandfather of Meshach Simpson Jr., and he commented that he saw him often. He too had commented that Banneker was a bookkeeper for the Ellicott brothers and that in fact he often weighed Guy's purchases of wheat and corn for him. He remarked that Banneker had little to do in general with people of color, "perhaps he was too busy," he suggested. Guy reported that when Banneker was in public he generally addressed others as "thee" and "thou." He noted that Banneker was not a "black man" but of a "thorn" color, which would now be described as chocolate color. Guy often laughed when he heard members of the Lett family speaking about "the dollars of Uncle Ben," and apparently he too gave little credence to Banneker's reported wealth.[30]

From his boyhood Banneker demonstrated considerable love and a great aptitude for mathematics in every form and particularly for mathematical puzzles, which he collected at every opportunity. Undoubtedly he recorded and preserved many examples over the years but the only ones to survive are several in the handsome new journal he purchased after his return from the Federal Territory. Shortly after returning home from the survey of Washington he copied the first puzzle into its pages. He identified the originator of the puzzle, or at least the person from whom he had obtained it, as Major Andrew Ellicott, presumably during the several months of their association in the Federal Territory.[31] (See Document 22)

Another puzzle of a somewhat different nature was one Banneker seems to have recorded for Gerard Hopkins, as its title indicates. Hopkins was a close friend and associate of George Ellicott's, and his wife was a cousin of George's wife Elizabeth. A man of learning and a minister of the Society of Friends, Hopkins was associated with Ellicott in the latter's endeavors to improve the condition of the Indians. In 1804 he had accompanied Ellicott on a visit to the Indians at Fort Wayne.[32] (For the problem and Banneker's solution, See Document 23)

The puzzles that Banneker collected and recorded were varied in type, but most of them were algebraic in form.[33] The subject matter often dealt with farm animals and simple objects found around the home,[34] as well as with subjects relating to his new scientific interests. (For other examples, see Documents 24, 25, 26 and 27). For many years the elderly farmer's interest in mathematical puzzles was well known to all who knew him, and they often brought examples to the Ellicott & Company store to be given to Banneker when opportunity arose.

Charles W. Dorsey described this interest in puzzles in his own account of Banneker. Dorsey worked as a clerk in the Ellicott store as a boy, from 1800 until he resigned to become a planter in Elkridge. He was a neighbor of Stout and lived with his family on the tract called "Three Brothers" near the Old Frederick Pike about a mile west of Ellicott's Lower Mills. He later became a lifelong friend of the Ellicotts. He recorded that he was about fifteen years of age when employed at the store and became acquainted with Banneker during the last six or seven years of the latter's life. "He was fond of, and well qualified to work out, abstruse questions in arithmetic," he recalled of Banneker.

> I remember he brought to the store one which he had composed himself and presented to George Ellicott for solution. I had a copy, which I have since lost, but the character and deportment of the man were so wholly different from anything I had ever seen in one of his color; his question made so deep an impression on my mind that I have ever since retained a perfect recollection of it, except two lines, which do not alter the sense.
>
> I remember George Ellicott was engaged in making out the answer, and cannot now say how he succeeded, but have no doubt he did. I have thus briefly given you my recollections of Benjamin Banneker. I was young when he died, and doubtless many incidents, from the time which has since elapsed, have passed from my recollection.[35]

The puzzle that Dorsey recorded was "The Cooper and the Vintner." It was not included in Banneker's manuscript journal, possibly because it had come to his attention near the end of his life. Dorsey reported that Benjamin Hallowell of Alexandria had solved this problem, stating

"Banneker's tub must be 24.745 inches; the less diameter, 14.8476." The puzzle appears in an even earlier source, Martha Tyson's manuscript memoirs of Banneker. (Document 24)[36]

His lifelong pursuit of arithmetical exercises from boyhood to old age—he continued to collect them in his journal as late as 1801—provides a circumstantial linking of his early attraction to mathematics with his later achievements with almanacs.[37] (See Document 25). It also may be possible to link Banneker to his African heritage by means of one or more of his puzzles that may have been derived from his grandfather and/or his father. The hare and hound puzzle, for example, is a classic, well known not only in European mathematical literature but even earlier in China and in Africa as well. Ron Eglash notes that the changes made in Banneker's version fit the numerology of both the Ifa and Fa divination systems of that part of western Africa in which Robert Banneky had his origins.

The "Quincunx," featured in one of Banneker's dreams, Eglash suggests, is geometric and clearly associates Banneker with his grandfather Bannaka. As defined in the *Oxford English Dictionary,* a "quincunx" is a Roman unit of measure, derived from the Latin *quincuncem* as meaning five twelfths. It describes an arrangement of five objects disposed in such a manner that four occupy the corners of a square or rectangle and the fifth is is located in the center. It is also a traditional arrangement for planting trees. In astrology it relates to an aspect of the planets in which these are at a distance of five signs or 150 degrees from each other.[38]

In Africa the quincunx is a symbol of importance for quite different reasons, as Eglash recently discovered during a sojourn in the region. Consequently he has been able to establish the quincunx as a symbol commonly encountered in that region of Africa known to both Bannaka and Robert Banneky. He noted that in fact it "is the most pervasive religious symbol in Senegal." Eglash provides an explanation of how Banneker may have become familiar with it:

> According to researchers at the Musée Nacional in Burkina-Faso, the figure originated in an animist amulet on which an X was drawn to indicate "power radiating in all directions." Islamic adaptation merely changed this to more two-dimensional, geometric forms, said to indicate "the light of Allah." These were often inscribed on leather neck bags which held Koranic writings. A portrait of the "Husband of the Queen of Walo" wearing such a

The Quincunx. Portrait of Tacé, the *Marosso* or husband of the queen of Walo and first general of the armies. Hung from around his neck is a leather bag decorated with the quincunx symbol for containing koranic writings, painted in 1853. From David Boilat, *Esquisses Sénégalaises* (1854). *Courtesy of the Museum of African Art, Smithsonian Institution.*

bag was painted in 1853. A variety of these forms, usually close to the standard quincunx shape, appeared on floor tiles, prayer mats, iron and leather work, and other material designs in both ancient and contemporary Wolof society. Since an important role of the quincunx is in protective amulets for children, it is not unreasonable to suggest that Bannaka had drawn or fabricated the quincunx design before Benjamin's birth, passed on some idea of its religious significance to his family, and that Benjamin recalled the design in the dream. It was clearly part of Banneker's geometrical armoury.[39]

Visitors to Banneker's home, particularly others than members of his family and his neighbors, generally were the exception rather than the rule. From time to time a curious tourist or two who had learned about the man who had made a clock would find their way to his log house. When a member of the so-called "gentry" called upon him, it was for Banneker a memorable event. One such visitor who came in the summer of 1796 was Susanna Mason, the wife of George Mason of Chester County, Pennsylvania.[40]

During the great yellow fever epidemic that swept through the region, the Masons had lost a son and a daughter and a slave child, and Mrs. Mason suffered from the fever as well. While George Mason set out on an expedition to the western territory to find a suitable and safe place in which to establish his family, his wife Susanna, having recovered, moved with her children to the home of a sister in Prince George's County near Baltimore. She was not destined to move westward, however, for one illness after another detained her and prevented her travel. Instead she moved about with her children from one friend's home to another, in Chester County, Philadelphia, and Baltimore. Meanwhile she took a great interest in the problems of those around her and established "a female association for the relief of the poor and afflicted" of Baltimore.

Among Susanna's close friends was her distant cousin, Cassandra Hopkins Ellicott, the wife of John Ellicott of Lower Mills. Cassandra had been widowed a few months earlier, and she welcomed Susanna's visit. It was during her prolonged stay with Cassandra that Susanna Mason learned about Banneker and his meteoric career from tobacco farmer to almanac-maker.[41] Her daughter, writing from notes that her mother had made after her visit to the Lower Mills, reported that Susanna, "who ever felt a deep interest in this department of the human family," desired to meet Banneker. Accompanied by her Ellicott cousin and several young friends, she walked to Banneker's farm. There they "found the venerable star-gazer under a wide-spreading pear tree, laden with delicious fruit; he came forward to meet us, and bade us welcome to his lowly dwelling. It was built of logs, one story in height, and surrounded by an orchard. In one corner of the room was suspended a wooden clock of his own construction, which was a true herald of departing hours." Banneker's cabin was humble, cluttered, and crude. "As no 'thrifty wifie's' smile had ever enlightened his abode, I have no remembrance that neatness and comfort were conspicuously depicted there." Banneker registered the names of his visitors in a "little book," then "diffidently, but very politely requested her acceptance of a manuscript almanack, which she received with evident marks of gratification, derived from this interview with him."[42]

Susanna Mason reacted warmly to the aged almanac-maker. Several days after her visit, she addressed a poetic letter to him that her daughter subsequently included in her *Selections*, a collection of her mother's writings. (Document 28) Susanna was particularly impressed with his scientific skills and concerned that

> Thou need'st to have a special care
> Thy conduct with thy talents square.
> That no contaminating vice,
> Obscure thy lustre in our eyes,
> Or cast a shade upon thy merit
> Or blast the praise thou might'st inherit. . . .[43]

Though he was obviously greatly impressed by the compliment, particularly from a member of the gentry, for a time Banneker did not attempt a reply. Not until the end of the following summer did he write to Mrs. Mason, explaining that his delay was due to ill health and begging to be excused for his poor penmanship. The letter in fact provides concrete evidence of his growing infirmity, for he was no longer able to write in the same beautiful script of which he had always been so proud. "Dear Female Friend," he began:

> I have thought on you every day Sinc I saw you last, and on my promise in respect of composing Some verses for your amusement, but I am very much indisposed and have been ever Since time, I have a constant pain in my head, a palpitation in my flesh, and I may Say I am attended with a

pleasure or delight gratify your curiosity in that particular at this present time, yet I Say my will is good to oblige you if I had it in my powers because you gave me good advice and edifying language in that piece of poetry which you was pleased to present unto me, and I can but love you and thank you for the same, and if ever it should be in my power to be Serviceable to you in any measure, your resonable requests shall be armed with the obedience of your Sincere well wisher — B. Banneker

N.B. the above is mean writing done by trembling hands BB[44]

Susanna Mason died in 1805, a year before Banneker's death. She passed away following a long illness, at the age of fifty-seven. The exchange of correspondence was a touching one, and one that Banneker cherished.

During his later years, as he found it increasingly difficult to move about, Banneker no longer was able to ride his horse to Ellicott's Mills, and to walk the distance required too great an effort. Jacob Hall's young grandson came by his house frequently, serving as his messenger and running his errands. The boy was impressed by this gentle old man who worked so assiduously among the books and papers scattered upon the great oval table opposite the fireplace, and he would fabricate excuses to run over to the Banneker farm and spend time with him. The boy often helped by milking the solitary cow that Benjamin kept, and sometimes shared his meals with the elderly astronomer.

Banneker cooked for himself, and meals were simple indeed. He kept a fire in his hearth most of the time, with a two-gallon iron kettle dangling from the crane. He would cut a large portion from the salt pork hung from one of the rafters and throw it into the kettle to simmer. When he thought it sufficiently boiled, he would make some corn dumplings, shaping the cornmeal in his hands until it achieved the desired consistency. After throwing the dumplings into the kettle, he returned to his work. When finally hunger pangs drove him to eat, he would put his work aside, clear a space on the table, and have his meal. Except for occasional greens from his garden, this was his constant fare. He drank only milk with his meals and never used coffee or tea.[45]

This glimpse of Banneker's life during his last few years was related to Bishop Payne almost half a century after Banneker's death by "Mr. H—, one of the local preachers residing at the Mills, who used to be his [Banneker's]

messenger and errand boy." "Mr. H——" was none other than Banneker's young companion, the grandson of Jacob Hall, Benjamin's old schoolmate, who later was employed as caretaker of the Ellicott family cemetery at the Lower Mills until his own death in 1843. Members of the Hall family continued to live in the vicinity of Banneker's farm to modern times, and a short distance from the site of the Banneker homestead is an old, abandoned private cemetery of the Hall family.

Though preoccupied with the stars, Banneker found necessary relaxation from his nocturnal studies in his garden and his orchard. He made various notations of these efforts:

> 1798 November the 30th, planted 170 pare [sic] tree Sprouts.[46]

> 1798 March 6th I planted in garden Nursery Some young pare [sic] trees, in the [part of page is torn away] . . . in the same row 15 red kind grew near the old pare.[47]

In his commonplace book Banneker recorded that on April 24, 1802, he worked in his field "holing" corn. Several entries noted charges to his tenants for pasturage. Entries made in the following year included:

> On the 26th of March, came Joshua Sanks with 3 or 4 bushels of turnips to feed the cows.

> 13th of April, 1803, planted beans and sowed cabbage seed.[48]

In general, despite the infirmities brought on by age, during his last decade and a half Banneker enjoyed life as never before. He had discovered an outlet for his scientific instincts which had proven to be rewarding financially as well as mentally, and each succeeding day and night promised a new adventure. His easy existence permitted him to devote more time and thought to natural phenomena. He wrote in his journal of the common things about him, with which he had been familiar all his life but which he now observed from a different point of view, because he had become more acutely aware of them. He made notes of those he considered to be sufficiently unusual. One of his observations, which was published and later widely reprinted, was a short paragraph on robber bees:

> In the month of January, 1797, on a pleasant day for the Season I observed

my honey bees to be out of their hives and Seemed very busy all but one hive. Upon examination I found all the bees had evacuated the hive and left not a drop of honey behind them, and on the 9th day of February ensuing, I killed the neighbouring hives of Bees, on a Special occasion, and found a great quantity of honey considering the season, which I imagine the Stronger had violently taken from the weaker and the weaker had persued them to their home resolved to be benefitted by their labour or die in the contest.[49]

In Banneker's time, beekeepers used hives called "skeps" that resembled inverted baskets made of plaited straw with two wooden cross-members inserted into the domed top of the structure, in which the bees built their comb. The bees commonly cultivated in Maryland in the eighteenth century were black German bees and had been known and used for more than two centuries. It was virtually impossible to remove the honey from a skep without destroying the hive. Beekeepers collected honey by blowing smoke, which is lethal to bees, into the hive before removing the comb.[50]

Banneker's brief statement on bees, which appeared in the accounts by Latrobe and Tyson,[51] seems to have led later writers to the conclusion that Banneker had published a treatise on bee culture.[52] This assumption may have been strengthened by the inclusion in his almanac for 1792 of a short parable about "The Two Bees." That Banneker was the author of the parable is doubtful, inasmuch as most of the literary content of his almanacs was provided by the printers. A careful search of Banneker's correspondence and writings and of the published literature has failed to bring to light any treatise on the subject.[53]

Banneker inherited his interest in beekeeping from his father, who established several hives on his farm soon after he acquired it. Whereas Robert's interest in bees had been primarily for the production of honey, which was then one of the few, and perhaps only, sweetening agents available for his family, Benjamin's interest was more extensive. In addition to the practical aspects of apiculture, Banneker had demonstrated that he was also an amateur naturalist, and he took great pleasure in watching the bees at work.

Of equal interest was a somewhat longer observation on the subject of "locusts" which Banneker recorded in his journal approximately three years later:

The first great Locust year that I can Remember was 1749. I was then about Seventeen years of age when thousands of them came and was creeping up the trees and bushes, I then immagined they came to eat and destroy the fruit of the Earth, and would occasion a famine in the land. I therefore began to kill and destroy them, but soon saw that my labor was in vain, therefore gave over my pretension. Again in the year 1766, which is Seventeen years after their first appearance, they made a Second, and appeared to me to be full as numerous as the first. I then, being about thirty-four years of age had more sense than to endeavour to destroy them, knowing they were not so pernicious to the fruit of the Earth as I did immagine they would be. Again in the year 1783 which was Seventeen years Since their Second appearance to me, they made their third; and they may be expected again in the year 1800, which is Seventeen years Since their third appearance to me. So that if I may venture So to express it, their periodical return is Seventeen years, but they, like the Comets, make but a short stay with us—The female has a Sting in her tail as sharp and hard as a thorn, with which she perforates the branches of the trees, and in them holes lays eggs. The branch soon dies and fall, then the egg by some Occult cause immerges a great depth into the earth and there continues for the Space of Seventeen years as aforesaid.[54]

Banneker signed a number of his entries, including this one, with his full signature, which suggests that he had intended to include them in the published almanacs, and thus distinguished them as his original work and not copied from other sources. The entry on the locusts, which was complete as written, was followed by this insert which he added some years later:

I like to forgot to inform, that if their lives are Short they are merry, they begin to Sing or make a noise from the first they come out of Earth till they die, the hindermost part rots off, and it does not appear to be any pain to them for they still continue on Singing till they die.[55]

Banneker's account described not the true locust or migratory grasshopper, which periodically devastated large sections of the American colonies several times in the mid- and late eighteenth century, but the seventeen-year locust or periodical cicada (*Tibicina septendecim*) which is prevalent on the North American continent.[56]

From his early childhood, Banneker was a deeply religious man. This quality, nurtured by his grandmother and supported by some of his readings, never led him to join a particular denomination. But he was especially interested in hearing traveling ministers or speakers when they held meetings and services in the vicinity, and he usually tried to attend. He favored the Society of Friends and frequently visited the Friends' meetings at Elkridge Landing. The Ellicott family made certain that he was informed of such occasions by sending a messenger to notify him. "We have seen Banneker in Elkridge Meeting house," Mrs. Tyson remarked, "where he always sat on the form nearest the door, his head uncovered . . . in quiet contemplation."[57]

When the Ellicotts first arrived in the region, they attended meetings at the nearest Friends Meeting House, which was in Elkridge, traveling on horseback over wooded trails since there were then no roads. The Meeting House at Elkridge was about a mile from Ilchester and stood atop Quaker Hill on the western side of the Patapsco River. That same year, the old Elkridge Meeting House, which had been used as a place of worship since 1670, was abandoned. Located in an attractive rural setting, the building was nevertheless old and small and uncomfortable, and access required crossing the Patapsco River. Later Banneker attended meetings in the Friends Meeting House erected by the Ellicott family in Ellicott's Lower Mills. "His life was one of constant worship in the great temples of nature and science," Tyson recalled in her second biographical account of Banneker. As places of worship grew in number, Banneker visited the various denominations, finally giving preference to the Society of Friends. "He presented a most dignified aspect as he leaned in quiet contemplation on a long staff, which he always carried after passing his seventieth year. 'And he worshipped leaning on the top of his staff.' His reverent deportment on these occasions added to the natural majesty of his appearance."[58]

Friends attended monthly meetings held at Indian Spring in what is now Prince George's County, near the Patuxent River. Soon after settling in Ellicott's Lower Mills, the Ellicott brothers donated land on which in 1800 was erected the Friends Meeting House for the new community. They built on the site of an old building adjacent to an extensive burial ground. When the new building opened at the Lower Mills, the congregation numbered 120 Friends. Meetings were held on the first day of each week and again on the fourth day following.

Society of Friends Meeting House at Ellicott's Lower Mills, which Banneker occasionally attended in his final years. Shown at right is the Ellicott family graveyard. From a lithograph by E. Sachse & Co., Baltimore, 1854. *Maryland Historical Society.*

Being familiar with Scripture from earliest childhood, when he spent long hours reading passages to his grandmother, Banneker kept a Bible of his own to the end of his life. He was thirty-two years of age when he acquired it, and it served him for his lifetime. Inscribed in the volume, in addition to a record of his own birth and his father's death, was the statement: "I bought this book of HONORA BUCKANAN, the 4th day of January, 1763."[59]

Interspersed throughout his manuscript journal are religious passages that Banneker apparently copied from his Bible for later reference and possibly for use on appropriate occasions. The religious notes appear to have been copied at random. One passage he considered worthy of preservation, "2 Kings Chap. 23, verse 11," relates to Josiah, the king of Jerusalem, who as a young man responded to the call of God and set about to reform the city: "And he took away the horses that the kings of Judah had given to the Sun."[60] On the same page Banneker inscribed a quotation from II Samuel 12:31, which was concerned with the same theme—the curse of cities, when

Jerusalem was as full of sorrow and strife caused by sin as any other city: "And he brought away the people that were therein and put them under Laws, and under harrows of iron, and under axes of iron, and made them pass through the brick-kiln."

Banneker also favored proverbs and occasionally copied them into his notes, again with the idea of using them in the almanacs, although this particular one was never included:

> Our distilled Spirits are like unto the water of the river of Phrygia, which, if drank sparingly, purges the brains and cures madness, but otherwise it infects the brains and creates madness. See Enticks Dictionary page 458.[61]

Another proverb or maxim Banneker found of interest was "Evil Communications Corrupts good manners." "I hope to live to hear that Good Communications Corrects bad manners," he added.[62]

Banneker was able to consider religion from a humorous point of view as well, as shown by the following anecdote preserved among his other notations:

> A very melting Sermon on being preached one day which caused all the Congregation to weep but one man, which attracted the notice of the people, after Sermon, a curious inquirer demanded his reason for not weeping as well as the rest of the congregation, he pertinently reply'd I do not belong to the parish.[63]

At various times during his adult life Banneker appears to have become interested in creative writing, even long before he became involved with the calculation of ephemerides for almanacs. He experimented with literary essays and attempted several that purported to be accounts of his dreams. Whether they actually were dreams he had experienced or fantasies that he had conceived cannot be ascertained. The earliest of these surviving literary efforts is a manuscript entitled "A Remarkable Dream" dated October 1762, almost a decade prior to Banneker's association with the Ellicott family and fully three decades before his involvement with almanacs.[64] (See Document 29)

Banneker copied several other examples of these dreams or fantasies into his journal. For the most part they seem to have been added during the earlier part of his so-called scholarly period. His continued preoccupation with developing a literary style as well as his emphasis on macabre subjects may have some significance beyond the text. Pervasive throughout these "dreams" is the feeling that Banneker was attempting to develop a form of literary self-expression. Were these actually dreams, or were they literary efforts? It is more likely that they were mystical fantasies, ranging from the search for Rasannah Crandolph's soul,[65] his skirmish with "the Infernal Spirit,"[66] the touching language of his encounter with a white fawn,[67] and finally his great distress over a child that had hurt its head. Some of these writings Banneker had copied into his manuscript journal from time to time, and others were written on separate loose sheets that had been gathered up together with his journal and borrowed books after his death when they were returned to George Ellicott.[68] (See Documents 29 through 33 inclusive.)

Whether Banneker had acquired elements of his African heritage from either his grandfather or his father, whether he had learned African myths, legends, traditions, or folklore or farming methods from them, remains a question. A clue that such may have been the case occurs in an untitled dream he dated December 5, 1791, copied into his manuscript journal:

> On the night of the fifth of December 1791, Being in deep Sleep, I dreamed that I was in a public Company, one of them demanded of me the limits Rasannah Crandolph's Soul had to display itself in, after it departed from her body and taken its flight. . . . When I returned I found the Company together and was able to Solve their Doubts by giving them the following answer: Quincunx. (Document 30)

Other journal entries provide occasional glimpses of Banneker's way of life: "Some say that it is dangerous to let blood in the Dog days, but I question it, because that, on the 30th Aug.^{T} 1796 which was 4 days before the expiration of the Dog Days, no harm ensues.— I bled John Minney ———." [69]

The identity of John Minney is uncertain, but Banneker noted that on August 10, 1792, he had sold to John Nimiy, a cooper, a section of sixty-four perches or two and one-half acres of his farm, Stout. The resemblance of the names suggests that they were one and the same, and that the recorder of the indenture may have been in error. For Banneker to have parted with a small section of his beloved farm at this time indicates that it must have been to a relative. It is not too farfetched to assume that John Minney, or

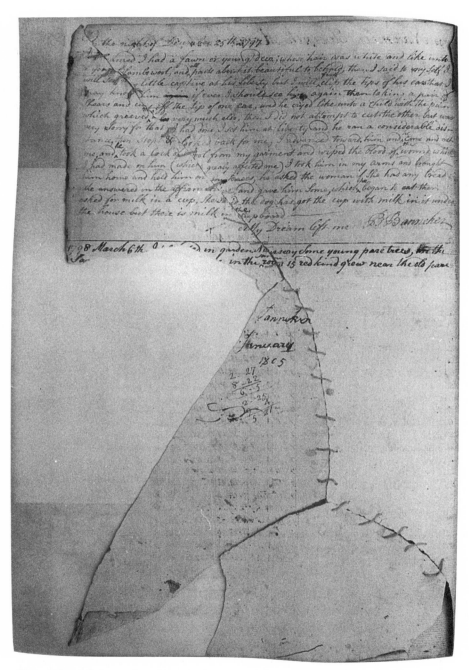

Torn and mended page from Banneker's manuscript journal containing his manuscript of the "Dream of the Fawn." *Maryland Historical Society.*

Nimiy, was the son-in-law of one of his sisters living nearby. The fact that he bled him also suggests that Minney was a close relative.

As the years wore on, Banneker reduced his activities to the most necessary chores, and even his astronomical endeavors diminished, although his interest continued as strong as ever. As his physical infirmities increased, it became more and more difficult for him to maintain his long nightly vigils observing the stars. This is reflected in the pages of his manuscript journal. He continued to make his calculations through the year of 1803 and completed those for January 1804. Random calculations for that year occur in the journal, but the ephemeris was never completed. The latest entry in the journal is the inscription "January 1805."

Despite his reduced activity, Banneker maintained a daily schedule. Each morning he set forth from his house upon a walk to observe his beloved hills, some of which rose nearby almost as guardians of his house and orchard and provided a windbreak from the winter gusts. Others were visible in the distance over the Patapsco River, where they provided a picturesque frame for the view.

On the morning of October 9, 1806, he took his walk as usual. It was a Sunday. The crisp autumn air was invigorating and he enjoyed bright sunshine as he followed his accustomed route. He met an acquaintance, and they stopped to talk for a short interval. Suddenly, Banneker felt unwell and excused himself. His acquaintance walked with him back to his house and waited until Banneker stretched himself out on his couch in the large room. He never spoke again, and in a short while he was dead.

Banneker's sisters and members of their families were immediately summoned and arrived quickly on the scene. His death had not come as a cruel surprise, for Banneker had lived exactly a month short of his seventy-fifth birthday. His family remembered his instructions and followed them to the letter. One of his nephews was dispatched promptly to carry the news to Ellicott's Mills. Pursuant to Banneker's directions for the disposition of his personal property, a nephew hitched a horse to a cart and loaded thereon all of those items which were to be returned to his old friend and neighbor George Ellicott. These included the old oval table, all of his scientific instruments, and the several books of reference on mathematics, astronomy, and surveying that Ellicott had loaned him. All had been gifts or loans from time to time from George, and the old astronomer considered it only fitting that they should be returned. To these were added the only items he truly treasured, his manuscript journal of astronomical calculations and his commonplace book.[70]

Banneker's sisters were concerned that his house and property might fall victim to theft and vandalism when news of his death became generally known. They recalled the disturbances he had experienced in the past few years from some who thought that he had gained wealth from his almanacs. Accordingly, between the Sunday afternoon that Banneker died, and the following Tuesday when his burial took place, his sisters Minta and Molly, assisted by several of their children, gathered at their brother's house and carefully sorted through his possessions, making a division between them of property that had not been returned to George Ellicott in Ellicott's Lower Mills. Household items, such as pillows, sheets, linen, and kitchen utensils including pots and pans, dishes, and cutlery were shared among the households of the two sisters and their married children. Several months prior to his death, Banneker had presented a featherbed to one of his sisters. She valued it highly, as one of the very few surviving possessions of her late brother and carefully preserved it. After a lapse of some years she felt something hard among the feathers, and upon examination she discovered a purse of gold coins. Banneker had apparently saved this small hoard for a rainy day in anticipation of his increasing infirmities and then forgotten its existence at the time he gave his sister the bed.

Objects of particular value, including his pocket watch, and perhaps also his musical instruments, the sisters took to their homes. Other items, such as his personal clothing and the sparse homemade furniture, were probably left for disposition to be made after the burial service. Inadvertently the famous wall clock he had made remained in place on the wall. Perhaps the sisters had not agreed who should acquire it and planned to remove it after the burial.

Banneker's burial took place two days after his death, on Tuesday, October 11. Just as his body was being lowered into the grave a few yards away from his house, the wooden building suddenly burst into flame. Before help could be summoned, the entire structure had burned to the ground, with all of its contents. Banneker's personal clothing, the few bits of furniture, his manuscript and printed copies of his almanacs, and the sparse collection of books in his personal library all were consumed, as well as the well-worn wooden striking clock that had served him for more than forty years.

The only one of his possessions known to have been preserved, other than the astronomical study materials, was Banneker's quarto Bible. It had been removed from his house after his death and before the funeral, probably by one of his sisters. It may in fact have been the copy used for his burial service. It remained in the possession of a member of his family well into the nineteenth century; its present location is not known.

Banneker had not prepared a last will and testament, and no inventory of his estate was made. He had previously arranged for the conveyance of his real estate to the Ellicott brothers immediately following his death. Since his house and contents were destroyed by fire at the time of his burial, no possessions to be probated survived the fire other than those already conveyed to George Ellicott. It seemed almost as if, at the end of his life, fate was determined to destroy every earthly vestige of the Negro sage.

Within weeks news of Banneker's death was brought to his sister Jemima and the Lett family in Virginia. As recounted by a member of the family, one day in the late autumn of 1806, they were in the fields putting in the hay, when they received a visitor, a Mr. Posey Steward (or Stewart), an old friend from Ellicott's Mills. He had come to notify Jemima and her family of the death of her brother. The Lett family became concerned about the disposition of Banneker's estate, for they always had maintained grand visions of the tobacco farmer's wealth without having any definite knowledge of its extent. Now they were eager to look into the matter, but lacking funds for travel and without knowing how to proceed, they eventually dropped the matter. Judson Lett subsequently reported, however, that some members of the family did travel to Baltimore County seeking their share of the Banneker estate.[71]

Banneker's death did not pass unnoticed. An obituary notice appeared in the *Federal Gazette* almost three weeks after his death, on October 28, 1806, which well described Banneker's way of life—modest, like his contributions.

> On Sunday, the 9th instant, departed this life at his residence in Baltimore county, in the 73d [sic] year of his age, Mr. BENJAMIN BANNEKER, a black man, and immediate descendant of an African father. He was well known in his neighborhood for his quiet and peaceable demeanor, and among scientific men as an astronomer and mathematician. In early life he was instructed in the most common rules of arithmetic, and thereafter,

with the assistance of different authors, he was enabled to acquire a perfect knowledge of all the higher branches of learning. Mr. B was the calculator of several almanacs which were published in this, as well as some of the neighboring states, and although of late years none of his almanacs were published, yet he never failed to calculate one every year, and left them among his papers, preferring solitude to mixing with society, and devoted the greatest part of his time in reading and contemplation, and to no books was he more attached than the scriptures. At his decease he bequeathed all his astronomical and philosophical books and paper to a friend.

Mr. Banneker is a prominent instance to prove that a descendant of Africa is susceptible of as great mental improvement and deep knowledge into the mysteries of nature as that of any other nation.[72]

X

"STOUT" FARM REDIVIVA: A RETURN TO THE PAST

On record now thy name's enrolled,
And future ages will be told,
There lived a man called Banneker,
An African astronomer.

Susanna Mason,
An Address to Benjamin Banneker. . . .

D URING THE CENTURY AND A HALF following Banneker's death the
pilgrim traveling to view the place where he lived would have
found little to recall memories of the self-taught astronomer
or of his time. To be sure there was evidence of technological progress in
the region and of its subsequent departure. Less than a mile away to the
southwest lies the picturesque community of Ellicott City, awaiting the
arrival of weekend tourists and collectors of antiques from nearby cities.
Many of its old buildings still stand; built of stern gray granite, they serve
as sober reminders of its industrial past as a thriving mill center of
national importance.

Through the center of town and proceeding along the route of the
National Turnpike flows the Patapsco River, whose roaring stream provided the power to turn the myriad mill wheels. One can discern little resemblance between the storied river that dominated the region and the docile
stream that now murmurs quietly along its worn-out rocky bed, passing

within a half mile of where Banneker once lived. This was once the great, untamed Patapsco that violently flooded its banks again and again bringing death and disaster to the region. Now it awakens but rarely, leaving its deceptively innocuous meandering to wreak sudden and unexpected havoc before resuming its slumbers once more.

The business section of Ellicott City spreads along its narrow, congested main street, and at the eastern end of the bridge over the Patapsco is the eight-story concrete building housing the plant of the Doughnut Corporation of America. The company's bins once held 500,000 bushels of wheat. Its main building is on the site of Ellicott's Lower Mills, where for more than half a century the Ellicotts made Patapsco Flour a widely known trade name.

But the Ellicott mills faced repeated disasters. First came the panic of 1837, when the plant was turned over to Charles Gambrill and Charles Carroll of Carrollton. Thirty-one years later a terrible Patapsco flood washed away the mill, bridge, dam, and several houses. Forty-two persons drowned. Across the road from the doughnut plant and facing the former millrace had stood the sturdy homes of several of the founding Ellicott brothers. West of them was the long, three-story building of yellow stone— the Ellicott & Company store.

To the north was the little factory community of Oella. It had its beginnings early in the nineteenth century as the Union Manufacturing Company. In addition to its surviving mills, now abandoned, lines of rowhouses, recently restored and attractive, retain the flavor of an Old World factory town. To the east lies Catonsville, once named Johnnycake for a roadside inn famed for its cornbread. Laid out in 1818 by Richard Caton, a son-in-law of Charles Carroll of Carrollton, not until some four decades later did it assume commercial interest with the establishment of the Kalb Pottery. The town developed slowly during the nineteenth century, but by the 1880s it emerged into a small commercial center. Sprawling through the old plantation region were the summer estates of wealthy Baltimoreans.

As the years passed the name of Benjamin Banneker gradually faded from memory, to be sporadically revived again and again by published accounts of his achievements. In 1953 the Maryland State Highway Commission finally erected a marker identifying the site of his farm. Little by little interest in Banneker grew, sparked in the 1960s by renewed interest in African-American history. (See Document 52)

Two decades passed, however, before there was sufficient interest for state historical authorities to attempt to identify the salient bounds of Banneker's farm from related land records. From time to time in his later years, Banneker had sold small portions of his hundred-acre farm, and just before his death he had conveyed to Ellicott & Company the remaining seventy-two acres on which his home and burial ground were located. By his agreement with the Ellicotts, the property reverted to them upon his demise. In 1851 George Ellicott sold fifty-two acres of the tract to Joshua Clements, who in turn sold twenty-five acres to Joshua Hynes ten days later. The Sydney map of 1850 shows the residences of both families, indicating that the Ellicotts had tenants living on the premises by the time they sold part of it. Following Banneker's demise and during the next century, most of the farm continued to be used for agricultural purposes.[1]

Later resurveyed as a tract named "West Ilchester," these bounds include parts of Cooper's Branch and the Old Frederick Road, the road leading to the Union Manufacturing Company Works, now called Oella Avenue, the second and third boundaries of "Stout," the first and second lines of "Stout," and a corner of the land sold by Banneker to John Barten. A corner of the remainder of the original "Stout" tract that had been resurveyed in 1761 for William Williams, it was bequeathed by his widow Mary Williams to her slaves. From these points of reference the final segment of Banneker's farm could be determined to have included the land on both sides of Oella Avenue between the Old Frederick Road and the line of the former Electric Railway, extending as far as the head of Cooper's Branch.[2] The land on which Robert and Mary Banneky, and later Benjamin, had toiled and lived for almost a century resisted the advances of modern technology for a time after their demise and succeeded in returning to nature in a state only a little less primeval than when they first owned it.

At a juncture of the manufacturing centers is the land Banneker used for tobacco culture, near the little-traveled section of the Old Frederick Road that runs from Ellicott City toward Catonsville. It extends on both sides of Oella Avenue, which twists and curves precariously northward after crossing Westchester Avenue and drops torturously into the hollow that is now Oella. Banneker's house was situated on the ridge overlooking Oella Avenue, the land dropping abruptly toward the ravine of Cooper's Branch, where one local tradition claims that the family burial ground was located. The old railway line was laid along part of the foot of the slope, and the Old

Frederick Road follows a wide plateau where once were open fields. The plateau, which commands an excellent view on all four sides of the region for a great distance, is covered with a thick undergrowth penetrated occasionally by sunlight and shadowed by tall second-growth trees. The line of the abandoned electric railway follows the diminished Cooper's Branch, now a muddy brook, which skirts the ravine at the foot of the plateau as it trickles westward to join the Patapsco River at Ellicott City.[3] From the time the Ellicott brothers purchased the land from Banneker in about 1799, the property remained unused in the possession of the Ellicott family until 1851, when George Ellicott sold part of it. Thereafter the property went through the hands of at least twelve owners who had it under cultivation at various times until 1972.[4]

In response to growing interest about Banneker and where he lived, in 1976 the confines of the farm were established with certainty. The actual boundaries were traced from an 1835 Howard County plat onto an 1803 Anne Arundel County plat of West Ilchester, and the confines of the farm were ascertained upon a current tax map of the region. Preliminary searches for the site were undertaken by a group of local citizens in 1979 and again in 1982. In 1983 a professional survey of the tract of the remaining seventy-two acres that Banneker had owned was identified.

It was not until some 180 years after Banneker's death that serious consideration was given to preserving his home site and converting part of his farm into a historical park. Very few sites related to the lives and work of significant African Americans have been preserved, for lack of tangible evidence. In Banneker's case there was ample supporting evidence not only of his achievments but also of the premises he had occupied.

Discussions continued for more than a decade before positive action was taken. Then, at a time when local interest in preserving the Banneker site was clearly on the rise, it was learned that a major part of the former Stout farm was about to be sold. Responding to this public interest, Baltimore County purchased 42.8 acres of Banneker's original acreage in January 1985. The tract encompassed the Banneker archeological site, containing the general location of the homestead and outbuildings. This was identified in 1983 by the Maryland Historical Trust of the State Department of Economic and Community Development from the presence of eighteenth-century artifacts.

High up on the knoll are the ruins of an old house. The remaining foundation with its great hearth was formed of blocks of the gray granite quarried at Ellicott City. It is said that a Negro cabin that had stood on this site in the nineteenth century had burned many years ago.

Standing on the same knoll "about half a mile from the Patapsco River" where in 1796 Susanna Mason had observed "a never failing spring beneath a large golden willow tree in the midst of his orchard" was Banneker's log house, which she described as a "lowly dwelling built of logs, one story in height and surrounded by an orchard." When her daughter set out to find it some forty years later, she was unsuccessful, as was the Reverend Daniel Alexander Payne who in 1845 also visited the site in search of Banneker's grave. His account suggests that the Banneker homestead had remained abandoned and relatively untouched since the time of his death, and that in fact the farm had not been under cultivation at least until the time of his visit.[5]

Six months after Baltimore County bought the tract, archeologists of the Maryland Historical Trust, funded by the Baltimore County Department of Recreation and Parks, began a search of the area. They recovered artifacts in an intensive investigation of the property in 1985 and 1986. The investigation focused on identification and study of core components from the Banneker farmstead site. After having tested various areas, the house site was determined to be site 18BA282. Investigation showed that two dwellings had occupied the site, the second of which was Banneker's log house that was destroyed by fire in 1806. There is evidence that an older, smaller, and less substantial building was replaced by the larger log house. Archaeological research determined the exact foundations of the two buildings and several other components of the Banneker homestead.

At the time he purchased the Stout tract, Robert Banneky and his young family probably had been living in a house he had built at Timber Point. Robert built his first, smaller, house on the Stout farm in 1737 or shortly thereafter. In the course of time as the family grew, more space was required and he erected a second and larger house a few years later, situated some fifty feet south of the first and placed upon a continuous stone foundation. Until this discovery by the archaeologists, there had been no knowledge of the existence of a second building.

Undoubtedly Banneker's log houses were constructed along the lines of a style used by Swedes settling in the Delaware Valley north of Maryland. During the colonial period, the design proliferated on the mid-Atlantic frontier. The second log house, built by Robert and in which Benjamin lived until his death, was constructed of logs upon stone piers. It had a large excavated storage cellar and a simple hearth with a mud-and-stick chimney. The building probably consisted of a single room measuring approximately sixteen by twenty feet. It can be compared to similar dwellings in the region. Banneker's nephew, Greenbury Morten, built in 1785 a one-story house measuring fourteen by sixteen feet, assessed in the 1798 Federal Direct Tax Assessment for Upper Patapsco Hundred at only $8.00. In about 1794, another neighbor, Edward Sugars, built a single-story, one-room house, measuring sixteen feet square and assessed at $12.00.

Since the Banneker dwelling had been erected near the crest of a hill that sloped gently to the north and northwest, its walls probably were supported by stone foundation piers set at periodic intervals. Evidence of the support of the earlier structure survives in the form of intermittent or discontinuous stone foundation piers or piles. On the eastern portion of the north wall was the building's doorway. The recovery of glass shards confirms the presence of at least one glazed window opening. The location of the simple hearth and chimney indicates that the hearthplace was more than five feet wide and one-and-a-half feet deep. Fragments of burned clay or fired daub recovered from the cellar fill suggest that the chimney was mud-and-stick or wattle and daub. In either case, the chimney was of wood and fireproofed with plaster or mud. Generally, chimneys were centrally located on an exterior gable end of the structure to reduce the threat of fire. A filled-in cellar hole is associated with the earlier building.[6]

No longer present or identifiable are the old arboreal landmarks—the tall Lombardy poplar that had marked the gable end of the house as recently as little more than a century ago, or the great old pear tree that shaded Banneker while he rested from his labors. Still, it remains a peaceful setting, and there has been little modern intrusion to this area, where Banneker "commanded a prospect of the near and distant hills of the Patapsco River, which have always been celebrated for their picturesque beauty."

A renewed search for the old Banneker family burial ground has proven unsuccessful, and neither of the two old tulip trees that grew so close together and marked the site can now be identified, nor can the old willow that shaded the Banneker spring a short distance away. A survey performed in 1985 of selected areas in and around Banneker's house by means of ground-penetrating radar and proton magnetometry failed to reveal any evidence of a graveyard. Following the information in Bishop Payne's report, the remote sensing survey covered the area southwest of the house, where it seemed likely that the graveyard would be found. Geophysical tests did not produce the hoped for results, but more intensive testing and a more rigorous consideration of factors that adversely affected the 1985 results may provide useful remote sensing data concerning the presence of subsurface features. The high residual magnetism of the soil and its rocky character may be one reason the tests failed.[7]

The archaeological excavation brought forth a full range of artifacts, including some 758 fragments of mid-eighteenth century kaolin clay pipes, bottle glass, handmade nails, fragments of earthenware, glazed stoneware, buttons, straight pins, a horseshoe, harness-leather ornaments, fragments of iron buckle frames, hooks, gun flints, hatpins, thimbles, and a variety of buttons. Other items recovered were the blade of a straight razor, slate marking pencils, a lens, and the frame of a mouth harp. Pigs' teeth, bits of charcoal, fish scales, and waste from gunflints also came to light.

Hand-wrought iron nails, nail fragments, and window glass shards ranging in color from light yellowish green to green tint were among the structural artifacts found. Melted glass undoubtedly resulted from the fire that burned the dwelling in 1806. Also found were evidence of sash-type windows, masonry debris including stone (largely mica schist), a few fragments of hand-made brick, and fragments of mortar or rough plaster. Much was learned about Banneker's life from the bits and pieces recovered from the site. A relatively high proportion of creamware and pearlware dating from the late eighteenth century to the mid-nineteenth century and the soil from which they were recovered revealed a very high concentration of potash in the top fill layer. This led archaeologists to conclude that this was the site of the house which had burned to the ground. The original building may have continued in use as an outbuilding or as a summer kitchen until about the 1780s when the cellar was filled in.[8] Evidence of fence posts were found in several places. An area approximately 160 feet east of the later house contained hand wrought nails and period artifacts and may have been the site of a barn or drying shed.

A large assemblage of faunal material indicated a reliance on both domestic and wild food sources in the earlier period. There were remains of large domestic animals such as hogs and cows and more than one hundred chicken bones, numerous egg shells, and remains of fish including

Excavation of site of Banneker's
home revealed a number of artifacts.
Maryland Historical Trust.

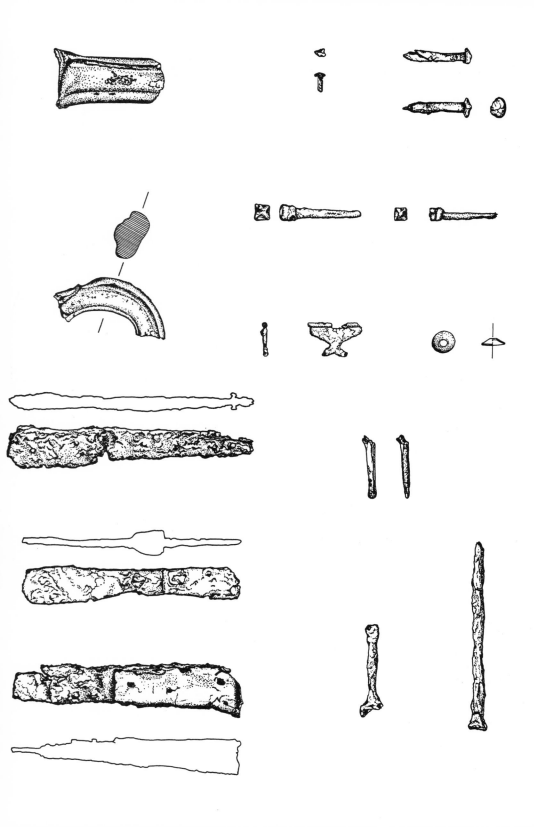

white perch and yellow perch which had been abundant in the nearby
Patapsco and its tributaries. Oysters, which were available in the tidewater
area as well as downriver also were common. The bones of grey squirrels
were also present, as were those of turkey and ruffed grouse. In the later
dwelling fewer examples of wildlife remains were to be found, probably
because meat and other foods were available from the Ellicott & Company
store at a time when age curtailed Banneker's hunting and fishing but
income from land sales and almanacs permitted him to buy food.[9]

A review of the surviving Banneker accounts with the Ellicott &
Company store for the years 1775 and 1776 reveals that in those years neither Banneker nor his mother purchased any meat from the store, apparently relying on their own livestock, hunting, and fishing. In his later years,
as his incomplete notations of purchases from 1799 to 1803 reveal, Banneker
continued to raise corn and vegetables and fruit from his orchard, but he
consistently purchased pork from the store.

Yet his purchases of gunpowder, lead shot, gun flints, and a gun lock
just four years before his death attest to the fact that he continued to hunt
and probably fish. During one year, from December 1798 to November 1799
Banneker purchased approximately seventy pounds of pork from the store,
but there is no record that he bought any pork for the nearly twenty
months from November 1799 to June 1801. This suggests that for two seasons he may have raised, butchered, and preserved sufficient pork for his
needs and that his increasing infirmities subsequently prevented him from
raising enough livestock.

Banneker was a pipe smoker, as confirmed by his purchase of clay
pipes and tobacco from the Ellicott & Company store, and by the nearly six
hundred mid-eighteenth-century kaolin pipe fragments recovered from
the site. His occasional purchase of tobacco from the Ellicott store indicates
that he had abandoned tobacco culture totally in his final years.

The lists of purchases from the Ellicott & Company store, in 1774 and
1775 by Mary and Benjamin Banneker, and then from 1795 to 1803 by
Benjamin alone, reveal other aspects of his life in both periods. During the
earlier period he made frequent purchases of rum in quantities of a quart
or a half gallon at a time. The purchase of fodder in the later period suggests that Banneker no longer was able to keep his own pastures mowed
and had to buy fodder for his horse and cows. During his last years, after he
had contracted with the Ellicott brothers for the sale of his property, fre-

quent purchases of pork, corn, and molasses appear. The cloth, thread, buttons, and related items may have been for the repair of his clothing by his sisters. He offset some of his purchases by selling mead and honey from his hives. Personal items recovered from the site included two razors, a comb, a penknife, a pocket watch, and an inkstand.

Some of these items or fragments thereof have been recovered from the archaeological excavation, though a wide variety of other objects, equally durable and which should be present on the site, have not been found. To some degree this can be plausibly explained by the probability that immediately after his death his two sisters who lived nearby, becoming concerned for the safety of their brother's possessions in an uninhabited house, removed them for distribution among their families. During the two days following Banneker's death on Sunday, October 9, until his burial on the eleventh, his sisters Minta and Molly undoubtedly went through his house together and selected items to be preserved for their own use or to be distributed to other members of the family. His personal clothing, pocket watch, penknife, inkstand and pens, his Bible, and possibly various other books, as well as pots and pans and other cooking utensils were removed. Notable by their absence from the artifacts recovered at the house site are remnants of useful everyday household wares; undoubtedly his sisters removed these objects for their own homes or those of relatives.[10]

XI

THE MAN
REMEMBERED

There is no reputation so great but
requires a little indulgence.

"Extracts from the Common-Place
Book of the Kentucky Philosopher,"
Banneker's Almanac for 1794

THE PHYSICAL APPEARANCE OF BANNEKER THE MAN is described in five separate accounts written by contemporaries who were acquainted with him during his lifetime. He is represented in one portrait claimed to have been drawn from life although obviously not so. Of the various biographical sketches and published references, only four are based upon contemporary sources. The descriptions of his physical appearance based upon personal observation are consistent in their portrayal of the amateur astronomer during the last decade of his life.

One of the most comprehensive of these accounts was compiled by Benjamin H. Ellicott. He lived during Banneker's lifetime and collected his information from various sources. He then communicated it in a letter to Moncure D. Conway, who published it in the *Atlantic Monthly* in January 1863. About Banneker, Ellicott wrote:

> During the whole of his long life he lived respectably and much esteemed by all who became acquainted with him, but more especially by those who could fully appreciate his genius and the extent of his acquirements. Although his mode of life was regular and extremely retired, — living alone, having never married, cooking his own victuals and washing his own clothes, and scarcely ever being absent from home, — yet there was nothing misanthropic in his character: for a gentleman who knew him thus

speaks of him: "I recollect him well. He was a brave-looking, pleasant man with something very noble in his appearance. His mind was evidently much engrossed in his calculations; but he was glad to receive the visits which we often paid him." Another writes: "When I was a boy I became very much interested in him, as his manners were those of a perfect gentleman: kind, generous, hospitable, humane, dignified, and pleasing, abounding in information on all the various subjects and incidents of the day, very modest and unassuming, and delighting in society at his own house. I have seen him frequently. His head was covered with a thick suit of white hair, which gave him a very dignified appearance. His dress was uniformly of superfine drab broadcloth, made in the old style of a plain coat, with straight collar and long waistcoat, and a broad-brimmed hat. His colour was not jet black, but decidedly negro. In size and personal appearance, the statue of Franklin at the Library in Philadelphia, as seen from the street, is the perfect likeness of him. Go to his house when you would, either by day or night, there was constantly standing in the middle of the floor a large table covered with books and papers. As he was an eminent mathematician, he was constantly in correspondence with other mathematicians in this country, with whom there was an interchange of questions of difficult solutions.[1]

The statue of Franklin to which Ellicott's correspondent referred was the one installed in 1790 in a niche above the doorway on the facade of the building housing the Library Company of Philadelphia. The statue was not in fact an accurate representation of Franklin. The figure had been based on sketches, not drawn from life, although the features were copied from a portrait bust of Franklin executed by the French sculptor Jean Jacques Caffieri. The implication in the statement, therefore, is not that Banneker resembled Franklin, but that he resembled the statue.[2]

Some recollections of Banneker were recorded also by Charles Worthington Dorsey, an employee of the Ellicott Mills, who recalled:

He was very precise in conversation and exhibited deep reflection. His deportment, whenever I saw him, was perfectly upright and correct, and he seemed to be acquainted with everything of importance that was passing in the country. . . . He was a large man and inclined to be fleshy. He was far advanced in years when I saw him.[3]

Thomas Ellicott, son of Andrew Ellicott (III) by a second marriage and younger half-brother of George Ellicott, described the amateur astronomer to his niece, Martha Tyson, in the following words:

I remember Benjamin Bannekers personal appearance very well. I remember much that was said about him by my elder Brothers, and other persons, at times, when I visited them at Ellicotts Mills; but as I never lived at that place, during Bannekers life term, I can say nothing that ought to be incorporated in to a Biographical memorial of his life.— I recollect he was quite a black man, of medium stature, of uncommonly soft and gentlemanly manners, and pleasant coloquial powers, and like other gentlemen of that day had not abstained from the use of intoxicating drink — though I think I never saw him improperly influenced by it. He owned I think about 50 acres of Land, about half a mile from the mills, which he conveyed to Ellicott & Co., a few years before his death, reserving to himself a life estate in it, and a yearly payment, during his life, of a Sum of money sufficient to supply his wants. How much that sum was, I do not remember, nor the time of his death.[4]

Finally there was Martha Tyson's own recollection of the philomath. As a child she had seen him at the Elkridge Meeting House. She recalled: "His ample forehead, white hair, and reverent deportment, gave him a very venerable appearance, as he leaned on the long staff (which he always carried with him) in contemplation."[5] Later, in her posthumously published account, she described him again in virtually the same words, but at greater length:

> The countenance of Banneker had a most benign and thoughtful expression. A fine head of white hair surmounted his unusually broad and ample forehead, whilst the lower part of his face was slender and sloping towards the chin. His figure was perfectly erect, showing no inclination to stoop as he advanced in years. His raiment was always scrupulously neat; that for summer wear, being of unbleached linen, was beautifully washed and ironed by his sisters. . . . In cold weather he dressed in light colored cloth, a fine drab broadcloth constituting his attire when he designed appearing in his best style.[6]

Although these details are meager, they nonetheless create a general impression of Banneker in his later years from which it is possible to visualize his appearance. They are considerably at variance, however, with the only contemporary portrait which was purportedly drawn from life. This first portrait appeared as a woodcut on the cover of the Banneker almanac for 1795 printed for the Baltimore distributor, John Fisher. No mention of the portrait is made within the almanac's contents, nor is any mention of it made among Banneker's papers, nor of those involved in the almanac's publication. The artist is not identified, but in her novelized biography of Banneker, Shirley Graham offered that the woodcut was the work of an artist from Philadelphia named Timothy Woods. No record of such an artist has been found in the literature nor in the city directories. The portrait may in fact have been executed by John Fisher, who was also an engraver, and who may have wished to enhance his edition of the almanac.

Little is known about Fisher, other than that he had lived in Philadelphia at the time of the Revolution. *The Journals of the Continental Congress* recorded on June 26, 1773, that John Fisher was owed twenty dollars for renewing copper plates for loan-office certification and for making two letters for the device utilized on thirty-dollar bills. At this time a number of the persons involved in various aspects of the book trade in Philadelphia moved to Baltimore, and Fisher may have been one of them.[7]

The woodcut appears to have been drawn by an artist who had neither seen Banneker nor heard a description of him but who obviously intended to render an idealized portrait of a black man. It represents a Negro male of medium frame in his late youth. At this time Banneker was in fact sixty-three years of age, suffering from arthritis or rheumatism, and his physical appearance may have already reflected to some degree his past illnesses and disabilities. He was described as being relatively fleshy, with a stocky build, which leaves no doubt that the portrait was in fact no more than an artist's conception of a young male Negro youth.

A portrait of Banneker in another edition of his almanac for 1795 was considerably less successful. The cover of the edition published by Samuel and John Adams at their Baltimore print shop featured what appears to have been an attempt to copy the portrait on the Fisher edition. The outline of the figure is identical in almost every detail but presumably the printers lacked a competent artist or draftsman on their staff, for the space within the outline is filled with vague, meaningless lines. It appears as if the portrait had been included in an effort to have the purchaser assume that the almanac was the one published for Fisher. The only resemblance to Banneker's physical appearance is that it was the image of a man of color.

The most accurate representation of Banneker known is a modern presentation, a mural painting of the survey of the Federal Territory featuring Banneker and Andrew Ellicott. It hangs in the Maryland House on the John F. Kennedy Highway in Aberdeen, Maryland. This mural by the late William A. Smith of Bucks County, Pennsylvania, is based upon Smith's careful research and study of descriptions of Banneker by his contemporaries and in the writings of Martha Tyson. The latter includes the account of Elizabeth Brooke Ellicott's supervision of his clothing for his journey to Alexandria.

The earliest published account of Banneker's life and achievements was the letter from Senator James McHenry included in the almanac for 1792. In addition to serving as an introduction to the almanac-maker's work, the letter was published separately again and again for the next year or so, usually without editorial comment or explanation. The first acknowledgment made of Banneker in print other than the McHenry letter was a brief reference in a work by Gilbert Imlay, published in 1793 in London, which did not mention Banneker by name. The reference to Banneker concerned an attack upon Thomas Jefferson's position on slavery. It was in this connection that Banneker's name was repeatedly brought to public notice within the next decade, distinguishing him as the only black man to question the statesman on his position.[8]

It is necessary perhaps to revisit briefly the topic of antislavery for a fuller understanding of its importance at this time. The cause of abolition in the New World had begun to engender growing sympathy as early as the end of the seventeenth century, particularly in New England. In 1729 Samuel Sewall had published his work entitled *Selling of Joseph,* a criticism of the slave trade, at a time when legislation against slavery was being prepared in Boston. This was followed by a mounting opposition among members of the Society of Friends against the purchase of slaves, and during the next century Quaker leaders, including John Woolman and Anthony Benezet, popularized the concept that slavery was un-Christian.

The doctrine of natural rights that had led to the American Revolution helped to emphasize the evils of slavery. Once again the Society of Friends assumed the burden of a national conscience. An exchange of correspondence between Quakers on both sides of the Atlantic developed into an antislavery movement that erupted into positive action in the new republic at the end of the war. Leaders of the American abolitionist movement exerted a strong effect on English Quakers who were leading the British antislavery movement.

The war of the American colonies to overthrow the British yoke was being compared to the enslavement of the Negro. Thomas Paine's tract

Mural painting of the Survey of the Federal Territory by the late William A. Smith, depicting Ellicott and Banneker. *Maryland House, John F. Kennedy Highway, Aberdeen, Maryland.*

Common Sense appeared in 1775, the same year in which was founded in Philadelphia the Society for the Relief of Negroes Unlawfully Held in Bondage. The first American antislavery society, with Benjamin Franklin as its president, it was incorporated in 1789. James Pemberton, whom Franklin succeeded, led the society in establishing similar satellite antislavery societies in several states. The first was in Maryland, under the leadership of Joseph Townsend.

During the next several years, while some of the American colonies enacted laws to prevent the future importation of slaves, motions against the slave trade also were being introduced into the British Parliament. By the end of the American Revolution, English Quakers had developed sufficient strength to launch an organized attack. They succeeded in consolidating the abolitionist forces in Great Britain sufficiently to present an Abolition Act in Parliament by 1787. This won the support of three British antislavery crusaders, the philanthropists William Wilberforce and Granville Sharp, and Prime Minister William Pitt. During the next few years the cause of abolition achieved increasing importance throughout the British Empire until it reached a climax with a great battle in Parliament in the spring of 1792.

Considerable influence on the movement in England was derived from events that had taken place elsewhere throughout the world during the previous year. The French Revolution had entered its most violent phase in 1791, and ensuing events in France brought about a violent reaction in England. At the same time the French Revolution affected its colonies overseas, and in 1791 the uprising of mulattoes in Santo Domingo resulted in massacres of white men on the island and the destruction of considerable property. A chain reaction developed, and slaves of other French islands revolted. Pitt seized the opportunity and changed his position from advocacy of the gradual abolition of slavery to urging immediate abolition. The House of Commons followed his lead and recommended the termination of the slave trade by 1796. The wild enthusiasm for the antislavery movement that had developed in England in 1792 did not last, however. Deliberations in the House of Lords succeeded in eroding its support the following year. By 1800 the movement had dwindled, and it was not until four years later that the campaign for the abolition of the slave trade was renewed.

During this period, American abolitionist societies avidly sought candidates to demonstrate the Negro's intellectual endowments as justification for awarding him equal rights. Given the fact that most blacks in America were, had been, or came from families that had been slaves, dramatic examples of Negro achievement were difficult to find in any numbers. Dr. Benjamin Rush had discovered James Derham, a black physician in New Orleans, and he also brought to light an untutored mathematical prodigy in Alexandria, Virginia, named Thomas Fuller. Phillis Wheatley had demonstrated her talents as a poet, and to the list could be added ministers Richard Allen and Absalom Jones of Philadelphia, as well as Prince Hall, a publicist of Boston. It was thus with considerable interest and enthusiasm that the Maryland and Pennsylvania Abolition Societies made every possible effort to bring Banneker to public notice after they had discovered him, for he was the unique example of black achievement in the sciences.

It was therefore no accident that, with the assured publication of his almanac for 1792, Banneker forwarded a manuscript copy of his ephemeris for that work to Thomas Jefferson, then secretary of state. Jefferson's personal interest in the sciences and in individuals of scientific achievement was well known, and his sincere desire to promote the sciences was undisputed. His position on the subject of slavery was also well known, and any comments he might make about Banneker's accomplishment would be useful for promoting the abolitionist movement.[9]

Banneker provided no indication in his letter that he was aware of Jefferson's position or writings relating to Negro slavery, and gave no indication whether he had read the latter's *Notes on the State of Virginia*. It seems likely, upon reflection, that Banneker's patrons were fully aware of the impact of the incident. But from what is known of Banneker's nature and integrity, it is most unlikely that he would have been party to a deliberate plot to place the statesman in an embarrassing position.

Banneker wrote his letter from the heart, with complete sincerity, meaning every word, although undoubtedly with the encouragement of others who were quite aware of how the ensuing correspondence could be used to serve the abolitionist movement. It was not in Banneker's character, as shown in those reported events prior to and following this correspondence, to seek Jefferson's attention. Although always satisfied with his own achievements and pleased with the acknowledgment made of them, at no time did Banneker appear to solicit praise. That he shared the same concern for the cause of slavery as did every member of his race is reflected in his letter to Jefferson and noted also in a brief poem he wrote during the same period. Martha Tyson commented on this aspect of Banneker's career:

> He appears to have been the pioneer in the movement in this part of the world, towards the improvement of his race; at a period of our history when the negro occupied almost the lowest possible grade in the scale of human beings, Banneker had struck out for himself a course, hitherto untravelled by men of his class, and had already earned a respectable position amongst men of science.[10]

Jefferson's reply to Banneker was straightforward and written very much in the same manner in which he responded to the many others who submitted their proposals or evidence of achievement in the field of science. Publication of the two letters in the Banneker almanac of 1793, in addition to their being issued as a separate pamphlet, must have made Jefferson realize the trap into which he had inadvertently fallen and the use that unquestionably would be made of it by his political enemies. In the ensuing controversy over Jefferson's candidacy for the presidency a few years later, he was attacked simultaneously from both sides—by those who foresaw in the liberation of Negro slaves a danger to the entire property system in the Southern states, and by those who supported the abolition of slavery. Banneker emerged from these attacks as the symbol of the oppressed Negro despite the fact that he was far from oppressed and had lived a half century and more in peaceful contentment.

Jefferson's critics and political opponents lost no time in pointing out the apparent inconsistencies between the statements in his reply to Banneker and the position he had taken on the subject of the Negro in his *Notes on the State of Virginia* some years earlier. The political pamphleteer and congressman from South Carolina, William Loughton Smith (ca. 1758–1812) was among the first to comment: "What shall we think of a *secretary of state* thus fraternizing with negroes, writing them complimentary epistles, stiling *them his black brethren,* congratulating them on the evidences of their *genius,* and assuring them of his good wishes for their speedy emancipation?"[11]

Smith's attack on Jefferson as a presidential candidate was vicious, and not at all times rational. He launched his barbs in both directions, for he described Banneker as "the reputed author of an Almanac," implying that he might have been given credit for the work of others. Again in 1800, Jefferson was the subject of an attack by lawyer and legislator Henry W. De Sassure (1763–1830) in a public statement that was subsequently published. As a candidate for the presidency, De Sassure found Jefferson vulnerable on a number of points, including his response to Banneker, and he attempted to demonstrate that Jefferson's election would be detrimental to the interests of the Southern states.[12]

The attacks continued, and in 1806 the satirist Thomas Green Fessenden (1771–1837) added his comments on then-President Jefferson's attitude on the subject. In his 1805 work, *Democracy Unveiled, or Tyranny Stripped of the Garb of Patriotism*, he launched a bitter poetic attack on Jefferson, again using the statesman's letter to Banneker to illustrate his position.[13]

In general, the published attacks on Jefferson sought to point out that his error may have been in not having endorsed Banneker's achievement as an example of intellectual activity but rather as evidence of moral eminence. If he had acknowledged Banneker's work as an example of scientific accomplishment, as had other prominent American figures in the field of science, such as David Rittenhouse and Andrew Ellicott, the presumed implication of Negro inferiority claimed in Jefferson's reply would not have emerged as a major issue.[14]

Following the occasional references appearing in connection with the attacks on Jefferson, Banneker was first memorialized in a work on Negro literature by Henri Gregoire (1750–1831), Bishop of Blois, which was published in Paris in 1808. Gregoire was a great libertarian who devoted his lifetime to the politically and socially oppressed. He produced the first study of Negro literature, in which he presented each of the arguments being made against the mental and moral faculties of the Negro with his own rebuttal to each of them. Gregoire collected biographical sketches of fifteen Negroes of note, including Banneker. In his brief account of the tobacco farmer, which featured Jefferson's reply to Banneker, Gregoire incorporated a number of factual errors. Gregoire's sources were the McHenry letter and the brief references he had found in the works of Imlay and Fessenden. He was not aware that Banneker had died two years earlier.[15]

Gregoire's presentation of Banneker's life tends to support the probability that Jefferson's letter to the Marquis de Condorcet with Banneker's manuscript had not been submitted to the Académie des Sciences. The bishop would have been the first to be informed of it, and would have exerted every effort to publicize it. As an active member of the Société des Amis des Noirs, he would have found Jefferson's communication particularly valuable as propaganda for the French antislavery movement. Even more conclusive is the fact that if Gregoire had known of the letter and the manuscript ephemeris he would have mentioned them in his correspondence with Jefferson on the subject of his book, a copy of which he had forwarded to him. Jefferson acknowledged the gift and closed his letter with the expressed hope that the Bishop would "accept my thanks for the many instances you have enabled me to observe of respectable intelligence in that race of men, which cannot fail to have effect in hastening the days of their relief. . . . Be assured that no person living, wishes more sincerely than I do, to see a complete refutation of the doubts I have myself entertained and expressed on the grade of understanding allotted to them by nature, and to find that in this respect they are on a par with ourselves."[16]

Jefferson's politeness to Gregoire was not completely sincere, as revealed in a letter which he wrote shortly thereafter to his friend Joel Barlow (1754–1812), the American poet and diplomat. He commented on his exchange of letters with Gregoire and on the latter's book in quite uncomplimentary terms. He described the work as having been assembled without discrimination or relation to truth or fiction. Furthermore, despite his own reply to Banneker, Jefferson had apparently had cause to reflect further and had come to the conclusion that he could not, after all, entertain a high opinion of either the amateur astronomer's work or his mental ability, as he wrote to Barlow:

> Bishop Gregoire wrote to me on the doubts I had expressed five or six and twenty years ago, in the *Notes on the State of Virginia*, as to the grade of understanding of the negroes. His credulity had made him gather up every story he could find of men of color (without distinguishing whether black, or of what degree of mixture), however slight the mention, or light the authority on which they are quoted. The whole do not amount in point of evidence, to what we know ourselves about Banneker. We know he had spherical trigonometry enough to make almanacs, but not without the suspicion of aid from Ellicot, who was his neighbor and friend, and never missed an opportunity of puffing him. I have a long letter from Banneker, which shows him to have had a mind of very common stature indeed. It was impossible for doubt to have been more tenderly or hesitatingly

expressed than that was in the *Notes on Virginia,* and nothing was or is further from my intentions, than to enlist myself as the champion of a fixed opinion, where I have only expressed a doubt. St. Domingo will, in time, throw light on the question.[17]

Jefferson's comments about Banneker come as something of a surprise after his letter acknowledging receipt of the manuscript ephemeris and the one he sent to the Marquis de Condorcet. His reference to "the suspicion of aid from Ellicot who was his neighbor and friend, and never missed an opportunity of puffing him" requires some comment. The Ellicott who was Banneker's neighbor and friend, namely, George, did not calculate ephemerides for almanacs, while Andrew Ellicott, who did make such calculations for a series of almanacs, was neither a neighbor nor particularly Banneker's friend. It is true that Jefferson had expressed himself on the Negro question most tenderly and hesitatingly in his *Notes on the State of Virginia,* but there is considerable question whether Banneker was aware of this work and had read it.

Jefferson's evaluation of Banneker was reflected also in a conversation he held with the young British diplomat, Sir Augustus John Foster, when the latter visited Monticello. Foster reported on the conversation in his notes, which were later published:

> Mr. Jefferson told me of a Negro named Bannister [sic], who died in the year 1806, at Baltimore, being a perfect black, the son of an African, and who had acquired considerable knowledge in mathematics so as to be able to solve very difficult problems. He annually published an almanac but the President asserted that in other respects he appeared to little advantage, particularly in his letters, he having received several from him, which were very childish and trivial. He told me, also, that the Negroes have, in general, so little foresight that though they receive blankets very thankfully from their masters on the commencement of winter and use them to keep off the cold, yet when the warm weather returns they will frequently cast them off, without a thought of what is to become of them, wherever they may happen to be at the time, and then not seldom lose them in the woods or the fields from mere carelessness.[18]

In 1836, the first published account of Banneker's career, other than what had appeared in his almanacs, was published in a volume of the letters and manuscripts of Susanna Mason collected by her daughter, Rachel.

In a memoir of her mother's life that formed part of the volume, Rachel Mason related that while she was visiting friends at Ellicott's Mills a short time prior to the book's publication, she was reminded of a visit to Banneker that her mother had made some years earlier. Thereupon, with several of her friends, Rachel set out across the countryside to revisit the site of the farm, only to discover that "memory has not chart whereby to direct our steps," and they failed to find it. Others in the region told her that the old astronomer's pear tree and the orchard still survived, although all evidence of the log house had perished long ago.[19] (For the full account see Document 34)

Although Martha Ellicott Tyson's own personal recollections of Banneker were limited only to what she recalled in her youth, she had often heard about him from her parents and others. To assist Rachel Mason in producing a narrative about Banneker, Martha Tyson interviewed his surviving relatives and the few people still alive who had been acquainted with Banneker in his lifetime. Among the latter were Jacob Hall, Banneker's boyhood friend, and John Henden, Banneker's cousin. Tyson's research was extremely thorough, and in her "Memoir," an undated manuscript, she wrote about her cousin and friend Rachel:

> After Rachel Mason had finished her memoir of her mother in 1836, she wished to prepare a narrative of the life of Benjamin Banneker, in order that the example of his fine talents, studious habits and ultimate attainments as an astronomer might be made useful to the people of color here as well as elsewhere; but aware at the same time that the value of such a work would be much increased if she could represent him (according to a concise account which had appeared in print), of being of strictly African parentage, she was anxious to procure proofs to that effect, and by the assistance of her friends made many enquiries on the subject, and I regret to say without the desired success, as I shall proceed to relate. At the date referred to, Banneker had been dead about 32 years but there still remained amongst the living a few persons who had been intimately acquainted with him — but before referring to them I asked my mother's opinion on the subject — she had often seen him previous to 1790, a period when he was looked upon as a very extraordinary man, and had always understood that his mother was a woman of mulatto complexion, very like an Indian in appearance and uncommonly intelligent and active. But being willing to establish the truth of the statement supporting his origin, she referred me to John Henden a man of color who she believed to be connected with the

Banneker family: — nor was she mistaken, he proved to be a near relation, being the son of Banneker's mother's sister. I ought not however omit to relate that John Henden had always been considered a man of strict integrity and was for a number of years employed by Ellicott & Co., and had charge of their stables. He told me he had been raised from a little child by old Molly Banneker who was his grandmother, and also the grandmother of Benjamin Banneker; she was a very industrious white woman & native of England, who came to this country when quite young. The account was confirmed by all the aged persons I conversed with on the subject who knew anything of the circumstances of the family.

Jacob Hall a very respected colored man who furnished some of the information recorded in the "Sketch" was originally the property of a gentleman and lady who had a residence on one of the hills near Ellicott's Mills. They were a benevolent pair and very kind to their slaves. They bequeathed by will to Jacob Hall and his two brothers Sharper and Will, and a sister named Hannah, each a small piece of land upon which their descendants now reside. In 1836 Jacob Hall was very far advanced in years, but with a mind in good preservation. He was considered a faithful chronicler of past events, and I have often listened to his details with interest.

Just before completing the "Sketch" which had been presented to the Historical Society I sent for a niece of Banneker named Harriet Henderson, in order to find if her account of her grandmother would coincide with John Henden's statement. She was young at the time of Banneker's death and was living as a small servant at the house of Ennion Williams at Elkridge Landing. Her account of Molly Welsh was similar to that I have given above with a few additional particulars, respecting the cause of her leaving England. Harriet Henderson lives at present in Washington she sometimes visits Baltimore. Moses Sheppard's servant George sent her to me and could say where she might be found. It was in George's family I found the old Bible which contained the record of Benjamin Banneker's birth.[20]

Sheppard's servant, George Barton, may have been a grandson of Banneker's aunt, Katherine, who had married James Boston [or Baslon, Barton?] in 1735, his name perhaps erroneously derived over the years, as had happened with Banneker's own. Although Harriet Henderson was stated to have been Banneker's niece, namely, the daughter of one of his sisters, she has not been further identified.

Several years after Banneker's death, his energetic sister, Minta Black, came to public attention as a victim of a current Maryland law relating to free Negroes. This was the statute of 1783 that denied to persons manumitted thereafter the privileges of office-holding, voting at elections, and giving evidence against white persons. In a court case involving white persons, Minta had been proposed as a witness on behalf of the plaintiff. The defendant objected to her appearance in the case, claiming that Minta was incompetent and should be disqualified. The plaintiff assured the court of her competence and pointed out that she was Benjamin Banneker's sister, having been born of the same parents, and descended of free parentage. He added that Banneker exercised all rights of a free man, that he had voted in elections and had been allowed to give evidence in courts of justice in cases in which free white men were concerned, and that consequently his sister qualified on the same basis. Minta had been born a free woman prior to the enactment of the statute. The court nevertheless determined that Minta would make an incompetent witness inasmuch as both the plaintiff and defendant were free white Christian individuals. The plaintiff had no choice but to accept the ruling.[21] (Document 47)

The name "Banneker" or versions thereof unquestionably appear to have been derived originally from "Bannka" or "Bannaka," the name of Benjamin Banneker's Senegambian grandfather, a name modified over the years in pronunciation. As a consequence, it appears to have been limited to members of the single family. Of considerable interest, therefore, is the presence in Baltimore County records of two individuals named "Baniker," Peter and Abraham, living at the same time and region as Benjamin Banneker. This circumstance appears to be too great a coincidence and must have some substance. Is it possible that Molly Welsh and Bannaka had a son in addition to their daughters? No record linking Peter and Abraham Baniker to Molly Welsh's family has been found.

Peter Baniker was a shoemaker who on September 1, 1794, adopted an orphan boy named Charles Philip Wise, then aged nine months, to whom he would eventually teach the trade of shoemaker.[22] Peter Baniker [Benecker] apparently died in 1802 or 1803, for an inventory of his goods and chattels and those of his widow, Mary Ann Baniker of Baltimore, included shoemakers' tools. Filed June 25, 1803, the inventory was compiled by Robert R. Richardson.[23]

The second individual bearing a version of the name was Abraham Banniker, born in 1773 and declared an orphan in October 1782. He was at age nine bound to Dutton Lane Jr., believed to have been a landowner. In 1785, Abraham, who was reported to having been then sixteen but was actually twelve, was apprenticed to George N. Griffith to learn shoemaking and farming. In 1798, Griffith occupied land in Middlesex Hundred owned by Henry Willis. The related documents are the following:

> Abraham Banniker an Orphan of the Age of nine years is bound to Dutton Lane Junior 'till he arrives at the Age of twenty one to be taught to Read, Write and Arithmetic as far as the Rule of Three or proportion to be provided good and sufficient Meat, Drink, Washing, Lodging and Apparel during the Term and at the Expiration thereof to have a compleat decent Suit of new Cloaths.[24]
>
> Abraham Banniker an Orphan Boy of the Age of 16 Years the 13th Day of next October is bound to George N. Griffith to be Taught the Trade of a Shoemaker and the Farming Business to be taught to Read Write and Arithmetick as far as the Rule of three to be found in sufficient meat Drink Washing Lodging and apparel and at the Expiration of his time Customary freedom Dues.[25]

Events in the decades that followed had the desirable effect of periodically reviving Banneker's name and acknowledging him to have been an outstanding member of his race. John H. B. Latrobe of Baltimore, the one chiefly responsible for the founding of the American Colonization Society in 1816, was also instrumental in establishing the Maryland Historical Society in 1844. He compiled an account of Banneker that he read before members of the society and published in the *Maryland Colonization Journal* the following year.

In the paper Latrobe drew upon original materials—Banneker's manuscript journal and commonplace book, both of which had been loaned to the Maryland Historical Society, presumably for his use. He had also assistance from Martha E. Tyson, and benefited from a compilation of information about Banneker from those who remembered him made by Benjamin H. Ellicott. Latrobe's biographical sketch is one of the most important sources on Banneker and provided the first comprehensive account of Banneker's life and achievements. It proved to be a popular account and was reprinted repeatedly. As Latrobe concluded in his memoir of Banneker,

> The extent of his knowledge is not so remarkable, as that he acquired what he did under the circumstances we have described. It might be said by

those disposed to sneer at his simple history, if there be any such, that after all he was but an almanac-maker, a very humble personage in the ranks of astronomical science. But that the almanac-maker of Pennsylvania, Delaware, Maryland and Virginia, from 1791 to 1802, should have been a free black man, is, to use the language of Mr. Jefferson, a fact to which his whole colour has a right for their justification against the doubts that have been entertained of them.[26]

At about the same time, the subject of Benjamin Banneker preoccupied yet another prominent figure in Baltimore. In 1845 the Reverend Daniel Alexander Payne had been assigned to the Bethel African Methodist Church. In the early part of that first year in his new assignment, the Reverend Payne learned about the self-taught astronomer and was intrigued by the story. He delivered a lecture about Banneker's life and work at his church to inspire the young men of his parish to pursue the sciences. In fact, he presented the lecture, whenever the opportunity arose, to raise funds for a monument over Banneker's grave.

On July 9, 1845, Payne and a committee of three fellow churchmen set out to find the site where Banneker was buried. Residents of Ellicott's Lower Mills conducted them across the fields of Banneker's farm and pointed out the location of the Banneker family graveyard. Payne subsequently reported:

> Beneath two tulip-trees, so grown as to seem one, lay the mortal remains of the black astronomer of Maryland. A few yards to the north-west of the grave was the site of his house, not a vestige of which could then be seen. It was marked only by a shallow cavity, at the south-eastern end of which stood a tall Lombardy poplar, said to be that which overshadowed the gable end of his house.[27]

Despite his efforts, Payne, who later become a bishop of the A.M.E. Church, failed to raise sufficient funds for erecting the monument he had proposed. Nonetheless, with the assistance of John H. B. Latrobe, he arranged to have a design for such a monument prepared by R. Cary Long Jr., a prominent Baltimore architect. That Payne and Latrobe succeeded in persuading Long to design the modest little monument is impressive, for Long, whose specialty was church architecture distinguished by a military Gothic style, had succeeded his father as the foremost architect of Baltimore. For a brief period, during which time Payne and Latrobe discussed with him the Banneker monument, he had become interested in

Egyptian style, particularly for cemetery structures. His design for the Banneker monument took the form of an Egyptian obelisk. Bishop Payne attempted to preserve the drawing in his papers (they now reside at the library at Wilberforce University), but apparently it has not survived.[28]

Bishop Payne's unsuccessful attempt to memorialize Banneker's grave did not diminish his interest in the astronomer. Between 1858 and 1862 he served as editor of the *Repository of Religion, Science and Literature* and wrote for the journal a series of articles on Banneker. In one of the last issues of the *Repository,* Payne featured "A Literary Curiosity — Letter from Benjamin Banneker to Hon. Thomas Jefferson." In introducing the article, which contained also Jefferson's response to Banneker, Payne noted: "The author of this letter was one of the most remarkable colored men who ever lived upon this continent... a man of uncommon mathematical genius." After continuing in this vein, Payne added, "in subsequent numbers of the Repository, I will give many other facts about this very remarkable man — one who has done quite as much as any other person to defend our race from the foul slander heaped upon them by their enemies — by those who delight to asperse us."[29]

An even greater effort to memorialize Banneker's name and accomplishments was made several decades after his death by Moses Sheppard, the Baltimore philanthropist. Sheppard spent a large part of his fortune on behalf of free blacks who had been manumitted by their masters but not set free by the heirs. He donated in funds and in books and by other means to Negroes in Africa. Sheppard (1771–1857), was a well-known Quaker who, although a native of Philadelphia, lived most of his life in Baltimore. During the American Revolution, espousal of the Loyalist cause by his father, Nathan Sheppard, resulted in the forfeiture of his property, thus forcing young Moses to seek his own career at an early age. He worked as a clerk with John Mitchell and later became his partner and finally his successor. After his retirement from business in 1832, he devoted all his energies and much of his wealth to the antislavery movement and was a strong supporter of the American Colonization Society.[30]

Sheppard provided funds for the education of Samuel McGill and other blacks who played an important role in the development of Liberia. He was also instrumental in preventing passage of a law to banish free Negroes from Maryland. A member of the Maryland Historical Society, he spent much time in its reading rooms, as well as at the Baltimore public library. Upon his death in 1857 his estate was bequeathed to the founding of the Sheppard asylum for the insane in Baltimore.

Sheppard became interested in Banneker after reading Latrobe's memoir and learning that Banneker's manuscript journal and common-place book were in the society's library, where an unidentified member of the Ellicott family had deposited them for safe-keeping in 1852. Martha E. Tyson noted that "the manuscripts . . . were enclosed in a rustic cover of parchment of antique appearance" and that Sheppard "had them bound in Russia leather."[31] She confirmed their identity, writing that the Banneker manuscripts comprised two separate volumes, a large volume of astronomical and other notations, and "his common-place book."[32] Latrobe had commented on how the old farmer's writing in these volumes impressed him. It "is very good and remarkably distinct, having a practised look, although evidently that of an old man, who makes his letters and figures slowly and carefully."[33] (See Documents 35–38 inclusive.)

When Sheppard discovered the journal in the library, he became particularly intrigued with the copies Banneker had made of his exchange of letters with Jefferson. Banneker had copied the original of his letter and of Jefferson's reply into his manuscript journal in his own handwriting, and Sheppard undertook to have this copy—not the original letters—reproduced in a large lithograph for distribution, together with a short descriptive text, which Latrobe may have prepared. Several distinct differences between the originals of the Banneker-Jefferson correspondence and the copies Banneker made in his journal are noteworthy. For instance, in the latter Banneker did not spell out his name in full as he had in the original, and in his copy he omitted both the footnote concerning his father's African origin and the second postscript concerning Crukshank.

Sheppard recorded the progress of this project in a series of letters he wrote to several significant figures of the day. The earliest, dated January 20, 1852, was addressed to Latrobe, with whom Sheppard had worked closely over a period of years in the antislavery cause.

I agreed with Hoen & Co to Lithograph Bannaker and Jefferson's letters, they got the original when you were absent. I wanted you to edit it, their shop is in one of Hopkins's row 2nd Street, will you take the trouble to call and give them any directions that you may see proper, would it not be well to insert that it is Bannaker's writing. I want a handsome Job.[34]

Early in May Sheppard sent a copy of the lithograph to Senator Charles Sumner of Massachusetts, a leading opponent of slavery, noting that perhaps the Banneker-Jefferson correspondence would not be unacceptable to the author of the "Law of Human Progress," which Sheppard stated he had read with considerable interest. Exactly a week later, he again wrote to Sumner, commenting on the latter's speech on the Iowa land grant, and then went on to remark, "I know that a single case proves nothing as to a race, there was Newton and I have internal evidence that all his race are not Newtons."[35] (See Document 39)

In July, Sheppard wrote to Dr. Samuel F. McGill at Cape Palmas in Liberia and described the lithograph he had arranged to have produced, which he noted had cost him sixty dollars. He expressed deep disappointment at the lack of response to the lithograph he had received in some quarters, and noted that white people seemed to have taken more interest in his project than members of Banneker's own race.[36] (See Document 40)

Sheppard's disappointment was understandable in view of his great investment in the advancement of the Negro, and he could not understand the failure of African Americans to express an interest in such an outstanding member of their race. The apparent lack of appreciation of Sheppard's endeavors is reflected to some degree in a brief, typewritten account of Banneker, undated and by an unknown author, found in the files of the Maryland State Archives in Annapolis. The account states that the Reverend John T. Raymond, a distinguished black Baptist clergyman, issued an edition of the Latrobe memoir with the comment: "I have snatched it from their (the Colonizationalists) foul purpose, in order to produce a contrary effect.— Our people are now too wise to be entangled in their meshes."

Later that year, Sheppard again corresponded with Dr. McGill and provided some valuable data concerning his interest in Banneker. On the same day Sheppard forwarded a copy of the lithograph to George M. Justice at Baltimore, with a note that it was done "To preserve from accident and oblivion something of a man who may be termed the Newton of his race." He speculated particularly on the possible effect the knowledge that he was of mixed blood may have had upon Banneker's own attitudes. (See Document 41)

Sheppard printed a limited edition of the lithograph at his own expense and forwarded copies to appropriate libraries as well as to many prominent individuals. Among those who received them were General John G. Chapman of Port Tobacco, Maryland, Judge Chambers of Chestertown, and Edward Everett (1794–1865) at the State Department in Washington.[37] Philanthropist and reformer Dorothea Dix (1802–87) in Washington wrote to Sheppard requesting a half dozen copies of the lithograph, which she planned to distribute to several members of Congress and public institutions.[38]

As Martha Tyson noted, Sheppard then had the manuscript journal bound in order to protect its contents. The binding he selected was of fine Russia leather, with marbled end-papers and six blank sheets added to the front and back of the manuscript. Banneker had begun a separate set of astronomical calculations on loose sheets of paper, and these six additional pages of notes were bound in at the end of the volume. The separate sheets were of smaller size, measuring 7-1/2 by 12-9/16 inches on paper watermarked with the cipher "McC" and the date "1798." The volume's front cover was decorated with an elaborate border stamped in gilt, and the name BANNEKER was printed in the upper center. Pasted inside the journal's front cover is the bookplate of the Maryland Historical Society. The notation of gift or donation has since been erased, although the date "1845" remains.[39]

Originally Banneker's manuscript volume was not intended as a gift from the Ellicott family to the society; it may have been deposited for safekeeping or more likely, as a loan to enable Latrobe to use it at his convenience during the time he was preparing his *Memoir* in 1844. The volume was not recorded in the society's accession records among the gifts received, and the circumstances of its temporary removal from the society's collections are almost as mysterious as those relating to its appearance in them. At an unknown later date, the society returned the volume to an Ellicott descendant, and it thereafter remained in the possession of that family until recently, when it has been once again returned to the society, as a permanent donation.[40]

The Maryland Historical Society again inadvertently became the center for the amateur astronomer's commemoration. On October 5, 1854, J. Saurin Norris, president of the First National Bank of Baltimore, read before a meeting of the society a biographical sketch of Banneker by an author then unidentified. On that same occasion, Norris presented to the society the gift of two original letters written by Banneker, one to George

Ellicott and the other to Susanna Mason, both of which have been quoted in this work. Also part of the gift was George Ellicott's personal copy of the Banneker almanac for 1792 on which he had inscribed his name. These were gifts donated by the family of George Ellicott and presented by the unidentified author of "A Sketch," who proved to be George Ellicott's daughter, Martha Ellicott Tyson. Norris was the husband of Henrietta Tyson, the niece of Nathan Tyson, Martha's husband, and thus related to the author by marriage.

Norris's presentation of *A Sketch* was one of the most important contributions to Banneker's memory. It was a compilation of facts collected from individuals in Baltimore County or their descendants who had known Banneker in his lifetime. Martha Tyson had begun collecting this information in 1836 at the suggestion and with the encouragement of her mother. Because of her valuable contribution to the memorialization of Banneker, it is appropriate to dwell briefly on Martha Tyson and her unusual career and her role in Banneker's story.

Born at Ellicott's Lower Mills on September 13, 1795, she was the second of George and Elizabeth (Brooke) Ellicott's four daughters. More than any other member of her family, she became interested in family history and even as a child was particularly observant of events at the Mills. She was eleven years of age when Banneker died, so that her personal memories of him were limited, but she remembered and treasured the accounts of him she heard from her father and mother, as well as from relatives and friends. On September 27, 1815, she married Nathan Tyson, a merchant miller and a son of Elisha Tyson, the celebrated philanthropist and antislavery advocate. Nathan and Martha Tyson were the parents of twelve children and were important members of the Society of Friends in Baltimore. Martha became an acceptable minister of the Society, remaining active in the organization until her death in 1873. In addition to *A Sketch of the Life of Benjamin Banneker; From Notes Taken in 1836,* read before the Maryland Historical Society and published in 1854, she was the author of *Settlement of Ellicott's Mills, With Fragments of History therewith Connected,* also read before the society and published in 1865. Martha Tyson's longer account of Banneker, *Banneker, the Afric-American Astronomer. From the Posthumous Papers of Martha E. Tyson* was published posthumously in 1884. Norris described Martha Tyson in a foreword to *A Sketch* as "a lady, who, from motives of delicacy, had chosen to withhold her name, . . . The Authoress was an immediate descendant of that branch of the Ellicott family, of Ellicott's Mills, from whom Banneker received much assistance in the prosecution of his studies."[41]

In the same work, Martha Tyson commented on the compilation of notes from which it was derived, without naming the compiler, "a writer of acknowledged merit, who believed that the astronomer's example of mental application, and subsequent attainments, might have a useful influence on his brethren, both in the United States, and in the African Colonies, and therefore wished to draw up a narrative of his life. But discouragement in the prosecution of the plan, having occured, the work was abandoned, and its intended author died in 1849." The notes had been returned to Martha Tyson, who prepared them in the form of the paper Norris presented to the society. The compiler of the notes, described as a "writer of acknowledged merit" was Rachel Mason, Susanna Mason's daughter and Martha's distant cousin, with whom she corresponded frequently in the decades preceding Rachel's death. In 1836, Rachel had brought together and published a volume of her mother's letters with a memoir. In one letter, written well after Martha Tyson had begun to collect data for her cousin's use, Rachel wrote that she had "received a message from thee . . . respecting B. Banaker. I have not materials to complete anything worth giving to the public, I think if I had, I should not feel competent to do it."[42] Rachel Mason believed that a publication about Banneker would be of greater interest to members of the Negro race if he could be represented therein to be "of strictly African parentage," and her failure to find that such was the case apparently dissuaded her from attempting it.[43] (See Document 42)

Rachel died in 1849 without even having begun the project, and it remained for Martha Tyson to fulfill it.[44] In preparing *A Sketch* for presentation to the Maryland Historical Society, Martha had several aims in mind. She had noted in an unpublished manuscript that Latrobe's *Memoir* misrepresented Banneker's parentage. In an effort to correct this misinformation, and to realize Rachel's plan, she had her *Sketch* presented to and published by the society.[45] (See Document 43). Almost a decade passed after the appearance of *A Sketch* before she sent a copy of it to Latrobe, along with other related materials. He replied graciously, noting that he had not been aware of her work prior to its arrival and that he now stood corrected in the matter of Banneker's parentage.[46] (See Document 44)

Before the Maryland Historical Society published *A Sketch*, questions arose concerning some of the statements therein, and the unidentified author was asked to make some revisions. A letter to Norris from Brantz Mayer, the society's librarian, expressed concern as to whether the article was strictly factual in matters dealing with race. He emphasized that opinions on the subject of slavery should be removed lest they provide further fuel to the society's critics. A comparison of the original manuscript with the published version reveals that considerable material was left out for this reason.[47] (See Document 45)

Meanwhile, Banneker's name and fame were perpetuated elsewhere, with the establishment of the Banneker Institute, of the City of Philadelphia. This organization was founded in a meeting of its incorporators held on September 9, 1853, who voted to form a "Young Men's Mutual Instruction Society." The name was not a satisfactory one, and it was soon changed to the "Alexandrian Academy" and later the "Alexandrian Institute." There is no evidence in the minutes for the first year that the organization limited its membership to Negro youth, but at a meeting held late in 1853 a motion was made "that a memorial be presented to the committee of the Institute for Colored Youth." At the meeting of April 13, 1854, the organization was renamed the "Banaker Institute."[48]

The institute flourished, and within the first decade it published a constitution and by-laws stating the objective of the organization to be primarily "the mental improvement of its members by means of lectures, debates and the formation of such committees in the various branches of knowledge, as may be deemed most effectual . . . ; secondarily, the diffusion of useful knowledge among all who may come within the pale of its influence."[49] Meetings were held at eight o'clock in the evening on the second Wednesday of each month, and membership consisted usually of about thirty young Negro men of Philadelphia. The institute received important press notices in November 1860, when it celebrated the eighth year of its existence on the 128th anniversary of Banneker's birth. The event was held at the "colored Masonic Hall" on South Eleventh Street, below Pine Street, and drew the black elite of Philadelphia. In honor of the occasion a bundle of Banneker's letters, owned by the Anti-Slavery Society, were exhibited to the audience.[50] (See Document 46)

The Banneker papers presented on the occasion were not in fact original documents but transcriptions made by hand and later deposited in the files of the Banneker Institute. Included among them were a number of letters sent by Townsend and Elias Ellicott to James Pemberton concerning Banneker and the publication of the almanac for 1792, the comments of David Rittenhouse and William Waring on Banneker's first ephemeris, and the certificate of its authenticity. Also included was the short poem by Banneker. The Institute continued to meet over the years in various public places in Philadelphia, including the Masons Hall and the Library Company of Philadelphia.[51]

Moncure D. Conway revived memories of Banneker once more during the Civil War, in a detailed account of his life published first in the *Atlantic Monthly* in 1863 and subsequently reprinted several times. Conway, the son of a Virginia slaveowner, achieved considerable note as an author and preacher. In his early writings he supported slavery, but he became such an outspoken opponent that in 1856 he was dismissed from his position as pastor of the Unitarian Church in Washington. He edited the *Commonwealth*, an antislavery newspaper, published several books and pamphlets, and lectured on the subject of antislavery in England. Conway's article about Banneker was a substantive publication and was reprinted widely in the United States. In 1864 the Ladies' London Emancipation Society reprinted it in London as a separate tract, and it became a useful work in supporting Union interests in Great Britain.[52]

Shortly before the close of the nineteenth century the first book-length biography of Banneker, and the first authoritative study of his life and work, was published. This tiny volume, based upon the notes compiled over many years by Martha Tyson, was intended to be an expansion of the earlier paper she had prepared and which Norris had read in 1854. Martha Tyson did not complete the work before her death in 1873; it remained in the form of posthumous notes that her daughter Anne Tyson Kirk edited. It is regrettable that Martha Tyson was unable to complete personally the project to which she had devoted so much attention over the years, for undoubtedly she would have been able to give it more substance.[53]

While preparing the manuscript for a publisher, Anne Kirk sought advice and encouragement from Frederick Douglass. Although her own letters to Douglass have not survived, a clear account of the discussion that ensued about the book can be derived from his replies. Inasmuch as these letters have not previously been studied or published, and since they relate so specifically to the perpetuation of the image of Banneker, their complete texts are presented herewith.[54]

In the first of the letters, dated March 4, 1878, Douglass replied in a most cooperative manner, encouraging Mrs. Kirk in her project. In answer to her question about its probable sale, he told her that a biography of "Benjamin Bannecker . . . if small and not made to cost more than fifty cents per copy, could sell and sell well among my newly emancipated people. We as a people are especially in need of just such examples of mental industry and success as I believe the life of Bannecker furnish." He then urged haste. "The sooner you give us the work the better and more timely it will be."[55]

Mrs. Kirk plodded along with her mother's notes, spending considerable time rewriting and editing. Because she was inexperienced as a writer, her negotiations with a publisher were disappointing. Possibly the times were not propitious, or the publisher's initial enthusiasm may have waned for some reason, but it is also true that after waiting a year for the manuscript he probably expected a better product than she submitted.

Kirk's dejection was reflected in her letter to Douglass a year later. He encouraged her once more to hurry. "I would not . . . have its publication delayed a week longer. The country needs it today. It will, I believe help my race immensely both as an incentive and a vindication." He was supportive. "I believe that a full narrative of the life of so exceptional a character as Bannecker will find a ready sale both in the North and in the South among colored and among white readers," he told her. And he had misgivings. "I wish I could see the Manuscript before you publish it. . . . There has been an attempt lately to make him son of a white woman by black father, and thus to credit the white race with whatever ability he possessed. I confess that my interest in him would would [sic] be measurably diminished if this should turn out to be true." Still, Douglass promised to do his utmost to promote the book, not the least of his efforts being a lecture on Banneker.[56]

Kirk struggled on with the manuscript for the next several years and in 1882 could finally report to Douglass that the work was ready for publication. Glad to learn she had not abandoned the project, Douglass predicted "a larger sale among the colored people of the country than any Book yet published. I think every colored man who reads will want it and those who cannot will want their children to read it. Bannecker has been much talked about of late, and many are curious to know all about him." Again, he warned of the practical problems of publication. Dismissing the prospect of advance sales, he told her, "People want to see before they purchase. If the

Book could be retailed at one dollar it can be sold at wholesale for fifty cents a copy. If I am right in this I will take fifty copies of the first Edition for gratuitous circulation. If a few others will do the same the Book can easily be set well afloat." He remained encouraging about the market for books by and about American blacks. "My own Book is selling very well — notwithstanding my many offences to popular sentiments — and the prejudice and envy excited by my success in life. The Story of Bannecker will not encounter any jealousies. He has been dead too long for that." He then returned to specifics. "Of how many pages do you intend to make the Book? A great many in buying books look [for] quantity as well as quality, and determine to buy or not to buy as they are suited or not suited by the former, without thinking of the latter."[57]

Anne Kirk's book finally was published, promising once more that the story of Banneker properly told would be available and that his name would attract increasing public attention as the nineteenth century approached its end. But the project was not yet free of problems. In 1884, after the manuscript had been completed and submitted to the publisher in Philadelphia, Mrs. Kirk died unexpectedly. It is likely that her difficulties in preparing the manuscript may have been due to illness in her final years. The literary property passed with her other assets into the hands of a trustee, and consequently relatively little if any distribution of the work was made. The book, in effect, emerged as a vanity press book, privately printed for the author, who presumably was to have been responsible for its distribution and sale. As a consequence of Mrs. Kirk's death, the edition remained relatively intact, and largely unsold and undistributed. Although it received several friendly reviews in 1884 in *The Critic,* the *Friends' Intelligencer,* and the *Baltimore Sun,* it remained virtually unknown to the reading public.

A review that appeared early in 1885 in *The Critic,* though unsigned, may have been written by Bishop Payne. Entitled "A Colored Astronomer," the review presented a favorable impression of the book and an impressive image of Banneker:

> Our colored brothers have had many opportunities within a generation past to show what they can do in the intellectual field, and they have not failed to take rank as orators, Congressmen, presiding officers at National Conventions, etc. They looked well lately under the flaring torch, taking their part in a Presidential election; but they have never furnished a more

BANNEKER,

THE

AFRIC-AMERICAN ASTRONOMER.

FROM THE POSTHUMOUS PAPERS

OF

MARTHA E. TYSON.

Edited by her Daughter.

"Act well your part, there all the honor lies."

PHILADELPHIA:
FRIENDS' BOOK ASSOCIATION,
No. 1020 ARCH STREET.
1884.

Title page of *Benjamin Banneker. The Afric-American Astronomer,* by Martha E. Tyson. The Author.

pleasing picture for the mind's eye to dwell on than that supplied in a small volume written some years ago by Mrs. Martha E. Tyson, edited by her daughter, Mrs. Anne T. Kirk, and published by the Friends' Book Association, of Philadelphia. In this volume, simple and quiet in style, we get a glimpse of life in the latter half of the last century — a semi-colonial life — about Ellicott's Mills in Maryland. The central figure of the picture is Benjamin Banneker, a thoroughly black negro, the grandson of an African prince, and with but a solitary ripple of white blood in his veins, and that ripple one which his princely blood seems to have utterly forgotten in two short generations. He was the calculator and maker of a series of almanacs by which the artless people of Maryland, Virginia, Delaware and Pennsylvania kept their reckoning in the time of Washington and Jefferson. The young fire-eaters of Virginia got up when the grandson of an African prince said it was sunrise, and the Pennsylvania farmer put out the lights and went to bed when Benjamin Banneker's almanac said the evening star had gone down. Banneker was a persistent student of astronomy, and attracted the attention of many eminent astronomers in his generation, and a manuscript copy of his first almanac probably lies to-day among the archives of the Academy of Science in Paris, sent there by Thomas Jefferson, the Secretary of State under Washington. Banneker was a free negro and held a vote, as did all free negroes in Maryland possessed of a certain amount of property. This right, in common with others, he lost in 1802, although he had twelve years before that date assisted Major Ellicott, his friend, in running the boundary lines of the District of Columbia, and had taken a hand in locating the Capitol, the President's house, and other buildings in the District, and consequently might have been held as accessory to the act by which the American eagle got a perching place and the American freeman a house to lay his head in. Mrs. Kirk, drawing from her mother's memoirs and her own personal recollections, makes an attractive picture of the simple-hearted, intelligent, and dignified negro in his plain home life, his astronomical studies out of doors at midnight, and his familiar association at the village stores with the superior race.[58]

Within the following year or two, one of Mrs. Kirk's relatives, Dr. Henry M. Fitzhugh, printed a modest notice that he distributed with complimentary copies of the book to a number of publishers. After describing the book's content and the reasons the edition was never distributed, he offered for sale the whole "'BANNEKER' property, consisting of copyright, stereotype plates and several hundred printed copies like the one attached, . . . to any publisher disposed to bring it before the world."[59]

Fitzhugh's efforts failed to arouse interest among publishers or substantially increase the public's awareness of Martha Tyson's little volume, thereby largely defeating its purpose. Tyson's posthumous book was the last work about Banneker to be based upon original materials. During the next several decades, numerous articles about Banneker's life and work appeared in periodicals and newspapers, but each was based on earlier publications without contributing any new information. Several were articles of some substance, such as a paper read by Philip LePhillips before the Columbia Historical Society in Washington in 1916 and published in its *Records* the following year. In addition, a biographical sketch by Henry E. Baker was published in the *Journal of Negro History* in 1918. A similar work was produced by Will W. Allen in 1921. All of these were based almost entirely upon earlier works, chiefly those by Latrobe and Tyson, from which they extracted freely.

In 1949 a highly fictionalized biography written for young people became popular and achieved wide distribution. But the blending of fact and fiction, though doubtless a compliment to the author's skill, provided yet more confusion concerning Banneker's achievements and their importance.

The identification of the site of Banneker's farm and home, first undertaken by Rachel Mason in 1836 and then pursued by Bishop Payne and his A.M.E. Church committee in 1845, remained ignored and forgotten until 1953. In that year the Maryland State Roads Commission considered erecting an appropriate marker to memorialize Banneker. In cooperation with the Maryland Historical Society, the commission collected and reviewed all available data relating to the location of Banneker's farm. In February 1954 a marker was installed on the premises of the Westchester Grade School on Westchester Avenue in Oella. Under the title "Benjamin Banneker 1731–1806" it bore the following inscription: "The self-educated Negro mathematician and astronomer was born, lived his entire life and died near here. He assisted in surveying the District of Columbia, 1791, and published the first Maryland almanac, 1792. Thomas Jefferson recognized his achievements."[60]

Despite inaccurately attributing to him the first Maryland almanac, the marker promised to bring recognition to the site. It proved to be not impervious to vandals, however, and had to be replaced twice, in 1968 and again in 1969, this time with a new plaque of cast aluminum and a revised inscription. The new installation proved to be quite as vulnerable to vandalism as the earlier ones. Not long after it was installed it was broken from its standard, leaving the site unidentified. (See Document 52)

The location of Banneker's home is derived primarily from a deed of partition made at the time of George Ellicott's death in 1832 and executed three years later by his executors and partners.[61] The property bounds described in this document include some of those defined in the indenture executed by Banneker with Ellicott & Company in 1799. A number of common points can be identified which verify that Banneker's remaining tract of seventy-two acres was unquestionably included in the former.[62]

Of particular interest is a parcel of land that originally adjoined a corner of Banneker's farm, owned in his lifetime first by William Williams, a merchant who maintained a store near the Patapsco River in the little community that is now Oella. After his death the land was owned by his widow, Mary M. Williams. In her last will and testament dated August 23, 1786, she included an unusual bequest, which may be unparalleled in the annals of slavery in Maryland. She bequeathed to the Quarterly Meeting of the Society of Friends of Baltimore "all my right of thirteen negroes," whom she named individually. She then went on to add as part of her bequest, "also ten acres of Land where James and Margaret [two of the Negroes previously listed] now live, being part of a tract of land called Mount Gilboa laying in Baltimore County for the use of the aforesaid Thirteen Negroes."

This was in itself an unusual gift and reflected the concern and interest of the testator. Mary Williams had more to add to her bequest, however. The remainder of her land she bequeathed to her brother-in-law, John Teale, who was also a neighbor, enjoining him "to hold in possession until such time as any Lawfull heir or heirs do claim any part of the aforesaid negroes as his or their property and my will is that at such times the aforesaid Quarterly Meeting do take from the aforesaid John Teale or any person claiming under him the aforesaid tract of Land and sell the same and apply the Money to the Setting at Liberty the aforesaid negroes which are at any time any otherwise Inthralled." No evidence can be found that it became necessary to purchase the freedom of the slaves to whom Mary Williams had been so loyal.[63]

Undoubtedly Banneker must have been acquainted with some of the Williams' slaves, especially James and Margaret, since his log house was within walking distance of the ten acres where they lived. It was probably on this ten-acre tract that a Negro community survived through the first half of the nineteenth century, for at the present intersection of Oella Avenue and Westchester Avenue the Mount Gilboa Chapel, erected in 1859, still stands. A neglected graveyard on the grounds bears a number of headstones, many overturned and overgrown, dating from the early decades of the nineteenth century and presumably marking the graves of members of this early black community.

In the nearly two centuries since Banneker's death, his achievements have been for the most part forgotten or misrepresented, and there have been few efforts to memorialize him. One or two public schools have been named for him. In November 1971, on the anniversary of Banneker's birthday, the secretary of the interior authorized the Tenth Street Overlook outside L'Enfant Plaza in Washington to be renamed and dedicated by the mayor as Benjamin Banneker Park. Once again, the reasons presented by the speakers on the occasion and widely reported in the press had been all based upon erroneous information: Banneker was hailed for his contribution to the plan of the city after L'Enfant was dismissed and Banneker "saved the plan by reconstructing it from memory." Despite the good intentions that had authorized the naming of the tiny park for Banneker, the premises were allowed to languish, and the four acres of land fell into disrepair. It was not until twenty-six years later, in November 1997, that the park again claimed public attention.

No monument marks Banneker's grave, and the site where his house once stood has only recently been identified. One may wander endlessly over the sloping hills and fields that once were part of his homestead and find no trace of his presence. Gone are all the things he knew—his father's orchard, the great chestnut tree that shaded his doorway and under which he rested, and the tall willow that grew beside the Indian spring. His acres no longer command "the prospect of the near and distant hills and the view of the once mighty Patapsco," of which he had been so fond.

Though all these vestiges of his life have disappeared, much still remains to be learned from Banneker's life. In a modern society increasingly concerned with the value and needs of the senior citizen, Banneker emerges as an outstanding example of the adage that it is never too late to learn, and to be productive. In his time, the age of sixty was considered to be old for most men, and it is only in recent years that the lifespan has been extended to fourscore and more. Banneker was fifty-nine when he first turned his attention to the study of mathematics and astronomy and taught himself in both without the guidance of others. In these studies he found an exciting and reinvigorating challenge that opened up a whole new world in the skies to him, and with the pursuit of which he filled his remaining years. His success pleased him, to be sure, primarily because it enabled him to continue to indulge the avocation that had brought him so much satisfaction and pleasure. He was appreciative of the opportunities given him, and grateful to those who contributed to his pursuit of knowledge. He did not believe that his attainments made him in any manner exceptional, or that renown was due him.

More than a century and a half after his death, the United States Postal Service honored Banneker with the issuance of a commemorative stamp. The fifteen-cent stamp was ceremonially issued at Annapolis, Maryland, on February 15, 1980, during the nationwide observance of Black History Month. The six-color stamp was designed by Jerry Pinkney of Groton-on-Hudson, New York, and modeled by Richard C. Sennett.[64]

Only a modest quantity of tangible memorabilia has survived to perpetuate Banneker's name, consisting chiefly of the materials preserved by generations of that branch of the Ellicott family that had provided his original inspiration and support. For the main part these constitute most of the items loaned to him by his benevolent neighbor George Ellicott and which he charged his family to return after his death. Preserved with loving care have been the old heavy oval gateleg table before which he sat for so many hours of his final years, the stretchers of which are well worn from the scraping of generations of feet including his own; his impressive volume of manuscript notes representing his astronomical studies capsulated into his final fifteen years; his pocket commonplace book which he always carried on his person; a few literary manuscripts; the candlesticks that illuminated his nightly vigils of the stars as he recorded his calculations; and finally a handful of borrowed texts which formed his fount of knowledge. Surviving also are a few letters, which like the entries in his journal, provide windows into the heart and mind of the aging philomath. Finally, copies of most of the numerous editions of his almanacs, which blazed so brightly for so brief a time, have found their way into various public collections.[65]

Meager though Banneker's material heritage may seem, it is nonetheless impressive and considerably greater in substance and significance than that which exists for many of his peers. For the past century and a half

Benjamin Banneker has been memorialized primarily as a member of the Negro race who achieved distinction. A study of his life and surviving memorabilia now makes it possible for him to be remembered instead, and for all time to come, for his achievements as a successful American man of science regardless of race. He retained always those characteristics that distinguished him among his contemporaries—a mild and philosophic temperament that never deserted him, a deep sense of religion without alignment to a particular creed, a pride in cleanliness and neatness of personal appearance that clad him always in dignity, a habitual kindness and generosity, and a gentlemanly mien that marked him all of his life.

Despite the public acknowledgment that came to him in his final years, Banneker remained always a modest man. He did not believe that his attainments made him great. His modesty was reflected in a quotation from a text in Banneker's almanac for the year 1794 :

> The pomp of honors may by kings be given
>
> To men, all equally the make of heaven:
>
> But true nobility's confin'd to none;
>
> It gilds the cottage and may leave the throne.[66]

Commemorative stamp honoring Benjamin Banneker issued by the U.S. Postal Service in 1980. *U.S. Postal Service.*

DOCUMENTS

❧❦❧

T HE MAJOR PORTION of the original materials upon which this biography is
based, including the manuscripts and correspondence relating to
Benjamin Banneker and to the survey of the Federal Territory, are either
privately owned or form part of large collections for which no convenient catalogue or index exists. To make this work as useful as possible, complete texts of
some of the documents quoted, and more extensive excerpts from others, are herewith presented. Each of the documents is fully identified in the *Reference Notes*.
Those excerpted from published sources are listed in section II of the *Bibliography*.
Original spelling has not been corrected.

Document 1.   Indenture from Richard Gist to Robert and
Benjamin Banneky, March 11, 1737 for purchase of the
farm "Stout."
Annapolis, Maryland Hall of Records. *Land Records,*
Liber HWS #1A, fol. 59. (Chapter II, pp. 25–27)

This Indenture made this tenth day of the month of March in the year of
our Lord one thousand seven hundred and thirty-seven Between Richard Gist of
Baltimore county in the province of Maryland Govt of the one part and Robert
Banneky and Benjamin Banneky his son of the county and province aforesaid of
the other part Witnesseth that the said Richard for and in consideration of the
sum of seven thousand pounds of Tobacco in hand paid to the said Richard Gist
the receipt whereof he doth hereby acknowledge and doth by these presents
acquit and discharge them the said Robert Bannaky and Benjamin Bannaky his
son their heirs and assigns forever from every part and parcel of Saith given
granted bargained and sold placed in escrow and confirmed unto Them the said
Robert Bannaky and Benjamin Bannaky his son their heirs and assigns forever
one hundred acres of land lying in the said county circumscribed by the bounds
hereafter . . . it being the moiety of two hundred Acres of Land formerly bought
by a certain John Whipps of Mr. Thomas Bale of said county . . . and being part

of a larger tract originally granted to the said Thomas Bale called Stout and by
the said Whip sold to the aforesaid Richard Gist on the nineteenth day of January
one thousand seven hundred and thirty three Beginning at a white oak found at
the beginning of bounded tree of the two hundred acres of land sold to John
Whipps as aforesaid the third bounded tree of the original tract called Stout and
runs . . . north twenty seven degrees west Eighty pr? southwest one hundred and
forty perches north twenty seven degrees west twenty six perches southwest sixty
perches south forty eight degrees east one hundred forty perches? north east thirty eight poles . . . by a direct line to the place of beginning containing and laid
out for one hundred acres of Land more or less, with all the improvements there
? and appurtenances thereto belonging and also all the estate rights & title interest claims endowed whatsoever of him the said Richard Gist.

This indenture made this tenth day of March in the year of our Lord one
thousand seven hundred and thirty seven between Richard Gist of Baltimore
County in the province of Maryland Government: of the one part and Robert
Bannaky and Benjamin Bannaky his son of the county and province aforesaid of
the other part, Witnesseth that the said Richard Gist for and in consideration of
seven thousand pounds of tobacco in hand paid to the said Richard Gist the
receipt whereof he doth hereby acknowledge and doeth by these presents acquit
and discharge them the said Robert Bannaky and Benjamin Bannaky his son
their heirs and assigns for ever from every part and parcell thereof HATH given
granted bargained and sold placed in escrow and confirmed unto them the said
Robert Bannaky and Benjamin Bannaky his son their heirs and assigns for over
one hundred acres of land lying in the said county circumscribed by the bounds
hereafter eschoffed it being the moiety of two hundred acres of Land (formerly)
bought by a certain John Whipps of Mr. Thomas Bale late of said county
deceased and being part of a larger tract originally granted to the said Thomas
Bale called Stout and by the said Whipps sold to the aforesaid Richard Gist on the
nineteenth day of January one thousand seven hundred and thirty three. BEGIN-
NING at a white oak being the beginning bounded tree of the two hundred acres
of land sold to John Whips as aforesaid and the third bounded tree of the original tract called Stout, and runs thence north twenty seven degrees west Eighty Ps
southwest one hundred and forty perches, north twenty seven degrees west twenty six perches, south west sixty perches, south forty eight degrees, west one hundred forty perches, northwest twenty six perches, north twenty seven degrees
west, thirty eight perches, thence by a direct line to the place of beginning containing and laid out for one hundred acres of Land more or less, with all the
improvements thereon and appurtenances thereonto belonging, and also all the
estate right title interest claims and demands whatsoever of him the said Richard
Gist his heirs and assigns for ever and the said Robert Banneky and Benjamin

Banneky his son there heirs and assigns and the said Richard Gist doth for himself and his heirs and assigns the said Land and premises? and every part and parcell thereto against thereof against the said Richard Gist his heirs and assigns and al and every other part and parecell whatsoever claiming or to claim from by or under him or through or by his l? or their causes . . . or any right title or interest thereunto or unto any part or parcel thru of warrant and flr over . . . unto the said Robert Bannekey and Benjamin Banneky his son their heirs and assigns for ever IN WITNESS whereof the said Richard Gist hath hereunto set his hand and seal the day and year first above written — Rich. Gist (seal)

Signed, sealed, and Delivered, before us —
Thos. Franklin
Thos. Sligh

     Baltimore County, Memorandum//that on the eleventh day of March one thousand and seven hundred and thirty seven came Richard Gist partie to the written deed and ackowledged the same to be his act and deed and the Land and premises within mentioned to be the right and title of the within Robert Banneky and Benjamin Banneky their heirs and assigns for ever
     — J. Sheridine
     T. Todd —
     March the 11th, 1737, Show Recd four shill for an .. fine of thre within one hundred acres of land for the use of the Lord Baltimore, by order of Benjamin Tasker Esq. /Gilbert Crockell. Recd. March the 11th, and recorded March the 12th, 1737. per J. Wells Stokes Clk Balt. City.

Document 2.   Minta Black's Account with the Maccubbin family.
          Annapolis, Maryland Hall of Records No. 1548,
          Ledger A of Zacharias Maccubbin, 1789-1802.
          Chancery Court exhibit. Courtesy of Robert
          J. Hurry, May 1988.(Chapter II, p. 47)

Midwife: delivered six of Maccubbin's chilren (1790–1800)
     delivered three slave children (1792–1795)
Spinning: spun 26-3/4 pounds of "Stocken Yarn" (1790–1792)
     spun 26 pounds of "cloth Yarn" (1792)
Tailoring: made 3 pair Mens Trowsers (1789)
     made 4 mens Shirts (1789)

     fol. 7

1789		£.s.d.
May 9	to 2 gal. Cyder some time ago	0.2.0
	3-1/2 lbs. Bacon	0.3.6
	5-1/2 " "	0.5.6
	2 gal. Cyder	0.2.0
May 23	4-1/2 lb. Bacon	0.4.6
	3 gal. Cyder	0.3.0
June 10	2 gal. Cyder	0.2.0
Sept. 4	To Cash	0.1.10-1/2
1790		
Jan. 11	To cash paid you on acct. of	
	Mrs. Maccubbin	0.7.6
April 14	" 1-1/2 bushel corn some time ago 0.7.6	
	Cash paid you	0.1.10-1/2
April 20	12-3/4 lb. Bacon	0.10.7-1/2
May 17	11 lb. Bacon	0.9.2
Dec. 4	2 gall. Cyder	0.1.4
1791		
Feb. 14	6-1/4 lb. Hogs Lard	0.6.8
July 19	1 Fletch Bacon, Wt. 28-1/2 lb.	1.3.9
1792		
Feb. 17	4-1/2 lb. Hogs Log [sic]	0.3.6-1/2
Feb. 23	3-1/2 lbs. Wool	0.6.6-3/4
Feb. 29	1-1/2 Bush. Indian Corn	0.6.0
1793		
April 11	l Bush. Indian Corn	0.5.0
	2 doz. eggs	0.1.6
May 25	4 lb. wool	0.7.6
	Cash	0.15.0
Sept. 6	24 lb. Wool	1.0.0
Oct. 27	Cash sent you by Will	0.7.6
Dec. 24	Cash	1.2.6
1794		
Jan. 25	Cash	0.4.0
Mar. 1	4-1/2 lb. Hogs Lard	0.5.3-3/4
June 26	1 Quarter Lamb, Wt. 6 lb.	0.3.0
Oct. 11	8 lb. Black Wool	0.15.0

	2 lb. White ditto	0.3.9
Nov. 27	Cash (one Dollar)	0.7.6
	Cash (four Dollars)	1.10.0
		————
		£12.16.1/2

[Carried over to fol. 57]

1795
Mar. 3	2-1/2 Bush. Indian Corn	0.12.6
Aug. 20	10-1/4 lb. Bacon	0.10.3
Sept. 17	16-1/2 lb. Bacon	0.16.6

1796
Sept. 16	To William Bell for the Amount	
	of my order on him in your favour 0.4.6	
Oct. 4	To Cash in full this time	1.3.1/4
		————
		£16.2.9-3/4

1796
Nov. 28	24 lb. Lambs Wool	2.5.0

1797
Feb. 4	2 lb. Hogs Lard	0.2.6
Mar. 29	To Cash	0.1.10-1/2

[Opposite fol. 7]

fol. 7	contra credit	

1789
May 23	By taking a dead Calf from a	
	Cow in April 1788	0.10.0
Aug. 3	By making 3 pr. Mens Trowsers	0.2.6
Aug. 14	By making 4 Mens Shirts	0.4.0
Sept. 19	By cash received of her	0.1.10-1/2

1790
Jan. 4	By delivering Mrs. Maccubbin	
	of a Daughter	1.10.0
Dec. 4	By Spinning 11-1/2 lb.	
	Stocken Yarn	0.14.4-1/2
Dec. 10	By Spinning 2-1/4 lb. ditto	0.2.9-3/4

1792
April 11   By Spinning 26 lb. Cloth Yarn   1.6.0

By delivering Mrs. Maccubbin
of a Son the 14th Sept. 1791   1.10.0

By delivering Mrs. Maccubbin
of a Daughter the 10th May 1793 1.10.0

Nov. 12   By delivering Negro Sall of
child the 9th Inst.   0.15.0

Dec. 11   By spinning 13 lb. stocken yarn 0.16.3

1794
Nov. 27   By delivering Negro Mary of
a Female Child   0.15.0

1795
Mar. 1   By delivering Mrs. Maccubbin
of a Daughter   1.10.0

Mar. 9   By taking a dead Calf from a cow 0.15.0

By Amount brought from Folio 7   13.2.9-3/4

Sept. 28   By delivering negro Ceicil of
Daughter this day   0.16.0

1796
Oct. 4   By delivering Mrs. Maccubbin
of a daughter this day   1.10.1

1800
May 28   By delivering Mrs. Maccubbin
of a Son this day   £2.9.4-1/2

[Folio 126]   Mary Black (Negro) Dr.

1802
Sept. 1   To 2 years rent of Lot #10 in
Macville ending this day   £9.0.0

1803
Sept. 1   To 1 year rent of Lot #10
in Macville ending this day   4.10.0

2 lb. wool   0.5.0

[opposite folio 126]

Contra cr.

1800
Oct. 30   By Spinning 14 lb. Cloth Yarn   0.17.6

	By ditto 12 lb. Stocken ditto	1.10.0
1801		
Aug.	By 12 days work @ 10-1/2	1.2.6
1802		
Nov. 13	By Spinning 14-1/2 lb. Cloth Yarn 0.18.1-1/2	
	By Cash rec.d of Pierpont	4.11.10-1/2
		————
		£9.0.0
1803		
Dec. 6	By sundry services as per	
	Settlement this day	£5.10.6-3/4

Document 3.   Letter from Joseph Townsend to James Pemberton, July 7, 1790.
See *Reference Notes*, n.15. (Chapter IV, p. 104)

George Mathews intending for your City I am desirous of embracing the Opportunity to inform thee that I rec.ᴰ by Elias Ellicott my Acceptable favour of the Pamphlets which is allowed by some of our Judges to be the first piece on the subject they have yet met with.— I was in hopes to have found amongst them some of Pinkney's Speech, as I have been often applied to for them by some of our Members — I think our Society would Cheerfully pay the expence of some of them if they are to be had — The bearer will be a safe hand [to send] them by — On 17th day last was our Stated Meeting where we recd. an Acct. from our Acting Committee of a large number of Slaves being liberated since last Meeting as likewise a very considerable number more whose cases are under the Consideration of the Court — One of the Committee informed me that there are nearly fifty Cases that will depend on the Determination of one [case] cause now in Court which I am in hopes will be so Handled as to be rendered Clear & the freedom of the whole obtained—Our Society continues to increase considerably, being now near two hundred Members, notwithstanding we have not as yet been a body form'd ten Months —

We have concluded to address our next General Assembly respecting the situation of the Negroes in the manner of last Year — And I expect it will be the case of our Approaching Yearly Meeting concerning which as we proceed therein I shall inform thee. . . .

Document 4. Excerpt from President Washington's letter to Thomas Jefferson, February 1, 1791, with instructions for Major Andrew Ellicott.
See *Reference Notes*, n.3. (Chapter V, p. 112.)

Nothing in the enclosed letter superceding [sic] the necessity of Mr. Ellicott's proceeding to the work in hand I would thank you, for requesting him, to set out on Thursday; or as soon after as can make it convenient: Also for preparing such instructions as you may conceive it necessary for me to give him for ascertaining the points we wish to know; first, for the *general* view of things and *next* for the more accurate and final decision.

Document 5. Excerpt from Thomas Jefferson's letter to Andrew Ellicott, February 2, 1791, with instructions for beginning the survey of the Federal Territory.
See *Reference Notes*, n.4. (Chapter V, p. 112.)

You are desired to proceed by the first stage to the Federal territory on the Potomac, for the purpose of making a survey of it. The first object will be to run the two first lines mentioned in the enclosed proclamation to wit: — the S.W. line 160 poles and the S. E. line to Hunting Creek or should it not strike Hunting Creek as has been suggested then to the River. These two lines must run with all the accuracy of which your art is susceptible as they are to fix the beginning either on Hunting Creek or the River, if the second line should strike the River instead of the Creek take and lay down the bearing and distance of the nearest part of the creek and also of any of its waters if any of them should be nearer than the creek itself; so also should either of these two lines cross any water of Hunting Creek let it be noted. The termination of the Second line being accurately fixed, either on the creek or river proceed to run from that at a beginning the four lines of experiment directed in the proclamation, this is intended as the first rough essay to furnish data for the last accurate survey. It is desirable that it be made with all the dispatch possible and with only common exactness, paying regard however to the magnetic variations. In running these lines note the position of the mouth of the Eastern Branch, the point of your first course there will receive the S. W. line from the Cape of the Eastern Branch — the Canal and particular distance of your crossing it from either end the position of Georgetown, and mouth of Goose Creek, and send by Post, A plat of the whole on which ultimate directions for the rest of the work shall be sent you, as soon as they can be prepared. Till these shall be received by you, you can be employed in ascertaining a true Meridian, and the latitude of the place, and running the meanderings of the Eastern Branch, and of the River itself, and other waters which will merit an exact place in the map of the Territory. You will herewith receive a draft on the Mayor of Georgetown to cover your expenses.

Document 6. Report of the survey's progress from Andrew Ellicott to Thomas Jefferson in a letter dated February 14, 1791.
See *Reference Notes*, n.10. (Chapter V, p. 123.)

I arrived at this town on Monday last, but the cloudy weather prevented any observations being made until Friday which was very fine. On Saturday the two first lines were completed. You will see by the enclosed plat that the second line does not touch any part of Hunting Creek unless the spring drain noted in the plat is to be considered a part of it. It appears to me that in order to make the plan as complete as possible it will be proper to begin the survey of the ten miles square at the Eastern inclination of the upper cape of Hunting Creek, marked on the plat. This plan will include all the Harbor and wharfs of Alexandria, which will not be the Case if the two first lines mentioned in the proclamation are to remain as now. I shall submit to your consideration the following plan for the permanent location which will I believe embrace every object of advantage which can be included within the ten miles square. [*Many erasures follow and writing is indistinct*]. . . as marked in plat A. The magnetic variations at this place is some-what uncertain, arising no doubt from some local cause. It was 20 easterly when the second line struck the river and at the end of the first line, it was nearly as much Westerly. The Latitude of Alexandria, I find to be about 33 48 20 N. This afternoon I intend beginning the rough survey which shall be executed with all possible dispatch, [*more erasures*]. You will observe by the plan which I have sug-gested for the Permanent Location a small deviation with respect to the compass from that mentioned in the Proclamation, the reason of which is that the Coup's in the Proclamation, strictly adhered to, would neither produce straight lines, nor contain quite the ten miles square, besides the utmost impropriety of running such lines without tolerable exactness.

Document 7. Excerpt from a letter from Andrew Ellicott to his wife, February 14, 1791.
See *Reference Notes*, n.11. (Chapter V, p. 123.)

I arrived at this Town on Tuesday last in good health but in consequences of bad weather, could not proceed to business till Friday last. I have been treated with great politeness by the inhabitants, who are truly rejoiced at the prospect of being included in the Federal district. I shall leave this town this afternoon to begin the rough survey of the ten miles square.

Document 8.   Excerpt from a letter written by Thomas Jefferson to Pierre Charles L'Enfant dated March 17, 1791.
See *Reference Notes*, n.16. (Chapter V, p. 126.)

You are advised to proceed to Georgetown, where you will find Mr. Ellicott employed in making a survey and map of the Federal territory. The special object of asking your aid is to have drawings of the particular grounds most likely to be approved for the site of the federal town and buildings. You will therefore be pleased to begin on the eastern branch, and proceed from thence upwards, laying down the hills, valleys, morasses, and waters between that and the Potomac, the Tyber, and the road leading from Georgetown to the eastern branch, and connecting the whole with certain fixed points of the map Mr. Ellicott is preparing. . . .

Document 9.   Communication from J. Saurin Norris to Martha E. Tyson, undated, concerning Banneker's role in the survey of the Federal Territory.
See *Reference Notes*, n.17. (Chapter V, p. 136.)

Whether Banneker went to the Federal Territory to assist the Commissioners to lay out the "District," or L'Enfant to lay out the City, is immaterial, — as in either case it is highly probable he must have met with all parties. —

The laying out of the District necessarily involved astronomical observations & calculations, as well as defining geographical position; while the survey of the City was merely a matter of engineering (after some initial point had been obtained), — and as Banneker's talent for astronomy was so predominant, it is natural to infer that it was to aid in the former work that he was retained —

The above considerations, with the recollection of Mrs. Eliz[h] Ellicott as corroboration, leave no doubt with me that it was especially to aid in the survey of the "District" that Banneker was employed,— and that while on that duty he made the acquaintance of Tho[s]. Jefferson, then Secretary of State. His letter to that Statesman is dated August 19, 1791, which was after his return from the District as he alludes to it in his letter.

Document 10.   Excerpt from an account of the installation of the Marker
at Jones Point in *The Alexandria Gazette,* April 21, 1791.
Chapter V, p. 128.

The mayor and the commonality, together with the members of the different
lodges of the town, at 3 o'clock waited on the commissioners at Mr. Wise's, where
they had arrived. After drinking a glass of wine to the following sentiment, viz.,
"May the stone we are about to place in the ground remain an immovable monument of the wisdom and unanimity of North America", the company then moved
on the Jones' Point in the following order:

"First, the Town Sergeant; second, the Hon. Daniel Carroll and the Mayor,
third; Mr. Ellicott and the recorder; fourth, such Aldermen and Councilmen as
were not free Masons; fifth strangers; sixth, the master of Lodge No. 22, with Dr.
David Steward at his right and Rev. James Muir at his left. Lastly the citizens, two
by two."

When Mr. Ellicott had ascertained the precise point from which the first
line of the District was to proceed, the master of the lodge and Dr. Steward,
assisted by some of the other brothers, placed the stone; after which a deposit of
corn, wine and oil was made upon it and the following observations were delivered by the Rev. Muir:

> *May this Stone long commemorate the goodness of God and those uncommon*
> *events which have given America a name among the nations. Under this Stone*
> *may Jealousy and Selfishness be forever buried! From this Stone may a super-*
> *structure arise whose glory, whose magnificence, whose stability, unequalled*
> *hitherto, shall astonish the World and invite even the Savage of the Wilderness*
> *to take shelter under its roof!*

Following the ceremony liquid refreshments were dispensed then the
assemblage returned from Jones' Point to Alexandria where a number of toasts
were offered, on the theme that "Of America it may be said as it was of Judea of
old, that it is a good land and large, O America, and prosperity within thy
palaces. May jealousy, that green-eyed Monster, be buried deep under the work
which this day we have completed, brethren and gentlemen, never to rise again
within the Federal District!"

Document 11.   Account of the selection of Banneker as assistant to Major Andrew Ellicott. From Martha E. Tyson, *A Sketch of the Life of Benjamin Banneker; From Notes Taken in 1836,* pp. 11–12.
(Chapter V, pp. 136–137.)

Major Ellicott selected Benjamin Banneker as his assistant upon this occasion, and it was with his aid that the lines of the Federal Territory, as the District of Columbia was then called, were run.

It was the work, also of Major Ellicott, under the orders of General Washington, then President of the United States, to locate the sites of the Capitol, President's house, Treasury, and other public buildings. In this, also, Banneker was his assistant.

Document 12.   Account of Banneker's behavior during the survey. From Martha E. Tyson, *Banneker, the Afric-American Astronomer. From the Posthumous Papers of Martha E. Tyson. Edited by Her Daughter* , p. 36.
(Chapter V, p. 137.)

. . . Banneker's deportment throughout the whole of this engagement, secured their respect, and there is good authority for believing, that his endowments led the commissioners to overlook the color of his skin to converse with him freely, and enjoy the clearness and originality of his remarks on various subjects.

Document 13.   Projection of a solar eclipse made by Banneker during the survey of the Federal Territory, from his manuscript journal.
See *Reference Notes*, n.35. (Chapter V, p. 137.)

This projection I laid down for April the third 1791 when the sun arose Centrally eclipsed at the City of Washington this is a back tryal to See how my present method would agree with the former

N.B Ferguson's Tables make the new Moon abbtit 30 minutes to Soon, Viz.

	d	h	m
April	3	10	30
I say	3	11	32 A.M.

Document 14. Letter from Andrew Ellicott from Philadelphia to the Commissioners, March 7, 1792.
See *Reference Notes*, n.41. (Chapter V, p. 142.)

Not hearing one syllable from you since I left George Town last December I am at a loss to know what preparations will be necessary for me to make in order to compleat such work as you may think advisable the ensuing season.— I shall at least want one assistant acquainted with practical astronomy and expert in the use of Instruments.— If you know of any person who has had practice in that way and who may be engaged at a moderate price in my opinion you will essentially serve the business by employing him.— M^R. Rittenhouse of this City and my Brothers are all whom I could undertake to recommend.— the former has never had less than eight dollars p^ER day since 1786 and neither of the later [sic] will return to the City of Washington for less than three dollars p^ER day which is the same they were offered by the Jenesco Company for all last season and a dollar short of what they are offered by the same Company to superintend their business the ensuing season.— In consequence of Maj^R. L'Enfant withdrawing himself from the business as soon as he arrived in this place we have been constantly employed in drawing a correct plan of the City and copying it for the Engraver and had we but have joined with him in withholding materials the whole expense of last summer would probably have been thrown away.

Since I have been in this City I have heard the expense incurred of last season frequently complained of but without offering to vindicate the necessity of every expense I will undertake to say that a piece of work of such magnitude was never executed in that manner so reasonably in this country before — of this I shall produce such proof when I come to George Town as I am sure will satisfy you.— As M^R. Jefferson is now waiting for a small sketch of the City, I am under the necessity of closing this before I intended.

Document 15. Excerpt from Andrew Ellicott's letter to his wife, April 10, 1793.
See *Reference Notes*, n.45. (Chapter V, p. 143.)

The singular situation into which I was thrown immediately on my arrival at this place and the doubtful issue prevented my writing until a final determination which was had yesterday. My victory was complete; and all my men reinstated in the City, after a suspension of one month. As my reputation depended on the determination, I neglected nothing in my power to defeat the Commissioners, but had to contend very unequally, owing to all my papers being seized by their order the day after I returned from Philadelphia. And this day they were all restored to me again. This victory has cost me at least £75. . . .

Document 16.   Excerpt from the Commissioners' letter to President
Washington dated March 23, 1794.
See *Reference Notes*, n.46. (Chapter V, p. 144.)

On Major Ellicott's evading the delivery of the papers we went with Colo Deakins to Prouts house where he then kept his Office and made a personal demand of them. He then told us that Dermott had stolen a plan of the City, describing it. Mr. Johnson remarked it was a severe charge for which he ought to be well grounded before he made it. Major Ellicott said he had stolen it, that it was in his Trunk and he could prove enough to obtain a Search Warrant, and if we could break open his Trunk we should find it.

Document 17.   Letter from Andrew Ellicott to Dr. William Thornton,
February 23, 1795.
See *Reference Notes*, n.48. (Chapter V, p. 144.)

It is with pleasure that I congratulate you on your appointment in the City of Washington. I am in hopes the change of the commissioners will have a good effect, and restore that confidence which the other commissioners by their strange conduct had forfeited.

I have been some time past engaged in drawing up a very long astronomical paper, which will be published the ensuing season, (for the philosophical society), in which I shall have occasion to mention the City of Washington.— The method pursued in executing that part of the plan in which I have been concerned will be explained: But I shall object to the injudicious alteration made since my expulsion from the City, in the street passing by the west end of the Hotel.— The centre of that street, was intended by the plan to pass thro' the centre of the market; but by this alteration will be thrown to the west of it, and the symmetry in that case, and in a great number of squares wholy destroyed.—

To understand the plan of the City some degree of science is certainly necessary, which I am confident is the reason why it was never comprehended by the former commissioners — They never could be taught to distinguish between the President's House, Hotel, and Capitol, on the plan. — Mr. Carroll, however, was enabled to point out Notley Young's, and Daniel Carroll's plans; which are much less conspicuous!! — The former commissioner's total ignorance of the subject, left them an easy prey to the duplicity of the designing, and their pride, and petulance, precluded them from receiving information. — They confided in the tales of one Dermott, who had plundered the office of my valuable papers, and from strong presumptive evidence had moved some very important signal stakes,— made erasures, and alterations on the general plan, and returned them as the errors of others! These facts were offered to be substantiated, but the commissioners refused to hear anything to his prejudice, fearing that he would either destroy one, or more of them, or that it would imply their fallibility, in attaching themselves to such a character. He is ignorant of the plan, and may therefore from that cause, or perhaps from vilany, pretend to disown many mistakes: But my Friend be upon your guard, for I assure you, that there is not a piece of work of equal magnitude in the universe, presented with equal accuracy.

Document 18. Notation from James Ferguson's *Tables and Tracts, Relative to Several Arts and Sciences*
(London, A. Miller and T. Cadell, 1767) copied by Banneker into his manuscript journal. It is to be noted that the entry is not a verbatim quotation from Ferguson.
See *Reference Notes*, n.4. (Chapter VI, p. 149–150.)

In the Calculation of New and full moons it is to be observed that when the Sun's distance from the Antibazon or North node of the Moon's obit [sic], it is more than 11 Signs, 18 degrees at time of the new Moon, since the Sun will be Eclipsed at that time. And when the Sun's distance from the Node is less than 0 Signs, 12 degrees or anything between 5 Signs 18 degrees and 16 Signs, 12 degrees, at the time of full moon, the Moon will be Eclipsed at that time.

Document 19. "A Plan for a Peace Office for the United States." A proposal formulated by Dr. Benjamin Rush and published in Banneker's Almanac for the year 1793.
See *Reference Notes*, n.5. (Chapter VII, p. 190.)

Among the many defects which have been pointed out in the federal constitution by its antifederal enemies, it is much to be lamented that no person has taken notice of its total silence upon the subject of an office of the utmost importance to the welfare of the United States, that is, an office for promoting and preserving perpetual peace in our country.

It is to be hoped that no objection will be made to the establishment of such an office, while we are engaged in a war with the Indians, for as the War-Office of the United States was established in time of peace, it is equally reasonable that a Peace-Office should be established in time of war.

The plan of this office is as follows:

I. Let a Secretary of Peace be appointed to preside in this office, who shall be perfectly free from all the present absurd and vulgar European prejudices upon the subject of government; let him be a genuine republican and a sincere Christian, for the principles of republicanism and Christianity are no less friendly to universal and perpetual peace, than they are to universal and equal liberty.

II. Let a power be given to this Secretary to establish and maintain free schools in every city, village and township of the United States; and let him be made responsible for the talents, principles, and morals of all his school-masters. Let the youth of our country be carefully instructed in reading, writing and arithmetic, and in the doctrines of a religion of some kind; the Christian religion should be preferred to all others; for it belongs to this religion exclusively to teach us not only to cultivate peace with all men, but to forgive, nay more — to love our very enemies. It belongs to it further to take away human life, and that we rebel against his laws, whenever we undertake to execute death in any way whatever upon any of his creatures.

III. Let every family in the United States be furnished at the public expense, by the Secretary of this office, with a copy of an American edition of the Bible. This measure has become the more necessary in our country, since the banishment of the Bible, as a school-book, from most of the schools in the United States. Unless the price of this book be paid for by the public, there is reason to fear that in a few years it will be met with only in courts of justice or in magistrate's offices; and should the absurd mode of establishing truth by kissing this sacred book fall into disuse, it may probably, in the course of the next generation, be seen only as a curiosity on a shelf in Mr. Peale's museum.

IV. Let the following sentences be inscribed in letters of gold over the door of every home in the United States:

The Son of Man Came into the World, Not To Destroy Men's Lives, But To Save Them.

V. To inspire a veneration for human life, and an horror at the shedding of human blood, let all those laws be repealed which authorize juries, judges, sheriffs, or hangmen to assume the resentments of individuals, and to commit murder in cold blood in any case whatever. Until this reformation in our code of penal jurisprudence takes place, it will be in vain to attempt to introduce universal and perpetual peace in our country.

VI. To subdue that passion for war, which education, added to human depravity, have made universal, a familiarity with the instruments of death, as well as all military shews, should be carefully avoided. For which reason, militia laws should everywhere be repealed, and military dresses and military titles should be laid aside: reviews tend to lessen the horrors of a battle by connecting them with the charms of order; militia laws generate idleness and vice, and therby produce the wars they are said to prevent; military dresses fascinate the minds of young men, and lead them from serious and useful professions; were there no uniforms, there would probably be no armies; lastly military titles feed vanity, and keep up ideas in the mind which lessen a sense of the folly and miseries of war.

In the seventh and last place, let a large room, adjoining the federal hall, be appointed for transacting the business and preserving all the records of this office. Over the door of this room let there be a sign, on which the figures of a lamb, a dove, and an olive-branch should be painted, together with the following inscriptions in letters of gold:

Peace on Earth—Good-Will To Man.

Ah! Why should Men Forget That They Are Brethren? Within this apartment let there be a collection of ploughshares and pruning-hooks made out of swords and spears; and on each of the walls of the apartment the following pictures as large as life:

1. A lion eating straw with an ox, and an adder playing upon the lips of a child.

2. An Indian boiling his venison in the same pot with a citizen of Kentucky.

3. Lord Cornwallis and Tippo Saib, under the shade of a sycamore-tree in the East-Indies, drinking Madeira wine out of the same decanter.

4. A group of French and Austrian soldiers dancing arm in arm, under a bower erected in the neighborhood of Mons.

5. A St. Domingo planter, a man of color, and a native of Africa, legislating together in the same colonial assembly.

To complete the entertainment of this delightful apartment, let a group of young ladies, clad in white robes, assemble every day at a certain hour, in a gallery to be erected for the purpose, and sing odes, and hymns, and anthems in praise of the blessings of peace.

One of these songs should consist of the following beautiful lines of Mr. Pope:

Peace o'er the world her olive wand extends,
And white-rob'd innocence from heaven descends;
All crimes shall cease, and ancient frauds shall fail,
Returning justice lifts aloft her scale.

Document 20. Preface to Banneker's Almanac for the year 1794 published by James Angell in Baltimore.
See *Bibliography*, Part I, Item 8. (Chapter VII, p. 194.)

Encouraged by the liberal Patronage bestowed, by an enlightened and philanthropic Public, on BENJAMIN BANNEKER's PENNSYLVANIA, DELAWARE, MARYLAND, and VIRGINIA ALMANACK, for the Year 1793, the Editor now presents them with one, for the Year 1794, calculated by his sable Friend, BENJAMIN, who, penetrated with Gratitude for the distinguished Approbation with which his former Astronomical Labours were received, has applied himself with redoubled Assiduity to bring the Calculations, now presented, to the greatest Degree of Accuracy a Work of the Kind is susceptible of.

That Africans and their Descendants are capable of attaining a Degree of Eminence in the Liberal Sciences BENJAMIN is not the only Proof — Among many which might be produced (without recurring to past Ages) we shall only mention PHILLIS WHEATLEY, who, in her eighth Year, was brought from Africa to Boston, and though labouring under the complicated disadvantages of Poverty and Slavery, and without the Benefit of School Education, before she had attained her 20th Year, composed a Number of Poems, which were published, in a small Volume, in 1772, from which the following, "*On the* WORKS *of* PROVIDENCE," is extracted:

"CREATION smiles, in various beauty gay, While day to night, and night succeeds to day: That Wisdom, which attends Jehovah's ways, Shines most conspicuous in the solar rays: Without them, destitute of heat and light, This world would be the reign of endless night: In their excess how would our race complain, Abhorring life, how hate its lengthen'd chain! From air adust what num'rous ills would rife! What dire contagion taint the burning skies! What pestilential vapours, fraught with death, Would rife, and overspread the lands beneath!"

No Pains having been spared to render the present Publication complete, the Editor, for himself and the *African descended* self-taught Astronomer, solicits a Continuance of that which BANNEKER's ALMANACK has hitherto experienced, and flatters himself its Patrons will find the Miscellany it contains not only entertaining but at the same time useful and instructive.

Document 21. Preface to Banneker's almanac for 1796 published by Edwards, Keddie, and Thomas, Andrews and Butler at Baltimore.
See *Bibliography*, Part I, Item 25. (Chapter VIII, p. 199.)

GENTLE READER,

To make an ALMANAC is not so easy a matter as some people think —
like a well furnished table, it requires to have a variety of dishes to suit every
palate, besides considerable skill in the cooking — Now, as it is impossible to suit
all the dishes to every particular taste, we hope you will not be offended, should
you find any not entirely to your liking, as we are certain there are a great many
which will suit you to a hair. We are persuaded you will not only be entertained
but instructed by our Almanac for we have ransacked all the repositories of
learning to cull a few flowers for your amusement. Moreover, Kind Reader, as we
believe, you would think the better of a man for having a decent coat on his back,
so we have exerted ourselves to make our Almanac appear in a more respectable
dress, than some other Almanac mongers have done, who, it would seem, have
thought their Almanacs not worthy a good coat.

But there is one dish we invite you to partake of, and we are prouder of it
than of all the rest put together; and to whom do you think are we indebted for
this part of our entertainment? Why, to a *Black Man* — Strange! Is a *Black* capable of composing an Almanac? Indeed, it is no less strange than true: and a clever,
wise, long-headed Black he is: it would be telling some whites if they had made as
much use of their *great school learning,* as this sage philosopher has made of the
little teaching he had got.

The labours of the justly celebrated Bannaker will likewise furnish you with
a very important lesson, courteous reader, which you will not find in any other
Almanac, namely that the Maker of the Universe is no respecter of colours; that
the colour of the skin is no ways connected with strength of mind or intellectual
powers; that although the God of Nature has marked the face of the African with
a darker shade than his brethren, he has given him a soul equally capable of
refinement. To the untutored Blacks, the following elegant lines of GRAY may be
applied.

> "Full many a gem of purest ray serene,
> The dark unfathom'd caves of ocean bear:
> Full many a flower is borne to blush unseen.
> And waste its fragrance on the desert air."

> Nor you ye proud, impute to these the blame
> If Afric's sons to genius are unknown,
> For Banneker has prov'd they may acquire a name
> As bright, as lasting as your own.

Document 22. Mathematical puzzle
> Recorded by Banneker in his manuscript journal.
> See *Reference Notes,* n. 33 (Chapter IX, p. 255.)

Question by Ellicott Geographer General

Divide 60 into four Such parts, that the first being increased by 4, the Second decreased by 4, the third multiplyed by 4, the fourth part divided by 4, that the Sum, the difference, the product, and the Qutient [sic] shall be one and the Same Number —

> Ans. first part 5.6 increased by 4 ( ) 9.6
> Second part 13.6 decreased by 4 ( ) 9.6
> third part 2.4 Multiplyed by 4 (is) 9.6
> fourth part 38.4 divided by 4 ( ) 9.6
> 60.0

Document 23. The Puzzle of the Hare and Hound
> Recorded by Banneker in his manuscript journal.
> See *Reference Notes,* n. 34 (Chapter IX, p. 256.)

Question for Hopkins

> When fleecy skies have Cloth'd the ground
> With a white mantle all around
> Then with a grey hound Snowy fair
> In milk white fields we Cours'd a Hare
> Just in the midst of a Champaign
> We set her up, away she ran,
> The Hound I think was from her then
> Just thirty leaps or three times ten
> Oh it was pleasant for to see
> How the Hare did run so timorously
> But yet so very Swift that I
> Did think she did not run but Fly
> When the Dog was almost at her heels
> She quickly turn'd, and down the fields
> She ran again with full Career
> And 'gain she turn'd to the place she were
> At every turn she gain'd of ground
> As many yards as the greyhound
> Could leap at thrice, and She did make,

Just Six, if I do not mistake
Four times She Leap'd for the Dogs three
But two of the Dogs leaps did agree
With three of hers, nor pray declare
How many leaps he took to Catch the Hare.

[Answer]

Just Seventy two I did Suppose,
An Answer false from thence arose,
I Doubled the Sum of Seventy two,
But still I found that would not do,
I mix'd the Numbers of them both,
Which Shew'd so plain that I'll make Oath,
Eight hundred leaps the Dog did make,
And Sixty four, the Hare to take.

$$4 \; : \quad 72 \; : \; : \quad 48$$

$$
\begin{array}{r}
48 \\ \hline
576 \\
288 \quad\;\; \\ \hline
4)\overline{3456} \\ \hline
864 \quad\;\; \text{ans.}
\end{array}
$$

Document 24. A Puzzle about Cattle,
Noted by Banneker in his manuscript journal.
(Chapter IX, p. 257.)

A gentleman Sent his Servant with £100 to buy 100 Cattle, with orders to give £5 for each Bullock, 20 Shillings for cows, and one Shilling for each Sheep, the question is to know what number of each sort he brought to his master.

Answer 19 bullocks at £5 each	£95
1 cow at 20s	1
80 sheep at 1s each	4
	100 proof

Document 25. A Puzzle about Triangles,
Recorded by Banneker in his manuscript journal.
(Chapter IX, p. 257.)

Suppose ladder 60 feet long be placed in a Street so as to reach a window on the one Side 37 feet high, and without moving it at bottom, will reach another window on the other side of the Street which is 23 feet high, requiring the breadth of the Street.

[No solution was recorded.]

Document 26. The Puzzle of the Cooper and the Vintner
Described by Charles W. Dorsey and published
in Tyson, *A Sketch* . . . .
See *Bibliography* Part II, Items 22 and 38; *Banneker, the Afro-American Astronomer*, W. W. Allen, p. 63. (Chapter IX, p. 257.)

A cooper and vintner sat down for a talk,
Both being so groggy that neither could walk;
Says cooper to vintner, "I'm the first of my trade,
There's no kind of vessel but what I have made,
And of any shape, sir, just what you will,
And of any size, sir, from a tun to a gill."
"Then," says the vintner, "you're the man for me.
Make me a vessel, if we can agree.
The top and the bottom diameter define,
To bear that proportion as fifteen to nine,
Thirty-five inches are just what I crave,
No more and no less in the depth will I have;
Just thirty-nine gallons this vessel must hold,
Then I will reward you with silver or gold,—
Give me your promise, my honest old friend."
"I'll make it tomorrow, that you may depend!"
So, the next day, the cooper, his work to discharge,
Soon made the new vessel, but made it too large;
He took out some staves, which made it too small,
And then cursed the vessel, the vintner, and all.
He beat on his breast, "By the powers" he swore
He never would work at his trade any more.
Now, my worthy friend, find out if you can,
The vessel's dimensions, and comfort the man!

[As noted by Tyson in an unpublished manuscript entitled "A Memoir," and by W. W. Allen, Benjamin Hallowell of Alexandria, Virginia was reported to have proposed as his solution 24.745 inches and 14.8476 inches for the diameters. Banneker had not provided a solution to the problem.]

Document 27. The Puzzle of Three Ages
Recorded by Banneker in 1801 in his manuscript journal.
(Chapter IX, p. 257.)

A, B and C, discoursing about their ages, Says A, if from double the Cube Root of B's age, double the biquadrate root of C's age betaken the remainder will be equal to the Squared Root [Fifth Root or Sursolid Root] of my age, says B, the square root of my age is equal to one fourth part of A's, and says C, the Square root of my age is one more than the Square root of B's, Required their several Ages —

A's)   (32 The Squared Root [Fifth Root or Sursolid root] of which is 2
B's) Age   (64 The Cube of Root of which is 4
C's)   (81 The biquadrate root [or Fourth Root] of which is 3.

The key word is Sursolid, a term used in place of "Squared" for the fifth root, according to *The Scholar's Arithmetic* (1801, 1807) by Daniel Adams. In his *Mathematical and Philosophical Dictionary* (1814), Peter Barlow defined "sursolid," which had already become archaic by that time, as "a term given by the early algebraists to what we now more commonly call a fifth power." No solution was recorded by Banneker.

Document 28. Poem about Banneker
Written by Susanna Mason and published posthumously by her daughter.
See *Bibliography*, Part II, Item 13. (Chapter IX, p. 260.)

An Address to Benjamin Banneker, an African Astronomer, who presented the author with a manuscript Almanack.

Transmitted on the wings of Fame,
Thine eclat sounding with thy name,
Well pleas'd I heard e'er was my lot
To see thee in thy rural cot,
That genius smil'd upon thy birth,
And application call'd it forth;
That time and tides thou couldst presage,
And traverse the celestial stage,
Where shining globes their circles run
In swift rotation round the sun;

Could'st tell how planets in their way,
From order ne'er were known to stray;
Sun, moon, and stars, when they will rise,
When sink below the upper skies;
When an eclipse shall veil their light,
And hide their splendor from our sight.
Now we'll apply thy wond'rous skill,
The wise may oft be wiser still.
Though saving knowledge to impart,
To guide the life and mend the heart,
Belongs to Him who rules the spheres,
Whose potent Arm all nature bears,
Whose sovereign wisdom governs all
If worlds consume or sparrows fall.
Yet nature in its wonted course
Some useful lessons may enforce.
A little star, like speck appears,
Scarce obvious 'mid the mightier spheres,
Into the wondrous field of space,
Eludes thy sight and runs its race,
Yet no account thou make'st of it,
Its waxing, waning, or exit;
What time it pass'd from mortal sight,
Or when again 'twill come to light'
But brighter orbs thou mark'st their way,
Observ'st their motions night and day;
Describ'st the speed at which they run,
And what their distance from the sun:
A speck in these is quickly seen,
If opaque bodies intervene,
Their native brightness to pervade,
And o'er their lustre cast a shade.
Now, as I've said, though thou art wise,
Permit me here to moralize.
Some men who private walks pursue,
Whom Fame ne'er ushered into view,
May run their race and few observe,
To right or left if they should swerve,
Their blemishes would not appear

Beyond their lives a single year.
But thou, a man exalted high,
Conspicuous in the world's keen eye,
On record now thy name's enrolled,
And future ages will be told,
There lived a man called Banneker,
An African astronomer.
Thou need'st to have a special care
Thy conduct with thy talent square,
That no contaminating vice,
Obscure thy lustre in our eyes,
Or cast a shade upon thy merit
Or blast the praise thou might'st inherit:
For folly in an orb so bright,
Will strike on each beholder's sight:
Nay, stand exposed from age to age,
Extant on some historian's page.
Now as thy welfare I intend,
Observe my counsel as a friend.
Let fair examples mark thy round
Unto thine orbit's utmost bound.
"The good man's path," the scriptures say,
"Shines more and more to perfect day."

Document 29. "A Remarkable Dream, 10th Mo. 1762."
A manuscript found among Banneker's miscellaneous papers.
See *Reference Notes*, n.64. (Chapter IX, p. 267.)

I thought I was dead and Beheld my Body lay like a corps, there seem'd to be a person in the appearance of a Man his Raiment somewhat of a sheep skin or bright fawn colour, who said follow me, he ascended a Hill on the Top of which was a Large Building, the outside appeared strongly Built, of Large rough Stone, I follow'd my guide to the House, but did not at first see the Beauty of it, to the full, it seem'd white and Bright, and a Large Company sitting, such a number as I never beheld, the farther we went in, the Brighter it appear'd, and more like the reflection of the Sun, the first step my guide made, seem'd to be more than half way the House, by what I Judg'd from the appearance of the length of the Building on the outside, while the guide stop'd I look'd at the Countenance of those I could see, which were many, but could not see the farther end, for the reflection of the Light, which appear'd brighter than when the Sun shin'd in its fullest Luster on a Summers day, there appeared a sweetness & composure in every countenance, far beyond what I ever seen in any person, while in the Body, and the luster reflected from the light, which extended to the Shirts of their Garments, which appeared like a plain robe or covering, in one piece; so that I was filled with admiration, I look'd to see if I could Distinguish Men from Women but could not, likewise if I could see any one I knew but knew none, on my first entrance into the House, I thought I had been at a Meeting of solid Friends, I looked to see from whence the Light came, but could not discern either Window or opening I then ask'd my guide what is this place he answered Heaven, then I looked to see what they sat on, but could not discern either seats or form the more I look'd, the more I admired and wanted to sit with 'em, but could not tell how, my guide Turned about to go out and look'd at me said follow, but I was so much delighted, that I was unwilling to follow he then Beckon'd and said Come, we had not gone far, before I stoped again, he stoped a little for me, and said again come, I followed, after halting, and Admiring the beauty I saw! in every countenance untill we got out, then the guide turn'd on the left hand, and we seem'd to I did not perceive the road we went, but could see my guide until we were where I beheld a Lofty grand arch of great width where we Entered into a Large Room, which I could not see to the end of, till we passed through: this Room appear'd grandly Wainscoted, and beautifully painted with different Collours, the first sight of this beautiful Room, abated my sorrow, which was very great, while we came down the descent, from leaving the other, I had but Just time to take a view of this fine place before a Number of persons, richly dressed passed us, who smell'd so strong of Brimstone, that I seem'd allmost suffocated all of them were talking to themselves, and before they came to us they look'd well, but when they came near, there appeared a Blackness on their lips, and seem'd to mutter to themselves, which was allso the manner of some that walked alone, I was seized with horror, and asked my guide what is this place and what are these, he Answered this place is Hell, and them are Miserable forever, they were when in the Body in Tumutts and will be so Everlastingly, at some distance sat an old Gentlewoman in a chair like a Bath Chair, a fine person very white and powdered and Grandly dress'd, I made up to her, to see if there was the same appearance of Misery in her, and was more shock'd than before, her lips were moving and from her Eyelids came small flames of fire, and Immediately after this as I look'd roun'd there appeared in my view a Woman Friend, plainly dress'd in a green apron, whom I remembered well when I was young, I often took notice of her, for the Solidity of her Deportment, particularly in Meeting, I eagerly made up to her, and said what art thou among the Miserable, tell me, tell me what brought the hither, she wept and said, no wrong that I have done between Man & Man, but unfaithfulness and disobediance to my God, brought me hither, I thought I wept as much as she, when I first look'd on her, she look'd sorrowful, then I turn'd to my guide, and said, let me go, he walked slowly on, and we met many like the other, in appearance, and smell, that I seem'd allmost suffocated with Brimstone, I then in great bitterness of spirit said to my guide, tell me am I to remain here forever, I thought a little time past, if I had died I had secured an Inheritance among the first we saw, my guide stood, and looking steadfastly at me said thou art not to remain here, but to return to the World again, if thou art faithful to thy God, thou mayest have an Inheritance among the first, but I have something else to show thee he went a little farther, when another arch appear'd, which divided, this place from a Large one, like a Chapple wherein abundance of people were assembled, to worship, and saying Amen, Lord have mercy upon us, Christ have Mercy upon us, these appear'd more plane in their dress and looked whiter, I said to my guide, these are not Miserable too, he said these are Miserable, these are they who thought to be saved by a profession of Religion, but have not the white robes of Righteousness they all came in by the way of this Room, some stop'd among the Worshipers, others went on to those who smell so strong of Brimstone, my distress now greater than before, for I thought I knew many of these who allso look'd at me, as if they knew me, and thought they appeared as if they worshiped, they looked to and fro, and seem'd much discompos'd, I again Intreated my guide to let me go, he walked gently out of this place and came again into the entrance of this House which is wide with a Large Gate, here stood a number in Black or dark Clothes, who did not seem to move forward to the others, when we came to the outside of the gate, I saw an Intimate Friend whom I much loved (this friend died in About a Month after) coming towards the Gate and two persons conducting him he look'd very Sorrowfull on me, and I on him, I asked him art thou agoing amongst the Miserable, what is thy offence, what hast thou done, Tell me, he Answered beware of Covetousness, and the love of Money, that brought me hither, we both wept much, and were greatly troubled, but I wanted to be gone, and followed my guide, and on looking back, saw some pulling, others pushing him, we were now in a large Enclosed field, in the field I saw many persons, some of whom are since Dead, out of it I could see no road, but my guide had me to a place, where there was just room to go Out, he stood and look'd at me, and earnestly said thou art now going into the World again Remember what thou hast seen, it is not enough to be honest to Man, thou must be honest and faithful to thy God Allso on this the thoughts of returning to the World affects me much for it seemed a Matter of doubt, whether I should be able to steer my Course, so as to be deemed worthy of admitance

Amongst the first I had a sight of, but standing speechless, and my guide standing still Faith suddenly sprung up in my mind, and I seem'd to say these Words: Lord those can'st if thou wilt preserve me thro' all, then I awoke, but the horror & distress I felt on my mind I am not capable of Expressing, I seem'd as if I fetch'd my breath in a room where Sulphur & Brimstone were Burning, often saying to my Nurse and those about me, I seem as if the smell of Brimstone was in my stomach.

Thought I could not live many Hours, nor do I believe I should if the Almighty in the Extendings of his Boundless — Goodness — had not had Reguard to me a poor unworthy Creature and caus'd that Suffocating smell to pass from me, and gave me to trust in that melted my spirit into contrition before him & Enabled me to vent my Sorrow in many Tears, after which my Toss'd mind was favoured with a Calm.

Document 30. The "Quincunx" Dream,
         Noted in Banneker's manuscript journal.
         See *Reference Notes,* 65. (Chapter IX, p. 268.)

On the night of the fifth of December 1791, Being a deep Sleep, I dreamed that I was in a public Company, one of them demanded of me the limits Rasannah Crandolphs Soul had to display itself in, after it departed from her Body and taken its flight. In answer I desired that he shew me the place of Beginning "thinking it like making a Survey on Land." He reply'd I cannot inform you, but there is a man about three days jorney from Hence that is able to satisfy your demand, I fortwith went to the man and requested of him to inform me place of beginning of the limits that Rasannah Crandolph's Soul had to display itself in, after the Separation from her Body; who gave me the answer, the Vernal Equinox, When I returned I found the Company together and I was able to Solve their Doubts by giving them the following answer Quincunx.

Document 31. "A Dream," dated "December 13, 1797,"
         Recorded in Banneker's manuscript journal.
         See *Reference Notes,* n.67 (Chapter IX, p. 268.)

I Dreamed I saw some thing passing by my door to and fro, and when I attempted to go to the door, it would vanish and reapted [sic] it twice or thrice, at length I let in the infernal Spirit and he told me that he had been concerned with a woman by the name of Beckey Freeman (I never heard the name as I remember) by some means we fell into a Skirmish, and I threw him behind the fire and endeavored to burn him up but all in vain — I know not what became of him but he was an ill formed being — Some part of him in Shape of a man, but hairy as a beast, his feet was circular or rather globular and did not exceed an inch and a half in diameter, but while I held him in the fire he said something respecting he was able to stand it, but I forget his words.

B. Banneker.

Document 32. Dream, dated "The night of December 25, 1797,"
Recorded in Banneker's manuscript journal.
See *Reference Notes*, 68. (Chapter IX, p. 268.)

I dreamed I had a fawn or young deer; whose hair was white and like unto lamb's wool, and all parts about it beautiful to behold. Then I said to myself I will set this little captive at liberty, but I will first clip the tips of his ear that I may know him if ever I should see him again. Then taking a pair of shears and cutting off the tip of one ear, and he cried like unto a child hath the pain which grieved him very much altho then I did not attempt to cut the other but was very sorry for that I had done I got him at liberty and he ran a considerable distance then he stopped and he looked back for at me I advanced toward him, and he came and met me and I took a lock of wool from my garment and wiped the blood of wound which I had made on him (which sorely affected me) I took him in my arms and brought him home and hold him on my knees, he asked the Woman if she had any trust and she answered him in the affirmative and gave him Some, which he began to eat and then asked for milk in a cup She said the dog had got the cup with milk in it under the house but there is milk in the cupboard.

My dream left me. B. Banneker.

Document 33. Dream, dated "April 24, 1802,"
Recorded in Banneker's manuscript journal.
See *Reference Notes*, n.69. (Chapter IX, p. 268.)

Being weary holing for corn, I laid down on my bed and fell into a deep sleep and dreamed I had a child in my arms and was viewing the back part of its head where it had been sore, and I found it was healed with a hole through the skin and Scull bone and came out at forehead, that I could see very distinctly through the child's head the hole being large enough to receive an ordinary finger —I called some woman to see the strange sight, and she put her spectacles on and Saw it, and she asked me if I had previously lanced that place in the Child's head, I answered in the affirmative.

N.B. the Child is well as any other.

Document 34.   Account of Rachel Mason's visit to Banneker's farm.
See *Reference Notes* (Chapter X, p. 260.)

In a late visit to Ellicott's Mills, two beloved friends and myself, who alike enjoy converse with Nature in her deepest solitudes, essayed to find the spot where the mental eye of this sable son of science had often pierced into futurity, and where his hand had recorded events as yet buried in its vast abyss. After mounting and descending successive hills, high and steep, and sometimes winding along the banks of the little streamlets that crossed our way, we found that memory had no chart whereby to direct our steps, and returned without accomplishing our purpose.

But I have heard from those who have passed that way, that a fire kindled by some unknown hand had consumed the cottage, and wasted every vestige belonging thereto. The pear tree and the orchard have not yet yielded to that Sovereign Power, which continued to inscribe this motto upon every terrestrial thing, "It shall perish."

Document 35.   Description of Banneker's Manuscript Journal, from Martha E. Tyson's unpublished manuscript
"A Memoir of Benjamin Banneker."
See *Reference Notes,* n.31. (Chapter XI, p. 305.)

All the manuscripts [of Banneker] were presented to the Maryland Historical Society in 1852, and were enclosed in a rustic cover of parchment of antique appearance. With a view to their preservation a member of the Society, the late Moses Sheppard, the founder of the Sheppard Asylum of Baltimore, had them bound in Russia leather.

Document 36.   Description of Banneker's Manuscript Journal, from Martha E. Tyson's *Banneker, The Afric-American Astronomer.*
See *Bibliography* Part II, Item 38. (Chapter XI, p. 305.)

It was a large volume of his manuscript and his common-place book. The former volume contains Banneker's observations on various subjects and copies of all his almanacs, as well as copies of his letter to Thomas Jefferson, and the reply of that statesman. We have extracted freely from these books. . . .

Document 37. Description of Banneker's Manuscript Journal,
from J. H. B. Latrobe's "Memoir."
See *Bibliography*, Part II, Item 14. (Chapter XI, p. 305.)

... the folio already referred to and now before the Society, contains the
calculations clearly copied, and the figures used by him in his work. The handwriting, it will be seen, is very good and remarkably distinct, having a practised
look, although evidently that of an old man, who makes his letters and figures
slowly and carefully.

Document 38. Engraved inscription appearing on facsimile
of the Banneker-Jefferson letters published by Moses
Sheppard as a broadside.
See *Reference Notes*, n.37. (Chapter XI, p. 305.)

The Letters, from which this facsimile is taken, are in the handwriting of
Banneker, who copied them into the volume of Manuscripts, in which they have
been preserved. His house and manuscripts were burnt soon after his decease,
except this book which was at a neighbor's, at the time.

Document 39. Excerpt from a letter written by Moses Sheppard
to Charles Sumner on May 3, 1852.
See *Reference Notes*, n.35. (Chapter XI, p. 306.)

Bannaker ... soon after his death his house and all his manuscripts were
burned, except one book which was at a neighbors. I have had it bound. There is
no Institution here in which it will not be subject to the same casualty as his
other papers. I therefore had the two letters lithographed to preserve as much of
Banneker in his own hand writing. I know that a single case proves nothing as to
a race, there was Newton, and I have internal evidence that all his race are not
Newtons. Pope's remark on Newton might with a little alteration be made applic-
able to Banneker. The Celestials "admire" such wisdom in an earthly shape and
show a Newton as we show an ape.

Document 40. Excerpt from a letter written by Moses Sheppard to
Dr. Samuel F. McGill in Liberia, July 5, 1852.
See *Reference Notes*, n.36. (Chapter XI, p. 306.)

... the whites take more interest in them than the blacks. After Latrobe published his biography of Bannaker, the colored people made a move to erect a monument to his memory, that died away. I then proposed to them to place a cenotaph of either marble or wood painted in each of their churches, they talked that off. I offered them a Lithographed copy of Bannaker's and Jefferson's letters to have framed and placed in their meeting houses, they have not accepted.

Document 41. Excerpt from a letter from Moses Sheppard to George M. Justice, November 18, 1852.
See *Reference Notes*, n.36. (Chapter XI, p. 307.)

The number of years in which Bannaker published almanacs is not known; a quantity of them were found in a loft at Ellicott's Mills used as waste paper; a new roof was put on the house and the rest of them were destroyed.

My investigations have convinced me that Bannaker's grandmother was a Scotch woman, he says in his letter to Jefferson that his color is of deepest dye, this must be understood in reference to those of the same mixture, a friend who lived near him and knew him well told me his color was "light black" or a dark mulatto, alieas a mulatto of "the deepest dye," strictly a quadroon reveres [sic].

Bannaker had two reasons to keep his mixture out of sight, one was that he was pleading the cause of the blacks, and he doubtless knew that it would be best to appear as one of them, and the other that his grandmother was a convict, this explanation is not designed to detract, as it cannot detract from the merits of the man, and his being rather intemperate, are circumstances that his biographer might omit, as his talents are the only question before the public. I send thee two of his Almanacs of 1792 and 96. I believe that one of 96 was the last one he published. . . After Latrobe published his memoirs of Bannaker, the colored people sent a deputation to ascertain the spot where his remains lay, about 15 miles from Baltimore, with the avowed intention of erecting a monument over him, but it was not done, they then talked of placing one in a cemetery near town, that ended in talk also. . . .

Latrobe's Memoirs were printed on a flying sheet that soon may disappear. Should that be its fate, the only Memorial or Monument of Bannaker will be the lithograph.

When we remember that Bannaker was destitute of all the means thought to be essential to the acquisition of astronomical knowledge, his asperations to understand the organization of the Solar system must have been sustained by a mind of unusual force, which places him in the case of great men of his age, and of every age. His case confirms the opinion of my own, if I may quote from myself, "That the Diety in the Creation of man did not restrict himself to any shade or form in which to wrap the ethereal essence that we call mind."

Document 42. Account of Rachel Mason's interest in Banneker, from an unsigned and undated manuscript written in the hand of Martha E. Tyson.
See *Reference Notes*, n.43. (Chapter XI, p. 309.)

After Rachel Mason had finished her Memoirs of her mother in 1836, she wished to prepare a narrative of the life of Benjamin Banneker, in order that the example of his fine talents, studious habits and ultimate attainments as an astronomer might be made useful to the people of color here as well as elsewhere; but aware at the same time that the value of such a work would be much increased if she could represent him, (according to a concise account which had appeared in print) as being of strictly African parentage, she was anxious to procure proofs to that effect, and by the assistance of her friends made many inquiries on the subject, and I regret to say without the desired success. . . .

Document 43. Note made by Martha E. Tyson concerning J. H. B. Latrobe's "Memoir."
See *Reference Notes*, n.45. (Chapter XI, p. 309.)

An able and interesting account of Ben Banneker was read before the H. S. [Historical Society] in 1845 by H. B. Latrobe, was published and extensively circulated — In this first memorial that had ever been prepared of him, appeared some details of his parentage which had then been misrepresented to the author and which were well known by many of the residents of Baltimore and its surrounding vicinity to be quite erroneous. The author of the following essay [A Sketch] who had often seen the old astronomer, and who had taken many notes connected with his history from aged persons who had known him well, yielded to the solicitation of influential members of the Society and prepared for them a new memorial which was read and published by them in the year 1854. . . .

Document 44. Excerpt from a letter written by John H. B. Latrobe to Martha E. Tyson, September 19, 1864.
See *Reference Notes*, n.46. (Chapter XI, p. 310.)

I have your note, with the Memoir of Banneker and the returned newspapers. You were quite right in supposing I had not seen the former. I stand corrected, now, on a point, which, I could have wished, for the argument, had been otherwise.— But the truth is the truth: and the capacity of the black color indicated, as us lawyers say, *aliunde* — I mean, of the native race without white admixture. The memoir I will put away as a valuable one, all the more so, because this particular copy has the autograph of a lady I very sincerely admire and respect.

Document 45. Excerpt from a letter by Brantz Mayer, Librarian of the Maryland Historical Society, to J. Saurin Norris concerning the manuscript of *A Sketch* . . . by Tyson, dated January 20, 1854.
See *Reference Notes*, n.47. (Chapter XI, p. 310.)

I think Mrs. Tyson's amendment of the sentence not only the best that has been made, but the best that could be made. My only desire in this matter was to have the fact explicitly stated that *Madame* Bannecker was a *white* woman. Whether her color is displayed at the *head* of the page or at its *foot*, matters very little. The tact of woman, in this, as in all other matters, has overcome the difficulty.

In regard to other alterations I have only to say that my chief anxiety is to have every thing omitted that can in any way connect our Society with *opinions* about Slavery or anti-Slavery. We may develop as many facts as we please about "the institution," but, as you know, there are so many "carpers and cavillers" about our Society, that I am anxious to give them no topic for fault finding.

You will oblige me very much if you will explain or show this to Mrs. Tyson, in order that she may understand exactly my position, and how much I was gratified by the perusal of her lucid and interesting narrative.

Document 46. Excerpt from a newspaper account of the anniversary celebration of the Banneker Institute held on November 9, 1860, in Philadelphia, from an unidentified Philadelphia newspaper, dated November 15, 1860.
See *Reference Notes*, n.50. (Chapter XI, p. 310–311)

Among the colored people of the country generally, few names are more honored than that of Benjamin Banneker, of Ellicott's Mills, Baltimore County, the 128th [actually 129th] anniversary of whose birth was celebrated last night by the elite among the colored people of Philadelphia, at the colored Masonic Hall, south Eleventh street, below Pine.

The occasion was the eighth anniversary of the Banneker Institute, a literary society comprising a membership of thirty young men, who meet at Benezet Hall, south Seventh street, and have amply illustrated the capacity of the colored people for a high degree of intellectual advancement. . . .

Document 47. Annapolis, Maryland. Hall of Records. *Report of Cases . . .
in the Court of Appeals of Maryland in 1810 . . . 1815,* vol. III
(1826), pp. 97–98. Courtesy of Frederick W. Jones and
Robert J. Hurry.
June 1810, Rusk vs. Sowerwine (Chapter XI, p. 301.)

. . . the plaintiff offered as a witness to that fact, a black woman named Minta;
and on the defendant's objecting to her, as an incompetent witness, the plaintiff
offered evidence that the witness, and the late Benjamin Bannaker, a black man of
Baltimore County, were born of the same parents, and that the witness and
Bannaker were always reputed to be free; and to be descended of free parentage,
and did actually enjoy freedom. That Bannaker exercised in his life the rights of a
free man in holding real property, in voting of elections, and being allowed and
permitted to give evidence in courts of justice in cases in which free white citizens were concerned; but it did not appear that at the times Bannaker was so
admitted as a witness, no objections were made to his competency. The Court
(Nicholson, Ch. J.) determined Minta to be an incompetent witness, the plaintiff
and defendant being free white Christian persons. The plaintiff accepted.

> *Reference to this incident is made by Jeffrey Brackett in* The Free Negro in Maryland
> *(Baltimore: Johns Hopkins University Studies, 1889) p. 268, and by James Wright in* The Free
> Negro in Maryland 1634–1860 *(New York: Octagon Books, 1971), reprint, p. 118. Neither
> author, however, identified Benjamin Banneker.*

Document 48. Freedom of John Henden and Alsey Henden (also
Hendon) Baltimore County Court (*Miscellaneous Papers*)
1811–1812
Tracking No. 2/16/53, Item 135. (Chapter XI, p. 300.)

10th Mo. 16th, 1811.
To whom it may concern:

The bearer hereof, John Hendon, a Man of colour having applied to us for
our Certificate respecting his and his Wife's Freedom:

We therefore certify on their behalf that we have known them for more
than twenty years, during most of which time he has been in our employ, and for
several years he and his family have lived on our lands as Tenants — That we
have always considered and believe them to be free persons & the Descendants of
the Banneker Family. —

Witness our Hands
Jno. Ellicott

Geo. Ellicott

Benj.ᵃ Ellicott

E. Ellicott.

Baltimore County Court

No. 1/16/53, Item 135.

Benjamin Ellicott, G. Ellicott, E. Ellicott to freedom of John Hendon and Alsey Hendon, 16 October 1811. Hendon was employed by the Ellicotts and lived on their land as tenants for about twenty years; always considered to be free persons and descendants of the Banneker family. Dark mulatto man, age circa 45 years, 5 feet 5 inches tall. "and he is descended from a few men and women of color of the name of Banneker."

"Alsey Hendon is the daughter age about 20 and a free mulatto woman."

Baltimore County to Wit

October 16, 1811 came Benjamin Ellicott one of the signers of the within certificate and of the Society of Friends and solemnly affirmed that he has known Hendon a dark mulatto man, aged about 45 years 5 feet 5 inches high for about twenty years, that he has always lived and worked about as a free man, and this affirmant believes that he is descended from a free man and woman of colour of the name of Banecker.

Thos. Griffith

Justice of the Peace.

Same time came John Hendon and made an oath that Alsey Hendon aged about 20 years 4 feet 11 inches high is the daughter of the deponent, and a free Mulatto Woman.

Thos. Griffith

Justice of the Peace.

[the former light yellow
the latter bright yellow
both Balti.State M.ᵒ]

Document 49. Annapolis, Hall of Records, *List of Free-born Black Men in Baltimore County*

Courtesy of Frederick W. Jones. (Chapter XI, p. 300.)

[The Register of Certificates granted by the Clerk of Baltimore County to free

Negroes (Not Manumitted) in Virtue of an Act of Assembly passed November Session 1805. Commencing on first of June 1806] lists 109 free born black men and 358 manumitted slaves who were registered between 1806 and 1816.

Page 1, Item No. 2

    20th March 1807 Greenbury [the name Benjamin crossed out] *Morton Free born [Color] Yellow or brown, scar on below the corner of his right Bale on top of the head. Age 50 5 feet 8 inches high.* [Nephew of Benjamin Banneker.]

Others listed who potentially may be of interest:

No.	17	1807	Negro Charles Moreton age	27	Baltimore County
	18	1807	Negro Violet Boston	40	Ann Arundel
	35	1807	Mulat. Ara Eliza Morton	21/22	Baltimore
	43	1809	Ephraim Black	31	Baltimore
	55		Negro James Hall	25	Baltimore
	70	1811	John Hendon	45	Baltimore
	71	1811	Alsey Hendon	20	Baltimore
	98	1813	Absalon Barton	30	Baltimore
	107	1813	Negro James Hall	32	Baltimore

Document 50. Itemized list of purchases made by Banneker at the Ellicott & Co. store in Ellicott's Lower Mills in the period 1774–1803. Noted in Ellicott Co. store ledger, Banneker's manuscript journal and Commonplace Book.

Ellicott & Co. Store Ledger

1774				
Sept.	8		To Ambio from Book W p. 34	£0.5.5-1/2
	12		To 2 lbs. shott & 1-1/2 lbs. powder	1.8-1/2
			1 quart Rum	1.2
	30		? sheets	2.11
Nov.	14		1 qt. Rum, 1/2 lb. chocolate	2.
			1 lb. Sugar, 1/2 lb. Candles	1.3
			By cash in full	14.6
	18		To Bush. Salt 1/9 for new	1.9

		1/2 gallons Rum, Paper of ink powder	3.3
		Hard buttons for Barten	1.
1775			
Jan.	11	1 quart Rum	1.2
	26	1 Bushel 36 lb. Wheat	cr. 10.9
		To cash in full	3.7
Feb.	12	Rum. A Remnant Cloth	13.2
		1 doz. Buttons	.6
	27	By Ballance brought from W Book	10.9
	28	12' Rum per order	1.2
Mar.	25	12' ditto (Rum)	1.2
	28	1 pt. Rum 1 gallon Molasses	2.1/2
July	3	1/2 gallon Rum	2.1/2
		By cash	1.6
	10	By Sam Morton	4.6
Jun	20	By cash in full	[June?]
		3.7	

Commonplace Book

1796			
May	4	To a watch 4. Dol.	£10.10
1799		Contra Credit	
Sept.	18	Recd of John Collin at sundry times	1.15.11
		Recd. fodder Recd. fodder	0.11.3
Nov.	23	Cash of wife	0.11.6
1799			
		Harriet Ducket debtor	
Nov.	17	To 1/2 pint honey	0.0.7
[Date not known]			
		William Hubbard, creditor	
Apr.	30	Cash lent him	0.0.10-1/2
		R2 b 2 c 1 Cl bl 2 debtor	
1795			
May	25	Cash lent her	0.7.6
Jun	22	Cash of her	
1799		John Collins Dr.	
		Cyder at sundry times	0.49

		2 quarts dry peaches	0.0.6
Nov.	27	1 peck peaches	0.0.11
Dec.	31	1 quart Mead	0.0.4

1800
Jan.	21	Cash lent wife (of John Collins)	0.1.10-1/2

Manuscript Journal

In account with Ellicott & Co.

1799
Jan.	15	Pork (previous to Dec. 22, 1798)	
	12	Almanac	
		9-1/2 lbs. pork	
Feb.	27	1 bushel corn	
Mar.	8	5 yards sheeting	
		6 skeins thread	
		1/4 lbs. pork	
		1-1/2 gallons molasses	
	19	1 bushel corn	
Apr.	1	7-1/2 lbs. pork	
		1/2 lb. tobacco	
		1 bushel corn	
	13	7-1/2 lbs. pork	
		1/2 gallons molasses	
May	6	1 bushel corn	
	7	4-1/2 lbs. pork	
		1/2 gallon molasses	
	31	6-1/2 lbs. pork	
Jun	1	l bushel corn	
	12	1 bushel corn	
July	1	1 paper of ink powder	
	12	1 bushel corn	
Aug.	9	1-3/4 (yds.?) nankeen	
		1-1/2 yards muslin	
		Twist thread and moulds	
		1 pair Stokings	
		Cash of George Ellicott	£0.12.0
	13	1/4 lb. gunpowder	
Sept.		Paid the taylor for making my jacket	

	21	9 lbs. pork	
Oct.	19	1/4 lb. powder and 1 lb. shot	
Nov.		Received of Elias Ellicott	$4.

1800

Jan.	20	1 pair Stockens	
	22	7-1/2 yds. Rushia Drilling [fabric]	
Feb.	7	4 yds. Ticklinburg	
	17	By paying Samuel 6 pair point	
Mar.	29	4-1/2 yards Russia sheeting	
		3-1/3 yds. Irish linen	
		8 skeins thread	
Apr.	16	Cash received	0.11.3
May	17	Cash from George Ellicott	4.7.0
	20	Paying the sheriff	0.7.6
July	1	Cash from George Ellicott	0.7.6
		1 peck salt	
Nov.	11	By cash a Dollar	0.7.6
	22	1-1/4 yards Coating	
		1-1/2 yards flannel	
		1/4 yards linen	
		Thread	
		1 pair Shoes	

1801

Jan.	31	2-1/2 yds. Rusia sheeting	
		3-1/2 yards. ditto; white linen	
		Thread	
Apr.	1	1 pair shoes @ $1.25	
May	9	1 Razor	
Jun	13	9 lbs. pork	
	18	1/2 bushel corn	
July	17	Paying the sheriff	
	20	1/2 bushel corn	
	13	6-1/2 yds. camblet	
		2 yds. brown holland	
		Silk twist and thread	
		Buckrem and moulds	
		4-1/2 kbs. pork	
Sept	2	Recd. 2-1/2 Dollars and 1/2 bushel corn	
Oct.	19	1 Razor at 1/2 Dollar	

		Paying the taylor for making a Coat	0.16.10-1/2
Nov.	2	2-1/2 yds. corduroy	
		1 dozen buttons	
		3/4 yds. Russia duck	
	28	Cash received £3.18.6	
Dec.	23	7-3/4 lbs. pork	
		Paid the taylor for making my Breches	

1802

Jan.	15	10-1/3 lbs. pork	
Feb.	2	1 pair shoes	
Mar.	3	7-3/4 lbs. pork	
	29	7-1/2 lbs. pork	
		A small w pail	
Apr.	15	A fine hat	$4
		7-1/4 lbs. pork	
		1/2 bushel corn	
May	10	11 lbs. pork	
	20	1 gunlock	
		1/2 bushel corn	
Jun	23	Paid the sheriff	
	26	3-1/4 yds. Irish linen	
		3-1/2 yds. linen	
		Thread and buttons	
July		1/2 bushel corn	
	8	Cash to pay for a Book	$3
		Cash recd. Said Day	$1
Aug.	4	1 padlock, 1/4 lb. powder, and shot	
		8 lbs. pork, 1/4 lb. soap	
Sept.	13	1/2 bushel corn	
		1 pair shoes @ 11.3	
Nov.	16	Cash received	1.18.3-1/2
		3-1/2 yds.Cloth	
		Trimming for a Great Coat	

1803

Jan.	10	1 pair shoes	
Mar.	22	1 yard Linen	
		1 pair Stockings, 1 pair Sect	
		1/4 lb. powder, 1 comb	
Apr.	18	1/2 gallon molasses. A pen knife	

	19	Recd. cash of John Ellicott	0.7.6
May	19	Paid the sheriff	
	20	20 yds. white muslin sheeting	
		2-1/2 yds. brown ditto. 1/2 gallon molasses	
		7-3/4 lbs. pork. Thread	
Jun		Paid Nannie Hall	
	18	7-1/4 lbs. pork	
		1/2 gallon molasses. 1 lb. soap	
July	9	1/2 lb. bacon. Paper and thread	
		1 handkerchief	
	13	1 lb. tobacco. A dose of castor oil	
	22	Cash 1 Dollar. 1/2 gallon molasses	
Aug.	11	8-1/2 lbs. pork	
Sept.	7	7 lbs. pork	
		1/2 gallons molasses. 1 lb. soap	
		8 lbs. pork	
		1/2 lb. powder. 2 lbs. shot	
		5 lbs. pork	
		1/2 lb. tobacco	
		1/2 gallons molasses. 2-1/2 lbs. candles	
Nov.		An ink stand	0.3.0
		1/2 lb. Tobacco	
		Cash of George Ellicott	£0.3.9

Document 51.   Indenture made between Benjamin Banneker and
Jonathan Ellicott and others, October 23, 1799.
(Chapter XI, p. 277.)

This Indenture made this Twenty third day of October in the year one thousand Seven hundred & ninety nine, Between Benjamin Banneker of Baltimore County State of Maryland of the one part and Jonathan Ellicott, Elias Ellicott, George Ellicott and John Ellicott of the other part Witnesseth that the said Benjamin Banneker for and in consideration of the sum of one hundred and Eighty pounds current money of the United States to him in hand paid by the said Jonathan, Elias, George and John Ellicott the receipt whereof the said Benjamin Banneker dothe hereby Acknowledge himself fully Satisfied contented and paid hath granted, bargained & sold aliened enfcoffed, released and confirmed unto the said Jonathan, Ellicott one fourth part, unto Elias Ellicott one fourth part unto George Ellicott one fourth part & unto John Ellicott one fourth

part their heirs and assigns forever as Tenants in common and not as Joint
Tenants, all his the said Benjamin Banneker's right Title interest claim and
Demand in and unto Seventy two Acres of Land being part of a tract of land
called "Stout" lying & being in Baltimore County aforesaid it being all the
remaining part of the said Banneker's land, which his father bought of a certain
Richard Gist on the tenth day of March in the year one thousand seven hundred
and thirty seven and which the said Banneker has not conveyed prior to the date
of this Indenture being bounded as follows, Beginning for the same at the third
boundary of the aforesaid tract of land called "Stout" then running with the second line of Stout reversed and with the Baltimore Company's land to John
Bartons land then bounding on said Bartons courses until it intersects the said
Ellicott land which they purchased of John Teal, and then with said land until it
intersects the land which the said Ellicotts bought of Abraham Walker then with
the said land until it intersects the northernmost corner of a part of Stout as conveyed by the said Banneker to Greenbury Morton then south easterly with and
bounding on the said Morton's land until it intersects land belonging to Thomas
Gibbons, then with and bounding on said Gibbons land to the place of
Beginning containing by estimation seventy two Acres of land more or less with
the Appurternances thereunto belonging or in any wise appurtaining and also the
reversion and reversions, remainder and remainders, rents, issues and profits of
the said land and Premises and all the Estate, right, title, and interest property,
Claim and Demand whatsoever of him the said Benjamin Banneker of in and to
the same and every part and parcel thereof To have and To Hold the one undi-
vided fourth part of the hereby granted land with the Appurtenances unto the
aforesaid Jonathan Ellicott his heirs and Assigns forever and the said Benjamin
Banneker for himself and his heirs and against all other persons whatsoever
claiming by from or under him the Said Benjamin Banneker his heirs or assigns
shall and will warrant and forever defend by these presents. In Witness whereof I
have hereunto set my hand and affixed my seal the day and year above

      Written
      /s/ Benjamin Banneker
      [seal]

signed, sealed and delivered)
  Received this 23rd day of
  October one thousand seven
  hundred and ninety nine in
  the presence of)
  of Jonathan Ellicott, Elias Ellicott,

George Ellicott & John Ellicott.
parties to the within deed
Benjamin Rish,
Amos Gillingham)
the sum of one hundred and eighty pounds it being the consideration
money within mentioned.
Witness Benjamin Rish; Amos Gillingham

B. Banneker.
    Be it remembered that on the 23rd day of October 1799 came the within
named Benjamin Banneker before the subscribers two of the Justices of the peace
for the County of Baltimore and acknowledged the within deed to be his Act &
Deed and the Lands and premises therein granted to be the right Title & Estate of
the within named Jonathan Ellicott, Elias Ellicott, George Ellicott and John
Ellicott their heirs and assigns forever
Geo. Buchanan
Wm. Russell

Received to be Recorded the 10th day of December 1799 same day Recorded and
Examined per Wm. Gibson.

Document 52.   Text of the public marker installed on Banneker's
              farm in Oella, Maryland, by the State Historical
              Sites Commission.
              (Chapter XI, p. 317.)

BENJAMIN BANNEKER

(1731–1806)

THE SELF-EDUCATED NEGRO

MATHEMATICIAN AND ASTRONOMER

WAS BORN, LIVED HIS ENTIRE LIFE

AND DIED NEAR HERE.

HE ASSISTED IN SURVEYING THE

DISTRICT OF COLUMBIA, 1791, AND

PUBLISHED THE FIRST MARYLAND

ALMANAC, 1792. THOMAS JEFFERSON

RECOGNIZED HIS ACHIEVEMENTS.

Maryland Historical Society.

REFERENCE NOTES

I. The Heritage and the Land

1. Charles Weathers Bump, "Indian Place-Names in Maryland," *Maryland Historical Magazine*, 2 (1907): 287–91.

2. Henry J. Berkley, "Extinct River Towns of the Chesapeake Bay Region," *Maryland Historical Magazine*, 19 (1924): 125–41.

3. *Laws of Maryland, Enacted at a Session of Assembly . . . 1763* (Annapolis: Jonas Green, 1766), Chapter 18.

4. Abbot Emerson Smith, *Colonists in Bondage, White Servitude and Convict Labor in America 1607–1770* (Chapel Hill: University of North Carolina Press, 1947), pp. 89–151. See also James Davie Butler, "British Convicts Shipped to American Colonies," *American Historical Review*, 2 (1897): 12–33; and Abbot Emerson Smith, "The Transportation of Convicts to the American Colonies in the Seventeenth Century," ibid., 39 (1934): 232–49. Basil Sollers, "Transported Convict Laborers in Maryland During the Colonial Period," *Maryland Historical Magazine*, 2 (1907): 17–47. Henry F. Thompson, "An Atlantic Voyage in the Seventeenth Century," *Maryland Historical Magazine*, 2 (1907): 319–26.

7. *The Maryland Gazette*, July 16, 1767.

8. Ibid., November 24, 1768.

9. [Martha E. Tyson], *Banneker, the Afric-American Astronomer. From the Posthumous Papers of Martha E. Tyson. Edited by Her Daughter* (Philadelphia: Friends' Book Association, 1884), p. 10 (hereinafter cited as Tyson, *Banneker).* See also Sollers, "Transported Convict Laborers in Maryland," pp. 17–29.

10. "Transportation of Felons to the Colonies," [author not identified], *Maryland Historical Magazine*, 27 (1932): 263–74.

11. For a discussion of the Indians of Baltimore County, see William B. Marye, "The Baltimore County 'Garrison' and the Old Garrison Roads," *Maryland Historical Magazine*, 16 (1921): 125–27.

12. Robert Sutcliffe, *Travels in Some Parts of North America, in the Years 1804, 1805, & 1806.* 2nd ed. (New York, 1815), pp. 107–8, 207.

13. Tyson, *Banneker*, p. 10.

14. Ibid, pp. 9–11.

15. Ron Eglash, "The African Heritage of Benjamin Banneker," *Social Studies of Science*, 27 (1997): 308–10.

16. Lucie G. Colvin, *Historical Dictionary of Senegal* (London: Scarecrow Press, 1981), p. 289; Pathé Daigne, cited in Eglash, "The African Heritage of Benjamin Banneker," pp. 309–10.

17. Joseph E. Holloway, ed., *Africanisms in American Culture* (Bloomington: Indiana University Press, 1990), pp. 4–5.

18. Peter D. Gamble, *The Wolof of Senegambia* in *Ethnographic Survey of Africa. Western Africa*, Part 14, edited by Daryll Forde (London: International African Institute, 1957); T. Alford, *Prince Among Slaves* (New York: Harcourt Brace & Co., 1977), passim.

19. *Laws of Maryland, 1752,* (Baltimore: Maryland Historical Society, 1883) Chapter 1.

20. Jeffrey R. Brackett, *The Negro in Maryland: A Study of the Institution of Slavery* (Baltimore: N. Murray, 1889), pp. 32–33, quoted from *Archives of Maryland*, Proceedings of the General Assembly, 1637–1664, pp. 533–34.

21. Carter G. Woodson, "The Beginnings of the Miscegenation of the Whites and Blacks," *The Journal of Negro History*, 3 (1918): 341.

22. J. Thomas Scharf, *History of Baltimore City and County from the Earliest Period to the Present Day, Including Biographical Sketches of Their Representative Men* (Philadelphia: Louis H. Everts, 1881), pp. 43–47; *Maryland, A Guide to the Old Line State* (New York: Oxford University Press, 1973), pp. 326–27.

23. *Maryland, A Guide to the Old Line State*, p. 309.

II. HOME AND FAMILY

1. "Freedom of John Henden and Alsey Henden," Item 135, No. 1/16/53, Baltimore County Court, Miscellaneous Papers 1811–1812, Maryland State Archives.

2. Ethan Allen, "History of St. Paul's Church," MS 13, Maryland Historical Society, courtesy of Charles J. Weiker. For a history of the parish, see Helen W. Ridgeley, "The Ancient Churchyards of Baltimore," *The Grafton Magazine of History and Genealogy*, 1 (1909): 8–14, and *Historic Graves of Maryland and the District of Columbia* (New York: Grafton Press, 1908); Tyson, *Banneker*, p. 25.

3. Parish Register, Marriages, folio 102, p. 153, no. 27, St. Paul's Parish, Baltimore, Maryland. The entry merely listed the marriage of "James Boston [or Baslon] to Katherine Banneker, May the 22nd, 1735, Negroes"; and Marriages, folio 111, p. 168. The entry states "William Black & Esther Banneker was married September 22, 1744."

4. Meshach Simpson Jr., "Notes of the Lett family history passed down from Meshach Lett and other family members." Courtesy of Charles Henry Lett and Charles J. Weiker. No record of the marriage has been found in the registers of St. Paul's Parish.

5. [Martha E. Tyson], *A Sketch of the Life of Benjamin Banneker, From Notes Taken in 1836* (Baltimore: John D. Toy, 1854), p. 4. (Hereinafter cited as Tyson, *A Sketch.*)

6. William B. Marye, "The Baltimore County 'Garrison' and the Old Garrison Roads," *Maryland Historical Magazine*, 16 (1921): 245. See also Colonel J. Thomas Scharf, *The Chronicles of* Baltimore; Being a Complete History of "Baltimore Town" and Baltimore City from the Earliest *Period to the Present Time* (Baltimore: Turnbull Brothers, 1874), pp. 12, 202.

7. Scharf, *Chronicles of Baltimore,* pp. 50–51.

8. Baltimore County Land Records, HWS #1A, fols. 58–59, Maryland State Archives; Liber DD, No. 5, F144; Baltimore County Deed IR No. PP. 137; Baltimore County Deed WG No. II; 602; Baltimore County Deed HWS No. M:26.

9. Baltimore County Rent Roll, Calvert Papers No. 883, folio 162. ". . . 27 Mar. 1701 for Capt. Tho. Bales." Maryland Historical Society.

10. On April 14, 1771, Williams sold part of this tract to Joseph, Andrew, Nathaniel, and John Ellicott and on the same date the Ellicott brothers purchased an adjacent tract called "Teal's Search" from Emmanuel Teal. These two parcels were subsequently developed by the Ellicott brothers into Ellicott's Lower Mills, now Ellicott City.

11. Additional Rent Roll of the Western Shore, Scharf Papers, Maryland Historical Society.

12. Debt Book, Baltimore County, No. 904, p. 69, Calvert Papers, Maryland Historical Society; Tax List, 1737 — Baltimore County — Upper Patapsco Hundred listed "James Bannacar and his wife . . . 2 taxables," Calvert Papers, Maryland State Archives. See also Baltimore County Debt Book, Calvert Papers, No. 904, p. 69, Maryland Historical Society.

13. "Narrative of a voyage to Maryland 1705–1706," Sloane MS. 2291, vol. 1, British Museum.

14. Thomas Glover, "Account of Virginia, 1671," in John Lowthorp, ed., *Philosophical* Transactions and Collections to the End of the Year 1700; Abridged and Dispos'd Under General *Heads by John Lowthorp,* 3 vols. (London, 1731), 2:574. See also William Tatham, *Essay on the Culture and Commerce of Tobacco* (London, 1800).

15. J. E. McMurtrey, *Tobacco Production,* Agricultural Information Bulletin No. 245, December 1961, pp. 27–29, 57.

16. Lewis Cecil Gray, *History of Agriculture in the Southern United States to 1860* (Washington, D.C.: Carnegie Institution, 1933), 1:218–19.

17. William Hand Browne, ed., *Archives of Maryland,* 73 vols. (Baltimore: Maryland Historical Society, 1883–), 13:552; 22:560; 24:106; and 26:331.

18. Aubrey C. Land, "Economic Base and Social Structure: The Northern Chesapeake in the Eighteenth Century," *Journal of Economic History,* 25 (1965): 642–66.

19. Tyson, *Banneker,* pp. 13–14.

20. Ibid. Members of the Hall family continued to live in the vicinity of Banneker's home to recent times.

21. Beatrice Lumpkin, "From Egypt to Benjamin Banneker; African Origins of False Position Solutions," Vita Mathematica. Historical research and Integration with Teaching. *National Mathematical Association Notes*, 40 (1996): 279–89. Banneker's puzzles and solutions are reviewed on pages 284–88. Correspondence with Professor Lumpkin, April 8 and 22, 1992. See also James Eaton, *A Treatise on Arithmetic* (Boston: Brown & Taggard, 1861), p. 203. On "Double Position," see also John Bonnycastle, *The Scholar's Guide to Arithmetic; or, A Complete Exercise Book for the Use of Schools*, 2nd ed. (London: For J. Johnson, 1780), pp. 121, 165; John J. White, *Arithmetic Simplified: Being a Plain, Practical System, Adapted to the Capacity of Youth, and Designed for Use in the Schools, in the United States* (Hartford: Geo. Goodwin & Sons, 1819); and David Eugene Smith, *History of Mathematics* (Boston: Ginn & Co., 1925), 2:437–40.

22. In the collection of the Division of Timekeeping, National Museum of American History, Smithsonian Institution.

23. Among Maryland's earliest clockmakers was the Philadelphia-trained Benjamin Chandlee, who established himself at Nottingham, Maryland, in 1712 and generated a family dynasty of clockmakers. At one point Hagerstown became a center for clockmaking, while at Annapolis William Faris was already in business making clocks by mid-century. See Chris Bailey, *Two Hundred Years of American Clockmaking* (New York: Prentice-Hall, 1975), pp. 37, 73–77; Edward E. Chandlee, *Six Quaker Clockmakers* (Philadelphia: Historical Society of Pennsylvania, 1943), pp. 21–37 et seq.; Brooks Palmer, *The Book of American Clocks* (New York: Macmillan and Company, 1950), passim; George H. Eckhardt, *Pennsylvania Clocks and Clockmakers* (New York: Devin-Adair Company, 1955), pp. 161–222; Paul Wilstach, *Tidewater Maryland* (Indianapolis: Bobbs, Merrill Co., 1931, passim.

24. Tyson, *Banneker*, pp. 31–32.

25. Ibid., 12–13.

26. Simpson, "Notes on the Lett family history," courtesy of Charles Henry Lett and Charles J. Weiker.

27. *Heads of Families at the First Census of the United States Taken in the Year 1790*, Census for Frederick County, Maryland, p. 62.

28. Simpson, "Notes on the Lett family history."

29. "Account of Minta Black with Zacharias McCubbins," No. 1548, Maryland State Archives. "Federal Direct Tax Assessment for Patapsco Upper Hundred," Item 3292, Department of Legislative Reference, Baltimore City Hall, lists McCubbins in 1798 as the owner of parts of tracts named Ashmans Hope, Bunker Hill, and "sundry other tracts in Patapsco Upper Hundred."

30. Tyson, *Banneker*, p. 11; Ledger of Ellicott & Co., 1774–1775, courtesy of Emmanuel Freeman.

31. Baltimore County Tax List for Patapsco Upper Hundred, 1773,

Department of Legislative Reference, Baltimore City Hall, lists "Benjamin Banneker, — 1 taxable." The item relating to the stray animal is recorded in Joppa, Maryland, Court Proceedings, f1761. Tyson, *Banneker,* pp. 12–13.

32.Tyson, *Banneker,* p. 12.

33. Robert Palmer, *Deep Blues* (New York: Penguin Books, 1981), passim. David P. Gamble, "The Wolof of Senegambia" in *Ethnographic Survey of Africa. Western Africa* (London: International African Institute, 1957), Part 14, pp. 11–12, 63–64, 77. Inasmuch as the Wolof lived in fairly close proximity with the Fulbe, they would have been familiar also with the *riti,* the one-stringed fiddle, and instruments played by wandering minstrels from other tribes.

III. FRIENDS AND NEIGHBORS

1. Charles W. Evans, *Biographical and Historical Accounts of the Fox, Ellicott, and Evans Families, and the Different Families Connected with Them* (Buffalo, N.Y.: Press of Baker, Jones & Co., 1882), pp. 10–74. Reprinted as *Fox Ellicott Evans American Family History* by Charles Worthington Evans, Martha Ellicott Tyson, G. Hunter Bartlett (Cockeysville, Md.: Fox Ellicott Evans Fund, 1976). See also Milton Drake, *Almanacs of the United States* (New York: The Scarecrow Press, 1962), Part 1, pp. 135–36, 218–20; Part 2, pp. 987, 991, 993, 1321–22.

2. Scharf, *History of Baltimore City,* pp. 47–50; *Maryland, A Guide,* pp. 308–9, 326–27; Silvio A. Bedini, "Philip Jones, Jr. and the Survey of Baltimore Town," *The Professional Surveyor* (January/February 1994): 52, and (March/April 1994): 50–51.

3. Martha E. Tyson, *Settlement of Ellicott's Mills, with Fragments of History therewith Connected, Written at the Request of Evan T. Ellicott* (Baltimore: Maryland Historical Society, 1871), pp. 25–26.

4. Ibid., p. 26.

5. John S. Tyson, "Sketches of the Settlement of Ellicott Mills for the Howard District Press, May 15, 1847." (Typewritten manuscript is privately owned and used with permission.)

6. Ibid., pp. 16–17; *Fox Ellicott Evans* (reprint), pp. 38–39.

7. Ledger of Ellicott & Co., 1774–1775, pp. 91, 103, 120, 523. (Collection of Mr. Emanuel Freeman).

8. Henry C. Peden Jr., *Revolutionary Patriots of Baltimore Town and Baltimore Town and County, 1775–1783* (Silver Spring, Md.: Family Line Publications, 1988), p. 123; Margaret M. Hodges, Unpublished Revolutionary Records of Maryland, MS., vol. 6, pp. 26–28, MdHS; "Oaths of Fidelity," *History Trails* (Cockeysville, Md., July 1976), p. 12.

9. *Fox, Ellicott, Evans* (reprint), pp. 22–24; Silvio A. Bedini, "Andrew Ellicott, Surveyor of the Wilderness," *ASCE Surveying and Mapping,* 36 (June 1976): 113–35; Silvio A. Bedini, "George Wall, Jr. and the Trigonometer," *The Professional*

Surveyor (September/October 1988): 59, 60.

10. "Tragedy Repeated Often in Ellicott City," *Ellicott City Times,* Centennial Edition, reprinted in *The Ellicott City Bicentennial Journal* (Summer/Fall 1972): 6B, 38B.

11. Several of the buildings can be identified with surviving original structures, including the homes of Jonathan and John Ellicott. The original sketch drawn by George Ellicott in 1782 and a description of it written in 1902 by his granddaughter, Lucy Tyson Fitzhugh, are in the collection of Mr. Emmanuel Freeman.

12. M. E. Tyson, *Settlement,* pp. 15–18.

13. Transferred by indenture dated December 31, 1774, a tract of 157 acres for £1,700 Maryland currency from Benjamin Hood to Joseph Ellicott.

14. Robert Gibson, *A Treatise of Practical Surveying; Which Is Demonstrated From Its First Principles,* 2nd ed. (Dublin: Printed for William Ross, 1768). This copy in its original leather binding was formerly owned by the late Dr. Robert T. Fitzhugh. On the flyleaf is the signature of George Wall Jr., with the date 1781 and the inscription, "James Hamilton, His Book." Also appearing on the title page are the signatures "Geo. Ellicott 1784" and "M. E. Tyson 1854."

15. Evans, et al., *Fox, Ellicott Evans American Family History,* pp. 2a, 3a, 4a, 12a.

16. M. E. Tyson, *Settlement,* p. 47.

17. Ferdinand-M. Bayard, *Voyage Dans l'Interieur des Etâts Unis, à Bath, Winchester, Dans la Vallée de Shenandoah, etc., etc., Pendant l'Été de 1791* (Paris, 1797), pp. 5–10. Detailed descriptions of the clock appear in Tyson, *Settlement,* pp. 57– 58; Richard E. Norton, "The Ellicott Clock," *Horology,* 7 (August 1940): 28–33; and George H. Eckhardt, "The Masterpiece of Joseph Ellicott, American Clockmaker," *Antiques,* (July 1934): 50–53.

18. George Wright, *Description and Use of Both the Globes, the Armillary Sphere, & The Orrery* (London, 1783). In the copy owned by George Ellicott (privately owned and used with permission), the title page has been torn out. However, on the half-title page are the notations: "Elizabeth Ellicott to her daughter M. E. Tyson 1852" and "Purchased by George Ellicott in 1790." The note quoted by Martha Tyson is pasted inside the front cover. Bound into the same leather-covered volume are three tracts by Joseph Priestley, "L.L.D. F.R.S. and a Lover of the Gospel," all published in 1784.

19. James Ferguson, *An Easy Introduction to Astronomy, For Young Gentlemen and Ladies: Describing the Figure, Motions and Dimensions of the Earth; the Different Seasons, Gravity and Light; the Solar Systems, the Transit of Venus, and its Use in Astronomy; the Moon's Motions and Phases; the Eclipses of the Sun and Moon; the Cause of the Ebbing and Flowing of the Tides, &c.* 4th ed. (London; Printed for T. Cadell in the Strand, 1779). The Ellicott copy, owned by the late Dr. Robert T. Fitzhugh, carries on the front flyleaf the story of its associations with the Ellicott family, and on the title page the words "Presented to M. E. Tyson by

her Mother, E.E., 1832," both in the handwriting of Martha E. Tyson. The copy
was donated to the Maryland Historical Society by the late Mrs. Robert Fitzhugh.

20. M. E. Tyson, *Settlement*, p. 47.

IV. WORK AND STUDY

1. In his letter to Goddard & Angell of August 10, 1791, which was
reproduced in the first issue of Banneker's almanac for 1792, James McHenry stated, "It is about three years since Mr. George Ellicott lent him [Banneker] 'Mayer's
Tables,' 'Ferguson's Astronomy,' 'Leadbetter's Lunar Tables,' and some astronomical instruments."

2. The eighteenth-century gate-leg table made of heavy maple and pine
boards, oval in shape, measures 29" x 67-1/2" x 49." It is oval with two D-shaped
drop-leaves, over a single drawer on ring-turned supports with two legs swinging
support leaves, joined by stretchers. The surface is considerably worn and grimy,
with numerous dents and scratches. When first seen by this writer in 1969 it was
labeled with a tag handwritten by Lucy Tyson Fitzhugh in the late nineteenth or
early twentieth century identifying the table as the one lent by George Ellicott to
Banneker.

3. James Ferguson, *Astronomy Explained Upon Sir Isaac Newton's Principles,
and made easy for those who have not studied Mathematics* (London, 1756, reprinted by J. F. and C. Rivington in at least nine editions). The copy used by Banneker
was owned by the Ellicott family.

4. [The Reverend Nevil Maskelyne, ed.] *Tabulae Motuum Solis et Lunae
Novae et Correctae. Auctore Tobia Mayer: Quibus Accedit Methodus Longitudinum
Promota, Eodem Auctore. Editae Jussu Praefectorum Rei Longitudinariae* (London,
William and John Richardson. Sold by John Nourse, John Mount, and Thomas
Page, 1770). Written on the title page is the inscription "George Ellicott 1784," and
a later one containing the words "Presented by George Ellicott to B. Banneker
and in the possession of the astronomer at his death. Martha E. Tyson 1854." A
note attached to the inner cover, signed "W. Kenworthy 1810," gives a formula for
correcting "Geo. Ellicott's Tables to agree with Nautical Almanac 1811."

5. Charles Leadbetter, *A Compleat System of Astronomy. In Two Volumes,
Containing the Description and use of the Sector, the Laws of Spheric Geometry; the
Projection of the Sphere Orthographically and Stereographically upon the Planes of
the Meridian, Ecliptic and Horizon; the Doctrine of the Sphere, and the Eclipses of
the Sun and Moon for thirty-seven years. Together with all the Precepts of
Calculation. Also new Tables of the Motions of the Planets, fix'd Stars, and the first
Satellite of Jupiter; of right and oblique Ascensions, and of Logistical Logarithms. To
the whole are prefix'd Astronomical Definitions for the Benefit of young Students,*
2nd ed. (London: J. Wilcox, 1742). The copy used by Banneker was owned in the
Ellicott family.

6. Letter from Benjamin Banneker to George Ellicott, dated October 13, 1789. Library, MdHS. The letter was donated to the society in 1854 by Martha E. Tyson, together with a letter of later date from Banneker to Susanna Mason and George Ellicott's personal copy of Banneker's almanac for the year 1792.

7. Ferguson, *Astronomy Explained* . . . , 9th ed. (London: J. F. & C. Rivington, 1794), pp. 335–40; Leadbetter, *A Compleat System of Astronomy*, pp. 5, 457–58.

8. Moses Coit Tyler, *History of American Literature* (New York: G. P. Putnam's Sons, 1878), 2:120.

9. Robb Sagendorph, *America and Her Almanacs: Wit, Wisdom & Weather, 1639–1970* (Boston: Little Brown & Co., 1970), pp. 21–27, 118–46; George Lyman Kittredge, *"The Old Farmer and His Almanac, Being Some Observations on Life and Manners in New England a Hundred Years Ago," Suggested by Reading the Earlier Numbers of Mr. Robert B. Thomas's Farmer's Almanac* (Boston: William Ware & Co., 1904), pp. 191–205.

10. Sam. Briggs, *The Essays, Humor and Poems of Nathaniel Ames, Father and Son, of Dedham, Massachusetts, From their Almanacks 1726–1775, With Notes and Comments* (Cleveland: n.p., 1891), pp. 9–22.

11. Tyson, *Banneker*, p. 31.

12. A. Rachel Minick, *A History of Printing in Maryland 1791–1800* (Baltimore, Enoch Pratt Free Library, 1949), pp. 74–87. See also Joseph Towne Wheeler, *The Maryland Press, 1777–1790* (Baltimore: Maryland Historical Society, 1938), pp. 43–44, 51–55.

13. The Baltimore Academy was established in 1786 on Charles Street under the patronage of the Reverend Doctors Carroll, West, and Allison, as a school for youth intended for the learned professions. Prior to this time the young men had to be sent to schools in Pennsylvania and abroad. The school survived for only a short period.

14. Minnick, *History of Printing in Maryland*, pp. 1–4.

15. Benjamin Banneker to Andrew Ellicott, May 6, 1790, Pennsylvania Abolition Society Manuscripts, vol. 2, folio 145, Historical Society of Pennsylvania (hereinafter PASM).

16. Joseph Townsend to James Pemberton, November 28, 1790, vol. 2, p. 233, PASM.

17. W. E. B. DuBois, *The Suppression of the African Slave-Trade to the United States of America, 1638–1870* (New York: Schocken Books, 1969), pp. 39–91.

18. Minutes of the society, vol. 1 (1787–1800), p. 133, PASM.

19. Joseph Townsend, "Some Account of the British Army, Under the Command of General Howe, and of The Battle of Brandywine, on the Memorable September 11, 1777 . . . ," *Proceedings of the Historical Society of Pennsylvania*, vol. 1, no. 7 (September 1846). Includes a biographical sketch of Joseph Townsend by Townsend Ward. See also *Minutes of the Proceedings of a Convention of Delegates From the Abolition Societies Established in Different Parts*

of the United States, Assembled at Philadelphia, On the First Day of January, One Thousand Seven Hundred and Ninety-Four, and Continued, by Adjournments, Until the Seventh Day of the Same Month, Inclusive (Philadelphia: Zachariah Poulson, Jr., 1794).

20. The constitution is quoted in its entirety, together with the first slate of officers and committee members, in William Frederick Poole, *Anti-Slavery Opinions Before the Year 1800* (Cincinnati: Robert Clarke & Co., 1873), pp. 50–54. The constitution is also quoted in John S. Tyson, *Life of Elisha Tyson, the Philanthropist* (Baltimore: B. Lundy, 1820), p. 20.

21. Letter from Joseph Townsend as secretary of the Maryland society to the Pennsylvania society, December 28, 1795, vol. 4, pp. 197ff, PASM. The Pennsylvania Abolition Society Manuscripts include periodic reports received from most of the other state antislavery societies at that time.

22. Letter from Joseph Townsend to James Pemberton, July 7, 1790, vol. 2, fol. 169, AM802, PASM. Noted by Pemberton on the cover of the letter, "Answ.d the 9th, and sent 50 of Pinkney's Speech."

23. The copy of the Banneker letter made by Pemberton for Ellicott is in a collection of Andrew Ellicott Papers in the Manuscript Division of the New York Historical Society. The original letter was filed by Pemberton among the papers of the Pennsylvania Abolition Society (see note 9 for this chapter).

24. The letter from Joseph Townsend to James Pemberton dated November 14, 1790, is in vol. 2, p. 223, PASM. In the same letter Townsend acknowledged the receipt of books and other materials for the Maryland society, as well as a circular letter relating to antislavery activities.

25. James Pemberton to Joseph Townsend, November 21, 1790. This letter has not been found, but Pemberton noted the date of his reply on the reverse of Townsend's letter of November 14.

26. Letter from Joseph Townsend to James Pemberton dated November 28, 1790, vol. 2, p. 233, PASM.

V. The Great Adventure

1. Bedini, "Andrew Ellicott, Surveyor of the Wilderness," pp. 113–35; Catherine Van Cortlandt Mathews, *Andrew Ellicott: His Life and Letters* (New York: The Grafton Press, 1908), pp. 81–104; Fox, Ellicott, Evans, *American Family History*, pp. 155–64.

2. Letter from Thomas Jefferson to Messrs. Johnson, Stuart, and Carroll dated January 15, 1791, Record Group 42, National Archives.

3. George Washington to Thomas Jefferson, February 1, 1791, State Department Papers, D.C. Miscellany, National Archives.

4. Thomas Jefferson to Andrew Ellicott, February 2, 1791, State Department Papers, D.C. Miscellany, National Archives.

5. Thomas Jefferson to the Marquis de Condorcet, August 31, 1791, in Paul Leicester Ford, ed., *The Works of Thomas Jefferson* (New York: Federal Edition, 1904), 5:379; quoted in full, 6:310–12. Jefferson's draft copy is in the Thomas Jefferson Papers, ff. 11477–478, Manuscripts Division, Library of Congress.

6. [Martha E. Tyson], "A Memoir of Benjamin Banneker, the Negro Astronomer. And Some Account of the People of The Times in Which he Lived, With Historical Extracts of Sketches of Primitive Maryland." Manuscript first draft written in 1865, of the work published as *Banneker, the Afric-American Astronomer,* op. cit. Manuscript privately owned; used with permission. (Hereinafter referred to as Tyson, Memoir.)

7. Gay M. Moore, *Seaport in Virginia, George Washington's Alexandria* (Richmond: Garrett and Massie, Inc., 1949) pp. 99–111; and Dorothy H. Kabler, *The Story of Gadsby's Tavern* (Alexandria, Virginia: Newell-Cole Company, 1952), pp. 9–19. The original hostelry was also known as the City Tavern during its early period.

8. Silvio A. Bedini, "The Rittenhouse-Ellicott Zenith Sector," *The Professional Surveyor,* 17 (No. 3, April 1997): 36–38, and 17 (No. 4, May–June 1997): 50–52.

9. Silvio A. Bedini, "The American Surveyor's Field Clock," *The Professional Surveyor,* 11 (No. 2, March/April 1991): 67–68, and 11 (No. 3, May/June 1991): 58–59.

10. Andrew Ellicott to Thomas Jefferson, February 14, 1791. From a draft in the possession of Ellicott descendants, quoted in Sally K. Alexander, "A Sketch of the Life of Major Andrew Ellicott," *Records of the Columbia Historical Society,* 2 (1899): 172–73. Reprinted also in Saul K. Padover, *Thomas Jefferson and the National Capital 1783–1818* (Washington: Government Printing Office, 1946) pp. 41–42.

11. Andrew Ellicott to Sarah Ellicott, February 14, 1791, in Alexander, "A Sketch," p. 173.

12. "A Letter from Andrew Ellicott, to Robert Patterson, in Two Parts. Part first contains a number of Astronomical Observations . . . April 2nd, 1795," *Transactions of the American Philosophical Society,* 4 (1799): 49–51.

13. Andrew Ellicott to Sarah Ellicott, March 20, 1791, in Alexander, "A Sketch," p. 173.

14. Ben: Perley Poore, *Perley's Reminiscences of Sixty Years of the National Metropolis* (Philadelphia: Hubbard Brothers, 1886), 1:480–82. See also Harold Donaldson Eberlein and Cortlandt Van Dyke Hubbard, *Historic Houses of George Town & Washington City* (Richmond: Dietz Press, 1958), pp. 713; and W. B. Bryan, "Hotels of Washington Prior to 1814," *Records of the Columbia Historical Society,* 7 (1904): 88.

15. *Gazette of the United States,* issue of March 5, 1791. The item bears the dateline from Georgetown, February 23.

16. Thomas Jefferson to Major Pierre Charles L'Enfant, March 17, 1791, in Andrew A. Lipscomb, ed., *The Writings of Thomas Jefferson* (Washington: Thomas Jefferson Memorial Association, 1904), 8:162.

17. Handwritten statement signed "J S N" and addressed to "Mrs. Tyson." (Privately owned; used with permission.)

18. *Georgetown Weekly Ledger*, March 12, 1791.

19. U.S. *v.* Martin F. Morris et al., *Records of the Supreme Court of the District of Columbia* (Washington, 1898), 7:2171–173.

20. "George-Town News," *Maryland Gazette*, March 8, 1791.

21. *Gazette of the United States*, Philadelphia, March 26, 1791.

22. J. C. Fitzpatrick, ed., *The Diaries of George Washington* (Boston: Houghton Mifflin Co., 1925), 4:152, diary entry for March 28–30, 1791.

23. William Tindall, *Standard History of the City of Washington from a Study of the Original Sources* (Knoxville: H. W. Crew & Co., 1914), p. 93.

24. *Alexandria Gazette*, April 21, 1791; also, under a dateline of April 26, 1791, from Alexandria in the *Maryland Journal* and the *Boston Advertiser*. It was carried in Boston's *Independent Chronicle* of May 22, 1791, and in the *Pennsylvania Journal* of May 4, 1791. The account of the ceremony appeared with an Alexandria dateline of April 21, 1791.

25. Marcus Baker, "Surveys and Maps of the District of Columbia." *The National Geographic Magazine*, 4 (November 1, 1894): 149–78. See also John Stewart, "Early Maps and Surveyors of the City of Washington, D.C.," *Records of the Columbia Historical Society*, 2 (1899): 57–60; and E. F. M. Faehtz and F. W. Pratt, with the assistance of Brainard H. Warner, *Washington in Embryo; Or, The National Capital from 1791 to 1800. The Origin of All Rights and Titles to Property in Washington, D.C.* (Washington, D.C.: privately printed, 1874).

26. These statements are based upon Andrew Ellicott's letter to his wife from Georgetown dated April 8, 1791, the Papers of Andrew Ellicott, Curtis Collection, Manuscripts Division, Library of Congress.

27. Andrew Ellicott to Sarah Ellicott, June 26, 1791, written from the "Surveyors Camp, State of Virginia." Quoted in Alexander, "A Sketch," p. 174. Andrew Ellicott [at Georgetown] to Sarah Ellicott, August 9, 1791, in Mathews, *Andrew Ellicott*, pp. 89–90. Andrew Ellicott to Sarah Ellicott, November 9, 1791, the Papers of Andrew Ellicott, Curtis Collection, Manuscripts Division, Library of Congress.

28. Tyson, *Banneker*, pp. 38–39.

29. [Andrew Ellicott], "Expences Insured [sic] on Surveying the Experimental and Permanent Lines of the District of Columbia," Papers of Thomas Jefferson, D. C. Miscellany, Series 3, Reel 57, courtesy of Frederick W. Jones, Manuscripts Division, Library of Congress; Silvio A. Bedini, "The Survey of the Federal Territory: Andrew Ellicott and Benjamin Banneker," *Washington History*, 3 (Spring/Summer 1991): 76–95, 137–38.

30. Tyson, *A Sketch*, pp. 11–12.

31. Tyson, *Banneker*, p. 36.

32. Tyson, *A Sketch*, pp. 11–12; repeated almost verbatim in Tyson, *Banneker*, pp. 36–39.

33. Tyson, *Banneker,* p. 37.

34. Benjamin Banneker to Thomas Jefferson, August 19, 1791, the Jefferson-Coolidge Papers, Manuscripts Division, Massachusetts Historical Society.

35. Banneker, Manuscript Journal, page facing calculations for May 1792; "A Letter from Andrew Ellicott to Robert Patterson . . . ," *Transactions of the American Philosophical Society,* 4 (1799): 49–51.

36. Jefferson to the Marquis de Condorcet, August 30, 1791, in Ford, ed., *The Works of Thomas Jefferson* (New York: G. P. Putnam Sons, 1904), 6:310–12.

37. Tyson, *Banneker,* pp. 38–39.

38. Pierre Charles L'Enfant to Thomas Jefferson, May 10, 1791, State Department Papers, D.C. Miscellany, National Archives.

39. *Maryland Journal and Baltimore Advertiser,* June 10, 1791.

40. Wilhelmus Bogart Bryan, *A History of the National Capital From Its Foundation Through the Period of the Adoption of the Organic Act* (New York: MacMillan, 1914), 1:165. In 1899 this building was marked with a plaque inscribed "Gen. Washington's Headquarters while surveying the city of Washington in 1791, erected by the Hiram Ripley Society, Daughters of the American Revolution."

41. Andrew Ellicott to the commissioners, March 7, 1792, at Philadelphia, Record Group 42, vol. 1, Public Buildings and Grounds, No. 811/2, National Archives.

42. Andrew Ellicott to Sarah Ellicott, September 3 and 11, 1792, the Papers of Andrew Ellicott, Curtis Collection, Manuscripts Division, Library of Congress.

43. Report on the completion of the survey dated January 1, 1793, from Andrew Ellicott to the commissioners, D.C. Miscellany, Manuscripts Division, Library of Congress. The same collection contains a letter from Andrew Ellicott to the commissioners dated January 8, 1793.

44. Letter from Andrew Ellicott to the commissioners dated January 29, 1793, Record Group 42, Public Buildings and Grounds, National Archives.

45. Letter from Andrew Ellicott to Sarah Ellicott, April lo, 1793, in Alexander, "A Sketch," p. 191.

46. The details of Ellicott's position in the controversy are set forth in two letters he addressed to President Washington, dated June 29, 1793, and February 28, 1794, and the commissioners' reply dated March 23, 1794. Record Group 42, Public Buildings and Grounds, National Archives.

47. "Letter from Andrew Ellicott to Robert Patterson, in Two Parts. Part first contains a number of Astronomical Observations. Part second contains the Theory and Method of calculating the Aberration of the Stars, the Nutation of the Earth's Axis, and the Semiannual Equation. Philadelphia, April 2nd, 1795," *Transactions of the American Philosophical Society* (Philadelphia, Thomas Dobson, 1799), 4:32–66.

48. Andrew Ellicott to Dr. William Thornton, February 23, 1795, J. Henley Smith Papers, folio 174V2–175V2, Manuscripts Division, Library of Congress. The text is quoted *in extenso* inasmuch as it has never been previously cited in relation

to the survey of the city of Washington.

49. Andrew Ellicott to Thomas Jefferson, April 13, 1801, Papers of Andrew Ellicott, Curtis Collection, Manuscripts Division, Library of Congress.

50. Julian P. Boyd, ed., *The Papers of Thomas Jefferson.* 1st series, 24 vols. (1990) (Princeton: Princeton University Press, 1974), 19:41–43, note 119.

VI. His First Almanac

1. Data courtesy Dr. Arnold E. Grummer, Curator of Museums, Institute of Paper Chemistry, Appleton, Wisconsin.

2. James Ferguson, *Astronomy Explained Upon Sir Isaac Newton's Principles,* chapter 21, par. 389.

3. Ibid.

4. James Ferguson, *Tables and Tracts, Relative to Several Arts and Sciences* (London, printed for A. Millar and T. Cadell, 1767).

5. Frederick R. Goff, "Early Printing in Georgetown (Potomak) 1789–1800," *Records of the Columbia Historical Society,* vols. 51–52, 1955, pp. 105–11.

6. For an account of Goddard's earlier career, see Joseph Towne Wheeler, *The Maryland Press 1777–1790* (Baltimore: Maryland Historical Society, 1938), pp. 1–10, 43–47, 72. Goddard's later work is described in Minick, *A History of Printing in Maryland,* pp. 1–5, 27–32, 74–78.

7. Minutes of the society, vol. 1, p. 133, PASM.

8. Elias Ellicott to James Pemberton, June 10, 1791, vol. III, p. 55, PASM.

9. Edward Needles, *An Historical Memoir of the Pennsylvania Society for Promoting the Abolition of Slavery: The Relief of Free Negroes Unlawfully Held in Bondage, and For Improving the Condition of the African Race. Compiled from the Minutes of the Society and Other Official Documents* (Philadelphia, Merrihew and Thompson, 1848), pp. 31–33. Also see Elias Ellicott to James Pemberton, July 21, 1791, vol. III, p. 75, PASM.

10. Scharf, *Chronicles of Baltimore,* pp. 256–59. A native of Baltimore County, Buchanan had studied medicine in Philadelphia before continuing his studies in Edinburgh and Paris, after which he returned to establish a practice in Baltimore.

11. *An Oration Upon the Moral and Political Evil of Slavery. Delivered at a public meeting of the Maryland Society for promoting the Abolition of Slavery and the relief of free Negroes and others unlawfully held in Bondage. Baltimore, July 4, 1791. By George Buchanan, M.D., Member of the American Philosophical Society* (Baltimore: Printed by Philip Edwards, 1793). Only a few copies are known, including one in the New-York Historical Society Library, and the copy from the personal library of George Washington preserved at the Boston Athenaeum. The Oration was described and reproduced in its entirety as an appendix to William Frederick Poole, *Anti-Slavery Opinions Before the Year 1800* (Cincinnati: Robert

Clarke & Co., 1873).

12. Brooke Hindle, *David Rittenhouse* (Princeton, N.J.: Princeton University Press, 1964), pp. 316–30.

13. David Rittenhouse to James Pemberton, August 6, 1791, vol. III, p. 81, PASM.

14. Minutes, vol. I, p. 115, PASM.

15. Statement by William Waring dated August 16, 1791, vol. III, p. 83, PASM.

16. "A List of Taxables of the Upper Hundred of Patapscoe 1737," City Hall, Baltimore, Maryland, Department of Legislative Reference, *Court Records of Baltimore City and Baltimore County.*

17. Benjamin Banneker to Thomas Jefferson, August 19, 1791, 7S. I. 38–43, Jefferson-Coolidge Papers, Massachusetts Historical Society.

18. Thomas Jefferson to Benjamin Banneker, August 30, 1791, in Paul Leicester Ford, ed., *The Works of Thomas Jefferson* (New York: G. P. Putnam's Sons, 1904), 4:309–10. Jefferson's file copy is in the *Thomas Jefferson Papers*, f. 11481, Library of Congress.

19. *Copy of a Letter from Benjamin Banneker, to the Secretary of State, with his Answer.* Philadelphia: Printed and Sold by Daniel Lawrence, No. 33, North Fourth-Street, Near Race. 1792.

20. "Letter from the famous self-taught ASTRONOMER, BENJAMIN BANNEKER, a black man, to THOMAS JEFFERSON, Esq. Secretary of State," *Universal Asylum and Columbian Magazine*, 2 (October 1792): 222–24.

21. Letter from Thomas Jefferson to the Marquis de Condorcet dated August 30, 1791, in Ford, ed., *The Works of Thomas Jefferson*, 6:310–12.

22. Thomas Jefferson to Jean Pierre Brissot de Warville, February 11, 1788, in Ford, ed., *The Works of Thomas Jefferson*, 5:388.

23. Private communication from the late Dr. Julian P. Boyd, editor of *The Papers of Thomas Jefferson*, dated January 29, 1970.

24. Letters from Mme. L. Hautecoeur, Conservateur en chef, Bibliothèque de l'Institut, February 17, 1970, and from Jean-Claude Nardin, March 14, 1970.

25. Private communications with R. Courier and Louis de Broglie, secretaries of the Académie des Sciences, March 17, 1969, and January 8, 1970, respectively; from Roger Pierrot of the Bibliothèque Nationale, May 12, 1969, and December 29, 1969; from Marcel Thomas of the same repository dated January 27, 1970; and from Jean-Claude Nardin, March 14, 1970.

26. The papers of the Société des Amis des Noirs have not been preserved as a whole. The private papers of Brissot are preserved by heirs and are not available for study. Those papers of the Société which have survived are in the collections of the Bibliothèque de l'Institut de France and in the Bibliothèque de l'Arsenal, but the Jefferson letter and enclosure are not among them. Nor are they to be found in the files of "Sequestered Papers," the personal papers seized at the homes of individuals condemned by the revolutionary courts, and which are preserved in Series T of the Archives Nationales.

27. George Ellicott to James Pemberton, August 24, 1791, vol. III, p. 87, PASM.

28. Poem signed by Benjamin Banneker and bearing the date October 19, 1791, Leon Gardner Collection on Negro History, Banneker Institute Papers, Historical Society of Pennsylvania. This poem is one of a number of holographic copies of original documents relating to Banneker contained in the Pennsylvania Abolition Society Manuscripts. The copies were made by an unknown individual for presentation at the November 9, 1860, meeting of the Banneker Institute. Quoted in an article, "The Banneker Institute," in an unidentified Philadelphia newspaper, issue of November 15, 1860.

29. Elias Ellicott to James Pemberton, August 31, 1791, vol. III, p. 93, PASM.

30. Benjamin Banneker to James Pemberton, September 3, 1791, vol. III, p. 95, PASM.

31. "Certificate in Regard to Genuineness of Banneker's Calculations," vol. III, p. 115, PASM.

These accounts form part of the ledger of Ellicott & Co. Letters relating to suits for collection of debts owed to a William Dilworth. They are in the Historical Society of Pennsylvania, Stauffer Collection, vol. 21, p. 1618 (letter of William Dilworth to Garrit D. Wolf dated July 14, 1808, and a copy of Dilworth's letter of the same date to T. Hollinshead), and in the society's Edward Carey Gardiner Collection, Miscellaneous Section (letter from Benjamin Wilson to Samuel Shoemaker re Dilworth's suit against a certain Marks, dated November 27, 1813). Ledger courtesy of Mr. Emanuel Freeman, who purchased it at public auction in September 1996.

32. Elias Ellicott to James Pemberton, September 5, 1791, PASM.

33. James Pemberton to William Goddard, September 9, 1791 (corrected draft), vol. III, p. 103, PASM.

34. William Goddard to James Pemberton, September 13, 1791, vol. III, p. 101, PASM.

35. *The Maryland Journal and Baltimore Advertiser,* December 21, 1790.

36. Ibid., December 21, 1791.

37. Banneker's Manuscript Journal, pages facing the ephemerides for October, November, and December, 1792 (hereinafter referred to as Manuscript Journal).

VII. The Years of Fulfillment

1. Early in November 1793 Angell took as his partner Paul James Sullivan. The partnership was dissolved in June 1794 and Angell again continued his business by himself until the end of October 1794, when he sold it to Francis Brumfield. See Joseph Towne Wheeler, *The Maryland Press, 1777–1790,* pp. 43–47.

2. *Banneker's Almanac for 1793* (Goddard and Angell), p. 2.

3. Dagobert D. Runes, ed., *Selected Writings of Benjamin Rush* (New York: Philosophical Library, 1947), pp. 19–23.

4. Benjamin Rush, *Essays, Literary and Moral* (Philadelphia: Thomas and William Bradford, 1798), pp. 183–88.

5. In a private communication dated February 10, 1970, Dr. Lyman H. Butterfield, editor of the *Letters of Benjamin Rush*, stated that he had no knowledge of any printing made of the essay prior to its appearance in Banneker's almanac for 1793. See *Letters of Benjamin Rush* (Princeton, N.J.: Princeton University Press, 1951), 2:542. Dr. Henry J. Cadbury, in private communications dated November 7 and November 14, 1969, also stated that he had had an impression that the essay had been published in an earlier form before its inclusion in the Banneker almanac, but he was not able to find such a published version despite an exhaustive search. The essay is mentioned also by Nathan G. Goodman in his biography, *Benjamin Rush, Physician and Citizen 1746–1813* (Philadelphia: University of Pennsylvania Press, 1934), p. 284, as well as by John Hope Franklin in *From Slavery to Freedom, A History of Negro Americans,* 3rd ed. (New York: Alfred A. Knopf, 1967), p. 158.

6. Joseph Townsend to Benjamin Banneker, May 8, 1793. This letter has not been located.

7. Benjamin Banneker to Joseph Townsend, May 14, 1793, Historical Society of Pennsylvania, *Dreer Collection, Astronomers and Mathematicians.* A brief description of this letter was published in the *Catalogue of the Collection of Autographs Formed by Ferdinand J. Dreer* (Philadelphia, 1890), 1:28.

8. Manuscript Journal, recto of page with calculations for January 1798.

9. Letter from Joseph Townsend to James Pemberton dated July 4, 1793, vol. 111, p. 246, PASM.

10. *Benjamin Banneker's Almanac for 1794* (James Angell), p. 2.

11. Benjamin Banneker to James Pemberton, March 22, 1794, New York Public Library, Manuscript Division, Miscellaneous Papers.

12. The original letter is in the collection of the Banneker-Douglass Museum, Annapolis, Maryland.

13. *Benjamin Banneker's Almanac for 1795* (Baltimore: S. & J. Adams), Preface, p. 2.

14. *Banneker's Almanac for 1795* (William Young), recto of cover.

15. *Benjamin Banneker's Almanac for 1796* (Edwards, Keddie, and Thomas, Andrews and Butler of Baltimore), Preface, p. 2.

16. This entry from Banneker's Commonplace Book is quoted by Tyson, both in *A Sketch*, p. 16, and in *Banneker,* p. 62.

17. The Irish-born George Keatinge was a prominent Baltimore bookseller, bookbinder, and publisher. He contracted with Jackson for the printing of a number of books and pamphlets bearing his imprint in 1796 and 1797. See Minick, *A History*, pp. 120–25.

18. *Banneker's Almanac for 1797* (Baltimore: Christopher Jackson), pp. 27–28.

19. *Banneker's Almanac for the Year 1797,* Richmond ed., p. 27; Baltimore eds. p. 26.

20. Sid Woolton, *The Little Book of Lydford* (Lydford, Privately printed, 1970), passim. Private communication from B. J. S. Watkins, rector of Lydford Church, March 1969. In a communication sent by a reader to *The (British) Horological Journal,* published in March 1959, p. 162, the same inscription was stated to have been found in Aberconway Churchyard in the same form in which it appeared in the almanac. A private communication to the writer from Gwilyn Berw Hughes, Rector of Conway Parish in Caernarvon, Wales, however, stated that the epitaph does not appear on any of the graves of that churchyard or of other village burial grounds in that area.

21. See, for example, Edward J. Wood, *Curiosities of Clocks and Watches From the Earliest Times* (London: Richard Bentley, 1866), p. 382; C. A. O. Fox, ed., *An Anthology of Clocks and Watches* (London: privately printed for the author, 1947), p. 29; Elizabeth Goudge, *The Dean's Watch* (Ann Arbor, Mich.: Servant Publications, 1960), "Epitaph in Lydford Churchyard;" D. H. Jackman, "Honest Watchmaker," *Clocks,* January 1991, pp. 24–5.

22. For a discussion of the reasons for the weakening of the antislavery movement by the turn of the eighteenth century, see Winthrop D. Jordan, *White Over Black, American Attitudes Towards the Negro 1550–1812* (Baltimore: Penguin Books, 1969), pp. 349–56.

23. Colonel J. Thomas Scharf, *Chronicles of Baltimore,* pp. 255–60.

24. "Report of Important Events in the History of the Maryland Society" [compiled by Joseph Townsend, Secretary], 1794, vol. IV, p. 31, PASM.

VIII. SCIENTIFIC CONSIDERATIONS

1. James Ferguson, *Astronomy Explained Upon Sir Isaac Newton's Principles,* p. 147

2. Ibid., chapter 18, "To Project an Eclipse of the Sun Geometrically."

3. Manuscript journal, page facing calculations for April 1792.

4. Ibid., page facing calculations for the year 1802.

5. Ibid., page facing calculations for the month of April 1793. See Ferguson, *Astronomy Explained Upon Sir Isaac Newton's Principles,* Plate 12, Figure 2, and pp. 344–45.

6. Ferguson, *Astronomy Explained Upon Sir Isaac Newton's Principles,* p. 368.

7. Manuscript journal, page facing calculations for January 1796.

8. Ibid., page facing calculations for March 1800.

9. Ibid., page facing calculations for May 1799.

10. *The Nautical Almanac and Astronomical Ephemeris* (London: H.M. Nautical Almanac Office, 1795). For an account of its history, see Eric G. Forbes, "The Foundation and Early Development of the Nautical Almanac," *Journal of the Institute of Navigation,* 18 (1965): 391–401.

11. Manuscript journal, page facing calculations for June 6.

12. Ferguson, *Astronomy Explained Upon Sir Isaac Newton's Principles*, chapter 18, "Of Eclipses: Their Number and Periods," p. 234. Since it is not presently known which edition of Ferguson's work was used by Banneker, it is not possible at this time to determine whether this footnoted material appeared in his copy.

13. Manuscript journal, page facing calculations for February 1794. The reference is to Charles Leadbetter, *A Compleat System of Astronomy . . .* , 2nd ed. (London, J. Wilcox, 1742), 2:204. The planetary symbols are, in order of their appearance, for Jupiter, Mars, the Sun, and Mercury.

14. Manuscript journal, page facing calculations for February 1802.

15. Ibid., page facing the ephemeris for November 1801.

16. Ibid., opposite ephemeris for May 1802.

17. Ibid., page facing the calculations for January 1798; the reference is to Leadbetter, op. cit., "Precept XIV. To Find in any Year, how many Eclipses there will be and in what Months they happen."

18. Leadbetter, op. cit., Section IV, The Doctrine of the Spheres.

19. See Ferguson, *Astronomy Explained Upon Sir Isaac Newton's Principles*, chapter 18, "To Project An Eclipse of the Sun Geometrically," p. 337.

20. *Banneker's Almanac for the Year 1797* (Baltimore, printed by Christopher Jackson for George Keatinge), p. 2.

21. Manuscript Journal, page facing calculations for May 1800. The eclipse notes are inscribed on the page facing calculations for April 1800. The longitude of the eclipse is given as 92 1/2° west and the latitude as 52°50' north, placing the eclipse center in central Canada, northwest of Lake Superior.

22. Ibid., page facing calculations for July 1800.

23. Ferguson, *Astronomy Explained Upon Sir Isaac Newton's Principles*, p. 340.

24. Manuscript journal, page facing calculations for January 1795

25. Ibid.

26. John Hamilton Moore, *The New Practical Navigator; Being an Epitome of Navigation; Containing the Different Methods of Working the Lunar Observations, and All the Requisite Tables Used with the Nautical Almanack, in Determining the Latitude and Longitude, and Keeping a Complete Reckoning at Sea* (London, J. Crowden, 1772). The first American edition was not published until 1799; Banneker used one of the numerous English editions. His copy has not survived.

27. The work is not identified; the quotation appears in Oliver L. Fassig, "A Sketch of the Progress of Meteorology in Maryland and Delaware," *Maryland Weather Service* (Baltimore: Johns Hopkins Press, 1899), 1:331.

28. Captain John Smith, *History of Virginia. The Sixth Voyage*, 1606. In *The Works of Captain John Smith*, edited by Edward Arber (Birmingham, 1884).

29. Thomas Campanius Holm, *Kort Beskrifning om Nya Sverige* (Stockholm, 1702).

30. Thomas Glover, "An Account of Virginia," *Philosophical Transactions of the Royal Society*, 67 (1667): 450.

31. John Clayton, "An Account of Several Observables in Virginia, more particularly concerning the Air," *Philosophical Transactions of the Royal Society*, 70 (1668): 781 ff.

32. John Bigelow, ed., *The Complete Works of Benjamin Franklin*, 3 vols. (New York: G. P. Putnam Sons, 1897), 2:76, 161–64. Letters to Jared Eliot datrd July 16, 1747, and February 13, 1750.

33. Richard Brooke, "Thermometrical Account of the Weather in Maryland for one year from September 1753," pp. 58 ff.; "Thermometrical account of the weather in Maryland for three Years from September 1754," pp. 70 ff.; and "Observations in Virginia and in his Voyage Thither, Particularly concerning the Air," *Philosophical Transactions of the Royal Society*, 51 (1759): pp. 79–82.

34. Weather forecasting based on the influence of the moon is discussed in Fassig, op. cit., p. 347 ff.; F. J. Walz, "Fake Weather Forecasts," *Popular Science Monthly*, 47 (October 1905): 503–13; and E. B. Garriott, "Long Range Weather Forecasts," U.S. Department of Agriculture, *Bulletin No. 35*, U.S. Department of Agriculture, Weather Bureau, 1904, pp. 37–43. See also A. J. Prahl, "The Hagerstown Almanack," *The American-German Review*, 8 (June 1942): 7–10; Dieter Cunz, "John Gruber and His Almanac," *Maryland Historical Magazine*, 47 (1952): 89–102.

35. For examples of such predictions see *Moore's Almanac*, by Francis Moore, M.D., London, for the years 1791–1800, and an almanac by the Reverend I. R. Hicks called *Word and Works*, January 1904.

36. Manuscript journal, page facing calculations for August 1797.

37. For discussion of weather prognostication prior to the development of instruments and institutions for the purpose see James Berry and W. F. R. Phillips, *Proceedings of the Second Convention of Weather Bureau Officials Held at Milwaukee, Wisconsin, August 27, 28, 29, 1901*, U.S. Department of Agriculture, Weather Bureau, Bulletin No. 31, pp. 111–67; passim; Edward B. Garriott, "Weather Folk-Lore and Local Weather Signs," U.S. Department of Agriculture, *Bulletin No. 33*, Weather Bureau No. 294, 1903; and Garriott, "Long-Range Weather Forecasts," op. cit.

38. *Banneker's Almanac for 1795* (Baltimore: S. & J. Adams).

39. D. Gernez, "Les Indications relative aux Marées dans les anciens livres de Mer," *Archives Internationales d'Histoire des Sciences*, no. 7, 1949, pp. 571–91.

40. Manuscript Journal, first page.

41. Ibid., page facing calculations for March 1792.

42. Ibid., page facing calculations for December 1798.

43. Ibid., page facing the ephemeris for October 1802.

44. Ibid., page facing the calculations for May 1792.

45. Ibid., page facing ephemeris for January 1793

46. Ibid., page facing calculations for the month of November 1802.

47. Charles W. Koontz, "A Comparison of Benjamin Banneker's Astronomical Data With Other Eighteenth Century Almanac Makers." Ellicott City, Unpublished manuscript, 1987.

IX. THE FINAL YEARS

1. "The stings of Poverty, Disease, and Violence, less pungent than those of guilty passion," *Banneker's Almanac for 1792* (Goddard & Angell), p. 28.

2. Shirley Graham, *Your Most Humble Servant* (New York, Julian Messner, 1949), p. 139, states that Benjamin's mother and oldest sister, Tillie, died in the summer of 1781, but no confirming documentation for this fact has been found.

3. "A List of Taxables for Patapsco Upper Hundred for the Year 1773 Taken by Abraham Walker Constable."

4. Manuscript journal, first page.

5. Ibid., page facing ephemeris for March 1799.

6. Ibid., page facing calculations for April 1799.

7. Ibid., page facing calculations for August 1802.

8. Tyson, *A Sketch*, p. 13, fn. 1.

9. Indenture for sale of land by Benjamin Banneker to Greenbury Morten dated December 20, 1785, witnessed on the following day and recorded on June 19, 1786. Baltimore County Land Records, 1785, WQ#Y, ff. 653–54, Maryland State Archives.

10. *The Maryland Journal*, August 8, 1783, p. 2.

11. Jeffrey R. Brackett, *The Negro in Maryland. A Study of the Institution of Slavery* (Baltimore: N. Murray, 1889), p. 187, fn. 1, and John Slattery, "Benjamin Banneker, The Negro Astronomer," *The Catholic World*, December 1883, p. 351.

12. Agreement between Banneker and Ellicott & Co., quoted in Tyson, *A Sketch*, p. 10.

13. Indenture of sale by Benjamin Banneker to John Barten [sic], dated April 2, 1792, Liber W. G. # H. H., folios 341–42, Baltimore County Land Records, Maryland State Archives.

14. Indenture of sale from Benjamin Banneker to John Nimiy dated August 10, 1792, witnessed May 7, 1793, and recorded October 17, 1793, Liber W. G. # M. M., folios 244–45, Baltimore County Land Records, Maryland State Archives.

15. Indenture of sale of land by Benjamin Banneker to Edward Shugar dated December 10, 1794, recorded December 18, 1794. Liber W. G. # P. P., folios 606–8, Baltimore County Land Records, Maryland State Archives.

16. Indenture for sale of land from Benjamin Banneker to Thomas Gibbons dated June 8, 1797, recorded June 26, 1797. Liber W. G. # 51, folios 197–99, Baltimore County Land Records, Maryland State Archives.

17. Indenture for sale of land from Benjamin Banneker to Thomas Gibbons dated October 22, 1799, recorded November 4, 1799. Liber W. G. # 60, folios 139–40, Baltimore County Land Records, Maryland State Archives.

18. Indenture for sale of land by Greenbury Morten to Thomas Gibbons dated October 22, 1799, ibid.

19. Indenture for sale of land by Benjamin Banneker to Jonathan Ellicott et

al. dated October 23, 1799. Liber W. G. # 60, ff. 408–10, Baltimore County Land Records, Maryland State Archives.

20. Manuscript journal, page facing calculations for November 1799.

21. Ibid., page facing calculations for January 1798.

22. Ibid., page opposite the calculations for January 1795.

23. Tyson, *Banneker*, p. 70.

24. Tyson, *A Sketch*, p. 10.

25. Ibid., p. 12.

26. Tyson, *Banneker*, p. 38.

27. Manuscript journal of the Reverend William Colbert, p. 81. Collection of the Union Library, Garrett Theological School, Evanston, Ill.

28. *Romans*, 6:23: "For the wages of sin is death, but the gift of God is life everlasting in Christ Jesus our Lord."

29. The identity of Banneker's third sister, Jemima Banneker Lett, came to light in 1983 during a genealogical search undertaken by Charles J. Weiker. He found the name in an article based upon a publication by Charles Henry Lett entitled *Oak Grove — A Pioneer Community* (Morgan County, Ohio Genealogical Society, 1983). The Lett family history published therein had been acquired by Lett from his grandfather, Judson Lett, son of James Lett and grandson of Aquila Lett Sr. who was a son of Jemima and her husband Samuel Delaney Lett. From the notes of Meshach Simpson Jr. reported as he received the information from Meshach Lett Sr., son of Jemima Lett. Courtesy of a descendant, Mr. Charles J. Weiker of Findlay, Ohio.

30. *Maryland Census for Frederick County, 1790. Heads of Families at the First Census of the United States Taken in the Year 1790 — Maryland*, p. 62. Courtesy of Mr. Charles J. Weiker. The comment that Banneker was employed as a bookkeeper at the Ellicott Lower Mills or the Ellicott & Company store occurs once or twice in reported recollections of Banneker by others and may have some basis in fact, although Martha Tyson made no mention of it in her writings.

31. Manuscript Journal, page facing calculations for March 1792.

32. Ibid., page facing the calculations for February 1792.

33. Ibid., page facing calculations for February 1797.

34. Ibid., page facing calculations for August 1798.

35. Tyson, *Banneker*, p. 54.

36. Ibid., pp. 55–56; William W. Allen. *Banneker The Afro-American Astronomer, From Data Collected by Will W. Allen Assisted by Daniel Murray, An Assistant Librarian of the Library of Congress* (Washington, D.C.: n.p., 1921), p. 63.

37. An association possibly exemplified in the Puzzle of the Three Ages. See Document 25.

38. *Oxford English Dictionary*. 20 vols. And supplement. 2nd edition (Oxford: Clarendon Press, 1989), 3:64.

39. Ron Eglash, "The African Heritage of Benjamin Banneker," *Social Studies of Science*, 27 (April 1997): 307–15, *vide* pp. 311–12.

40. [Rachel Mason], *Selections from the Letters and Manuscripts of the Late Susanna Mason; With a Brief Memoir of her Life, By Her Daughter* (Philadelphia, Rackliff & Jones, 1836), pp. 16–17.

41. Evans, *Biographical and Historical Accounts of the Fox, Ellicott, and Evans Families*, pp. 32–33.

42. Mason, *Selections from the Letters*, pp. 242–46.

43. Ibid., pp. 244–46.

44. Letter from Benjamin Banneker to Susanna Mason dated August 26, 1797, Manuscripts Department, Maryland Historical Society.

45. Daniel Alexander Payne, *Recollections of Seventy Years* (Nashville, Tenn.: Publishing House of the A.M.E. Sunday School Union, 1888), p. 78.

46. Manuscript journal, page facing calculations for December 1798.

47. Ibid., page facing calculations for December 1799.

48. Banneker's Commonplace Book.

49. Manuscript journal, page facing calculations for June 1798.

50. Everett Franklin Phillips, *Beekeeping* (New York: Macmillan, 1928), pp. 263–64; A. I. Root, *The ABC and XYZ of Bee Culture* (Medina, Ohio: The A. I. Root Co., 1966), pp. 343–45, 568–70, 579.

51. John H. B. Latrobe, "Memoir of Benjamin Banneker, Read Before the Historical Society of Maryland," *Maryland Colonization Journal*, new series, vol. 2, no. 29, May 1845, p. 360, and Tyson, *Banneker*, p. 62.

52. Such a treatise is mentioned in the entry about Banneker in *Who Was Who in America 1607–1896*, rev. ed. (Chicago: A. N. Marquis Co., 1963), p. 39, as well as in Lerone Bennett Jr., *Before the Mayflower: A History of the Negro in America 1619–1962* (Chicago: Johnson Publishing Company, 1962), p. 332, and Wilhelmena S. Robinson, *Historical Negro Biographies* (New York: Publishers Co., 1968), p. 9.

53. *Banneker's Almanac for 1792* (Baltimore: Goddard and Angell), pp. 24–25.

54. Manuscript journal, page facing calculations for June 1800.

55. A. S. Taylor, "Grasshoppers and Locusts of America," *Annual Report of the Board of Regents of the Smithsonian Institution of the Year 1858* (Washington, 1859), pp. 203ff. See also John T. Schlebecker, Jr., "Grasshoppers in American Agricultural History," *Agricultural History*, 27 (July 1953): 85–93.

56. J. G. Myers, *Insect Singers: A Natural History of the Cicada* (London: G. Routledge and Sons, 1929).

57. Tyson, *A Sketch*, p. 14.

58. Tyson, *Banneker*, p. 67.

59. Tyson, *A Sketch*, p. 4, and Tyson, *Banneker*, p. 12.

60. Manuscript journal, page facing calculations for October 1800.

61. Ibid., page facing calculations for November 1795.

62. Ibid., page facing calculations for August 1800; quoted in Tyson, *A Sketch*, p. 13, and Tyson, *Banneker*, p. 64.

63. Manuscript journal, page facing calculations for August 1800.

64. A four-page manuscript written in Banneker's hand but unsigned. (Privately owned; used with permission.)

65. Manuscript journal, page facing calculations for March 1793.

66. Ibid., page facing calculations for February 1797.

67. Ibid., page facing calculations for December 1799.

68. Ibid., page facing calculations for August 1802.

69. Ibid., page facing calculations for February 1798.

70. Tyson, *A Sketch*, pp. 17–18, and Tyson, *Banneker*, pp. 70–72.

71. Notes of Meshach Simpson Jr., reported to have been received from Meshach Lett, Jemima's son. Courtesy of Mr. Charles J. Weiker.

72. *The Federal Gazette*, and *Baltimore Daily Advertiser*, October 28, 1806.

X. "Stout" Farm Rediviva: A Return to the Past

1. Wayne E. Clark, Proposed Archeological Program for the Systematic Survey of the Benjamin Banneker Property in Baltimore County, Maryland, submitted to the Baltimore County Department of Parks and Recreation, Maryland Historical Trust, 1982.

2. J. C. Sidney, *Map of the City and County of Baltimore from Original Surveys* (Baltimore: J. C. Stephens, 1850); [G. M. Hopkins], *Atlas of Baltimore County, Maryland. Surveyed and Published under the Direction of G. M. Hopkins* (Philadelphia, 1877).

3. John W. McGrain, "Benjamin Banneker's property lines at last discovered" (1976) manuscript on file with the Maryland Historical Trust in Annapolis. Later published as "Banneker's Property Lines Discovered," *The Catonsville Times*, August 19, 1976, pp. 1A, 103. 4. In the century and a half following Banneker's death, his land passed through the hands of at least twelve owners before it was acquired by the Department of Parks and Recreation of Baltimore County.

5. Rachel Mason, *Selections from the Letters and Manuscripts of the Late Susanna Mason*; Payne, *Recollections*.

6. Robert J. Hurry, *An Archeological Survey of the Benjamin Banneker Property, Baltimore County, Maryland*, MHT Manuscript Series No. 34 (Baltimore: Maryland Historical Trust, 1983).

7. Robert J. Hurry. "Archeological Investigations of the Benjamin Banneker Homestead (18BA282) Baltimore County, Maryland." For Baltimore County Department of Recreation and Parks, 1997. Draft.

8. For information about log house construction see George W. McDaniel, *Hearth and Home: Preserving a People's Culture* (Philadelphia: Temple University Press, 1982) and C. A. Westlager, *The Log Cabin in America* (New Brunswick, N.J.: Rutgers University Press, 1969).

9. Communication from Richard J. Hughes, July 3, 1997.

10. Hurry, *An Archeological Survey of the Benjamin Banneker Property,* pp. 17– 19; Hurry, "Archeological Investigations of the Benjamin Banneker Homestead," pp. 276–393; Document 50; Harriet Jackson Scarupa, "Digging for the Facts About Benjamin Banneker," *American Visions,* 2 (August 1987): 16– 21.

XI. THE MAN REMEMBERED

1. John H. B. Latrobe, in "Memoir of Benjamin Banneker . . ." *Maryland Colonization Journal,* new series, vol. 2, no. 29, May 1845, p. 362.

2. Charles Coleman Sellers, *Benjamin Franklin in Portraiture* (New Haven: Yale University Press, 1962), pp. 203–5.

3. Tyson, *A Sketch,* p. 19, and Tyson, *Banneker,* p. 54.

4. Thomas Ellicott replied to Martha Tyson's request for information about Banneker in a letter dated "Avondale 12 mo 21st. 1857" addressed to "My dear Niece Martha E. Tyson," formerly in the possession of the late Dr. Robert T. Fitzhugh.

5. Tyson, *A Sketch,* p. 14.

6. Tyson, *Banneker,* pp. 67–68.

7. Mantle Fielding, *Dictionary of American Painters, Sculptors and Engravers* (Philadelphia, privately printed, 1926). Fisher is described as a "renewer of copper plates for certificates" in H. Glenn Brown, *A Directory of the Book Arts and Book Trade in Philadelphia to 1820, Including Painters and Engravers* (New York: New York Public Library, 1950).

8. Gilbert Imlay, *A Topographical Description of the Western Territory of North America,* 2nd ed. (London, 1793), pp. 212–13.

9. For a clear analysis of Jefferson's position on Negro slavery see Daniel J. Boorstin, *The Lost World of Thomas Jefferson* (New York: Holt, 1948), Chapters 2 and 4, and Jordan, *White Over Black,* chapter 12.

10. Tyson, *A Sketch,* p. 7.

11. [William Loughton Smith*]*, *The Pretensions of Thomas Jefferson to the Presidency Examined; And the Charges Against John Adams Refuted* (Philadelphia, 1796), pp. 7–14, *vide* p. 10.

12. Henry W. De Sassure, *Address to the Citizens of South Carolina* (Charleston, S.C.: For W. P. Young, 1800), p. 16.

13. Thomas Green Fessenden, *Democracy Unveiled or Tyranny Stripped of the Garb of Patriotism by Christopher Caustic* (New York, 1806), vol. II, p. 52.

14. An enlightening discussion of Jefferson's position in relation to Banneker is to be found in Jordan, op. cit., pp. 449–57. See also "Thomas Jefferson's Thoughts on the Negro," *Journal of Negro History,* 3 (1918): 55–89.

15. Henri Gregoire, *De la littérature des Negres, Ou Recherches sur leurs facultés intellectuelles, leurs qualités morales et leur littérature* (Paris, Chez Maradan,

1808), pp. 211–12. An English translation appeared two years later with the title, *An Enquiry concerning the Intellectual and Moral Faculties and Literature of Negroes; Followed with an Account of the Life and Works of Fifteen Negroes and Mulattoes.* Translated by D. B. Warden (Brooklyn: Thomas Kirk, 1810).

16. Letter from Thomas Jefferson to Bishop Henri Gregoire, dated February 25, 1809, Ford, ed., *The Works of Thomas Jefferson,* 11:99–100.

17. Letter from Thomas Jefferson to Joel Barlow dated October 8, 1809, in H. A. Washington, ed., *The Writings of Thomas Jefferson* (Washington, D.C.: Taylor & Maury, 1853), 5:475–76. The letter is included also in Ford, op. cit., p. 261.

18. [Rachel Mason], *Selections from the Letters and Manuscripts of the Late Susanna Mason,* pp. 242–46.

19. [Sir Augustus John Foster], *Jeffersonian America. Notes on the United States of America Collected in the Years 1806–7 and 11–12, by Sir Augustus John Foster, Bart.* Edited by Richard Beale Davis (San Marino, Cal.: The Huntington Library), pp. 148–49.

20. Martha E. Tyson, *Memoir.* Erratic pagination.

21. *Report of Cases . . . in the Court of Appeals of Maryland in 1810 . . . 1815,* 3 (1826), pp. 97–98, Maryland State Archives. Courtesy Robert J. Hurry and Frederick W. Jones.

22. Baltimore County, *Proceedings of the Orphan's Court,* Book 3, p.105, 1 September 1794.

23. Baltimore County, *Proceedings of the Orphan's Court,* October 1782.

24. Baltimore County, *Proceedings of the Orphan's Court,* Section 3, 1792–1798, p. 1205, 1 September 1794. LDS film 13685.

25. Baltimore County, *Proceedings of the Orphan's Court,* October 1782, p. 185.

26. Latrobe, "Memoir," pp. 353–64.

27. Bishop Daniel Alexander Payne, D.D., L.L.D., *Recollections of Seventy Years.* Compiled and arranged by Sarah C. Bierce Scarborough, edited by Rev. C. S. Smith (Nashville, Tenn; Publishing House of the A.M.E. School Union, 1888), pp. 77– 78. See also Josephus R. Coan, *Daniel Alexander Payne, Christian Educator* (Philadelphia: The A.M.E. Book Concern, 1935), p. 78.

28. T. Buckler Ghequiere, "The Messrs. Long, Architects," *The American Architect and Building News,* 1 (1876): 207; Richard Hubbard Howland and Eleanor Patterson Spencer, *The Architecture of Baltimore* (Baltimore: Johns Hopkins Press, 1953), pp. 54–59, 97–99; and Wilbur H. Hunter Jr., "Robert Cary Long, Jr., and the Battle of the Styles, *Journal of the Society of Architectural Historians,* 16 (March 1957): 28–30.

29. *Repository of Religion, Science and Literature,* vol. 4, no. 7, mentions the articles by Bishop Payne.

30. For a biographical sketch of Moses Sheppard see *Appleton's Cyclopedia of American Biography* (New York, 1894), 5:496–97. Sheppard's interest in

Banneker is mentioned in Bliss Forbush, *Moses Sheppard, Quaker Philanthropist of Baltimore* (Philadelphia: J. B. Lippincott, 1968), pp. 241–43.

31. Martha E. Tyson's comment occurs in her manuscript, *A Memoir*.

32. Tyson, *Banneker,* p. 71.

33. Latrobe, "Memoir," p. 358.

34. Letter from Sheppard to John H. B. Latrobe dated January 20, 1852, Moses Sheppard Papers, RG 5, box 2, folder ser. 3,h, the Friends Historical Library, Swarthmore College. (Hereinafter Moses Sheppard Papers.)

35. Letter to Charles Sumner dated May 3, 1852, ibid., Moses Sheppard Papers.

36. Letters to Dr. Samuel F. McGill at Cape Palmas, Liberia, July 5, 1852, and November 18, 1852; also letter to George M. Justice, November 18, 1852, Letter Book A, RG 5, box 2, folder ser. 3,h, Moses Sheppard Papers.

37. Copies of the lithograph exist in the Historical Society of Pennsylvania, Maryland Historical Society, New York Public Library, and other collections. Sheppard maintained a record of the copies of the lithograph that he distributed in his Letter Books, now preserved among the Moses Sheppard Papers.

38. Letter from Miss Dorothy Dix to Sheppard, June 29, 1852, Letter Book A, RG 5, box 2, folder ser. 3,h, a, Moses Sheppard Papers.

39. A note made in 1910 by Martha Ellicott Tyson's daughter, Lucy Tyson Fitzhugh, on the reverse side of a letter from Frederick Douglass to Anne Tyson Kirk dated March 4, 1878, stated "Moses Sheppard had bound in Russia leather a large manuscript book of Bannekers, containing calculations & many interesting things — we also have it. L T F 1910 Westminster, Md."

40. The manuscript journal, formerly owned by the late Dr. Robert Tyson Fitzhugh, has been donated to the Maryland Historical Society in his memory by his widow.

41. Tyson, *A Memoir,* p. 2 of the manuscript copy in the hand of Martha E. Tyson, presumed to be a draft of the original paper read before the Maryland Historical Society.

42. Letter from Rachel Mason to Martha E. Tyson, December 5, 1847, privately owned.

43. Statement without topical heading, signed by Martha E. Tyson and undated, privately owned.

44. Martha E. Tyson, "A Memoir," manuscript; [Will W. Allen], *Banneker the Afro-American Astronomer,* pp. 62–63.

45. Unsigned and undated statement by Martha E. Tyson, privately owned.

46. John H. B. Latrobe to Martha E. Tyson, September 19, 1864, privately owned.

46. From a handwritten statement signed by Martha E. Tyson but not dated, privately owned.

47. Brantz Mayer of the Maryland Historical Society to J. Saurin Norris, January 20, 1854, privately owned. Eight hundred copies of *A Sketch* were

published, of which two hundred were forwarded to Mrs. Tyson, according to a letter dated January 15, 1855, to her from Lewis Mayer, assistant librarian of the Maryland Historical Society, privately owned.

48. Historical Society of Pennsylvania, Leon Gardner Collection of American Negro History, "Minute Book of the Banneker Institute (Literary) 1854," Ams 32.

49. *Constitution and by-laws of The Banneker Institute of the City of Philadelphia* (Philadelphia: G. T. Stockdale, 1864). Copy in Leon Gardner Collection of American Negro History, Ams 32.

50. An article entitled "The Banneker Institute" in an unidentified Philadelphia newspaper for November 15, 1860, in the collection of the John Carter Brown Library.

51. The Minutes of the Banneker Institute for the years 1854–59, in addition to four other volumes of rolls, receipts, etc., are in the Manuscripts Department of the Historical Society of Pennsylvania. The transcriptions are in a folder marked "Banneker Institute Papers" in the Leon Gardner Collection on Negro History, Historical Society of Pennsylvania.

52. Moncure D. Conway, "Benjamin Banneker, The Negro Astronomer," *The Atlantic Monthly* (January 1863): pp. 79–84; reprinted as Tract No. 9, *Benjamin Banneker, The Negro Astronomer. Reprinted from The Atlantic Monthly,* by M. D. Conway (London, Printed and Published for the Ladies' London Emancipation Society, by Emily Faithfull, Printer and Publisher in Ordinary to Her Majesty, Victoria Press, April 1864), 15 pp.

53. [Martha E. Tyson], *Banneker, The Afric-American Astronomer. From the Posthumous Papers of Martha E. Tyson. Edited by Her Daughter* (Philadelphia, Friends' Book Association, 1884), 72 pp.

54. These three letters from Frederick Douglass to Anne Tyson Kirk, among Tyson family papers owned by the late Dr. Robert T. Fitzhugh, were donated to the Maryland Historical Society by his widow.

55. The following note is inscribed on the reverse side of the letter by Martha Tyson's daughter Lucy Tyson Fitzhugh: "The book to which Frederic Douglas refers in this letter, was edited by Anne Tyson Kirk from the posthumous papers of her mother, Martha E. Tyson. It was published by the Friends' Book Association, 1020 Arch Street, Philadelphia, in 1884. The table upon which Banneker made his calculations & mathematical books were loaned him by my grandfather George Ellicott & are now in my possession. L T F 1910—."

56. Letter from Frederick Douglass to Anne T. Kirk, revision.

57. Letter from Douglass to Anne T. Kirk.

58. Payne, review

59. The size of the edition was relatively small, and unsold copies may have been destroyed.

60. The research was directed by John H. Scarff with the assistance of William B. Marye of Baltimore, who contributed a comprehensive study of

Baltimore County land records. The statement that Banneker produced the first almanac in Maryland is in error.

61. Baltimore County Land Records, Liber T. K. No. 260, folios 1–46, dated May 2, 1835, Maryland State Archives. Roger Brooke, Joshua Pearce and Nathan Tyson, Trustees for the Estate of George Ellicott, deceased, and Jonathan, John, and Elias Ellicott.

62. Ibid., Liber W. G. No. 60, folio 410, dated October 23, 1799. Benjamin Banneker to Ellicott & Co.

63. Baltimore County Wills, Liber 4, folios 392–93, filed December 3, 1789. Maryland State Archives Mary Williams was a sister of Thomas Johnson.

64. The stamp is reproduced courtesy of the Stamp Service, United States Postal Service, Washington, D.C. A study made by William B. Marye for the Historical Sites Commission, now filed in the Maryland Historical Society.

65. Tyson, *Banneker*, pp. 64–65.

66. From "Worth Superior to meer Birth and Title," *Banneker's Almanack and Ephemeris for. . . 1794* (Philadelphia: Crukshank, 1793), p. 10.

BIBLIOGRAPHY
✾✾✾

I. Banneker's Letters and Almanacs

1. *Copy of a Letter from Benjamin Banneker, to the Secretary of State, with his Answer.* Philadelphia: Printed and Sold by Daniel Lawrence, No. 33. North Fourth-Street, Near Race, 1792.

Letter to Thomas Jefferson dated August 19, 1791 transmitting a copy of the writer's almanac, and discussing the subject of slavery. Jefferson's reply is dated August 30, 1791.

2. *Benjamin Banneker's Pennsylvania, Delaware, Maryland, and Virginia Almanack and Ephemeries, For the Year of Our Lord, 1792; Being Bissextile, or Leap-Year, and the Sixteenth Year of American Independence, which commenced July 4, 1776. Containing, the Motions of the Sun and Moon, the true Places and Aspects of the Planets, the Rising and Setting of the Sun, and the Rising, Setting and Southing, Place and Age of the Moon, &c.—The Lunation, Conjunction, Eclipses, Judgment of the Weather, Festivals, and other remarkable Days; Days for holding the Supreme and Circuit Courts of the United States, as also the usual Courts in Pennsylvania, Delaware, Maryland, and Virginia.— Also, Several useful Tables and valuable Receipts.— Various Selections from the Commonplace-Book of the Kentucky Philosopher, an American Sage; with interesting and entertaining Essays, in Prose and Verse—the Whole comprising a greater, more pleasing, and useful Variety, than any Work of the Kind and Price in North-America.* Baltimore: Printed and Sold, whole-sale and Retail, by William Goddard and James Angell, at their Printing-Office, in Market-Street.—Sold, also, by Mr. Joseph Crukshank, Printer, in Market-Street, and Mr. Daniel Humphreys, Printer in South-Front Street, Philadelphia—and by Messrs. Hanson and Bond, Printers in Alexandria [1791].

3. *Benjamin Banniker's Pennsylvania, Delaware, Maryland and Virginia Almanack and Ephemeris for 1792.* Baltimore: William Goddard and James Angell [1791].

4. *Banneker's Almanac for 1792.* By Benjamin Banneker. Philadelphia: Printed for William Young, Bookseller, No. 52, the Corner of Chestnut and Second Streets [1791].

5. *Banneker's Almanack, and Ephemeris For the Year of our* Lord, *1793; Being the First After Bissextile or Leap-Year: Containing The Motions of the Sun and Moon; The True Places and Aspects of the Planets; The Rising and Setting of the Sun; Rising, Setting, and Southing of the Moon: the Lunations, Conjunctions, Eclipses; and the Rising, Setting, and Southing of the Planets and Noted Fixed Stars.* Philadelphia: Printed and Sold by Joseph Crukshank, No. 87, High Street [1792]. (Listed by Evans, but no locations given.)

6. *Benjamin Banneker's Pennsylvania, Delaware, Maryland and Virginia Almanack and Ephemeris, For the Year of our Lord 1793; Being the first after Bissextile, or Leap-Year, and the Seventeenth Year of American Independence, which commenced July 4th, 1776: Containing the Motions of the Sun and Moon, the true Places and Aspects of the Planets, the Rising and Setting of the Sun and the Rising, Setting and Southing, Place and Age of the Moon, &c.— The Lunations, Conjunctions, Eclipses, Judgment of the Weather, Festivals, and other remarkable Days; Days for holding the Supreme and Circuit Courts of The United States, as also the Usual Courts in Pennsylvania, Delaware, Maryland, and Virginia.— Also, Several useful Tables and valuable Receipts.—Various, Selections, from the Commonplace-Book of the Kentucky Philosopher, an American Sage; with interesting and Entertaining Essays, in Prose and Verse—the Whole Comprising a Greater, more Pleasing, and Useful Variety, than any Work of the Kind and Price in North-America [Four Lines of verse].* Baltimore: Printed and Sold Wholesale and Retail, by William Goddard and James Angell, at their Printing-Office, in Market-Street [1792].

7. *Banneker's Almanack and Ephemeris for the Year of our Lord 1794; Being the Second After Bissextile or Leap Year: Containing the Motions of the Sun and Moon; The True Places and Aspects of the Planets; The Rising and Setting of the Sun; Rising, Setting, and Southing of the Moon; The Lunations, Conjunctions and Eclipses; and the Rising, Setting and Southing of the Planets and Noted Fixed Stars.* Philadelphia: Printed and sold by Joseph Crukshank, No. 87, High Street.

8. *Benjamin Banneker's Pennsylvania, Delaware, Maryland and Virginia Almanac and Ephemeris. For the Year of our Lord, 1794* . . . Baltimore: Printed and sold, wholesale and retail by James Angell, at his Printing-Office in Market-Street [1793].

9. *Benjamin Banneker's Almanac for 1794.* Philadelphia: Printed for William Young, Bookseller, No. 52, the Corner of Chestnut and Second Streets [1793].

10. *The Virginia Almanack for 1794.* By Benjamin Banneker. Petersburg: Printed for William Prentis [1793].

11. *Bannaker's New-Jersey, Pennsylvania, Delaware, Maryland and Virginia Almanac, or Ephemeris, For the Year of our Lord 1795; Being the Third after Leap-Year,—the Nineteenth Year of American Independence, and the Seventh of our Federal Government—Which may the Governor of the World prosper. Containing the Motions of the Sun and Moon; the true Places and Aspects of the Eight Planets, the Rising and Setting of the Sun; the Rising, Setting, Southing, Node, Age and Latitude of the Moon, &c.—Also, the Lunations, Conjunctions, and Eclipses; remarkable Days;*

judgment of the Weather; length of Days and Nights; the Time that Courts are held in New-Jersey, Pennsylvania, Delaware, Maryland and Virginia; Post-Roads, with a Variety of instructive and entertaining Matter in Prose and Verse. Wilmington: Printed by S. & J. Adams [1794].

12. *Bannaker's Wilmington Almanac, or Ephemeris, For the Year of Our Lord 1795; Being the Third after Leap-Year;— the Nineteenth Year of American Independence, and the Seventh of our Federal Government—Which May the Governor of the World prosper!— Containing the Motions of the Sun and Moon; the true Places and Aspects of the Eight Planets; the Rising and Setting of the Sun; the Rising, Setting, Southing, Node, Age and Latitude of the Eclipses; remarkable Days and Nights; the Time that Courts are held in New-Jersey, Pennsylvania, Delaware, Maryland and Virginia, Post-Roads, with a Variety of instructive and entertaining Matter in Prose and Verse.* Wilmington: Printing by S. & J. Adams, for Frederick Craig [1794].

13. *Banneker's Almanac, For the Year 1795: Being the Third after Leap Year. Containing, (Besides every Thing Necessary in an Almanac,) An Account of the Yellow Fever, Lately Prevalent in Philadelphia; With the Number of those who Died, from the First of August till the Ninth of November, 1793.* Philadelphia: Printed for William Young, Bookseller, No. 52, the Corner of Chestnut and Second Streets [1794].

14. *Benjamin Bannaker's Pennsylvania, Delaware, Maryland and Virginia Almanac, for the Year of our Lord 1795; Being the Third after Leap-Year.* [Portrait of Banneker]. Philadelphia: Printed for William Gibbons, Cherry Street [1794].

15. *Benjamin Bannaker's Pennsylvania, Delaware, Maryland, and Virginia Almanac, For the Year of our Lord 1795; Being the Third after Leap-Year.* [Portrait of Banneker]. Philadelphia: Printed for Jacob Johnson & Co. No. 147 Market-Street [1794].

16. *Bannaker's Wilmington Almanac, or Ephemeris for the Year of Our Lord 1795; Being the Third After Leap-Year.* Wilmington: Printed by S. & J. Adams [1794].

17. *Bannaker's Wilmington Almanack for the Year of Our Lord 1795; Being the Third After Leap-Year.* Wilmington: S. & J. Adams for W. C. Smyth [1794]. (Listed by Evans as No. 1397 but no copies are known.)

18. *Benjamin Bannaker's Pennsylvania, Delaware, Maryland and Virginia Almanac for 1795.* Wilmington: S. & J. Adams [1794]. (Listed by Evans as No. 1398 but no copies are known.)

19. *Banneker's New-Jersey, Pennsylvania, Delaware, Maryland and Virginia Almanac, or Ephemeris for 1795.* Baltimore: S. & J. Adams [1794].

20. *New-Jersey & Pennsylvania Almanac, For The Year of our Lord 1795; Being the Third after Leap-Year, and the Twentieth of American Independence, after the Fourth of July. Containing, Besides the usual Requisites of an Almanac, A Variety of Entertaining Matter, in Prose and Verse. To Which is Added, An Account of the Yellow Fever, in Philadelphia. The Astronomical Calculations By Benjamin Banneker, An African.* Trenton: Printed and Sold, Wholesale and Retail by Matthias Day [1794].

21. *Bannaker's New-Jersey, Pennsylvania, Delaware, Maryland and Virginia*

Almanac, or Ephemeris, For the Year of our Lord 1795; Being the Third after Leap-Year. [Portrait of Bannaker]. Wilmington: Printed by S. & J. Adams [1794].

22. *The Pennsylvania, Delaware, Maryland and Virginia Almanack, for the Year of our Lord, 1795.* Baltimore: Printed by James Angell for Fisher and Coale [1794]. (Listed by Charles W. Evans but no locations given; Drake No. 2239.)

23. *The Pennsylvania, Delaware, Maryland and Virginia Almanack for the Year of our Lord, 1795; Being the Third after Leap-Year.* Wilmington: Printed and sold by S. and J. Adams [1794].

24. *Benjamin Bannaker's Pennsylvania, Delaware, Maryland and Virginia Almanac, For the Year of Our Lord 1795; Being the Third After Leap Year.* Baltimore: Printed for, and Sold by John Fisher, Stationer [1794]. (Portrait of Banneker on title page.)

25. *Bannaker's Maryland, Pennsylvania, Delaware, Virginia, Kentucky and North Carolina Almanack and Ephemeris For the Year of our Lord 1796; Being Bissextile, or Leap-Year; The Twentieth Year of American Independence and Eighth Year of the Federal Government.* Baltimore: Printed for Philip Edwards, James Keddie, and Thomas, Andrews and Butler; and Sold at their respective Stores, Wholesale and Retail [1795].

26. *Bannaker's Virginia and North Carolina Almanack and Ephemeris for the Year of our Lord 1797; Being First after Bissextile, or Leap-year; The Twenty-First Year of American Independence, and Ninth Year of the Federal Government.* Petersburg: Printed by William Prentis and William Y. Murray [1796].

27. *Bannaker's Virginia, Pennsylvania, Delaware, Maryland and Kentucky Almanack and Ephemeris, for the Year of Our Lord 1797; Being First Year after Bissextile, or Leap-Year; The Twenty-First Year of American Independence, and Ninth Year of Federal Government.* Baltimore: Printed by Christopher Jackson, No. 67 Market Street for George Keatinge's bookstore [Copyright secured] [1796].

28. *Bannaker's Virginia, Pennsylvania, Delaware, Maryland and Kentucky Almanack and Ephemeris, for the Year of Our Lord 1797; Being First After Bissextile, or Leap-Year; The Twenty-First Year of American Independence, and the Ninth Year of Federal Government.* Richmond: Printed by Samuel Pleasants, jun. near the Vendue Office [by privilege] [1796].

29. *Bannaker's Maryland and Virginia Almanack and Ephemeris, for the Year of Our Lord 1797; Being First After Bissextile, or Leap-Year. The Twenty-First Year of American Independence, and Ninth Year of the Federal Government.* Baltimore: Printed by Christopher Jackson, for George Keatinge's Wholesale and Retail Book-Store, No. 140 Market-street [1796].

II. WORKS RELATING TO BANNEKER

In addition to the twenty-eight editions of Banneker's almanacs issued over a period of six years, and the pamphlet containing his correspondence with

Thomas Jefferson, the published literature relating to Benjamin Banneker consists of numerous references and biographical sketches published in a great variety of periodicals and books from 1792 to the present time. To assist scholars and students in further studies of Banneker's work or of related aspects of the history of science in America, such references and accounts as can presently be compiled are listed herewith. The annotations designate original material or indicate when possible the sources of other work. Of the more than one hundred sources containing information about the life and work of Benjamin Banneker, only five are biographical sketches based upon contemporary sources utilizing information from acquaintances of Banneker in his lifetime. These are the accounts published by James McHenry, Susanna Mason, and John H. B. Latrobe, in addition to the two works by Martha Ellicott Tyson. It is upon these that the numerous other accounts and references have principally relied for their information, frequently perpetuating minor errors of dates and data. In order to illustrate how interest in Banneker has fluctuated over the years, these references are presented chronologically by date of publication. The list is undoubtedly incomplete, and additional references may come to light from time to time. Perhaps the present work will stimulate the discovery of additional original information and publications about Banneker.

1. "Account of Benjamin Banneker, a free Negro." *Universal Asylum* (November 1791): 300–301. Reprint of the letter from James McHenry to Goddard & Angell, written August 20, 1791, and published in Banneker's almanac for 1792. (See also Items 2 and 3.) James McHenry's letter to James Pemberton dated August 20, 1791 was reprinted in *The Bee, or Literary Weekly Intelligencer* [Edinburgh], vol. 13, 1793, pp. 291–93.

2. "Account of a Negro Astronomer. A Letter from Mr. James McHenry to the Editors of the Pennsylvania, Delaware, Maryland and Virginia Almanack, containing particulars respecting Benjamin Banneker, a free Negro." *New York Magazine, or Literary Repository,* 1791, vol. 2, pp. 557–58. Reprint of McHenry's letter of August 20, 1791. (See also Items 1 and 3.)

3. "A letter from mr. James McHenry, to messrs. Goddard and Angel, containing particulars reflecting Benjamin Banneker, a free negro." *American Museum,* Philadelphia, (September 1792): 185–87. Reprint of McHenry's letter of August 20, 1791. (See also items 1 and 2.)

4. "Letter from the famous self-taught ASTRONOMER, BENJAMIN BAN-NEKER, a black man, to THOMAS JEFFERSON, Esq. Secretary of State." *Universal Asylum* (October 1792): 222–24. Reprint of Banneker's letter to Jefferson and the latter's reply. (See also Bibliography, Part I, item 1.) This correspondence was also reprinted under the title "From a Virginia Newspaper To The Printer" as a front page feature in *The Providence* [R.I.] *Gazette and Country Journal,* November 3, 1792.

5. "Account of Benjamin Banneker, A Negro Calculator, Prefixed to His Pennsylvania, Delaware, Maryland, and Virginia Almanack and Ephemers, For the Year of Our Lord 1792. Baltimore, Printed and Sold by W. Goddard and J. Angell. For the Bee." *The Bee, or Literary Weekly Intelligencer, . . .* by James Anderson, LLD,

Edinburgh, vol. 13, 1793, pp. 291–93. Reprint of McHenry's letter of August 20, 1791. (See also items 1, 2 and 3.)

6. Gilbert Imlay. *A Topographical Description of the Western Territory of North America.* 2nd ed. London, 1793, pp. 212–13. In the second edition of this work (first published in 1792), reference is made to an unnamed New England Negro who had composed an ephemeris. Imlay's statement is mentioned by Gregoire (item 11), with a speculation as to whether Imlay was referring to Banneker or to another Negro savant in the American colonies. Imlay's passage is in rebuttal to Jefferson's argument in his *Notes on the State of Virginia* and other writings, in which the latter had asked:

> if the world has produced more than two poets acknowledged to be such by all nations, how many mathematicians, how many great inventors in arts and sciences had Europe, north of the Alps, when the Romans crossed those mountains? and then he says, "it was sixteen centuries before a Newton could be formed." And after asking these questions, he [Jefferson] absurdly expects that black poets and mathematicians are to spring up like mushrooms.
>
> However, a black in New England has composed an ephemeris, which I have seen, and which men, conversant in the science of astronomy declare exhibits marks of acute reason and genius.

7. [George Buchanan]. *An Oration Upon the Moral and Political Evil of Slavery. Delivered at a Public Meeting of the Maryland Society for Promoting the Abolition of Slavery, and the Relief of Free Negroes, and others unlawfully held in Bondage.* Baltimore, July 4th, 1791. By George Buchanan, M.D., Member of the American Philosophical Society. Baltimore: Printed by Philip Edwards, 1793, p. 10. Brief mention of Banneker as an outstanding member of his race, along with Phillis Wheatley and others.

8. William Loughton Smith. *The Pretensions of Thomas Jefferson to the Presidency Examined; And the Charges Against John Adams Refuted. Addressed to the Citizens of America in General; And Particularly to the Electors of the President.* United States, October 1796, pp. 7–14. This pamphlet constitutes a vicious attack on Jefferson, particularly in his role as a philosopher. Smith dwelt at length upon the apparent inconsistencies in Jefferson's published statements on the Negro and on slavery. He made extensive use of Jefferson's remarks on skin pigmentation in his *Notes on Virginia,* cited Jefferson's reply to Banneker as further evidence of insincerity, questioned whether Jefferson did in fact forward Banneker's ephemeris to de Condorcet, and then attacked de Condorcet for the absurdities he claimed to have found in his constitution.

9. Henry W. De Sassure. *Address to the Citizens of South Carolina.* Charleston, S.C.: For W. D. Young, 1800, p. 16. Discussion of Jefferson's position on slavery, quoting his reply to Banneker in part.

10. Thomas Green Fessenden. *Democracy Unveiled or Tyranny Stripped of the Garb of Patriotism by Christopher Caustic.* New York, 1806, 2:52n. Refers to

Jefferson's apparent reversal of attitude toward the Negroes as expressed in his reply to Banneker. Fessenden was quite as vicious in his attack on Jefferson as he was, by implication, in his comments on "Banneker, *said to be* [italics S.A.B.] the author of an almanack, &c.," and on "the wonderful phenomenon of a Negro Almanack, (probably enough made by a white man). . . ."

11. Bishop Henri Gregoire. *De la littérature des Nègres, ou Recherches sur leurs facultés intellectuelles, leurs qualités morales et leur littérature; suivies de Notices sur la vie et les ouvrages des Nègres qui se sont distingués dans les Sciences, les Lettres et les Arts.* Paris: Chez Maradan, Libraire, 1808, pp. 211–12. This work was translated into English and published in the United States two years later with the title *An Enquiry concerning the Intellectual and Moral Faculties and Literature of Negroes; Followed with an Account of the Life and Works of Fifteen Negroes and Mulattoes.* Translated by D. B. Warden. Brooklyn: Thomas Kirk, 1810. Among the sketches of fifteen Negroes is one of Banneker, which incorporates a number of errors. It mentions briefly the almanacs for 1794 and 1795 without reference to the earlier or later issues. The author was apparently unaware that Banneker had died two years prior to the publication of his book. He mentioned a letter to Banneker from Jefferson but not the letter which Banneker had sent to him. Footnotes mention the two almanacs as well as the works of Fessenden (item 10) and Imlay (item 6).

12. Alexander Mott. *Biographical Sketches and Interesting Anecdotes of Persons of Colour. To Which is Added a Selection of Pieces of Poetry.* New York: Mahlon Day, 1826, p. 219. The biographical sketch of Banneker consists of a single paragraph, which appears to be merely a translated summary of the sketch published by Bishop Gregoire (item 11).

13. [Susanna Mason]. *Selections from the Letters and Manuscripts of the Late Susanna Mason; With a Brief Memoir of Her Life, By Her Daughter.* Philadelphia: Rackliff & Jones, 1836, pp. 242–46. Included among the letters and writings of Susanna Mason are an account of her visit to Banneker's home about 1796, with a poem she composed about him after her visit (Document 34). One of the earliest first-hand accounts about Banneker.

14. John H. B. Latrobe. "Memoir of Benjamin Banneker, Read Before the Historical Society of Maryland." *Maryland Colonization Journal,* New Series, vol. 2, no. 23, May 1845, pp. 353–64. The first published account devoted exclusively to the life and work of Banneker; provides much of the authenticated data subsequently copied by later writers. Latrobe indicated that his sketch was based on memoranda collected by Benjamin H. Ellicott of Baltimore, to which he added "the materials furnished by his record book."

15. John H. B. Latrobe. "Memoir of Benjamin Banneker." *The African Repository (Colonizationist).* No copy of this article has been found.

16. [John H. B. Latrobe]. "Memoir of Benjamin Banneker." *The New National Era.* No copy of this article has been found.

17. "Benjamin Banneker: The Colored Astronomer of Maryland." *Plea For the Oppressed And Enslaved.* Austinburg (Ohio), February 2, 1847, vol. 1, no. 3, pp. 1–2.

The full front page and part of a second page of this small journal are devoted to an anonymous presentation of Banneker as an example of intellectual achievement of a member of the Negro race. It consists chiefly of a comprehensive sketch of his life and accomplishments, largely derived from Latrobe's "Memoir" (item 14). The journal *Plea For the Oppressed and Enslaved* was published by the Ladies' Anti-Slavery Society of Ashtabula County, Ohio, and approximately 4,000 copies of each issue were distributed without charge. According to an editorial note, the present issue was the last to be published.

18. Benjamin Kurtz. "The Learned Negro." *The Lutheran Observer* [Lancaster, Pennsylvania], vol. 16, no. 31, August 25, 1848, pp. 134–35. An article of one and one-third columns, preceded by a note stating:

> For the gratification of our readers we have prepared a hasty sketch of Banneker, the Learned Negro, which will be found in another column, and will doubtless be read with interest. The facts we have collected from a pamphlet, enti-tled: Memoir of Benjamin Banneker, read before the Maryland Historical Society, at the monthly meeting, May 1, 1845, by John H. Latrobe, Esq. (See item 14.)

19. Wilson Armistead. *A Tribute for the Negro: Being a Vindication of the Moral, Intellectual, and Religious Capabilities of the Coloured portion of Mankind; With Particular Reference to the African Race.* Manchester: William Irwin, 1848, pp. 126, 350– 56. This English work was widely distributed by the antislavery move-ment. The title page indicated that the American agent for the publication was "Wm. Harned, Anti-Slavery Office, 61, John Street, New York; and may be had of H. Longstreth and G. W. Taylor, Philadelphia." It is a compilation from other pub-lished works about the Negro. Banneker is mentioned in two parts of the work. In Chapter XI, in which "The African race [is] examined in an Intellectual point of view," he is described among Negroes having made achievements in the arts and sciences. He was identified as "Richard" Banneker, and the author noted that "his calculations were so thorough and exact, as to excite the approbation of Pitt, Fox, Wilberforce, and many other eminent persons. An almanac which he composed, was produced in the British House of Commons, as an argument in favour of the mental cultivation of the Coloured people, and of their liberation from their wretched thraldom." This section was based on the biographical sketch of Banneker published by Gregoire (item 11) and so stated. In a later section a short biography of Banneker features his correspondence with Jefferson, which is quot-ed in full. Reference is made also to the comment by Imlay (item 6) concerning an American Negro who calculated an almanac.

20. William G. Allen. *Wheatley, Banneker, and Horton: With Selections from the Poetical Works of Wheatley and Horton, and the letter of Washington to Wheatley, and of Jefferson to Banneker.* Boston: Daniel Laing, Jr., 1849, pp. 28–38, "Benjamin Banneker" by John H. B. Latrobe. A condensed version of Latrobe's memoir as published in the *Maryland Colonization Journal* (item 14), of which selected para-graphs are included verbatim. In his Introduction, Allen states:

The sketches of Wheatley, Banneker and Horton were written by white persons distinguished for character and standing. It is worthy of remark that not one of the writers is identified with the anti-slavery movement; but on the contrary two of them reside in slave States. This fact, with the letters of Washington and Jefferson, will add to the interest of these sketches and confirm their authenticity. . . .

Banneker excelled in the department of intellect to which the colored man has usually been regarded as being but illy adapted. He was an astronomer and mathematician. He was also a mechanic of the highest order,—working not by patterns but by principles. The sketch here presented was read before the Maryland Historical Society. The copy used for the present work has on the title page an inscription stating that it was a presentation from "Wm. H. Minton to the Banneker Institute" and that a former owner was J. B. White Jr. It is now in the collection of the Historical Society of Pennsylvania.

21. "A Negro Almanac-Maker." *The Leisure Hour* (London), no. 56, January 20, 1853, pp. 54–58. Anonymous account of Banneker based on Latrobe's "Memoir" (item 14), with errors in dates and data.

22. [Martha E. Tyson]. *A Sketch of the Life of Benjamin Banneker; From Notes Taken in 1836. Read by J. Saurin Norris, before the Maryland Historical Society, October 1854.* Baltimore: John D. Toy [n.d.], 20 pages. "A Sketch" was compiled by Martha E. Tyson with the encouragement of her mother, Mrs. George Ellicott, to provide material for a biography of Banneker planned by Rachel Mason, daughter of Susanna Mason (see item 13). Rachel Mason abandoned the project shortly before her death in 1849, and Mrs. Tyson then prepared the paper for the society to serve as a correction for erroneous data previously presented by Latrobe (item 14). She interviewed various individuals who had known Banneker in his lifetime, as well as surviving relatives, in order to produce what is one of the most valuable original sources on Banneker. J. Saurin Norris, who read *"A Sketch"* before the Maryland Historical Society, was Mrs. Tyson's nephew-in-law.

23. [Moncure D. Conway]. "Banneker The Black Astronomer." *The Southern Literary Messenger,* vol. 23, New Series vol. 2, July 1856, pp. 65–66. Brief, relatively accurate account of Banneker and his works, containing a few minor errors. (See also items 26 and 27.)

24. [Daniel Alexander Payne]. "A Literary Curiosity — Letter from Benjamin Banneker to Hon. Thos. Jefferson." *Repository of Religion and Literature and of Science and Art,* vol. 4, no. 7, July 1862, pp. 168–71. The first of a series of articles about Banneker which the Reverend Daniel Alexander Payne planned to publish in the *Repository,* of which he served as editor from 1858 to 1862. It consists primarily of the letters exchanged between Banneker and Jefferson, with a brief summary of Banneker's life. Payne mentioned that Banneker's letter to Jefferson had been brought to his attention by John H. Pinder, a teacher in Ebenezer Sabbath School. (See also item 39.) Payne commented:

> If our young men would but follow the noble example set by this black son of Maryland, they would by their intellectual culture, correct deportment, pure

habits and chaste manners, prove their manhood and equality, and compel the respect of all who now hate our race unless they be so stupified by prejudice and malice towards one portion of God's creatures that no truth—no ray of light—can reach them.

25. William Wells Brown. "A Celebrated Colored American: Benjamin Banneker." *Sunday Dispatch* (Philadelphia), September 1, 1861. Fairly extensive biographical sketch of Banneker, including several erroneous statements; quotes largely from his letter to Jefferson and the latter's reply.

26. Moncure D. Conway. "Benjamin Banneker, The Negro Astronomer." *The Atlantic Monthly,* January 1863, pp. 79–84. A concise account of Banneker's life and accomplishments based on the articles by Tyson (item 22) and Latrobe (item 14). Includes some clarification of Banneker's involvement in astronomical studies not provided in other accounts. There is no original material. A version was reprinted in *Sharpe's London Magazine,* vol. 37, 1863, pp. 133–34.

27. [Moncure D. Conway]. *Benjamin Banneker, The Negro Astronomer. Reprinted from "The Atlantic Monthly". By M. D. Conway. Tract No. 9.* London, Printed and Published for the Ladies' London Emancipation Society, by Emily Faithfull, Printer and Publisher in Ordinary to Her Majesty, Victoria Press, Princes Street, Hanover Square, April 1864. This pamphlet, a reprint of Conway's article (item 26), was sold for 1d., or 5s., per hundred copies and consists of fifteen pages. The reverse of the cover bears the names of the officers and committee members of the Ladies' London Emancipation Society.

28. Lydia Maria Child. *The Freedmen's Book.* Boston: Ticknor and Fields, 1865, pp. 14–23. Sketch of Banneker's life and work based on Latrobe (item 14) and Tyson (item 22). Well written and generally accurate, although the author repeats the legendary and the unsubstantiated claim that in 1803 Jefferson invited Banneker to visit him at Monticello, and there are some errors in dates picked up from the sources stated.

29. Martha E . Tyson. *A Brief Account of the Settlement of Ellicott's Mills, With Fragments of History therewith Connected, Written at the Request of Evan T. Ellicott, Baltimore 1865.* Fund Publication No. 4. Baltimore: Maryland Historical Society, 1871. 63 pages. As stated, a summarized account of the arrival of the Ellicott brothers from Buckingham, Bucks County, Pennsylvania, their purchase of land, and establishment of their mills.

30. Commissioner of Education, *Report on the Condition and Improvement of the Public Schools. Submitted to the Senate and House of Representatives June 1868 and 1870.* Washington: Government Printing Office, 1871, pp. 297–98, 300. The work is contained in *Executive Documents Printed by Order of the House of* Representatives During the Second Session of the Forty-First *Congress, 1869–1870.* Washington: Government Office, 1870. The essay "Banneker, the Astronomer" is a short survey of Banneker's career, with numerous erroneous dates and details, prepared by M. B. Goodwin and addressed to Henry Barnard, Commissioner of Education, as part of a report on "Schools of the Coloured Population." This is the

account of a debate in the U.S. Senate in March 1864, when Charles Sumner proposed an amendment prohibiting exclusion of blacks from the bill incorporating the Metropolitan railroad of Washington. The proposed amendment prompted Senator Reverdy Johnson to respond spiritedly—if not quite accurately—to Senator Saulsbury's disparagement of the Negro race with an erroneous reference to Banneker, although he did not mention his name:

> Many of those born free have become superior men. One of them was employed in Maryland in surveying, several of our boundary lines — Mason's and Dixon's particularly — and some of the calculations made on that occasion, astronomical as well as mathematical in the higher sense, were made by a black Maryland man who had been a slave.

31. William Frederick Poole. *Anti-Slavery Opinions Before the Year 1800.* Cincinnati: Robert Clarke & Co., 1873, pp. 10, 27–28. The letters between Banneker and Jefferson are quoted in relation to Jefferson's published statements on the subject of slavery. The oration of Dr. George Buchanan (item 7) is reproduced in its entirety.

32. "A Learned American Negro." *The Chronotype,* vol. 1, no. 1, 1873. Published by the American College of Heraldry and Genealogical Registry, pp. 24–26. Unsigned brief résumé of Banneker's life and work based on earlier sources.

33. Mary Clemmer Ames. *Ten Years in Washington. Life and Scenes in the National Capital, As a Woman Sees Them.* Hartford: A. D. Worthington & Co.; Chicago: L. Lloyd & Co., 1874, pp. 49–50. Contains a short description of Banneker's career based on other sources, including Latrobe (item 14) and possibly Conway (item 26).

34. David MacRae. *Amongst the Darkies.* Glasgow: John S. Marr & Sons, 1876, repr. 1880, pp. 28–30. In a tour of the southern states MacRae visited many schools for Negro children. In this work he incorporated accounts of outstanding Negroes in all fields of endeavor, including a brief account of Banneker's life and achievements which he used to illustrate the fallacy of the assertion that "The negro has strong emotions and may orate and poetise, but he is destitute of invention and contrivance." Based upon other published sources, the account perpetuates erroneous dates and such apocryphal claims as that in 1803 Banneker was invited to visit Jefferson at Monticello.

35. George W. Williams. *History of the Negro Race in America from 1619–1880.* 2 vols. New York: G. P. Putnam's Sons, 1883, 1:386–98. Comprehensive account of the life and work of Banneker based on Tyson (item 22) and Latrobe (item 14). The writer noted, "William Wells Brown, William C. Neill, and all the Colored men whose efforts I have seen, have made a number of very serious mistakes respecting Banneker's parentage, age, accomplishments, etc. *He was of mixed blood.* His mother's name was not Molly Morton, but one of his sisters bore that name." He stated that his account was based on the works of Latrobe and Norris and other material in the Maryland Historical Society.

36. [John R. Slattery]. "Benjamin Banneker, The Negro Astronomer." *The*

Catholic World, 38 (December 1883): 342–54. Biographical sketch based on Latrobe (item 14) and Tyson (item 22).

37. *Letters of Lydia Maria Child, With a Biographical Introduction by John G. Whittier and an Appendix by Wendell Phillips.* Boston: Houghton Mifflin and Company, 1883, p. 184. In a letter to Miss Eliza Scudder written from Wayland in 1864, Lydia Child commented on Lincoln and Johnson with particular reference to antislavery demonstrations in Nashville and in Baltimore where there was erected "the triumphal arch in the streets of Baltimore, whereon, with many honored historical names, were inscribed the names of Benjamin Banneker and R. R. Forten, two colored men! Glory to God! This is marvellous progress!"

38. Martha E. Tyson. *Banneker, the Afric-American Astronomer. From the Posthumous Papers of Martha E. Tyson. Edited by Her Daughter.* Philadelphia: Friends' Book Association, 1884. This account of Banneker is the most extensive and authoritative of all the published sources on the subject. It is an amplification of item 22, to which were added data collected from surviving contemporaries who had known Banneker.

39. [Daniel Alexander Payne]. "A Colored Astronomer." *The Critic*, January 31, 1885. A short account of Banneker's background, his accomplishments as an almanac-maker, and an exaggerated, incorrect mention of his role in the survey of the Federal Territory, refers to Tyson, *Banneker, the Afric-American Astronomer.*

40. Rev. William J. Simmons. *Men of Mark: Eminent, Progressive and Rising.* Cleveland: George M. Rewell & Co., 1887, pp. 344–51. The chapter on Banneker is based primarily on the work of Latrobe (item 14) as taken from Williams (item 34).

41. Daniel Alexander Payne. *Recollections of Seventy Years.* Nashville: Publishing House of the A.M.E. Sunday School Union, 1888, pp. 77–78. Payne, who was appointed historiographer of the A.M.E. Church and became bishop in 1850, describes a lecture he presented on Banneker and his visit on July 9, 1845, with members of his parish, to the site of Banneker's home and grave. Of particular interest is his interview with a local preacher who as a boy did errands for Banneker. (See also item 24.)

42. Jeffrey R. Brackett. *The Negro in Maryland, A Study of the Institution of Slavery.* Baltimore: N. Murray, 1889, see Chapter 5, pp. 180, 187 n1. Reference is made, without identification, to the case of Greenbury Morten, a free Negro who had been in the habit of voting and was unaware of the new amendment of the Maryland Constitution of 1810 limiting the right of suffrage to whites. His vote was refused at the polls. Morten was Banneker's nephew. The source for the incident mentioned was given as Latrobe's "Memoir" (item 14).

43. Edward A. Johnson. *A School History of the Negro Race in America, From 1619 to 1890, With a Short Introduction as to the Origin of the Race; Also a Short Sketch of Liberia.* Raleigh: Edwards and Broughton, 1890, pp. 32–35. A short chapter on "Benjamin Banneka, Astronomer and Mathematician" provides a brief description of his life and achievements, based on earlier sources, with no new information.

44. Florian Cajori. *The Teaching and History of Mathematics in the United States.* Bureau of Education Circular of Information No. 3, 1890 [Whole Number 167]. Washington, Government Printing Office, 1890, p. 43. Banneker and his achievements are briefly described in relation to early American mathematicians. The information is credited to Williams (item 34).

45. Gabrielle Marie Jacobs. "The Black Astronomer." *The Chautauquan,* vol. 29, New Series Vol. 20, April–September, 1899, pp. 585–89. A well-written and quite accurate biographical sketch of Banneker encompassing the important details of his life and work, based primarily on Latrobe (item 14).

46. F. R. Diffenderffer. "Andrew Ellicott." *Historical Papers and Addresses of the Lancaster County Historical Society.* Vol. 4, 1899–1900, p. 67. Short statement describing Banneker's role in the survey of the city of Washington, with a brief biographical sketch of his life and achievements. The author stated that the association of Banneker in the survey was brought to his attention by a Dr. Joseph H. Dubbs.

47. Letter to the Editor, *Washington Star,* October 21, 1901. Criticizes of President Roosevelt for inviting Booker T. Washington to the White House, and relates the event to Jefferson's invitation to Banneker to visit him at Monticello.

48. Emily Emerson Lantz. "Suburban Baltimore." *Baltimore Sunday Sun,* October 22, 1905. Includes brief mention of Banneker.

49. Emily Emerson Lantz, "Maryland Heraldry; History of Distinguished Families and Personages." *Baltimore Sun,* March 12, 1905. Brief reference to Benjamin Banneker and his association with George Ellicott in a history of the Ellicott family.

50. Prof. Silas X. Floyd. *The New Floyd's Flowers, Short Stories for Colored People Old and Young.* Washington, D.C.: Austin Jenkins Co., 1905, pp. 220–24. Includes a chapter on "Benjamin Banneker, the Negro Astronomer," which addresses itself to "The little colored boys and girls of America." Contains exaggerated claims, such as that Banneker produced the first clock of which every part was made in America and the earliest almanacs prepared for general use in this country. As the author indicates, his account is based in large part on Conway (item 26).

51. Catherine Van Cortlandt Mathews. *Andrew Ellicott, His Life and Letters.* New York: The Grafton Press, 1908, p. 86. This is the only definitive biography of Andrew Ellicott to the present time; it was commissioned by the family. The author stated that during the first period of the survey of the Federal City early in 1791, "Major Ellicott was at this time hard at work upon the survey, assisted by Mr. Briggs, Mr. Fenwick, his brother Benjamin Ellicott and a unique character, Benjamin Banneker, the negro mathematician and astronomer." There is a further reference to Banneker in a footnote.

52. John W. Cromwell. *The Negro in American History.* Washington: The American Negro Academy, 1914, pp. 86–97, chapter 19, "Benjamin Banneker." A fairly accurate account of Banneker's life, based on Latrobe (item 14) and incorporating the several errors in dates and data noted therein. Reference is made also to the

article by Jacobs (item 43), to Bishop Payne (item 24) and to the public school named for Banneker in Washington, D.C.

53. William Tindall. *Standard History of the City of Washington, From a Study of Original Sources.* Knoxville: H. W. Crew & Co., 1914, p. 57. In a mention of Major Andrew Ellicott's assistants in the survey of the Federal Territory, the author included Banneker, "a protege of Major Ellicott and of his father." A brief description of Banneker's achievements follows. Banneker was not a protégé of either Andrew or Joseph Ellicott.

54. Letters to the Editor concerning Banneker, *The Washington Evening Star,* October 21 and 30, 1916. One writer, W.A.L., stated that Jefferson invited Banneker to dine with him at the Executive Mansion and that he had also invited Banneker to Monticello. Another, B., disputed these statements on the basis that they were not included in the accounts by Latrobe (item 14) and Tyson (items 22 and 37). To this, W.A.L. replied that Tyson's information was collected fifty years after Banneker's death from those who knew him and were too young to have known of the Jefferson invitations. No evidence of such invitations has been found. (See also item 28.)

55. Phillip LePhillips. "The Negro, Benjamin Banneker; Astronomer and Mathematician, Plea for Universal Peace." *Records of the Columbia Historical Society,* 20 (1917): 114–20. Paper read by LePhillips before the Society on April 18, 1916, based entirely on earlier published sources.

56. Fred. E. Woodward. "A Ramble Along the Boundary Stones of the District of Columbia With a Camera." *Records of the Columbia Historical Society,* 20 (1917): 65–66. In an article about the original boundary stones of the Federal City, Woodward provides another account of Banneker's presence during the survey, without supporting documentation and with various inaccuracies about his life and associations.

57. "Thomas Jefferson's Thoughts on the Negro." *The Journal of Negro History,* 3 (1918): 55–89. General discussion of Jefferson's expressions about the inferiority of the Negro. Banneker is discussed in Section 5, pp. 69–71, which includes Jefferson's letters to Marquis de Condorcet, Joel Barlow, and Henri Gregoire.

58. Henry E. Baker. "Benjamin Banneker, The Negro Mathematician and Astronomer." *The Journal of Negro History,* 3, (1918): 99–118. At the time of writing, Baker was an Assistant Examiner at the U.S. Government Patent Office, and based his account on the Tyson work on Banneker (item 37) which he obtained from one of her descendants, Mrs. Tyson Manly. Other sources included the accounts in *The Leisure Hour* (item 21) and *The Atlantic Monthly* (item 26), as well as the *Sketch* by Tyson (item 22), *The Southern Literary Messenger* (item 23), *The Catholic World* (item 35), Latrobe's "Memoir" in the *Maryland Colonization Journal* (item 14), as well as the work of LePhillips published in the *Records of the Columbia Historical Society* (item 51). Despite erroneous statements about the division of the farm and Banneker's involvement with the survey of the Federal Territory, the article is a generally accurate presentation of the data already provided by the basic sources.

59. Elizabeth Ross Haynes. *Unsung Heroes.* New York: Du Bois and Dill, 1921, pp. 153–64, Chapter 8, "Benjamin Banneker, Astronomer and Surveyor 1732–1804." A fictionalized account of Banneker's childhood and later life based on the work of Tyson (item 21) and the English reprint of the article by Conway (item 27). There is no new material, and the dates of birth and death are inaccurate.

60. William W. Allen, assisted by Daniel Murray. *Banneker, the Afro-American Astronomer.* Washington, D.C., 1921, 80 pp. This compilation is based on the later Tyson work (item 37) and on the articles by LePhillips (item 51) and Baker (item 54). It was read before the Banneker Association of Washington by Daniel Murray, Assistant Librarian of the Library of Congress, with an introduction in which Murray puts forward the fictional claim that it was by means of Banneker's memory that L'Enfant's plans for the city of Washington were preserved.

61. George F. Bragg Jr. *Men of Maryland.* Baltimore: Church Advocate Press, 1925, pp. 38–40, 155–57. Short sketch of Banneker's life, with numerous errors in details; copies of the correspondence with Jefferson.

62. Henry D. Hyde. "Maryland Negro Distinguished as Scientist in 1792." *Baltimore Sun,* [n.d.] 1926. A brief newspaper article recounting the highlights of Banneker's achievements, prompted by the acquisition of a copy of Banneker's almanac for 1792 by the Maryland Historical Society. In an effort to dramatize his subject, the author perpetuated some of the errors in dates and data from earlier accounts.

63. "The Learned Negro." *The Journal of Negro History,* 14, (April 1929): 238–42. Transcription of the article in *The Lutheran Observer,* August 25, 1848 (item 18). Although the author is not identified, it is believed to have been written by the *Observer's* editor, the Reverend Benjamin Kurtz. A concise biographical account with discrepancies in dates, based on Latrobe (item 14) and the two Tyson accounts (items 22 and 37).

64. Helen Alpert-Levin. "A Negro Genius of His Day." *Baltimore Sun,* July 2, 1929. A short account of Banneker's life and achievements, based probably on Latrobe (item 14). There are no new data, and a few errors have been incorporated from the sources consulted.

65. Thomas O. Fuller. *Pictorial History of the American Negro.* Memphis: Pictorial History, Inc., 1933, pp. 37, 342–47. In addition to a brief mention of Banneker among other outstanding Negro figures of his time, the volume includes a short "Biography of Benjamin Banneker" by John H. B. Latrobe, which is a condensed version of his more detailed "Memoir" (item 14).

66. Josephus R. Coan. *Daniel Alexander Payne, Christian Educator.* Philadelphia: The A.M.E. Book Concern, 1935, p. 78. A brief comment on a lecture delivered by Bishop Payne about Banneker, and his visit to the farm and Banneker's grave in July 1845, based on Payne's *Recollections of Seventy Years* (item 39). Reference is made also to a series of articles on Banneker by Payne in the periodical *Repository of Religion, Science and Literature* (item 24).

67. "Jefferson's Dilemma." *Letters* (Time, Inc.), vol. 2, no. 7, April 1, 1935, pp.

3–4. Letter from J. N. G. Finley and a reply by the editor, discussing Jefferson's comments on Banneker in his letters to de Condorcet and Barlow. In a supplementary biographical account of Banneker by the editor, there are numerous erroneous dates and data.

68. Benjamin Brawley. *Early Negro American Writers.* Chapel Hill: University of North Carolina Press, 1935, pp. 75–86. Thoughtful and careful account of Banneker's life and achievements based on the two works by Tyson (items 22 and 37) with a useful evaluation of the major published sources.

69. Michael Kraus. "Slavery Reform in the Eighteenth Century: An Aspect of Transatlantic Intellectual Cooperation." *Pennsylvania Magazine of Biography and History*, 60 (January 1936): 62–63. In a description of the influence of the Society of Friends in the antislavery movement on both sides of the Atlantic, reference is made to a lengthy article about Banneker in *The Bee* published in Edinburgh (item 5).

70. Henry J. Cadbury. "Negro Membership in the Society of Friends." *The Journal of Negro History*, 21 (April 1936): 208–9. In a brief and accurate summary of his life, Banneker is described as a Negro well known to the Society of Friends. Reference is made to the fact that although he did not join any denomination, he frequently attended the meetings of Friends at Ellicott's Mills, based on Tyson's account (item 37).

71. Benjamin Brawley. *Negro Builders and Heroes.* Chapel Hill: University of North Carolina Press, 1937, Chapter 5, "Benjamin Banneker: Astronomer," pp. 25–29, 295. Brief account based on Brawley's earlier work (item 64), with no new material.

72. Dorothy B. Porter. "Early American Negro Writings: A Bibliographical Study." *The Papers of the Bibliographical Society of America.* New York: The Bibliographical Society of America, 1945, 39:204–5, 213, 221–25. A brief account of Banneker's life and the publication of his almanacs, including a check list of nineteen issues of the almanacs. The author states erroneously that Banneker studied Latin, Greek, German, and French. The principal source is the article by Baker (item 54).

73. Saul K. Padover. "Benjamin Banneker: Unschooled Wizard." *The New Republic*, February 2, 1948, pp. 22–25. Brief account of Banneker highlighting the outstanding events culled from the accounts of Latrobe (item 14) and Tyson (item 22), with some errors in dates and data.

74. Shirley Graham. *Your Most Humble Servant.* New York: Julian Messner, 1949. This work is a full-length fictionalized biography of Benjamin Banneker for children, based primarily on the published accounts of Banneker by Latrobe (item 14) and Tyson (items 22 and 37), and supplemented by fictitious incidents to complete gaps in the story. Reviews that appeared in various journals, including the *Maryland Historical Magazine*, 45 (1950): 63–64) and the *Washington Afro-American*, Afro Magazine Section, February 7, 1950, pp. 3–5, unfortunately selected for comment those incidents which are apparently fictional, thus creating new fictions.

75. William W. Harrison. "Banneker as Builder." *Baltimore Evening Sun,*

February 24, 1950. Communication to the editor relating to Banneker's role in the survey of Washington, based on earlier published sources.

76. H. Paul Caemmerer. *The Life of Pierre Charles L'Enfant, Planner of the City Beautiful: The City of Washington.* Washington, D.C.: National Republic Publishing Co., 1950, pp. 131, 199. This useful source work on the history of the national capital reproduces on p. 131 a painting by Garnet W. Jex. Entitled "The Planning of Washington," it shows President Washington on the scene with Ellicott, L'Enfant, the City Commissioners, James Hoban, Isaac Roberdeau, and Banneker. The original is in the library of George Washington University in Washington, D.C. The author describes Banneker as one of the assistants of L'Enfant, whereas he was in fact Ellicott's assistant. There are no other references to Banneker.

77. William B. Settle. "The Real Benjamin Banneker." *The Negro History Bulletin,* 16 (January 1953): 90–91; (February 1953): 105–8; (March 1953): 129–35; (April 1953): 153–58. This four-part series presents the story of Banneker's life in an interesting manner and generally with accuracy. The author acknowledges the "Memoir" by Latrobe (item 14), and the two articles by Tyson (items 22 and 37), as his basic sources, supplemented by the account in the work by Bragg (item 57), Mason (item 13), and Conway (item 26).

78. William B. Marye. "Benjamin Banneker, His Dwelling Place." MS. General clipping file, Maryland Historical Society.

79. Sir Augustus John Foster. *Jeffersonian America. Notes on the United States of America Collected in the Years 1805–6–7 and 11–12.* San Marino, Cal.: Huntington Library, 1954) pp. 148–50.

80. E. Franklin Frazier. *The Negro in the United States.* rev. ed. New York: Macmillan, 1957, p. 494. Includes a passing mention of Banneker's almanac among outstanding prose works produced by Negroes as a protest against slavery.

81. John C. Schmidt. "Benjamin Banneker's Unusual Career." *Baltimore Evening Sun,* April 3, 1960, p. 7. Short account of Banneker's life and work containing erroneous statements relating to his correspondence with Jefferson and his involvement in the survey of the Federal City.

82. T. F. Mulcrone. "Benjamin Banneker, pioneer Negro mathematician." *The Mathematics Teacher,* 54, (January 1961): 32–37. A carefully researched account of Banneker's life, with particular emphasis on his interest and work in mathematics.

83. Benjamin Quarles. *The Negro in the American Revolution.* Chapel Hill: The University of North Carolina Press, for the Institute of Early American History and Culture, 1961, pp. 43, 187–88. Brief references to Banneker's letter to Jefferson and of Jefferson's opinion of Banneker based on the former's correspondence.

84. Lerone Bennett, Jr. *Before the Mayflower: A History of the Negro in America 1619–1962.* Chicago: Johnson Publishing Company, 1962. Contains a comparison of Banneker and Phillis Wheatley, and a short account of Banneker's life. Accurate, except for the statement that "Banneker also wrote a dissertation on bees and put together what was probably the first clock made in America."

85. Russell L. Adams. *Great Negroes Past and Present.* Chicago: Afro-

American Publishing Co., 1963, pp. 11, 18, 49. A picture-book treatment, with a one-page biography of Banneker and two other references.

86. Silvio A. Bedini. *Early American Scientific Instruments and Their Makers.* United States National Museum Bulletin No. 231. Washington, D.C.: Government Printing Office, 1964, pp. 22–25. A brief account of Banneker's scientific career and his role in the survey of the Federal Territory, with illustrations of his letter of October 13, 1789, and the portrait from the Fisher edition of the almanac for 1795.

87. District of Columbia Board of Education Curriculum Dept. *The Negro in American History, A Curriculum Resource Bulletin for Secondary Schools.* Washington, D.C.: [Mimeograph], 1964, pp. 19– 20. Features one paragraph on Banneker, erroneously stating that he was the first American to make a clock, that he "predicted the location of stars," and that he was appointed a professional member "of the commission headed by Major Pierre Charles L'Enfant."

88. Jack L. Hodge. "He Looked and Remembered." *Baltimore News-American,* February 7, 1965. Brief newspaper account of Banneker's restoration of the plans for the Federal City from memory, which is fiction.

89. "Banneker's Memory Saved Capital Plans." *Catonsville* [Md.] *Herald-Argus,* April 15, 1965. Brief account of Banneker's life, probably based on Graham (item 70), and erroneously claiming that from memory he was able to restore the plans of L'Enfant.

90. John W. Caughey, John Hope Franklin, Ernest R. May. *Land of the Free, A History of the United States.* New York, Benziger Brothers, 1966, pp. 192–93. Includes a brief and inaccurate mention of the survey of the Federal City, claiming that the commissioners for the survey were Pierre L'Enfant, Benjamin Banneker, and George Ellicott.

91. William Loren Katz. *Eyewitness, The Negro in American History.* New York: Pitman Publishing Corp., 1967, pp. 29–31, 61– 62. Brief account of Banneker's career and contributions, which are stated to have been in "the fields of science, mathematics, and political affairs," illustrated with a fictional portrait from Allen's work (item 56) and the title page of the almanac for 1793. Among the misstatements are the claims that Banneker produced the first clock made entirely with American parts, that Jefferson promised Banneker that he would end slavery, that George Ellicott worked with Banneker in the survey of Washington, that Banneker was appointed to the commission after a suggestion Jefferson made to Washington, and that Banneker selected the sites of the principal buildings. The fiction that Banneker re-created L'Enfant's plan from memory is again presented, and his almanacs are said to have been published for a period of ten years.

92. John Hope Franklin. *From Slavery to Freedom.* New York: Alfred A. Knopf, 1967, pp. 157–59, 662–63. A short account of Banneker's role in the antislavery movement, apparently based on the works of LePhillips (item 51) and Baker (item 54).

93. "Voices from Negro History." *International Afro-American Museum,* [Detroit], 2 (Spring 1967). A short boxed column with numerous erroneous state-

ments. Illustrated with a portrait, which has been exchanged with that of Jan Matzeliger, the subject of the adjacent column.

94. Wilbur Pinder Jr. "History Bypasses Early American Genius." *Catonsville Herald-Argus* and *Baltimore Evening Sun,* March 8, 1967. Brief newspaper accounts of Banneker based on Graham's work (item 70).

95. [John Hope Franklin]. "An Intellectual argued with a Founding Father." *Life Magazine,* November 22, 1968. Brief statement of Banneker's achievements, emphasizing in particular Banneker's correspondence with Jefferson.

96. Winthrop D. Jordan. *White Over Black: American Attitudes Towards the Negro, 1550–1812.* Chapel Hill: University of North Carolina Press, 1968, pp. 449–57, 486. Discussion of Jefferson's attitude toward Banneker and Banneker's achievements, with thorough documentation, although some details of Banneker's life are incorrect.

97. Phillip T. Drotning. *Black Heroes in Our Nation's History.* New York, Cowles Co., Inc., 1968, pp. 34–35. Brief statement concerning Banneker's participation in the survey of the city of Washington. The author identifies the surveyor as George Ellicott and claims that Banneker assisted L'Enfant in reconstructing the latter's plan from memory, and that Banneker and L'Enfant selected the sites for the Capitol and President's House.

98. Wilhelmena S. Robinson. *Historical Negro Biographies.* Inter-National Library of Negro Life and History. New York: Publishers Company, 1968, p. 9. A short account in which Banneker is identified as an "engineer" who published almanacs until 1802; states that "He published also a treatise on bees and computed the cycle of the seventeen-year locust."

99. John Hines. *The Genius of Benjamin Banneker. A Play.* New York: New Dimensions Publishing Co., 1969. Based upon a series of achievements attributed to Banneker, all of them incorrect.

100. Maxwell Whiteman, ed. *Banneker's Almanack, and Ephemeris for the Year of Our Lord 1793; Being the First After Bissextile or Leap Year; and Banneker's Almanac, for the Year 1795: Being the Third after Leap Year.* Philadelphia: Historic Publications, Afro-American History Series No. 202, 1969. Reprint of two of Banneker's almanacs, with a short introduction describing Banneker's career and identifying several of the basic sources.

101. Peter M. Bergman. *Chronological History of the Negro in America.* New York: Harper & Row, 1969, pp. 31–32, 71, 146. Brief account of Banneker and his accomplishments, perpetuating inaccuracies in dates and other details.

102. James W. Gibbs. "'Black Genius' Benjamin Banneker." *Bulletin of the National Association of Watch and Clock Collectors,* 69, vol. 13, no. 12, pp. 1155–57. Brief résumé of Banneker's life, with misstatements relating to Banneker's association with David Rittenhouse, the claim that he made the first clock in Maryland, etc.

103. J. W. Haywood, Jr. "Banneker Monument" (Letter to the editor), *Washington Post,* April 5, 1969. Proposes the creation of a suitable monument to Banneker for his role in the survey of the city of Washington.

104. Otto Lindenmeyer. *Black History: Lost, Stolen, or Strayed.* New York: Avon Books, 1970, pp. 37, 40–47. Brief account of Banneker's life and achievements, including the fable that he was able to restore from memory the details of L'Enfant's map, and the statement that following L'Enfant's dismissal he was employed to continue the survey of the national capital with Andrew Ellicott as his assistant. Another story, for which there is no known documentary basis, is that the Philadelphia publisher of his almanac "was so skeptical of Banneker's prediction of a solar eclipse that he challenged the astronomer to a wager before beginning to set type."

105. Sarah Gilbert. "He helped put Washington on the map, Benjamin Banneker." *Potomac Magazine, The Washington Post,* January 11, 1970, pp. 23–27. An account of Banneker's role in the survey of Washington, based largely on the novelized biography by Graham (item 70) and perpetuating the fictions originally published in that work. Illustrated with the sketch first published in Allen's work (item 56), which is also fiction.

106. Robb Sagendorph. *America and Her Almanacs, Wit, Wisdom & Weather 1639–1970.* Boston: Little, Brown & Co., 1970, p. 123. Brief mention of Banneker's almanacs with a reproduction of the cover of the almanac for 1796.

107. Claude Lewis. *Benjamin Banneker, The Man Who Saved Washington.* New York: McGraw-Hill Book Company, 1970. Juvenile. Written for a young audience, this work incorporates many of the erroneous legends, such as Banneker's purchase of Anola, a slave girl, employment as a surveyor in the Federal Territory, his purported recovery of L'Enfant's design for the city of Washington, etc.

108. "Letters." *New York Times Sunday Book Review,* November 1, 8, and 29, 1970. Comments on the absence of a biographical sketch of Banneker in the *Dictionary of Scientific Biography* (New York, Charles Scribner's Sons, 1970).

109. Lois Mark Stalvey, *The Education of a Wasp.* New York: William Morrow & Co., 1970, pp. 148–49. States that Banneker "had been omitted from 'standard' histories" because the author had "never before questioned or noticed that almost every historical figure I have been offered was white and presumably Protestant" and because it would have been embarrassing to Jefferson.

110. Silvio A. Bedini. "Benjamin Banneker and the Survey of the District of Columbia." *Records of the Columbia Historical Society of Washington,* 1969–70, pp. 7–30. Detailed account of Banneker's participation in the survey as a scientific assistant of Major Andrew Ellicott during the winter and spring of 1791.

111. Margaret Goff Clark. *Benjamin Banneker Astronomer and Scientist.* Champaign, Ill.: Garrard Publishing Co., 1971. Juvenile. A fictionalized biography for young children, presenting the salient events of Banneker's life based on the more accurate earlier accounts, including Latrobe (item 14), Tyson (items 22 and 37), and Graham (item 70).

112. Letitia Woods Brown [and Elsie M. Lewis]. *Washington From Banneker to Douglass 1791–1870.* Washington, D.C.: National Portrait Gallery, 1971. Exhibition catalogue.

113. Richard Claxton Gregory. "The Myth of the Founding Fathers." in *No*

More Lies: The Myth and Reality of American Slavery, edited by James R. McGraw. New York: Harper & Row, 1971, pp. 64–100. Places the exchange of letters between Banneker and Jefferson into modern idiom. The statesman blames the Congress for striking out the anti-slavery clause of the Declaration of Independence.

114. Sidney Kaplan. *The Black Presence in the Era of the American Revolution 1770–1800*. New York: The Graphic Society, Ltd., 1973; Washington, D.C.: Smithsonian Institution, National Portrait Gallery, 1973, pp. 42–50. Exhibition catalogue with same title based upon above by Lisa W. Strick. Material on Banneker appears to have been based for the most part on *The Life of Benjamin Banneker* by Silvio A. Bedini (1972).

115. Charles W. Evans. *Biographical and Historical Accounts of the Fox, Ellicott and Evans Families, And the Different Families Connected with Them*. Buffalo: Press of Baker, Jones, 1882, repr. 1976. Reprint of Evans (1882) with excerpts from Tyson, "Settlement," Bartlett, "Andrew and Joseph Ellicott," Norris, "A Sketch," and foreword by Silvio A. Bedini.

116. Julian P. Boyd, ed. *The Papers of Thomas Jefferson*. 25 vols. Princeton: Princeton University Press, 1974, 19:4–47. *Vide* fn. 119 on pp. 41–43. In this extensive footnote, the late Dr. Boyd attempted to evaluate the exact nature of Banneker's participation in establishing the experimental and permanent lines of the survey of the Federal Territory.

117. Fawn M. Brodie. *Thomas Jefferson. An Intimate History*. New York: W. W. Norton, 1974, p. 423. Brodie relates Jefferson's discussion with the British diplomat Sir Augustus John Foster, noting that Foster had gravely annoyed Jefferson by emphasizing British moral superiority over Americans on the subject of slavery. Although acknowledging Banneker's mathematical abilities, Jefferson is portrayed as having belittled his literary ability.

118. John McGrain. "Banneker's Property Lines Discovered." *The Catonsville Times*, August 19, 1976. Based upon McGrain's unpublished manuscript.

119. Silvio A. Bedini. "Andrew Ellicott, Surveyor of the Wilderness." *Surveying and Mapping*, 36 (1976): 113–35. Biographical sketch of Ellicott, featuring the survey of the Federal Territory and mentioning Banneker in passing.

120. Silvio A. Bedini, "Benjamin Banneker, the First Black Man of Science," *Science and Children*, vol. 13, No. 4, January 1976, pp. 19–21.

121. [Benjamin Banneker.] *A Chronology of the Life of Benjamin Banneker: Son of Maryland 1731–1806*. Annapolis: Commission on Afro-American History and Culture, N.D. Compiled from *The Life of Benjamin Banneker* by Silvio A. Bedini.

122. John Hope Franklin. *Racial Equality in America*. The 1976 Jefferson Lecture in the Humanities presented by the National Endowment for the Humanities. Chicago: University of Chicago Press, 1976, pp. 12–34. States that the fact that the ideology of the American Revolution was not actually egalitarian was illustrated by Jefferson himself. Jefferson's attitude towards Banneker and Wheatley is analyzed.

123. John Chester Miller. *The Wolf by the Ears: Thomas Jefferson and Slavery.* New York: The Free Press, 1977, pp. 76–77. Discussion of the Banneker-Jefferson exchange of letters, noting that Jefferson had "secured for Banneker an appointment as surveyor in the District of Columbia where the new Federal City was to be built."

124. Robert J. Hurry. *An Archeological Survey of the Benjamin Banneker Property, Baltimore County, Maryland.* Baltimore County Department of Recreation and Parks. Maryland National Trust Manuscript Series No. 34. November 1983.

125. Harriet Jackson Scarupa. "Digging for the Facts About Benjamin Banneker." *American Visions,* 2 (August 1987): 16–21. The first published account of the archeological investigation of the Banneker homestead.

126. Charles W. Koontz. *A Comparison of Benjamin Banneker's Astronomical Data with Other 18th Century Almanacs.* Unpublished manuscript. Ellicott City, Md., 1987.

127. Matthew Scott. "Benjamin Banneker, Laying the Foundation of a Great City." *Modern Black Man* (March 1987): 76–77. Brief and erroneous account of Banneker's role in the survey of the Federal Territory — "relaid the cornerstones of the city from memory."

128. Silvio A. Bedini. "Benjamin Banneker, First Black Man of Science." *National Society of Black Engineers Journal,* 3 (February 1988): 28–33, cover illus.

129. Jeri Ferris. *What Are You Figuring Now? A Story About Benjamin Banneker.* Minneapolis: Carolrhoda Books, Inc., 1988. Juvenile. For very young readers.

130. Kevin Conley. *Benjamin Banneker.* New York: Chelsea House, 1989. Juvenile. For young readers.

131. Silvio A. Bedini. *Thomas Jefferson: Statesman of Science.* New York: Macmillan Publishing Company, 1990, pp. 212, 222–25.

132. Silvio A. Bedini. "The Survey of the Federal Territory: Andrew Ellicott and Benjamin Banneker." *Washington History,* 3 (Spring/Summer 1991): 76–95, 137–38. Account of the survey and Banneker's role. Includes first report of Ellicott's expense account listing Banneker's employment in the survey of the Federal Territory.

133. Silvio A. Bedini. "He Did Not Hold the Horses!" *The Professional Surveyor* (November/December 1993): 50–52. Clarifying Banneker's role in the survey of the Federal Territory and disclaiming the several legends.

134. Beatrice Lumpkin. "From Egypt to Benjamin Banneker. African Origins of False Position Solutions." In *Vita Mathematica. Historical Research and Integration with Teaching, Mathematical Association of American Notes,* Ronald Calinger, ed., 40 (1996): 279–89. With analysis of some of Banneker's mathematical puzzles.

135. Ron Eglash. "The African Heritage of Benjamin Banneker." *Social Studies of Science,* 27, (April 1997): 307–15. Discussion of the African origins of Banneker's

grandfather Bannka, of the significance of of the quincunx symbol, and Banneker's mathematical puzzles.

136. Robert J. Hurry. *Archeological Investigations of the Benjamin Banneker Homestead (18BA282), Baltimore County, Maryland.* Maryland Historical Trust Manuscript Series No. 34. Comprehensive report of the archeological investigation of the Banneker homestead site from its inception. 1997.

III. REFERENCE WORKS

Boubacar Barry. *Le Royaume du Waalo. Le Sénégal avant la Conquête.* Paris: François Maspero, 1972. Part II, Chapter 2.

Bascom, William R.. *Ifa Divination* (Bloomington, Ind.: Indiana University Press, 1969).

Boilat, Père David. *Esquisses Sénégalaises* (Paris: Karthala, [1853], 1984).

Bonnycastle, John. *The Scholar's Guide to Arithmetic; or A Complete Exercise-Book for the Use of Schools* (London: For J. J. Johnson, 1780).

Brigham, Clarence S. "An Account of American Almanacs and Their Value for Historical Study." *Proceedings of the American Antiquarian Society,* October 1925, vol. 15, Part 2, pp. 190–209.

Colvin, Lucie Gallistel. *Historical Dictionary of Senegal* (London: Scarecrow Press, 1981), pp. 288–90. Gamble, Peter D. *The Wolof of Senegambia* in *Ethnographic Survey of Africa. Western Africa,* Part 14, edited by Daryll Forde. London: International African Institute, 1957, pp. 11–12, 63–64.

Holloway, Joseph E., "The Origins of African-American Culture." In *Africanisms in American Culture,* Joseph E. Holloway, ed. Bloomington: Indiana University Press, 1990, pp. 2–18.

Kittredge, George Lyman. *"The Old Farmer and His Almanacs, Being Some observations on Life and Manners in New England a Hundred Years Ago." Suggested by Reading the Earlier Numbers of Mr. Robert B. Thomas's Farmer's Almanacs.* Boston: William Ware & Co., 1904.

McDaniel, George W. *Hearth and Home: Preserving a People's Culture.* Philadelphia: Temple University Press, 1982.

Maryland, A Guide to the Old Line State. New York: Oxford University Press, 1973.

Palmer, Robert. *Deep Blues.* New York: Penguin Books, 1981.

Petitto, Andrea L. "Practical Arithmetic and Transfer. A Study Among West African Tribesmen." *Journal of Cross-Culture Psychology,* 13, (1982): 15–28.

Prussin, Labelle. *Hatumere: Islamic Design in West Africa.* Berkeley: University of California Press, 1986.

Sagendorph, Robb. *America and Her Almanacs: Wit, Wisdom & Weather 1639–1970.* Boston: Little Brown & Co., 1970.

Scharf, J. Thomas. *History of Baltimore City and County from the Earliest*

Period to the Present Day, Including Biographical Sketches of Their Representative Men. Philadelphia: Louis H. Everts, 1881.

    Smith, David Eugene. *History of Mathematics.* 2 vols. New York: Ginn and Company, 1925, 2:437–42.

    Weslager, C. A. *The Log House in America from Pioneer Days to the Present.* New Brunswick, N.J.: Rutgers University Press, 1969, pp. 135–45.

    Wroth, Laurence C. *The Colonial Printer.* Charlottesville: University Press of Virginia, 1965.

INDEX

References to illustrations are noted in italics

THE AUTHOR

SILVIO A. BEDINI, a native of Ridgefield, Connecticut, was appointed Curator of the Division of Mechanical and Civil Engineering of the National Museum of History and Technology of the Smithsonian Institution in Washington, D.C. in 1961. He became Assistant Director in 1965 and then Deputy Director in 1971, in which position he remained until 1977, when he was appointed the Smithsonian Institution's Keeper of the Rare Books. Upon his retirement in 1987 he was named Historian Emeritus.

Following studies at Columbia University 1935–1942, he was in military service 1942-1945. In 1970 he received an honorary LL.D. from the University of Bridgeport. He is a Fellow of the Washington Academy of Sciences and a member of the American Philosophical Society, the American Antiquarian Society, the Society of American Historians, the History of Science Society, the American Historical Association, and the Antiquarian Horological Society.

The author of several hundred articles and some sixteen books chiefly in the field of the history of science, he was a recipient of the Abbott Payson Usher Award of the Society for the History of Technology in 1962, and was awarded the Paul Bunge Prize in 1994.

Among his books and monographs are:

The Mace and the Gavel: Symbols of Authority in America (*Transactions*, American Philosophical Society, 1997)

The Pope's Elephant (Manchester, England, Carcanet Press, 1997)

Science and Instruments in Seventeenth Century Italy (London, Ashgate Publishing Ltd., 1994)

The Trail of Time (Cambridge: Cambridge University Press, 1990)

The Pulse of Time. Galileo Galilei, the Determination of Longitude and the Pendulum Clock, (Florence: Leo S. Olschki, 1991)

Thomas Jefferson Statesman of Science (New York: Macmillan Publishing Company, 1990)

Clockwork Cosmos. Bernardo Facini and the Farnese Planisferologio (Vatican City: Biblioteca Apostolica Vaticana, 1985)

Thomas Jefferson and His Copying Machines (Charlottesville: University Press of
    Virginia, 1984)

At The Sign of the Compass and Quadrant. The Life and Times of Anthony Lamb
    (*Transactions,* American Philosophical Society, 1984)

Declaration of Independence Desk; Relic of Revolution (Smithsonian Institution
    Press, 1981)

Thinkers and Tinkers. Early American Men of Science (New York: Charles
    Scribner's Sons, 1975)

The Life of Benjamin Banneker (New York: Charles Scribner's Sons, 1972)

Moon, Man's Greatest Adventure (With Werner von Braun and Fred R. Whipple)
    (New York: Harry N. Abrams, 1970)

Mechanical Universe. The Astrarium of Giovanni de' Dondi (With Francis R.
    Maddison (*Transactions,* American Philosophical Society, 1966)

Early American Scientific Instruments and Their Makers (Washington:
    Smithsonian Institution Press, 1964)

The Scent of Time (*Transactions,* American Philosophical Society, 1963)

Ridgefield in Review (New Haven: Walker-Rackliff, 1958)

Designed by Gerard A. Valerio, Bookmark Studio, Annapolis, Maryland

Composed in Trajan and Minion by Sherri Ferritto, Typeline, Annapolis

Printed on Finch Opaque Vellum and bound in Holliston Kingston cloth by
United Book Press, Inc. Baltimore

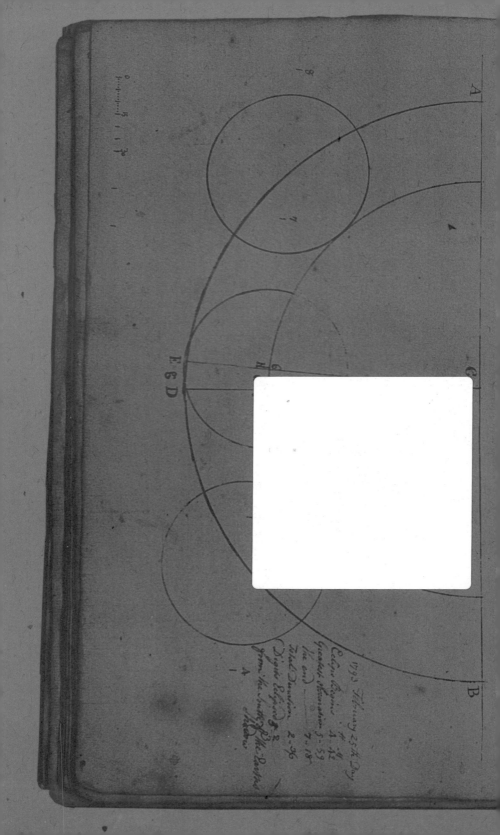